discover
GREAT BRITAIN

OLIVER BERRY
**DAVID ELSE, DAVID ATKINSON, FIONN DAVENPORT,
BELINDA DIXON, PETER DRAGICEVICH, NANA LUCKHAM,
ETAIN O'CARROLL, ANDY SYMINGTON, NEIL WILSON**

DISCOVER GREAT BRITAIN

London (p51) Shop till you drop, soak up the culture, savour the sights: Britain's capital has enough for a lifetime of visits.

Southern England (p107) From Cornwall's craggy cliffs to Brighton's buzzing nightlife, the south is one nonstop adventure.

Central England (p161) Stop off at Shakespeare's birthplace or punt down the river in Cambridge.

Northern England (p199) Forget the tired old stereotypes: the north's had a revival, and it's high time you joined the party.

Wales (p245) Governed by its own Celtic culture, Wales has always stood one step removed from the rest of the nation.

Edinburgh & Glasgow (p275) Soak up the atmosphere in the two cities before exploring the stormy Scottish frontier.

Scotland's Highlands & Islands (p313) Looking for that landscape of lochs and lonely glens? This is where you'll find it.

↘CONTENTS

SCOTLAND'S HIGHLANDS & ISLANDS p313

EDINBURGH & GLASGOW p275

NORTHERN ENGLAND p199

CENTRAL ENGLAND p161

WALES p245

LONDON p51

SOUTHERN ENGLAND p107

Northern Islands

Unst
Yell Fetlar
Toft Yell
Shetland Islands
Mainland
Lerwick
Yell Sound
Ulsta
Colgrave Sound
Foula
North Sea
Fair Isle

See Northern Islands inset

Same scale as main map

Westray Sanday
Rousay
Orkney Islands
Mainland Stronsay
Stromness Kirkwall
Hoy South Ronaldsay
John O'Groats

LEGEND

Freeway
Primary Road
Secondary Road
Railway

0 ___ 100 km
0 ___ 60 miles

ELEVATION

1000m
700m
500m
300m
200m
100m
0

THE GREAT GLEN p333

Take an unforgettable road-trip through Scotland's most spectacular landscape

EDINBURGH p286

History, heritage, art, architecture: Scotland's premier city packs it in

HADRIAN'S WALL p240

Trace the history of this masterpiece of Roman engineering

THE LAKE DISTRICT p228

Wander the hills which inspired William Wordsworth, Beatrix Potter and Arthur Ransome

John O'Groats
Duncansby Head
Thurso
Scrabster
Melvich
Bettyhill
Durness
Tongue
Kinlochbervie
Lochinver
Ullapool
Gairloch
Harris
Tarbert
Lewis
Stornoway
North Uist
Lochmaddy
Benbecula
South Uist
Lochboisdale
St Kilda
Barra
Helmsdale
Brora
Bonar Bridge
Invergordon
Dingwall
Inverness
Nairn
Elgin
Grantown-on-Spey
Aviemore
Cairngorms National Park
Braemar
Huntly
Banff
Fraserburgh
Peterhead
Aberdeen
Stonehaven
Montrose
Brechin
Forfar
Arbroath
Blairgowrie
Pitlochry
Dunkeld
Aberfeldy
Crieff
Perth
Dundee
St Andrews
Kinross
Kirkcaldy
Loch Ness
Fort Augustus
Great Glen
Kyle of Lochalsh
Portree
Isle of Skye
Uig
Dunvegan
Mallaig
Eigg
Rum
Fort William
Ben Nevis (1344m)
Glen Coe
Grampian Mountains
Trossachs National Park
Loch Lomond
Stirling
Falkirk
EDINBURGH
Haddington
Dunbar
Berwick-upon-Tweed
Holy Island
Lammermuir Hills
Peebles
Galashiels
Melrose
Kelso
Coldstream
Jedburgh
Hawick
Southern Uplands
Newcastleton
Isle of Coll
Isle of Tiree
Isle of Mull
Tobermory
Craignure
Lochaline
Oban
Lochgilphead
Isle of Colonsay
Isle of Jura
Isle of Islay
Dunoon
Greenock
Dumbarton
Glasgow
Motherwell
Lanark
Kilmarnock
Ayr
Girvan
Ardrossan
Brodick
Isle of Arran
Lochranza
Kintyre
Larne
BELFAST
Cairnryan
Newton Stewart
Galloway Forest Park
Kirkcudbright
Dumfries
Dunfermline
Berwickshire
Wooler
Alnwick
Northumberland National Park
Hadrian's Wall Haltwhistle
Brampton
Carlisle
Lake District
Workington
Pennines
Durham
Darlington
Middlesbrough
Hartlepool
Sunderland
South Shields
Tynemouth
Newcastle-upon-Tyne
Newcastle
NORTHERN IRELAND

CASTLE HOWARD p230
Play lord of the manor at England's quintessential country estate

YORK p225
Climb to the top of York's famous minster for bird's-eye views across the city

LONDON p51
From urban thrills to world-class sights, nowhere tops the capital city

MT SNOWDON p274
Brave the trails and marvel at the views from Wales' highest mountain

BATH p145
From Georgian crescents to Roman hot-tubs, beautiful Bath is a feast for the senses

STONEHENGE p143
Ponder the motives of Britain's ancient builders at this world-famous stone circle

BRIGHTON p122
Party hard or sit back and chill in this funky seaside city

THE EDEN PROJECT p157
Three giant greenhouses form the centrepiece for this stunning ecological adventure

BELGIUM

FRANCE

IRELAND

DUBLIN

Isle of Man

52°N

2°E

0° (Greenwich)

3°W

51°N

50°N

Map place names

St-Omer, Boulogne-sur-Mer, Calais, Folkestone, Dover, Ramsgate, Margate, Canterbury, Ashford, Maidstone, Chatham, Sheppey, Southend-on-Sea, Basildon, Colchester, Ipswich, Felixstowe, Woodbridge, Lowestoft, Great Yarmouth, Norwich, Bury St Edmunds, Haverhill, Cambridge, Newmarket, King's Lynn, Ely, Peterborough, Stamford, Huntingdon, Bedford, Milton Keynes, Stevenage, Luton, St Albans, Watford, Harlow, Chelmsford, LONDON, Crawley, Royal Tunbridge Wells, Bexhill, Eastbourne, Seaford, Brighton, Hove, Bognor Regis, Chichester, Portsmouth, Ryde, Isle of Wight, Southampton, Winchester, Basingstoke, Reading, Windsor, Guildford, Andover, Newbury, High Wycombe, Aylesbury, Oxford, Banbury, Abingdon, Witney, Swindon, Cirencester, Cheltenham, Gloucester, Stroud, Bath, Bristol, Newport, CARDIFF, Barry, Warminster, Salisbury, Stonehenge, Avebury, Leamington Spa, Stratford-upon-Avon, Warwick, Coventry, Rugby, Northampton, Leicester, Loughborough, Nottingham, Derby, Litchfield, Birmingham, Wolverhampton, Worcester, Hereford, Ludlow, Shrewsbury, Stafford, Stoke-on-Trent, Hay-on-Wye, Abergavenny, Monmouth, Merthyr Tydfil, Port Talbot, Swansea, Llanelli, Carmarthen, Tenby, Pembroke, Milford Haven, Haverfordwest, Fishguard, Cardigan, Aberystwyth, Newtown, Llandrindod Wells, Welshpool, Llangollen, Wrexham, Chester, Newcastle, Worksop, Chesterfield, Sheffield, Doncaster, Scunthorpe, Grimsby, Gainsborough, Lincoln, Newark-on-Trent, Boston, Skegness, Leeds, Bradford, Halifax, Huddersfield, Bolton, Manchester, Liverpool, Birkenhead, Rhyl, Llandudno, Conwy, Bangor, Holyhead, Amlwch, Anglesey, Caernarfon, Pwllheli, Porthmadog, Blaenau Ffestiniog, Dolgellau, Barmouth, Wigan, Southport, Blackburn, Preston, Blackpool, Fleetwood, Lancaster, Morecambe, Barrow-in-Furness, Ulverston, Kendal, Windermere, Ingleton, Settle, Skipton, Ilkley, Harrogate, Ripon, Thirsk, York, Selby, Beverley, Hull, Bridlington, Scarborough, Castle Howard, Ramsey, Peel, Castletown, Douglas, Dundalk, Rosslare Harbour, Wexford, Waterford, Dungarvan, Cashel, Ilfracombe, Barnstaple, Bideford, Bude, Launceston, Okehampton, Tavistock, Bodmin, Wadebridge, Padstow, Newquay, Truro, Falmouth, Penzance, Land's End, St Ives, Redruth, Plymouth, Tiverton, Exeter, Exmouth, Torquay, Dorchester, Weymouth, Poole, Bournemouth, Dartmouth, Minehead, Taunton, Yeovil, Glastonbury, Wells, Frome, Bristol, Lundy, Isle of Scilly

National Parks
North York Moors National Park, Yorkshire Dales National Park, Lake District National Park, Peak District National Park, Snowdonia National Park, Brecon Beacons National Park, Pembrokeshire Coast National Park, Exmoor National Park, Dartmoor National Park, New Forest, Norfolk Broads National Park, Cotswolds, Cambrian Mountains, Chiltern Hills

Motorways
M1, M2, M3, M4, M5, M6, M11, M18, M20, M23, M25, M27, M32, M40, M42, M50, M54, M56, M62, M65, A1, A9, A30, A38, A55, A595

↘ THIS IS GREAT BRITAIN

The clue's in the name: Great Britain might only appear to be a speck on the world map, but this plucky little island can pack a heftier punch than a country 10 times its size.

Few places manage to cram so much history, heritage and spectacular scenery into such a tiny space. Twelve hours is all you need to cover the country from tip to tip, but you could spend a lifetime getting to grips with Britain – from the ancient relics of Stonehenge and Hadrian's Wall to the great medieval cathedrals of Salisbury, Ely and Canterbury and the magnificent country houses of Chatsworth and Castle Howard. This is an island entranced by its past, but it's a long way from a dusty old relic – sneak a peek at the gleaming skyscrapers stacked up along London's skyline or the futuristic biomes of the Eden Project, and you'll realise there's plenty of life left in this elegant old girl yet.

This past–future schism is just one of many contradictions you'll stumble across on your British travels. Contrariness and eccentricity are hardwired into the national

character: after all, Britain is really three countries rolled into one, and its constituent nations haven't always made easy bedfellows down the centuries. The process of devolution over the last decade has only served to underline their differences, and you're bound to be struck by just how different things feel in Britain's corners these days – whether it's moseying along Edinburgh's Royal Mile, admiring the cutting-edge architecture around Cardiff Bay or exploring one of London's lively street markets.

'It's Britain's contradictory character that makes it such a fascinating place'

But while it's sometimes hard to get a handle on, in many ways it's Britain's contradictory character that makes it such a fascinating place to visit. With a sensory smorgasbord of picture-pretty villages, stately cities, world-class museums and stunning national parks, not to mention countless miles of coast and countryside to explore, Britain's an awfully big adventure packed into a conveniently pint-sized package.

1

⬎ LONDON

'If you're tired of London, you're tired of life,' wrote Samuel Johnson in the 18th century. Britain's **capital city** (p51) is still its most essential sight. You could spend a lifetime in London and never discover all its secrets. It's inspiring, infuriating and intoxicating in equal measures – but you won't be bored.

Oliver Berry, Lonely Planet Author, UK

↘ OXFORD & CAMBRIDGE

Long-standing rivalries notwithstanding, Oxford and Cambridge both offer a highly educational look at student life over the last 800 years. In Oxford (p127) you're following the footsteps of Tolkien, Lyra, CS Lewis and Inspector Morse; in Cambridge (p188) the top attractions are the beautiful colleges and the chance to punt on the river.

Etain O'Carroll, Lonely Planet Author, UK

↖ AVEBURY & STONEHENGE

If there's one monument that sums up Britain, it has to be Stonehenge (p143). Despite numerous theories no-one's still exactly sure what the ancient builders were up to. Nearby Avebury (p148) is actually Britain's biggest stone circle, but receives far fewer visitors.

Oliver Berry, Lonely Planet Author, UK

1 ORIEN HARVEY; 2 WAYNE WALTON; 3 GLENN BEANLAND

1 London Eye (p77), England; 2 Cambridge (p188), England; 3 Stonehenge (p143), England

⬃ CLEANING UP IN BATH

4

After a day shopping and discovering Bath's Georgian architecture, enjoy a session at **Thermae Bath Spa** (p149) – Britain's only natural thermal spa. The tourist board claims that it uses the same warm, mineral-rich water that the Romans used 200 years ago. Hopefully they've changed it since then.

Judith Holford, traveller

5

⬃ CHATSWORTH

England's stately homes are our greatest national treasures. Wherever you travel there's bound to be a stunning country house within easy reach. My favourite is **Chatsworth** (p176) – it's full of fascinating art and antiques, but the real highlight is the glorious building itself.

Susie Berry, traveller, UK

⬇ YORK MINSTER

'Too much history' was how a friend once described **York** (p225), but if the past is your thing then York will press all the right buttons. And there's still plenty to do, even if you're more interested in shopping, pubs and restaurants than old stones and tales of yore.

Clifton Wilkinson, Lonely Planet Staff

6

4 SIMON GREENWOOD; 5 GLENN BEANLAND; 6 NEIL SETCHFIELD

4 Roman baths (p145), Bath, England; 5 Chatsworth (p176), England; 6 York Minster (p225), England

↘ PINT DOWN THE PUB

Whether it's a quick after-work drink or a celebration of whatever kind, the traditional **pub** (p348) is still the centre of socialising in Britain. And as well as making new friends over a pint, these days you can also often get decent pub grub to go with your drink.

Sally Schafer, Lonely Planet Staff

7

8

⬈ VISITING THE LAKE DISTRICT

Visiting England's beautiful Lake District (p228) is like taking a step into the idyllic past. Shimmering blue lakes contrast with green fields and trees, while sheep keep pasture over rolling hills and vales, quaint villages cluster along the shoreline and sailboats glide across the water.

Kathleen Stinner, traveller, USA

⬈ GREENWICH

9

London's full of history, but one of the most fascinating areas is Greenwich (p83), which in bygone centuries was the centre of British maritime power. It feels like it's hardly changed in the last hundred years – you can visit the famous Royal Observatory and the National Maritime Museum, or just admire the wonderful London views.

Paul Collins, traveller, UK

7 WILL SALTER; 8 DAVID TOMLINSON; 9 TRAVIS DREVER

7 Beer taps; 8 Lake District (p228), England; 9 Old Royal Naval College (p84), Greenwich, England

10

↘ PORTMEIRION

Cult TV fans mustn't miss this **fantasy land** (p273), where the 1960s show *The Prisoner* was filmed. Created between the 1920s and 1970s by the classic English eccentric Sir Clough Williams-Ellis, it borrows from a bewildering range of architectural styles. All together, now: 'I am a not a number! I am a free man!'

↘ FISH AND CHIPS

11

Britain's contributions to the culinary world may be limited (and often, sometimes unfairly, criticised), but for a simple and tasty meal nothing beats fresh **fish and chips** (p350) doused in salt and vinegar. Best spot to enjoy them: at the seaside after a ride on the rollercoaster.

⬈ THE BALTIC, GATESHEAD

Not long ago Newcastle-upon-Tyne and neighbouring Gateshead were firmly in the doldrums, but over the last couple of decades these towns have been completely transformed. Top spot goes to the world-beating Baltic (p237), which gives London's Tate Modern a serious run for its money.

James Grant, traveller, UK

⬈ KELVINGROVE ART GALLERY & MUSEUM

Glasgow's *numero uno* educational haven (p304) has a multitude of weird and wonderful artefacts, from the majestic stuffed elephant which greets you upon arrival, to Salvador Dali's *Christ of St John of the Cross*. You'll be hard-pressed not to find something which piques your interest.

Zaineb Al-Hussani, traveller

10 PATRICK HORTON; 11 HOLGER LEUE; 12 DOUG MCKINLAY; 13 NEIL SETCHFIELD

10 Portmeirion (p273), Wales; 11 Fish and chips; 12 Baltic – The Centre for Contemporary Art (p237), Gateshead, England; 13 Kelvingrove Art Gallery & Museum (p304), Glasgow, Scotland

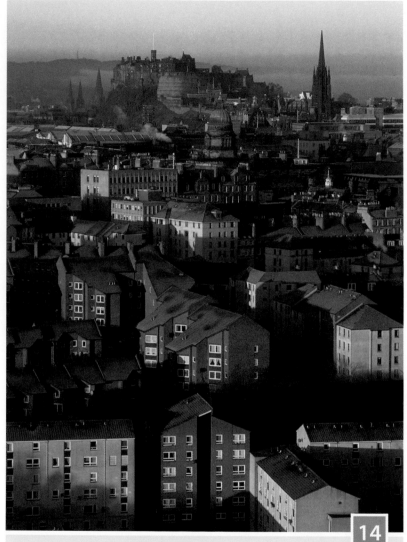

14

↘ EXPLORING EDINBURGH

Edinburgh (p286) is a city rich in history. The city buzzes with the sound of locals, travellers and the bagpipes on Princes Street. Looking up you can see the castle watching over the city, walk on cobbled streets and visit Underground Edinburgh to get an insight into the history of the city.

Louise Griffiths, traveller, Australia

↘ ISLE OF SKYE

Even a simple day trip to the misty, magical Isle of Skye (p340) can be enough to refresh your spirit. Enjoy spectacular, rugged scenery and, on a fair day, wave to the Outer Hebrides seen off in the distance. Whether you spend a day or a month here, you'll want to return.

Marg Gibson, traveller, Canada

15

14 JONATHAN SMITH; 15 GARETH MCCORMACK

14 Edinburgh Castle and Old Town from Arthur's Seat (p290), Scotland; 15 Cuillin Hills (p341), Isle of Skye, Scotland

⬇ SNOWDONIA

Spend the days climbing mountains, riding rapids and hiking trails in **Snowdonia National Park** (p271), arguably Wales' most beautiful area. Afterwards, retire to your luxury hotel or cosy bed-and-breakfast for some well-deserved R&R and let your mind wander and your body recuperate from all that exertion.

David Atkinson, Lonely Planet Author, UK

16

↘ PADSTOW

The gorgeous Cornish pocket town of **Padstow** (p155) is a hive of activity when the summer sun shines – the pubs and shops overflow on to the pavements where jovial tourists and locals enjoy a chilled cider with some fish and chips or Cornish pasties, legs dangling over the jetty. Watch out for the seagulls!

Pru Engel, traveller, UK

↘ HAY-ON-WYE

Bookworms beware! The secondhand bookshops in the Welsh border town of **Hay-on-Wye** (p266) are so numerous that you may find yourself spending more time and money here than you'd planned. On the other hand, there are definitely worse ways and places to lose yourself...

David Atkinson, Lonely Planet Author, UK

16 EOIN CLARKE; 17 GLENN BEANLAND; 18 PHILIP GAME

16 Snowdonia National Park (p271), Wales; 17 Harbour, Padstow (p155), England; 18 Bookshop, Hay-on-Wye (p266), Wales

↘ EXPERIENCING THE EDEN PROJECT

Ever wondered what it feels like to live on the moon? Then you mustn't miss a trip to these three gigantic **biomes** (p157) plonked at the bottom of a converted clay pit in St Austell in Cornwall. In a single day you can explore the world's natural habitats from the humid tropics to the dusty desert.

19

20

⬃ THE GOWER PENINSULA

There's nothing like coming across a piece of the picturesque **Gower coastline** (p262) that you have all to yourself. The blustery sea breeze refreshes you and the only obstacle in your path is sheep poo. Travelling during the shoulder season does have its perks.

Martin Chiu, traveller, Canada

19 GLENN BEANLAND; 20 CHERYL FORBES

19 Eden Project (p157), Cornwall, England; 20 Gower Peninsula (p262), Wales

21

↘ CANTERBURY CATHEDRAL

The first time I clapped eyes on this amazing cathedral (p119), they very nearly popped out of their sockets. I've visited lots of England's great cathedrals over the years but, for me, nowhere compares to Canterbury Cathedral. It's a marvellous medieval wonder.

Leo Burrell, traveller, UK

↘ WHISKY GALORE

22

Central Scotland is famous for its whiskies, and if you can't tell your Glenfiddich from your Glenlivet, this is definitely the place to learn. Most of the major makers offer guided tours (p326) around their distilleries, and you won't escape without tasting a wee dram or two.

Simon Dukes, traveller, UK

⬎ TOWER OF LONDON

23

Europe's best-preserved **medieval fortress** (p73) lives up to all the expectations. Wander around on your own to discover quieter corners or join a Beefeater Tour for insights into the Tower's 1000-year history. Don't miss the Crown Jewels, the Bloody Tower and the scaffold site with a list of the unfortunates to have died here.

Peter Dragicevich, Lonely Planet Author, New Zealand

24

⬎ SEASIDE FUN IN BRIGHTON

It might be one of England's oldest seaside resorts, but **Brighton** (p122) still has plenty of life in it. The pier and the beach are good fun during the day, but it's in the evening when the bars, restaurants and clubs start filling up that the city rediscovers its Regency decadence.

Nana Luckham, Lonely Planet Author, UK

21 Cloisters, Canterbury Cathedral (p119), England; 22 Whisky and shortbread; 23 Tower of London (p73), England; 24 Carousel, Brighton (p122), England

↘ STIRLING CASTLE

Many of the great events of Scottish history have been played out within the walls of Stirling's brooding **stronghold** (p330), and it's well worth your while taking the time to delve into the castle's stormy past. While you're nearby, don't forget to visit the National Wallace Monument.

25

GRANT DIXON

Stirling Castle (p330), Scotland

↘ GREAT BRITAIN'S TOP ITINERARIES

JUST THE CLASSICS

FIVE DAYS LONDON TO LONDON

If time is tight you'll have to pack in the sights, so we've stripped this trip down to include the bare essentials. If you've got more time, consider extending the itinerary with local day-trips from each key area.

❶ LONDON

Let's face it – you'll need more than a couple of days to properly explore the nation's capital, **London** (p51), and even then you'll only have time to scratch the surface. But if you're on a really tight time-frame, you'll have to plan your sightseeing with military precision. At the very least, try to tick off the **Tower of London** (p73), the **British Museum** (p72), the **Tate Modern** (p79) and **Greenwich** (p83). If you can spare a few more days, you could also add in some shopping and museum time in **Kensington and Knightsbridge** (p78), take in the city's skyline from the **London Eye** (p77), browse for a bargain at **Portobello Road Market** (p102) and perhaps venture out to the Royal Botanical Gardens at **Kew** (p85).

❷ OXFORD

One you've 'done' the capital, head west to spend a day exploring elegant **Oxford** (p127), England's most famous university town, whose first college was founded way back in the 13th century. Famous writers including Philip Pullman, JRR Tolkien and CS Lewis were all inspired by the architecture and atmosphere of this superbly scenic city, and we bet you will be, too. If your itinerary allows, a side-trip to the fabulous

RIGHT: JON DAVISON; LEFT: JULIET COOMBE

Left: Brasenose College, Oxford (p127); Right: Shopping at Portobello Road Market (p102), London

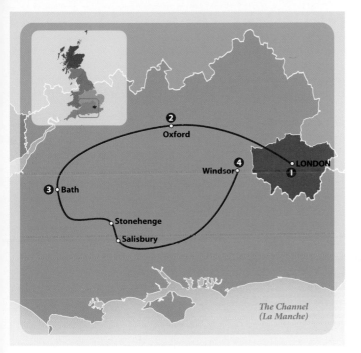

stately home of **Blenheim Palace** (p133) will provide you with a perfect introduction to the rarefied world of the English stately home.

❸ BATH
Day four is reserved for beautiful **Bath** (p145), renowned for its Georgian architecture, classy restaurants and top shopping, not to mention one of the best-preserved Roman baths in Europe. You should also have time for a quick detour via the great circle of **Stonehenge** (p143) but it's really worth allowing more time if you can – an extra afternoon will allow you to take a guided tour, understand the history and geography of the ancient monument and explore some of the other nearby ancient sites associated with Stonehenge. You could even extend your trip into nearby **Salisbury** (p144), famous for its magnificent medieval cathedral and sky-topping spire (the tallest in England).

❹ WINDSOR
On the final day, turn eastwards and head back towards the big smoke via the monumental fortress of **Windsor Castle** (p137), arguably England's most impressive royal residence. Don't miss the Changing of the Guard at 11am sharp.

NATIONAL TREASURES

10 DAYS CAMBRIDGE TO EDINBURGH

This south-to-north trip takes its cue from the nation's architectural treasures, starting amongst the colleges of Cambridge before travelling north to Edinburgh's Royal Mile.

❶ CAMBRIDGE & AROUND

Begin by exploring the historic colleges of **Cambridge** (p188), a city awash with elegant architecture, dreamy bridges and landmark buildings. Nearby are the wonderful cathedrals of **Ely** (p193) and **Peterborough** (p194). Having paid your religious respects, it's time for more secular pleasures: the great stately homes of **Ickworth** (p178) and **Burghley House** (p178), where you'll gain a glimpse into the lavish lifestyles once enjoyed by the nation's aristocratic upper-crust.

❷ BLENHEIM PALACE

Further west is **Blenheim Palace** (p133), the ancestral home of the Duke of Marlborough as well as the birthplace of one of the nation's favourite cigar-chomping statesmen, Winston Churchill.

❸ CHATSWORTH HOUSE

Still not tired of playing lord of the manor? Then how about finishing this leg of the tour with a day exploring the undisputed queen of English country estates at **Chatsworth** (p176).

❹ YORK

After sampling southern England's architectural splendours, it's time to bend your gaze northwards. Cross the glorious **Yorkshire Dales**

GLENN BEANLAND

Blenheim Palace (p133), Oxfordshire, England

(p224) en route to graceful **York** (p225). Famous architectural land-marks include the medieval streets known as the **Shambles** (p226), the old **city walls** (p225) and a rather marvellous **minster** (p225).

❺ CASTLE HOWARD

A short spin on from York brings you to **Castle Howard** (p230), a jaw-dropping slice of architectural extravagance which provided the back-drop for the TV adaptation of Evelyn Waugh's *Brideshead Revisited*.

❻ HADRIAN'S WALL

Continue north for an unforgettable stroll along Britain's great mas-terpiece of Roman engineering, **Hadrian's Wall** (p240). Much of the wall has survived the centuries essentially intact, and you can see the remains of several Roman garrison forts, including **Chesters** (p241) and **Housesteads** (p243).

❼ EDINBURGH

Beyond the wall it's a simple skip over the Scottish border to admire Edinburgh's architectural highlights, including **Edinburgh Castle** (p287), **Holyroodhouse** (p291), the **Royal Mile** (p287) and the con-troversial new **Scottish Parliament** (p290).

ONE TRIP, THREE NATIONS

TWO WEEKS EDINBURGH TO BRIGHTON

Righto, chaps – it's time for a big 'un. This grand tour takes in the very best Britain's three constituent nations have to offer, from the wilds of Scotland right down to the chalky-white cliffs of Dover.

❶ EDINBURGH

Begin with at least a day in Edinburgh (p286), allowing time for the Royal Mile (p287), the Castle (p287), Princes St (p292) and an after-dark ghost tour (p293). Travel north via historic Stirling Castle (p330) en route to the scenic Cairngorms (p338), arguably the most dramatic of all Britain's national parks. Lively Inverness (p336) makes a good base for exploring much of central Scotland – a trip to a whisky distillery (p337) is a must, especially if you're feeling the Scottish chill.

❷ GLASGOW

Swing south via Loch Ness (p334) and Glen Coe (p334) before spending a day sampling the sights of Glasgow (p300), such as the impressive collections at Kelvingrove Art Gallery & Museum (p304), the Hunterian Museum (p304) and the Gallery of Modern Art (p301).

❸ NEWCASTLE-UPON-TYNE

Entering England, head south via Northumberland National Park (p243) to Newcastle-upon-Tyne (p235), with its funky suburbs, such as Ouseborn (p204), and innovative museums and galleries such as the Baltic (p237) and the Great North Museum (p237).

DENNIS JOHNSON

Urquhart Castle (p335) and Loch Ness, Scotland

❹ LAKE DISTRICT

Alternatively you could set a course for the **Lake District** (p228), once the home of the Romantic poets and now one of England's most popular national parks. Take a boat-trip on **Windermere** (p230) or **Ullswater** (p235) and visit Wordsworth's cosy home at **Dove Cottage** (p233).

❺ YORK

It's a hop, skip and a jump to the windswept **Yorkshire Dales** (p224) en route to **York** (p225), possibly Britain's most attractive city, and one of the very few that still preserves much of its medieval character – top attractions include the atmospheric Viking centre of **Jorvik** (p220) and the network of higgledy-piggledy streets known as the **Shambles** (p226).

❻ MANCHESTER/LIVERPOOL

After York, take your pick from nearby **Manchester** (p212), famous for its world-conquering football team and world-class museums, or **Liverpool** (p217), home to lots of lively galleries and top-notch museums.

❼ SNOWDONIA NATIONAL PARK

It's over the border again into Wales for another splendidly scenic drive via **Llandudno** (p268) and **Conwy Castle** (p269) into the snow-capped surroundings of **Snowdonia National Park** (p271). If time allows, a hike to the top of **Mt Snowdon** (p274) is highly recommended.

❽ CARDIFF

The **Welsh capital** (p256) is well worth a day of your time – be sure to see the **castle** (p258) and the **National Museum** (p256). If you're a Dylan Thomas devotee you might like to visit the poet's home in **Laugharne** (p263) instead.

❾ STRATFORD-UPON-AVON

Head back across the border and veer east via Shakespeare's birthplace at **Stratford-upon-Avon** (p177), where you can visit the Bard's **former homes** (p177) or catch a performance courtesy of the **Royal Shakespeare Company** (p181).

❿ OUTER LONDON

If you've already done **Oxford** (p127), then you should have time to explore some of outer London's attractions, including the Royal Botanic Gardens at **Kew** (p85) and the monarch's modest weekend retreat, **Hampton Court Palace** (p85).

⓫ BRIGHTON TO DOVER

You could then head either into the **capital** (p51), or alternatively skip the big city altogether in favour of the buzzy seaside city of **Brighton** (p122) and a visit to the stately cathedral at **Canterbury** (p119) before reaching journey's end at the **White Cliffs of Dover** (p121).

GLENN BEANLAND

Stratford-upon-Avon (p177), England

PLANNING YOUR TRIP

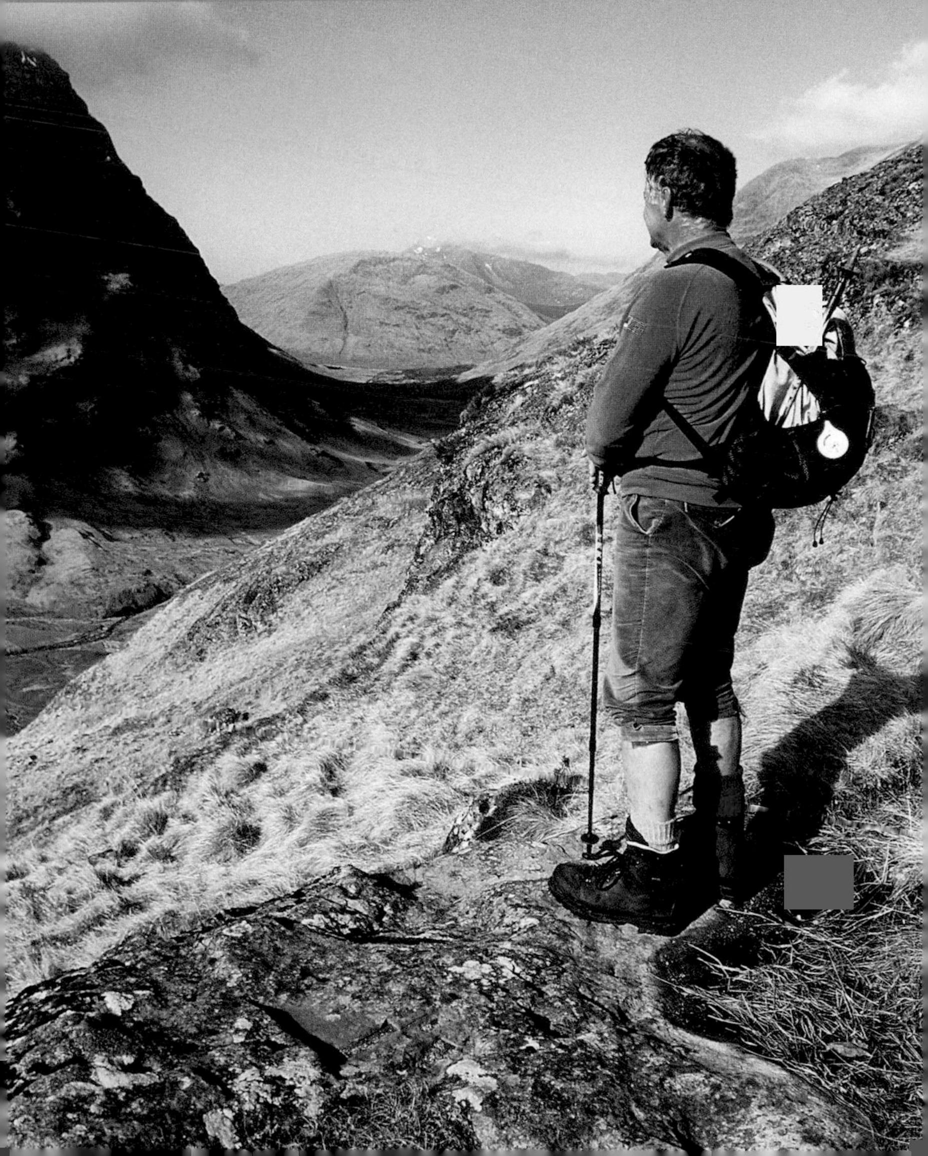

PLANNING YOUR TRIP

GREAT BRITAIN'S BEST...

GREAT BRITAIN'S BEST...

MONUMENTS

- **Nelson's Column** (p65) Raised to commemorate Nelson's landmark victory at the Battle of Trafalgar.
- **Palace of Westminster** (p69) The seat of British political power for centuries – don't forget to set your watch to the chimes of Big Ben.
- **Angel of the North** (p240) The nation has taken Anthony Gormley's rust-red winged sculpture firmly to its hearts.
- **Stonehenge** (p143) Ancient Britons built it almost 4000 years ago; now over a million people make a pilgrimage every year.
- **National Wallace Monument** (p330) Dedicated to the Scottish freedom fighter William Wallace, who inspired Mel Gibson to discover his dodgiest accent yet in *Braveheart*.

MUSEUMS

- **British Museum** (p72) The cultural equivalent of the nation's attic.
- **Natural History Museum** (p78) Where beasties big and small take centre stage.
- **Imperial War Museum** (p78 & p213) London and Manchester both have their own outpost of this award-winning war museum.
- **National Museum of Scotland** (p291) The main trove for Scotland's treasures.
- **Kelvingrove Art Gallery & Museum** (p304) This Glaswegian gem is eclectic, eccentric and all-round wonderful.

LEFT: GLENN BEANLAND; RIGHT: GRANT DIXON

Left: Natural History Museum (p78), London; Right: Snowdon Mountain Railway (p272), Wales

↘ HIKING

- **The Lake District** (p228) Follow in the footsteps of Wordsworth, Coleridge and co.
- **The Cairngorms** (p338) As close to wilderness as Britain gets.
- **The Peak District** (p174) Where to go if you prefer your walks wild and windy.
- **Snowdonia** (p271) Where Britain's mountaineers test their mettle.
- **The Yorkshire Dales** (p224) Green and pleasant in every sense.

↘ ISLANDS

- **The Isles of Scilly** (p159) Isolated islands off Cornwall's westerly tip.
- **Skye** (p340) 'Over the sea to Skye,' goes the old song, although these days you can just cross the bridge.
- **Shetland** (p329) Goodbye, Scotland; next stop the Arctic.
- **Orkneys** (p329) Some of Britain's oldest remains have been discovered at this island archipelago located off Scotland's northern tip.

↘ TRAIN TRIPS

- **Settle-Carlisle Railway** (p225) This famous route cuts across northern England, traversing hills, dales and umpteen viaducts en route.
- **Great Western Railway** (p139) The London-Bristol line is one of England's most historic railways, not to mention one of its most scenic.
- **Snowdon Mountain Railway** (p272) Catch a lift to the top of Snowdon.
- **Heart of Wales** (p262) This marvellous route cuts across the Welsh countryside from Swansea to Shrewsbury.
- **West Highland Railway** (p334) Travel the west Scottish coast from Glasgow to Fort William and beyond.

↘ NIGHTLIFE

- **London** (p99) Nowhere parties quite like the capital.
- **Brighton** (p122) This seaside getaway is a must for night-owls.
- **Newcastle-upon-Tyne** (p235) Newcastle's nightlife revolves around Jesmond and Ouseburn.
- **Manchester** (p216) Pubs and clubs aplenty in England's second city.
- **Liverpool** (p222) The Beatles kicked things off at the Cavern Club; now Ropewalks is the centre of the action.

THINGS YOU NEED TO KNOW

⬊ AT A GLANCE

- **ATMs** Widely available in towns and cities
- **Bargaining** Unusual except at markets
- **Credit Cards** Visa and MasterCard accepted practically everywhere
- **Currency** Pound (Scottish notes are legal tender in England)
- **Language** English in England and Scotland (with a bit of Gaelic); English and Welsh in Wales
- **Tipping** Not required, but generally 10% to 15% for good service in restaurants
- **Visas** Not required for most western nationalities

⬊ ACCOMMODATION

- **Hostels** The budget traveller's choice. Accommodation is usually in dorms, but the locations are often brilliant.
- **B&Bs & Guesthouses** The traditional British B&B has come on in leaps and bounds in recent years. The best places would give most boutique hotels a run for their money.
- **Hotels** Britain has some fantastic midrange and top-end hotels, but prices certainly aren't cheap as you move up the luxury ladder. You'll pay a premium in city hotels, especially in London.

⬊ ADVANCE PLANNING

- **Two months ahead** Make accommodation reservations, especially if you're visiting London and other busy areas during a busy period.
- **One month ahead** Arrange train tickets and car hire to secure the cheapest deals. Reserve tables at high-profile restaurants.
- **Two weeks ahead** Confirm opening times and prices for visitor attractions.
- **One week ahead** Check the weather forecast. Then ignore it.

⬊ BE FOREWARNED

- **Public holidays** Much of Britain shuts up shop for bank holidays, although many sights stay open. Everything's closed on Christmas Day.
- **School holidays** Everything's busier during school holidays around Easter, summer and Christmas – see p389.
- **Traffic jams** A fact of life, especially during the morning and evening rush hours and in summer. You'll find it easier to stick to public transport in the big cities.

⬊ COSTS

- **Under £100 per day** Will limit you mainly to budget B&Bs and restaurants.
- **£100 to £200** Double room in a midrange B&B or hotel, with cash left over for attractions and an evening meal.

- **More than £200** Will allow you to travel in serious style, staying at the best hotels and eating at top restaurants.

↘ EMERGENCY NUMBERS

- ☎ **999** Fire, police & ambulance

↘ GETTING AROUND

- **Air** Budget carriers fly between major cities, but it's often just as quick to take the train.
- **Bus** National Express coaches link urban areas, but once you get out into the countryside coverage can be patchy.
- **Train** This is a fast and efficient way of getting around, although you'll have to book well ahead for the best deals.
- **Car** Having your own car will allow you to reach those more out-of-the-way spots.

↘ GETTING THERE & AWAY

- **Fly** Britain's main airports, Heathrow (p394) and Gatwick (p394), are both just outside London. Other busy regional airports include Edinburgh (p297), Glasgow (p307), Manchester (p216) and Liverpool (p222).
- **Train** The zippy Eurostar (p395) connects London St Pancras with Paris and the rest of Europe, or you can cross the channel with your own car thanks to the Eurotunnel (p395).
- **Sea** Ferry services (p396) serve UK ports including Dover, Portsmouth, Weymouth, Newcastle and Liverpool.

PLANNING YOUR TRIP

THINGS YOU NEED TO KNOW

MANFRED GOTTSCHALK

Traditional telephone box, Scottish Highlands

↘ TRAVEL SEASONS

- **Spring** Quieter sights and generally good weather means this is an attractive time to travel.
- **Summer** The main holiday season means traffic, attractions and national parks are at their busiest, despite the fact that the weather's unreliable.
- **Autumn** Another relatively quiet season, especially if you time your visit for late September and October.
- **Winter** Often cold and wet, but if you're looking for peace and quiet it can be a good time to travel. Remember that many popular attractions close down for the winter.

↘ WHAT TO BRING

- **Rain jacket** The rumours about the weather aren't exaggerated.
- **Comfortable shoes** Hard to enjoy the endless strolls without them.
- **Small day-pack** For carrying that rain jacket when the sun does shine.
- **Listening skills** English is the main language, but the difference in accents across Britain is incredible.

GARETH MCCORMACK

Cuillin Hills (p341), Isle of Skye, Scotland

GET INSPIRED

BOOKS

- **Oliver Twist** (1837) Fagin, the Artful Dodger, Bill Sykes – need we say more?
- **Sense and Sensibility** (1813) Jane Austen's quintessential tale of English manners.
- **Brighton Rock** (1938) Gangland classic by Graham Greene.
- **Cider with Rosie** (1959) Laurie Lee's charming memoir of his Gloucestershire childhood.
- **The Remains of the Day** (1989) Kazuo Ishiguro's Booker Prize–winner about a buttoned-up butler.
- **White Teeth** (2000) Zadie Smith's literary debut explores life in multicultural London.
- **Last Orders** (1996) Graham Swift's moving novel follows four born-and-bred Londoners.

FILMS

- **Brief Encounter** (1945) David Lean's classic of English reserve and unstated love.
- **Chariots of Fire** (1981) Oscar-winning story of British Olympic endeavour, set against Oxford's dreaming spires.
- **Withnail & I** (1986) Cult comedy about two out-of-work actors on a disastrous Lake District holiday.
- **Trainspotting** (1996) Danny Boyle's breakthrough based on Irvine Welsh's heroin-laden novel.
- **Four Weddings and a Funeral** (1994) Box-office smash starring Hugh Grant in full floppy-haired flow.

- **Shaun of the Dead** (2004) Zombie comedy-horror: ballsy, bloody and British through-and-through.

MUSIC

- **Sergeant Pepper's Lonely Hearts Club Band** (The Beatles) The Fab Four's finest moment needs no introduction.
- **Village Green Preservation Society** (The Kinks) Poppy melodies and wry English observations courtesy of Ray Davies.
- **Exile On Main Street** (The Rolling Stones) Classic album recorded before the Stones needed walking frames.
- **London Calling** (The Clash) Punk with a point.
- **Different Class** (Pulp) Tales of English eccentricity from lanky northern wordsmith Jarvis Cocker.

WEBSITES

- **BBC** (www.bbc.co.uk) News and entertainment courtesy of the national broadcaster.
- **British Council** (www.britishcouncil.org) British culture, arts and science.
- **Visit Britain** (www.visitbritain.com) Official tourism website; accommodation, attractions, events and much more.
- **National Rail** (www.nationalrail.co.uk) Online resource for train travel.
- **UK Tea Council** (www.tea.co.uk) All you need to know about the national tipple.

CALENDAR

Tug-of-war, Braemar Gathering (p49)

JONATHAN SMITH

FEBRUARY

JORVIK VIKING FESTIVAL
Mid-February sees horned helmets galore, plus mock invaders and Viking longship races in Jorvik (p226), York.

MARCH

UNIVERSITY BOAT RACE
This historic rowing contest between rivals Oxford and Cambridge Universities has been held yearly since 1856 (apart from the odd break in the world wars). It takes place in late March or early April; see http://theboatrace.org.

APRIL

GRAND NATIONAL
Half the country has a flutter on the nation's favourite horse race, notorious for its testing course and high jumps. The race takes place on the first Saturday in April at Aintree, Liverpool.

MAY

FA CUP FINAL
The highlight of the football season for over a century. Teams from all England's football divisions battle it out in a knock-out tournament, culminating in the heady spectacle of the Cup Final at Wembley Stadium in early May.

CHELSEA FLOWER SHOW
Top international garden designers descend on west London for the Royal Horticultural Society's flower show late in the month (see http://rhs.org.uk/chelsea). Top gardens take away gold, silver and bronze medals, while the punters take away the plants in the last-day giveaway.

COOPER'S HILL CHEESE-ROLLING COMPETITION

Simple concept, centuries old: a big lump of cheese is rolled down a very steep hill, chased by hundreds of locals. The winner keeps the cheese. Losers may have broken legs. Go to www.cheese-rolling.co.uk for details and pics.

⬎ JUNE

COTSWOLDS OLIMPICKS

Since 1612 the locals of Chipping Camden have been testing their mettle in their annual sports day (www.olimpickgames.co.uk), featuring eccentric events such as shin kicking, sack racing and climbing the slippery pole. Held in early June (sometimes late May).

TROOPING THE COLOUR

Military bands and bear-skinned grenadiers march down Whitehall in this martial pageant to mark the Queen's official birthday in June (despite the fact that her actual birthday in on 21 April).

ROYAL ASCOT

It's sometimes hard to tell which matters more – the fashion or the fillies – at the annual spectacle of Royal Ascot. Expect top hats, designer frocks and plenty of frantic betting. See ascot.co.uk.

WIMBLEDON LAWN TENNIS CHAMPIONSHIPS

The last British champion was way back in 1977, but that doesn't seem to dampen the nation's enthusiasm for their annual tennis-fest at **Wimbledon** (p380), held over two rapid-fire weeks in late June.

GLASTONBURY FESTIVAL

England's favourite musical mudfest (www.glastonburyfestivals.co.uk), held (nearly) every year on Michael Eavis' dairy farm in Pilton, Somerset; still a rite of passage for every self-respecting British teenager.

⬎ JULY

T IN THE PARK

Scotland's answer to Glastonbury – an open-air festival featuring hot-ticket acts from the pop, rock and dance scenes. Check out the latest line-up at www.tinthepark.com.

VERONICA GARBUTT
Royal Ascot

↘ CALENDAR

| JAN | FEB | MAR | APR |

INTERNATIONAL EISTEDDFOD
Lively **mix of cultures** (p272) from Wales and far beyond, held in mid-July in the lively town of Llangollen. The National Eisteddfod takes place a month later in August.

LATITUDE FESTIVAL
More than just a music festival, this relative newcomer to Britain's festival calendar (www.latitudefestival.co.uk) packs in poetry, literature, comedy and drama, too. Held in Henham Park, Southwold.

EDEN SESSIONS
The famous biomes of the **Eden Project** (p157) are transformed into Cornwall's most spectacular live-music venue in July/August. Go to www.edenproject.com/sessions to book your tickets online.

↘ AUGUST

EDINBURGH FRINGE FESTIVAL
Edinburgh's world-famous arts gathering sees hundreds of theatre companies, comedians and musicians congregate throughout August and into September. Runs alongside the Edinburgh International Festival. Book tickets and plan your festival at www.edfringe.com.

GREEN MAN FESTIVAL
Set near Crickhowell, this mid-month festival (www.thegreenmanfestival.co.uk) takes a more alternative approach than many of the UK's other mainstream festivals. The Black Mountains setting is rather lovely too.

NOTTING HILL CARNIVAL
London's most colourful festival is a multicultural feast of music, dancing and costumed street parades that cel-

DOUG HOUGHTON / ALAMY

Outdoor ice rink at New Year, Edinburgh

| MAY | JUN | JUL | AUG | SEP | OCT | NOV | DEC |

ebrates the city's African-Caribbean community. Get inspired at www.the nottinghillcarnival.com.

READING FESTIVAL
England's second-oldest music festival (readingfestival.com; predated only by Glastonbury). Poppier than it used to be, but still a good bet for big-name bands. It shares many acts with its sister festival in Leeds, held a little later in the month.

BIG CHILL
An eclectic and relaxed mix of live music, club events, DJs, multimedia and visual art, held in the grounds of Eastnor Castle in Herefordshire. You'll find the low-down at www.bigchill .net.

Glastonbury Festival (p47)

check out the competition at birdman .org.uk. First weekend in September.

▶ SEPTEMBER

BRAEMAR GATHERING
With more than 20,000 people (including the royals), 'gathering' is an understatement for this famous Highland knees-up (www.braemargathering.org). First Saturday of the month

INTERNATIONAL BIRDMAN COMPETITION
Competitors dressed as batmen, fairies and flying machines compete in an outlandish celebration of self-powered flight in Bognor Regis. The furthest flight takes the top £30,000 prize – so far no-one's got anywhere near the hallowed 100m goal. Find your wings and

▶ NOVEMBER

BONFIRE NIGHT   5 NOV
Bonfires and fireworks across Britain fill the skies in commemoration of Guy Fawke's failed Gunpowder Plot of 1605 (a terrorist attempt to blow up Parliament).

▶ DECEMBER

NEW YEAR CELEBRATIONS   31 DEC
Get drunk and kiss strangers as the bells chime midnight. The biggest crowds are in London's **Trafalgar Sq** (p65) and Edinburgh's **Princes St** (p292).

↘ LONDON

LONDON

GREATER LONDON

GREATER LONDON

INFORMATION
Royal Free Hospital................**1** C1

SIGHTS & ACTIVITIES
Chapel...**2** H5
Cutty Sark..................................**3** G5
Hampstead Heath.................**4** C1
Imperial War Museum...........**5** E4
Lord's Cricket Ground...........**6** C2
National Maritime Museum.**7** G6
Old Royal Naval College......**8** G5
Painted Hall...............................**9** G5
Royal Observatory...............**10** H6
Tate Britain **11** E5
Wallace Collection **12** D3
Westminster Cathedral.......**13** D4

SLEEPING
Luna & Simone Hotel **14** D5
St Alfege's **15** G6

EATING
Bermondsey Kitchen...........**16** F4
Song Que **17** G2

ENTERTAINMENT
Almeida......................................**18** E2
Battersea Arts Centre **19** C6
Brixton Academy **20** E6
Shepherd's Bush Empire **21** A4

SHOPPING
Greenwich Market................**22** G6
Selfridges...................................**23** D3

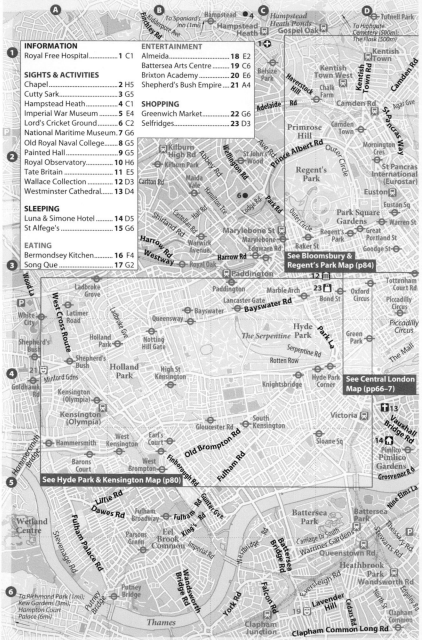

See Bloomsbury & Regent's Park Map (p84)

See Central London Map (pp66–7)

See Hyde Park & Kensington Map (p80)

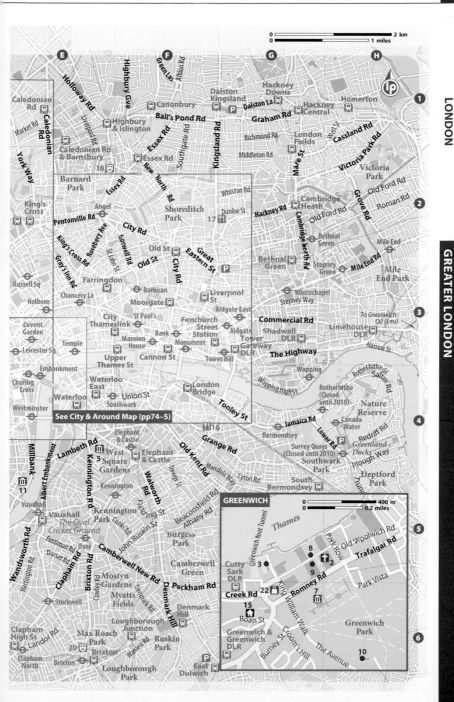

LONDON HIGHLIGHTS

1   THE TOWER OF LONDON

BY JOHN KEOHANE, CHIEF YEOMAN WARDER AT THE TOWER OF LONDON

The Yeoman Warders (or Beefeaters as we're often known) have been a part of the Tower's history since at least 1485. Our official role is to guard the Tower and the Crown Jewels. To qualify you must have served at least 22 years in the Armed Forces and have earned a Long Service and Good Conduct Medal.

↘ JOHN KEOHANE'S DON'T MISS LIST

❶ A TOWER TOUR

To understand the Tower and its history, a guided tour with one of the Yeoman Warders is essential. Very few people appreciate that the Tower is actually our home as well as our place of work; all the Warders live inside the outer walls, which once housed stables and workshops. The Tower is rather like a miniature village – visitors are often rather surprised to see our washing hanging out beside the castle walls!

❷ CROWN JEWELS

Visitors often think the Crown Jewels are the Queen's personal jewellery collection. They're not, of course; the Crown Jewels are actually the ceremonial regalia used during the Coronation. The highlights are the Sceptre and the Imperial State Crown, which contains the celebrated diamond known as the Star of Africa. People are often surprised to hear that the Crown Jewels aren't insured (as they could never be replaced).

Clockwise from top: Sightseers, Tower of London; Close-up of the Tower; Guard on alert; Changing of the Guard; Tower view from the Thames

CLOCKWISE FROM TOP: WAYNE WALTON; NEIL SETCHFIELD; BRIAN CRUICKSHANK; VERONICA GARBUTT; DOUG MCKINLAY

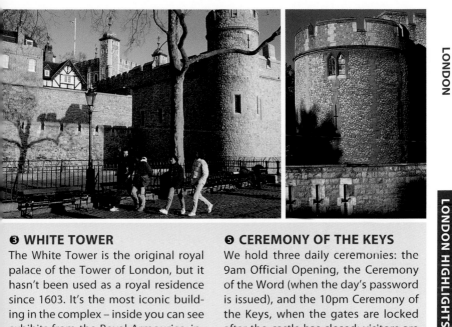

❸ WHITE TOWER

The White Tower is the original royal palace of the Tower of London, but it hasn't been used as a royal residence since 1603. It's the most iconic building in the complex – inside you can see exhibits from the Royal Armouries, including a suit of armour belonging to Henry VIII.

❺ CEREMONY OF THE KEYS

We hold three daily ceremonies: the 9am Official Opening, the Ceremony of the Word (when the day's password is issued), and the 10pm Ceremony of the Keys, when the gates are locked after the castle has closed; visitors are welcome to attend the latter, but must apply directly to the Tower in writing.

❹ RAVENS

A Tower legends states that if its resident ravens ever left, the monarchy would topple – a royal decree states that we must keep a minimum of six ravens at any time. We currently have nine ravens, looked after by the Ravenmaster and his two assistants.

↘ THINGS YOU NEED TO KNOW

Top tip Booking online will allow you to dodge the queues **Photo op** Standing on the battlements overlooking the Thames **Did you know?** The Yeoman Guards' famous red-and-gold ceremonial outfits cost around £7000 **For full details on the Tower of London, see p73**

LONDON HIGHLIGHTS

2 | BRITISH MUSEUM

BY PAUL COLLINS, CURATOR IN THE MIDDLE EAST AT THE BRITISH MUSEUM

The British Museum is one of London's great wonders. As our slogan suggests, it's truly a museum of the world; in the space of a day you can explore the history and culture of all the world's great civilisations. It's a real privilege to work here.

⬎ PAUL COLLINS' DON'T MISS LIST

❶ ENLIGHTENMENT GALLERY (ROOM 1)

This magnificent room contains an informative display that shows how collectors, antiquaries and travellers viewed and classified objects at the time the museum was founded (1753). It's an excellent introduction to the British Museum and its collections.

❷ ASSYRIAN LION HUNT FROM NINEVEH (ROOM 10)

These are some of the greatest carvings from the ancient world. They originate from the city of Nineveh, in what is now modern-day Iraq. They've become especially important given the events of recent years in Iraq.

❸ CLOCKS & WATCHES GALLERY (ROOMS 38–9)

These rooms contain a collection of mechanical devices for telling the time. It's quite a strange experience to be surrounded by the ticking, striking and chiming the hours of hundreds of clocks!

Clockwise from top: Great Court, British Museum; British Museum's main entrance; Enlightenment Gallery; National Portrait Gallery

LONDON

LONDON HIGHLIGHTS

❹ EAST STAIRS

An impressive collection of casts of Persian, Mayan and Egyptian reliefs line the stairs. These were made in the 19th and early 20th centuries, and are historically important as the original objects left at the sites have been damaged or have disappeared.

❺ NATIONAL PORTRAIT GALLERY

As well as visiting the British Museum, I'd encourage everyone to pay a visit to this wonderful **art gallery** (p65), which contains Britain's finest collection of historic portraits, from the early Tudors right through to the modern day; the rooftop cafe has the most wonderful view over Trafalgar Sq.

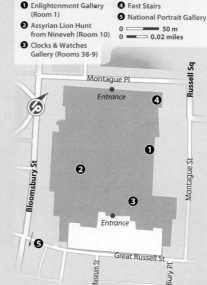

❶ Enlightenment Gallery (Room 1)
❷ Assyrian Lion Hunt from Nineveh (Room 10)
❸ Clocks & Watches Gallery (Rooms 38-9)
❹ East Stairs
❺ National Portrait Gallery

0 ———— 50 m
0 ———— 0.02 miles

↘ THINGS YOU NEED TO KNOW

Best time to visit Weekdays are quieter than weekends **How long will I need?** At least half a day **Top tip** Audioguides (£3.50) let you explore at your own pace **Tours** Free 30-minute guided tours are offered throughout the day **For full details on the British Museum, see p72**

LONDON HIGHLIGHTS

↘ TATE MODERN

This run-down power station was once a real eyesore, but since the inspired decision to transform it into the **Tate Modern** (p79) in the late 1990s it's helped reinvigorate the nation's interest in modern art. The permanent collection takes in everyone from Andy Warhol to Pablo Picasso, but it's the big-ticket exhibition in the Turbine Hall which inevitably sparks the most excitement.

↘ SHAKESPEARE'S GLOBE

The original theatre where Bill Shakespeare premiered some of his most famous plays burned down in 1613, but this modern-day **reconstruction** (p77) used traditional materials and building techniques to bring the Bard's open-air playhouse back to life. It offers a fascinating insight into Shakespeare's theatrical world; take a guided tour or, better still, join the groundlings for an afternoon performance.

5

↘ LONDON EYE

All right, all right – it might be touristy, but this famous **Ferris wheel** (p77) is still a must-do. Jump into one of the space-age pods and enjoy a half-hour spin offering one of the finest views in all of London, stretching out to 25 miles on a good day. Book online and you won't even have to queue much.

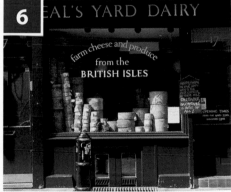

6

↘ SHOP TILL YOU DROP

If you're looking to splash some cash, you won't be short on options in London. For big-name boutiques and department stores, go to the **West End** (p71). For something more exclusive, head for the streets of **Knightsbridge and Kensington** (p78). For quirkier souvenirs try the tucked-away shops of **Covent Garden** (p71) or one of the busy **markets** (p102).

7

↘ GET LOST IN GREENWICH

Many visitors never venture south of the river, but it's worth making the trip to **Greenwich** (p83). This elegant area was once the centre of British maritime power, and relics of that seafaring heritage linger on at the **National Maritime Museum** (p85), the **Royal Observatory** (p85) and the **Old Royal Naval College** (p84).

3 NEIL SETCHFIELD; 4 MANUEL HARLAN/ HAKESPEARE'S GLOBE IMAGE LIBRARY; 5 DOUG MCKINLAY; 6 CHRISTOPHER WOOD; 7 PAUL BIGLAND

3 Turbine Hall, Tate Modern (p79); 4 Shakespeare's Globe (p77); 5 London Eye (p77); 6 Neal's Yard Dairy, Covent Garden (p71); 7 Old Royal Naval College (p84)

LONDON

LONDON'S BEST...

LONDON'S BEST...

⇘ THINGS FOR FREE

- The **British Museum** (p72) and London's other flagship museums.
- Marvel at the masterpieces of the **National Gallery** (p65).
- Wander, window-shop and watch street art in **Covent Garden** (p71).
- Catch the **Changing of the Guard** (p70).
- Have a picnic in **Hyde Park** (p81).

⇘ PLACES TO CHILL

- **Regent's Park** (p82) John Nash's glorious city park.
- **Hampstead Heath** (p83) North London's oasis of greenery.
- **Kew Gardens** (p85) The nation's botanical gardens.
- **Highgate Cemetery** (p83) Seek out the tombs of the great and good.
- **Richmond Park** (p86) Country park just outside central London.

⇘ CITY VIEWS

- **London Eye** (p77) Book well ahead for this London landmark.
- **Greenwich** (p83) Survey the cityscape from the Royal Observatory.
- **Westminster Cathedral** (p69) Climb the tower for views of Old London Town.
- **Parliament Hill** (p83) Hampstead Heath's highest point.
- **Tower Bridge** (p73) Get another perspective on the River Thames.

⇘ BOUTIQUE SLEEPS

- **Soho Hotel** (p89) Funky Firmdale hotel styled by designer *du jour* Kit Kemp.
- **Zetter** (p90) Contemporary lines in a converted warehouse.
- **Sanderson** (p90) Super-chic, super-modern and super-expensive.
- **Hempel** (p91) Five-star West London luxury.
- **Rookery** (p90) Step back into East End history.

Left: Hyde Park (p81); Right: Westminster Bridge, Houses of Parliament and Big Ben (p69)

THINGS YOU NEED TO KNOW

⬏ VITAL STATISTICS

- **Telephone code** ☎ 020
- **Population** 7.51 million
- **Area** 609 sq miles

⬏ NEIGHBOURHOODS IN A NUTSHELL

- **Trafalgar Square** (p65) The heart of the city.
- **Westminster & Pimlico** (p68) The hub of British political power.
- **St James's & Mayfair** (p70) Playground of the rich, famous and royal.
- **West End** (p71) London's hectic commercial centre.
- **Holborn & Clerkenwell** (p73) Where Dickensian London lives on.
- **The City** (p73) London's financial powerhouse.
- **Hoxton, Shoreditch & Spitalfields** (p95) Once grimy, now quirky and creative.
- **Chelsea, Kensington & Knightsbridge** (p78) The capital's poshest addresses.
- **North London** (p82) Residential neighbourhoods with a twist.
- **Greenwich** (p83) Where Britannia ruled the waves.

⬏ ADVANCE PLANNING

- **Two months before** Sort your hotel room and theatre tickets.
- **Two weeks before** Make restaurant reservations.
- **One week before** Prebook for the London Eye, Madame Tussaud's, St Paul's and the Tower of London.

⬏ RESOURCES

- **Visit London** (www.visitlondon.com) The main event.
- **BBC London** (www.bbc.co.uk/london) London-centric low-down from the Beeb.
- **Evening Standard** (www.thisislondon.co.uk) Latest news from the city's daily rag.
- **Urban Path** (www.urbanpath.com) Up-to-date tips.

⬏ EMERGENCY NUMBERS

- **Police/Fire/Ambulance** (☎ 999)
- **Samaritans** (☎ 0845-790 9090)

⬏ GETTING AROUND

- **Bus** Good for sightseeing; not good for traffic.
- **Tube** The speediest way to get around town.
- **Walk** around Soho, Covent Garden, Bloomsbury and the West End.
- **Boat** The city looks pretty seen from the river.

⬏ BE FOREWARNED

- **Exhibitions** High-profile seasonal exhibitions at museums and galleries often charge extra and are sold out weeks ahead.
- **Restaurants** You'll need to book for the big-name establishments.
- **Public Transport** Oyster cards (p104) offer the best value.
- **Rush hour** Many public transport tickets aren't valid in rush hour.

LONDON

THINGS YOU NEED TO KNOW

DISCOVER LONDON

Everyone comes to London with a preconception of the metropolis. Whatever yours is, prepare to have it shattered by this endlessly fascinating, amorphous city.

Don't believe anyone who claims to know London – you could spend a lifetime exploring it and find that the slippery thing's gone and changed on you. One thing is constant: that great serpent of a river enfolding the city in its sinuous loops, linking London both to the green heart of England and the world. The Empire may be long gone but the engines of global capital continue to be stoked by the side of the River Thames. This only adds to London's vibrant, finger-on-the-pulse persona. It's also what makes it the third-most expensive city in the world. With endless reserves of cool, London is one of the world's great cities, if not the greatest.

LONDON IN...

Two Days

Only two days? Start in **Trafalgar Square** (p65) and see at least the outside of all the big-ticket sights: **London Eye** (p77), **Houses of Parliament** (p69), **Westminster Abbey** (p68), **St James's Park and Palace** (p70), **Buckingham Palace** (p70), **Green Park** (p70), **Hyde Park** (p81) and **Kensington Gardens & Palace** (p81) and then motor around the **Tate Modern** (p79) until you get booted out. In the evening, explore **Soho** (p71). On day two race around the **British Museum** (p72) then head to the **City** (p73). Take a walk around this history-packed square mile, finishing in the **Tower of London** (p73). Head to the East End for an evening of **ethnic food** (p95) and **hip bars** (p98).

Four Days

Take the two-day itinerary but stretch it to a comfortable pace. Stop at the **National Gallery** (p65) while you're at Trafalgar Sq, explore inside Westminster Abbey and **St Paul's Cathedral** (p76) and allow half a day for the Tate Modern, British Museum and Tower of London. On your extra evenings, check out **Camden** and **Islington** (p97) or splurge on a slap-up dinner in **Chelsea** (p96).

One Week

As above, but add in a day each for **Greenwich** (p83), **Kew Gardens** (p85) and **Hampton Court Palace** (p85).

LONDON

HISTORY

HISTORY

London first came into being as a Celtic village near a ford across the River Thames, but it wasn't until after the Roman invasion, in the year AD 43, that the city really began to take off. When William the Conqueror won the watershed Battle of Hastings in 1066, he and his forces marched into London where he was crowned king. The throne has passed through various houses since (the House of Windsor has warmed its cushion since 1910), with royal power concentrated in London from the 12th century.

The mother of all blazes, the Great Fire of 1666, virtually razed the place, destroying most of its medieval, Tudor and Jacobean architecture. One plus was that it created a blank canvas upon which master architect Sir Christopher Wren could build his magnificent churches.

Georgian London saw a surge in artistic creativity with the likes of Dr Johnson, Handel, Gainsborough and Reynolds enriching the city's culture while its architects fashioned an elegant new metropolis. In 1837 the 18-year-old Victoria ascended the throne. During her long reign (1837–1901), London became the fulcrum of the expanding British Empire, which covered a quarter of the earth's surface.

Although London suffered relatively minor damage during WWI, it was devastated by the Luftwaffe in WWII when huge swathes of the centre and East End were flattened and 32,000 people were killed.

London became the capital of cool in fashion and music in the 'Swinging Sixties'.

CLOCKWISE FROM TOP: ORIEN HARVEY; NEIL SETCHFIELD; CHRISTER FREDRIKSSON; NEIL SETCHFIELD

Clockwise from top left: London Eye (p77); Portobello Road Market (p102); Hyde Park (p81); Outdoor drinks and dining, Soho (p71)

The party didn't last long, however, and London returned to the doldrums in the harsh economic climate of the 1970s. Recovery began – for the business community at least – under the iron fist of Margaret Thatcher, elected Britain's first woman prime minister in 1979.

In 2000 the modern metropolis got its first Mayor of London (as opposed to the Lord Mayor of the City of London), an elected role covering the City and all 32 urban boroughs.

Snatching victory from the jaws of Paris (who were the favourites), the city won its bid to host the 2012 Olympics and celebrated with a frenzy of flag-waving. Work is continuing in earnest in the East End to transform a 200-hectare site into the Olympic Park, complete with new legacy venues and an athletes' village that will be turned into housing post-Olympics.

ORIENTATION

The M25 ring road encompasses the 609 sq miles that is broadly regarded as Greater London. The old City of London (note the big 'C') is the capital's financial district, covering roughly a square mile bordered by the river and the many gates of the ancient (long-gone) city walls: Newgate, Moorgate etc. The areas to the east of the City are collectively known as the East End. The West End, on the City's other flank, is effectively the centre of London nowadays. Surrounding these central areas are dozens of former villages (Camden, Islington, Clapham etc), each with its own High Street, which were long ago swallowed by London's sprawl.

MAPS

No Londoner would be without a pocket-sized London A-Z, which lists nearly 30,000 streets and still doesn't cover London in its entirety.

INFORMATION
MEDICAL SERVICES

Hospitals with 24-hour accident and emergency units:

Royal Free Hospital (Map pp52-3; ☎ 7794 0500; Pond St NW3; ⊖ Belsize Park)

St Thomas' Hospital (Map pp66-7; ☎ 7188 7188; Lambeth Palace Rd SE1; ⊖ Waterloo)

University College Hospital (Map p84; ☎ 0845-155 5000; 235 Euston Rd WC1; ⊖ Euston Sq)

MONEY

You can change cash easily at banks, travel agents and post offices, where rates are usually fair. If you use bureaux de change, check commission rates and exchange rates; some can be extortionate.

American Express (Amex; Map pp66-7; ☎ 7484 9610; 30-31 Haymarket SW1; ☽ 9am-6pm Mon-Sat, 10am-4pm Sun; ⊖ Piccadilly Circus)

Thomas Cook (Map pp66-7; ☎ 0845-308 9570; 30 St James's St SW1; ☽ 9am-5.30pm Mon, Tue, Thu & Fri, 10am-5.30pm Wed; ⊖ Green Park)

DANGERS & ANNOYANCES

Considering its size and disparities in wealth, London is generally safe. That said, keep your wits about you and don't flash your cash unnecessarily. When travelling by tube, choose a carriage with other people in it and avoid deserted suburban stations. Watch out for pick-pockets on crowded tubes, night buses and streets.

When using ATMs, guard your PIN details carefully. Don't use one that looks like it's been tampered with as there have been incidents of card cloning.

SIGHTS
TRAFALGAR SQUARE

Trafalgar Sq is the public heart of London, hosting rallies, marches and feverish New Year festivities. Formerly ringed by gnarling traffic, the square's been tidied up and is now one of the world's grandest public places. At the heart of it, Nelson surveys his fleet from the 43.5m-high **Nelson's Column** (Map pp66–7), erected in 1843 to commemorate Nelson's 1805 victory over Napoleon off Cape Trafalgar in Spain. At the edges of the square are four plinths, three of which have permanent statues, while the **fourth plinth** (Map pp66–7) is given over to temporary modern installations.

NATIONAL GALLERY

Gazing grandly over Trafalgar Sq through its Corinthian columns, the **National Gallery** (Map pp66-7; ☎ 7747 2885; www.nationalgallery.org.uk; Trafalgar Sq WC2; admission free; ☼ 10am-6pm Sat-Thu, to 9pm Fri; ⊖ Charing Cross) is the nation's most important repository of art. Four million visitors descend annually to admire its 2300-plus Western European paintings, spanning the years 1250 to 1900.

Highlights include Turner's *The Fighting Temeraire* (voted Britain's greatest painting), Botticelli's *Venus and Mars* and Van Gogh's *Sunflowers. Da Vinci Code* fans will make a beeline for Leonardo's *The Virgin of the Rocks,* the sister of the one hanging in the Louvre. The medieval religious paintings in the Sainsbury Wing are fascinating, but for a short, sharp blast of brilliance you can't beat the truckloads of Monets, Manets, Cézannes, Degas and Renoirs in rooms 43 to 46.

Free one-hour guided tours leave at 11.30am and 2.30pm daily.

NATIONAL PORTRAIT GALLERY

The fascinating **National Portrait Gallery** (Map pp66-7; ☎ 7312 2463; www.npg.org.uk; St Martin's Pl WC2; admission free; ☼ 10am-6pm Sat-Wed, to 9pm Thu & Fri; ⊖ Charing Cross) is like stepping into a picture book of English history.

Founded in 1856, the permanent collection (around 10,000 works) starts with the

Steps outside the National Gallery

ORIEN HARVEY

CENTRAL LONDON

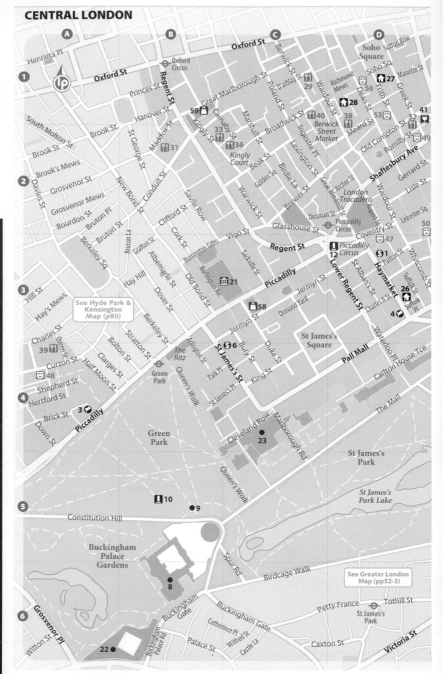

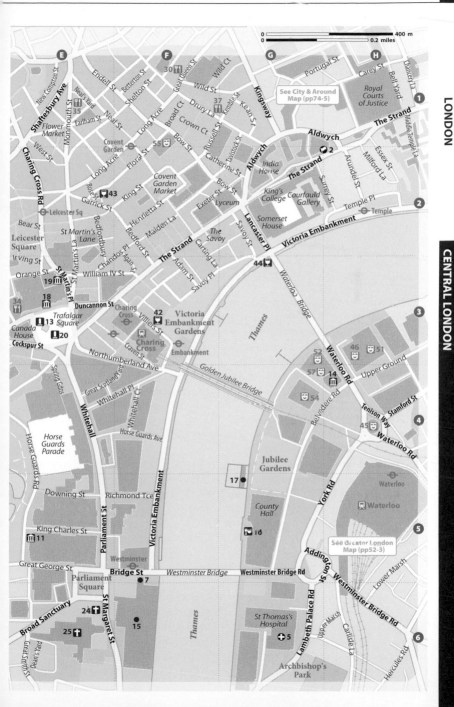

INFORMATION		
American Express (Main Office)	1	D3
Australian High Commission	2	H2
Japanese Embassy	3	A4
New Zealand Embassy	4	D3
St Thomas's Hospital	5	G6
Thomas Cook (Main Office)	6	C4

SIGHTS & ACTIVITIES		
Big Ben	7	F5
Buckingham Palace	8	B6
Canada Gate	9	B5
Canada Memorial	10	B5
Churchill Museum & Cabinet War Rooms	11	E5
Eros Statue	12	D3
Fourth Plinth	13	E3
Hayward Gallery	14	H4
Houses of Parliament	15	F6
London Aquarium	16	G5
London Eye	17	G5
National Gallery	18	E3
National Portrait Gallery	19	E3
Nelson's Column	20	E3
Royal Academy of Arts	21	C3
Royal Mews	22	A6
St James's Palace	23	C4
St Margaret's Church	24	E6
Westminister Abbey	25	E6

SLEEPING		
Haymarket Hotel	26	D3
Hazlitt's	27	D1
Soho Hotel	28	D1

EATING		
Breakfast Club	29	C1
Great Queen Street	30	F1
Hibiscus	31	B2
Kettners	32	D1
Mother Mash	33	B2
National Gallery Dining Rooms	34	E3
Neal's Yard Salad Bar	35	E1
Sacred	36	C2
Sarastro	37	F1
Spiga	38	D1
Tamarind	39	A4
Yauatcha	40	C1

DRINKING		
Coach & Horses	41	D1
Gordon's Wine Bar	42	F3
Lamb & Flag	43	E2
Queen Mary	44	G3

ENTERTAINMENT		
BFI IMAX	45	H4
BFI Southbank	46	H3
Comedy Store	47	D3
Curzon Mayfair	48	A4
Curzon Soho	49	D2
Leicester Square Half-Price Ticket Booth	50	D2
National Theatre	51	H3
Purcell Room	(see 52)	
Queen Elizabeth Hall	52	G3
Ronnie Scott's	53	D1
Royal Festival Hall	54	G4
Royal Opera House	55	F1
Soho Theatre	56	D1
Southbank Centre	57	G4

SHOPPING		
Fortnum & Mason	58	C3
Liberty	59	B1

Tudors on the 2nd floor and descends to contemporary figures. Among the modern mob, look out for a full-length painting of Dame Judi Dench, a 3-D depiction of JK Rowling and a photographic study of David Bowie, seated in a seedy toilet with a dead-looking Natasha Vojnovic across his lap.

WESTMINSTER & PIMLICO
WESTMINSTER ABBEY
Not merely a beautiful place of worship, **Westminster Abbey** (Map pp66-7; ☎ 7222 5152; www.westminster-abbey.org; 20 Dean's Yard SW1; adult/child £12/9, tours/audio guides £5/4; ☯ 9.15am-4.30pm Mon, Tue, Thu & Fri, to 6pm Wed, to 2.30pm Sat; ⊖ Westminster) serves England's history cold on slabs of stone. Every monarch since William the Conqueror has been crowned here, with the exception of a couple of unlucky Eds who were murdered (Edward V) or abdicated (Edward VIII) before the magic moment. Look out for the incongruously ordinary-looking **Coronation Chair**.

The original church was built in the 11th century by King (later Saint) Edward the Confessor, who is buried in the chapel be-

hind the main altar. Henry III began work on the new building in 1245 but didn't complete it; the French Gothic nave was finished in 1388. Henry VII's magnificent Late Perpendicular–style **Lady Chapel** was consecrated in 1519 after 16 years of construction.

Apart from the royal graves, keep an eye out for the many famous commoners interred here, especially in **Poet's Corner** where you'll find the resting places of Chaucer, Dickens, Hardy, Tennyson, Dr Johnson and Kipling as well as memorials to the other greats (Shakespeare, Jane Austen, Emily Bronte etc).

The octagonal **Chapter House** (☯ 10.30am-4pm) dates from the 1250s and was where the monks would meet for daily prayer before Henry VIII's dissolution of the monasteries. Used as a treasury and 'Royal Wardrobe', the cryptlike **Pyx Chamber** (☯ 10.30am-4pm) dates from about 1070. The neighbouring **Abbey Museum** (☯ 10.30am-4pm) has as its centrepiece death masks of generations of royalty.

Parts of the Abbey complex are free to visitors. This includes the **Cloister**

(🕑 8am-6pm), which featured prominently in *The Da Vinci Code,* and the 900-year-old **College Garden** (🕑 10am-6pm Tue-Thu Apr-Sep, to 4pm Oct-Mar). Adjacent to the abbey is **St Margaret's Church** (Map pp66-7; 🕑 9.30am-3.30pm Mon-Fri, to 1.30pm Sat, 2-5pm Sun), the House of Commons' place of worship since 1614.

On weekdays, Matins is at 7.30am, Holy Communion at 8am and 12.30pm, and Choral Evensong at 5pm. There are services throughout the day on Sundays.

HOUSES OF PARLIAMENT

Coming face-to-face with one of the world's most recognisable landmarks is always a surreal moment, but in the case of the **Houses of Parliament** (Map pp66-7; ☎ 0870-906 3773; www.parliament.uk; Parliament Sq SW1; ⊖ Westminster) it's a revelation.

Officially called the Palace of Westminster, the oldest part is **Westminster Hall** (1097), which is one of only a few parts that survived a catastrophic fire in 1834. However, the palace's most famous feature is its clock tower, aka **Big Ben** (Map pp66-7). Ben is actually the 13-ton bell, named after Benjamin Hall, who was commissioner of works when the tower was completed in 1858.

When Parliament is in session, visitors are admitted to the **House of Commons Visitors' Gallery** (admission free; 🕑 2.30-10.30pm Mon & Tue, 11.30am-7.30pm Wed, 10.30am-6.30pm Thu, 9.30am-3pm some Fri). The **House of Lords Visitors' Gallery** (admission free; 🕑 2.30-10pm Mon & Tue, 3-10pm Wed, 11am-7.30pm Thu, from 10am some Fri) is also open.

When parliament is in recess there are guided **tours** (75min tours adult/child £12/5) of both chambers and other historic areas.

WESTMINSTER CATHEDRAL

Begun in 1895, the neo-Byzantine **Westminster Cathedral** (Map pp52-3; ☎ 7798 9055; www.westminstercathedral.org.uk; Victoria St SW1; admission free; 🕑 7am-7pm, ⊖ Victoria) is the headquarters of Britain's once suppressed Roman Catholic Church. The distinctive 83m red-brick and white-stone **tower** (adult/child £5/2.50) offers splendid views of London and, unlike St Paul's dome, you can take the lift. Call ahead to book a Cathedral tour (£5).

TATE BRITAIN

Unlike the National Gallery, it's Britannia that rules the walls of **Tate Britain** (Map pp52-3; ☎ 7887 8008; www.tate.org.uk; Millbank SW1; admission free; 🕑 10am-5.50pm; ⊖ Pimlico). Reaching from 1500 to the present, it's crammed with local heavyweights like Blake, Hogarth, Gainsborough, Whistler, Spencer and, especially, Turner, whose

CHRIS MELLOR

Big Ben and statue of Winston Churchill

work dominates the **Clore Gallery**. The always-controversial (and often painfully conceptual) annual Turner Prize is exhibited in the gallery from October to January.

There are free hour-long guided tours, taking in different sections of the gallery, held daily at noon and 3pm, as well as additional tours at 11am and 2pm on weekdays.

CHURCHILL MUSEUM & CABINET WAR ROOMS

The **Cabinet War Rooms** (Map pp66-7; ☎ 7930 6961; www.iwm.org.uk; Clive Steps, King Charles St SW1; adult/child £12/free; ☙ 9.30am-6pm, last entry 5pm; ⊖ Westminster) were Prime Minister Winston Churchill's underground military HQ during WWII. Now a wonderfully evocative and atmospheric museum, the restored and preserved rooms (including Churchill's bedroom) capture the drama of the time.

ST JAMES'S & MAYFAIR

BUCKINGHAM PALACE

Built in 1803 for the Duke of Buckingham, **Buckingham Palace** (Map pp66-7; ☎ 7766 7302; www.royalcollection.org.uk; The Mall SW1; adult/child £16/8.75; ☙ 9.45am-6pm late Jul-late Sep; ⊖ St James's Park) replaced St James's Palace as the monarch's London home in 1837. Nineteen lavishly furnished staterooms are opened up to visitors when Her Majesty the Queen takes her holidays. The tour includes **Queen Victoria's Picture Gallery** (76.5m long, with works by Rembrandt, Van Dyck, Canaletto, Poussin and Vermeer) and the **Throne Room**, with his-and-hers pink chairs initialled 'ER' and 'P'.

CHANGING OF THE GUARD

If you're a fan of bright uniforms, bearskin hats, straight lines, marching and shouting, join the throngs outside the palace at 11.30am (daily from May to July and on alternate days for the rest of the year, weather permitting), when the regiment of guards outside the palace changes over in one of the world's most famous displays of pageantry.

ROYAL MEWS

Indulge your Cinderella fantasies while inspecting the exquisite state coaches and immaculately groomed royal horses housed in the **Royal Mews** (Map pp66-7; ☎ 7766 7302; Buckingham Palace Rd SW1; adult/child £7.50/4.80; ☙ 10am-5pm Aug & Sep, 11am-4pm mid-Mar–Jul & Oct; ⊖ Victoria).

ST JAMES'S PARK & ST JAMES'S PALACE

With its manicured flowerbeds and ornamental lake, **St James's Park** is a wonderful place to stroll and take in the views of Westminster, Buckingham Palace and St James's Palace. The striking Tudor gatehouse of **St James's Palace** (Map pp66-7; Cleveland Row SW1; ⊖ Green Park), initiated by the palace-mad Henry VIII in 1530, is best approached from St James's St to the north of the park. This was the residence of Prince Charles and his sons before they shifted next door to **Clarence House** (1828), following the death of its previous occupant, the Queen Mother, in 2002.

GREEN PARK

Green Park's 47-acre expanse of meadows and mature trees links St James's Park to Hyde Park and Kensington Gardens, creating a green corridor from Westminster all the way to Kensington. Although it doesn't have lakes, fountains or formal gardens, it's blanketed with daffodils in spring and semi-naked bodies whenever the sun shines.

The only concession to formality is the **Canada Memorial** (Map pp66–7)

LONDON

near **Canada Gate** (Map pp66–7), which links the park to Buckingham Palace. At its western end is **Hyde Park Corner**, where you'll find the **Australian** and **New Zealand War Memorials** (Map p80).

WEST END

Synonymous with big-budget musicals and frenzied flocks of shoppers, the West End is a strident mix of culture and consumerism. Elegant **Regent St** and frantic **Oxford St** are the city's main shopping strips. At the heart of the West End lies **Soho**, a grid of narrow streets and squares hiding gay bars, strip clubs, cafes and advertising agencies. Lisle and Gerrard Sts form the heart of **Chinatown**. Its neighbour, pedestrianised **Leicester** (les-ter) **Sq** heaves with tourists – and buskers, inevitably.

PICCADILLY

Named after the elaborate collars (picadils) that were the sartorial staple of a 17th-century tailor who lived nearby, Piccadilly became the fashionable haunt of the well-heeled (and collared), and still

boasts establishment icons such as the Ritz Hotel and Fortnum & Mason department store (p101). It meets Regent St, Shaftesbury Ave and Haymarket at neon-lit, turbo-charged **Piccadilly Circus**, home to the popular but unremarkable **Eros statue** (Map pp66-7; ⊖ Piccadilly Circus).

Set back from Piccadilly, the grandiose **Royal Academy of Arts** (Map pp66-7; ☎ 7300 8000; www.royalacademy.org.uk; Burlington House, Piccadilly W1; admission varies; ◷ 10am-6pm Sat-Thu, to 10pm Fri; ⊖ Green Park) hosts high-profile exhibitions and a small display from its permanent collection.

COVENT GARDEN

A hallowed name for opera fans due to the presence of the esteemed Royal Opera House (p100), Covent Garden is one of London's biggest tourist traps, where chain restaurants, souvenir shops, balconied bars and street entertainers vie for the punters' pound.

In the 18th and 19th centuries, the area immediately north of Covent Garden was the site of one of London's most notorious

SIGHTS

DOUG MCKINLAY

Football game, Regent's Park (p82)

slums, the 'rookery' of St Giles. Much of it was knocked down in the 1840s to create New Oxford St, but the narrow lanes and yards around Monmouth St still carry an echo of the crammed conditions of the past.

BLOOMSBURY

With the University of London and British Museum within its genteel environs, it's little wonder that Bloomsbury has attracted a lot of very clever, bookish people over the years. **Russell Square**, its very heart, was laid out in 1800 and is one of London's largest and loveliest.

BRITISH MUSEUM

The largest museum in the country and one of the oldest and finest in the world, this famous **museum** (Map p84; ☎ 7323 8000; www.thebritishmuseum.org; Great Russell St WC1; admission free; ☺ 10am-5.30pm Sat-Wed, to 8.30pm Thu & Fri; ⊖ Tottenham Court Rd or Russell Sq) boasts vast Egyptian, Etruscan, Greek, Oriental and Roman galleries among many others.

Before you get to the galleries, you'll be blown away by the **Great Court**, which was restored and augmented by Norman Foster in 2000. The courtyard now boasts a spectacular glass-and-steel roof, making it one of the most impressive architectural spaces in the capital. In the centre is the **Reading Room**, with its stunning blue-and-gold domed ceiling, where Karl Marx wrote the *Manifesto of the Communist Party*.

Among the must-sees are the **Rosetta Stone**, discovered in 1799 and the key to deciphering Egyptian hieroglyphics; the controversial **Parthenon Sculptures**, which once adorned the walls of the Parthenon in Athens; the stunning **Oxus Treasure** of 7th- to 4th-century BC Persian gold; and the Anglo-Saxon **Sutton Hoo** burial relics.

You'll need multiple visits to savour even the highlights here; happily there are 14 half-hour free 'eye opener' tours between 11am and 3.45pm daily, focusing on different parts of the collection. Other tours include the 90-minute highlights tour at 10.30am, 1pm and 3pm daily

Timepiece sundial sculpture by Wendy Taylor and Tower Bridge

DAVID TOMLINSON

(adult/child £8/5), and there is a range of audio guides (£3.50).

HOLBORN & CLERKENWELL

In these now fashionable streets, it's hard to find an echo of the notorious 'rookeries' of the 19th century, where families were squeezed into damp, fetid basements, living in possibly the worst conditions in the city's long history. This is the London documented so vividly by Dickens, whose sole surviving London residence, now the **Dickens House Museum** (Map pp74-5; ☎ 7405 2127; www.dickensmuseum .com; 48 Doughty St WC1; adult/under 16yr/concession £5/3/4; ☒ 10am-5pm Mon-Sat, 11am-5pm Sun; ⊖ Russell Sq) is where his work really flourished – The Pickwick Papers, Nicholas Nickleby and Oliver Twist were all written here. The handsome four-storey house opened as a museum in 1925, and visitors can stroll through rooms chock-a-block with fascinating memorabilia.

THE CITY

For most of its history, the City of London was London. It's only in the last 250 years that the City has gone from being the very essence of London and its main population centre to just its central business district. But what a business district it is – you could easily argue that the 'square mile' is the very heart of world capitalism.

TOWER OF LONDON

If you pay only one admission fee while you're in London, make it the **Tower of London** (Map pp74-5; ☎ 0844-482 7777; www .hrp.org.uk; Tower Hill EC3; adult/child £17/9.50; ☒ 10am-5.30pm Sun & Mon, 9am-5.30pm Tue-Sat Mar-Oct, 10am-4.30pm Sun & Mon, 9am-4.30pm Tue-Sat Nov-Feb; ⊖ Tower Hill).

A former royal residence, treasury, mint and arsenal, it became most famous as a prison when Henry VIII moved to Whitehall Palace in 1529 and started dishing out his preferred brand of punishment. On the small green in front of the church stood Henry VIII's **scaffold**, where seven people were beheaded, including Anne Boleyn and her cousin Catherine Howard (his second and fifth wives).

The most striking building is the huge **White Tower**, with its solid Romanesque architecture and four turrets, which today houses a collection from the Royal Armouries. On the 2nd floor is the **Chapel of St John the Evangelist**, dating from 1080 and therefore the oldest church in London.

To the north is the **Waterloo Barracks**, which now contains the spectacular **Crown Jewels**. On the far side of the White Tower is the **Bloody Tower**, where the 12-year-old Edward V and his little brother were held 'for their own safety' and later murdered, probably by their uncle, the future Richard III. Sir Walter Raleigh did a 13-year stretch here, when he wrote his History of the World, a copy of which is on display.

On the patch of green between the Wakefield and White Towers you'll find the latest in the tower's long line of famous ravens, which legend says could cause the White Tower to collapse should they leave. Their wings are clipped in case they get any ideas.

To help get your bearings, take the hugely entertaining free guided tour with any of the Tudor-garbed Beefeaters. Hour-long tours leave every 30 minutes from the Middle Tower; the last tour's an hour before closing.

TOWER BRIDGE

London was still a thriving port in 1894 when elegant Tower Bridge was built. Designed to be raised to allow ships to pass, electricity has now taken over from

CITY & AROUND

500 m
0.3 miles

SIGHTS & ACTIVITIES
Barbican	**1** D4
Design Museum	**2** F8
Dickens House Museum	**3** A4
Dr Johnson's House	**4** B5
London Dungeon	**5** E7
Shakespeare's Globe	**6** C7
St Katharine Dock	**7** F7
St Paul's Cathedral	**8** C6
Tate Modern	**9** C7
Tower Bridge Exhibition	**10** F7
Tower of London	**11** F7

SLEEPING
Clink	**12** A2
Malmaison	**13** C4
Rookery	**14** B4
Zetter Hotel	**15** B4

EATING
Bleeding Heart Restaurant & Bistro	**16** B4
Breakfast Club	**17** B1
Delfina	**18** E8
Duke of Cambridge	**19** C1
Fifteen	**20** D2
Garrison	**21** E8
Hoxton Apprentice	**22** E2
Konditor & Cook	**23** D7
Konditor & Cook	**24** E5
Konstam at the Prince Albert	**25** A2
Little Bay	**26** A3
Magdalen	**27** E8
Oxo Tower Brasserie	**28** B7
S&M Cafe	**29** B1
Smiths of Smithfield	**30** B4

DRINKING
Commercial Tavern	**31** F4
George Inn	**32** D7
Jerusalem Tavern	**33** B4
Ten Bells	**34** F4

ENTERTAINMENT
Barbican Centre	(see 1)
Comedy Cafe	**35** E3
Old Vic	**36** B8
Sadler's Wells	**37** B2
Young Vic	**38** B8

SHOPPING
Borough Market	**39** D7
Brick Lane Market	**40** F3
Camden Passage Market	**41** B1
Spitalfields Market	**42** F4

See Greater London Map (pp52-3)

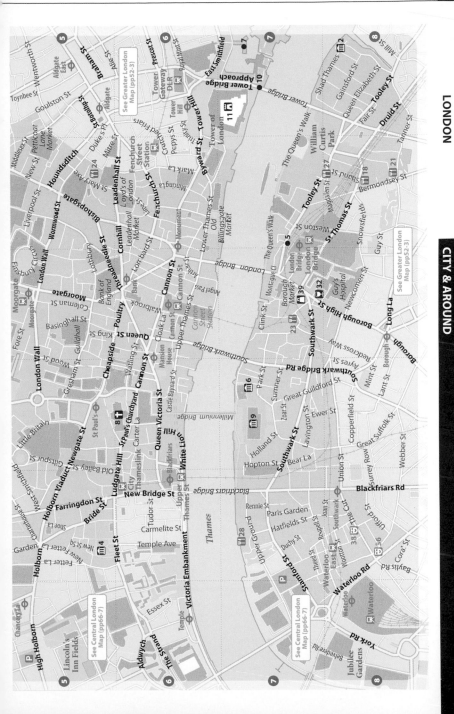

PHILIP GAME

St Paul's Cathedral from the Millennium Bridge

↘ ST PAUL'S CATHEDRAL

Dominating the City with a dome second in size only to St Peter's in Rome, St Paul's Cathedral was designed by Sir Christopher Wren after the Great Fire and built between 1675 and 1710.

Inside, some 30m above the main paved area, is the first of three domes (actually a dome inside a cone inside a dome) supported by eight huge columns. The walkway round its base is called the **Whispering Gallery**, because if you talk close to the wall, your words will carry to the opposite side 32m away. It can be reached by a staircase on the western side of the southern transept (9.30am to 3.30pm only). It is 530 lung-busting steps to the **Golden Gallery** at the very top, and an unforgettable view of London.

The **Crypt** has memorials to up to 300 military demigods including Wellington, Kitchener and Nelson, whose body lies below the dome. But the most poignant memorial is to Wren himself. On a simple slab bearing his name, a Latin inscription translates as 'If you seek his memorial, look about you'.

Audio tours lasting 45 minutes are available for £4. Guided tours (adult/child £3/1) leave the tour desk at 11am, 11.30am, 1.30pm and 2pm (90 minutes). Evensong takes place at 5pm most weekdays and at 3.15pm on Sunday.

Things you need to know: Map pp74-5; ☎ 7236 4128; www.stpauls.co.uk; adult/child £10/3.50; ⏱ 8.30am-4pm Mon-Sat; ⊖ St Paul's

the original steam engines. A lift leads up from the modern visitors' centre in the northern tower to the **Tower Bridge Exhibition** (Map pp74-5; ☎ 7403 3761; www .towerbridge.org.uk; adult/child £6/3; ⏱ 10am-6.30pm Apr-Sep, 9.30am-6pm Oct-Mar; ⊖ Tower Hill), where the story of its building is recounted with videos and animatronics.

BARBICAN

Like Marmite, you either love or hate the concrete **Barbican** (Map pp74-5; ☎ 7638 4141;

www.barbican.org.uk; Silk St EC2; ⊖ Barbican). The Barbican Centre (p100) is at its heart. It also houses the **Barbican Art Gallery** (☎ 7638 4141; Level 3; adult/child £8/6; ⏰ 11am-8pm Thu-Mon, 11am-6pm Tue & Wed), home to temporary exhibitions of contemporary art, and the smaller **Curve Gallery** (☎ 7638 4141; Level 0; admission free; ⏰ 11am-8pm).

DR JOHNSON'S HOUSE

The Georgian **house** (Map pp74-5; ☎ 7353 3745; www.drjohnsonshouse.org; 17 Gough Sq EC4; adult/child £4.50/1.50; ⏰ 11am-5.30pm Mon-Sat May-Sep, to 5pm Mon-Sat Oct-Apr; ⊖ Chancery Lane) where Samuel Johnson and his assistants compiled the first English dictionary (between 1748 and 1759) is full of prints and portraits of friends and intimates, including the good doctor's Jamaican servant to whom he bequeathed this residence.

SOUTH OF THE THAMES

SHAKESPEARE'S GLOBE

While today's Londoners might nab a budget flight to Amsterdam to behave badly, in Shakespeare's time they'd cross London Bridge to Southwark. Free from the city's constraints, you could hook up with a prostitute, watch a bear being tortured for your amusement and then head to the theatre, the most famous of which was the **Globe** (Map pp74-5; ☎ 7401 9919; www.shakespeares-globe.org; 21 New Globe Walk SE1; adult/child £9/6.50; ⏰ 10am-6pm May-Sep, last entry 5pm, to 5pm Oct-Apr; ⊖ London Bridge), where a clever fellow was producing box-office smashes like *Macbeth* and *Hamlet*.

Originally built in 1599, the Globe burned down in 1613 and was immediately rebuilt. The Puritans, who regarded theatres as dreadful dens of iniquity, eventually closed it in 1642. Its present incarnation was the vision of American actor and director Sam Wanamaker, who sadly died before the opening night in 1997.

Admission includes a guided tour of the open-roofed theatre, faithfully reconstructed from oak beams, hand-made bricks, lime plaster and thatch. Plays are still performed here, and while Shakespeare and his contemporaries dominate, modern plays are also staged (see the website for upcoming performances). As in Elizabethan times, 'groundlings' can watch proceedings for a modest price (£5; seats are £15 to £35), but there's no protection from the elements and you'll have to stand.

DESIGN MUSEUM

The whiter-than-white **Design Museum** (Map pp74-5; ☎ 7403 6933; www.designmuseum.org; 28 Shad Thames SE1; adult £8.50; ⏰ 10am-5.45pm; ⊖ Tower Hill) is a must for anyone interested in beautiful, practical things. The permanent collection has displays of modern British design and there are also regular temporary exhibitions including the annual *Designs of the Year* competition.

LONDON DUNGEON

Older kids love the **London Dungeon** (Map pp74-5; ☎ 0871-423 2240; www.thedungeons.com; 28-34 Tooley St SE1; adult/child £19.95/14.95; ⏰ 10.30am-5pm, longer hours some weeks, check website; ⊖ London Bridge), as the terrifying queues during school holidays and weekends testify. It's all spooky music, ghostly boat rides, macabre hangman's drop-rides, fake blood and actors dressed up as torturers and gory criminals (including Jack the Ripper and Sweeney Todd).

LONDON EYE

It may seem a bit Mordor-ish to have a giant eye overlooking the city, but the **London Eye** (Map pp66-7; ☎ 0870 5000 600; www.londoneye.com; adult/child £15.50/7.75; ⏰ 10am-8pm Jan-May & Oct-Dec, to 9pm Jun &

Sep, to 9.30pm Jul & Aug; ⊖ Waterloo) doesn't actually resemble an eye at all, and, in a city where there's a CCTV camera on every other corner, it's probably only fitting.

This 135m-tall, slow-moving Ferris wheel (although we're not supposed to call it that for all kinds of technical reasons) is the largest of its kind in the world. Passengers ride in an enclosed egg-shaped pod that takes 30 minutes to rotate completely and offers a 25-mile view on a clear day. It's so popular that it's advisable to book your ticket online to speed up your wait (you also get a 10% discount), or you can pay an additional £10 to jump the queue.

Joint tickets for the London Eye and Madame Tussauds can be purchased (adult/child £35/25), as well as a 40-minute, sight-seeing **River Cruise** (adult/child £12/6) with a multilingual commentary.

LONDON AQUARIUM

One of the largest in Europe, the **London Aquarium** (Map pp66-7; ☎ 7967 8000; www.londonaquarium.co.uk; County Hall SE1; adult/child £14/9.75; ⊙ 10am-6pm, last entry 5pm; ⊖ Waterloo) has three levels of fish organised by geographical origin, but you'll be peering over children's excited heads during holidays. Check the website for shark-feeding times.

HAYWARD GALLERY

Part of the Southbank Centre (p100), the **Hayward** (Map pp66-7; ☎ 0871 663 2587; www.southbankcentre.co.uk/visual-arts; Belvedere Rd SE1; admission prices vary; ⊙ 10am-6pm Sat-Thu, to 10pm Fri; ⊖ Waterloo) hosts a changing roster of modern art (video, installations, photography, collage, painting etc).

IMPERIAL WAR MUSEUM

You don't have to be a lad to appreciate the **Imperial War Museum** (Map pp52-3; ☎ 7416 5000; www.iwm.org.uk; Lambeth Rd SE1; admission free; ⊙ 10am-6pm; ⊖ Lambeth North) and its spectacular atrium with spitfires hanging from the ceiling, rockets (including the massive German V2), field-guns, missiles, submarines, tanks, torpedoes and other military hardware.

CHELSEA, KENSINGTON & KNIGHTSBRIDGE

Known as the royal borough, residents of Kensington and Chelsea are certainly paid royally, earning the highest incomes in the UK (shops and restaurants will presume you do too).

VICTORIA & ALBERT MUSEUM

A vast, rambling and wonderful museum of decorative art and design, the **Victoria & Albert** (V&A; Map p80; ☎ 7942 2000; www.vam.ac.uk; Cromwell Rd SW7; admission free; ⊙ 10am-5.45pm Sat-Thu, to 10pm Fri; ⊖ South Kensington) is part of Prince Albert's legacy to Londoners in the wake of the Great Exhibition.

Spread over nearly 150 galleries, it houses the world's greatest collection of decorative arts, including ancient Chinese ceramics, modernist architectural drawings, Korean bronze, Japanese swords, cartoons by Raphael, Asian and Islamic art, Rodin sculptures, actual-size reproductions of famous European architecture and sculpture (including Michelangelo's *David*), Elizabethan gowns, ancient jewellery, an all-wooden Frank Lloyd Wright study and a pair of Doc Martens.

NATURAL HISTORY MUSEUM

A sure-fire hit with kids of all ages, the **Natural History Museum** (Map p80; ☎ 7942 5725; www.nhm.ac.uk; Cromwell Rd SW7; admission free; ⊙ 10am-5.50pm; ⊖ South Kensington) is crammed full of interesting stuff, starting with the giant dinosaur skeleton that

Tate Modern

ORIEN HARVEY

↘ TATE MODERN

It's hard to miss this surprisingly elegant former power station on the side of the river, which is fortunate as the tremendous Tate Modern really shouldn't be missed. Focusing on modern art in all its wacky and wonderful permutations, it's been extraordinarily successful in bringing challenging work to the masses, becoming one of London's most popular attractions.

Outstanding temporary exhibitions (on the 4th floor; prices vary) continue to spark excitement, as does the periodically changing large-scale installation in the vast Turbine Hall. The permanent collection is organised into four main sections. On floor three you'll find *Material Gestures* (postwar painting and sculpture, including Mark Rothko's affecting *Seagram Murals*) and *Poetry and Dream* (Pablo Picasso, Francis Bacon and surrealism). On the 5th floor, *Idea and Object* showcases minimalism and conceptual art, while in *States of Flux,* cubism and futurism rub shoulders with pop art (Roy Lichtenstein, Andy Warhol) and Soviet imagery.

Things you need to know: Map pp74-5; ☎ 7887 8888; www.tate.org.uk; Queen's Walk SE1; admission free; ☪ 10am-6pm Sun-Thu, to 10pm Fri & Sat; ⅙ ; ⊖ Southwark

greets you in the main hall. In the main dinosaur section, the fleshless fossils are bought to robotic life with a very realistic 4m-high animatronic Tyrannosaurus Rex and his smaller, but no less sinister-looking, cousins. The **Darwin Centre** (☎ 7942 5011) houses some 22 million zoological exhibits, which can be visited by prearranging a free tour.

SCIENCE MUSEUM

With seven floors of interactive and educational exhibits, the **Science Museum** (Map p80; ☎ 0870-870 4868; www.science museum.org.uk; Exhibition Rd SW7; admission free; ☪ 10am-6pm; ⊖ South Kensington) covers everything from the Industrial Revolution to the exploration of space. There is something for all ages, from vintage cars, trains

See Central London Map (pp96–7)

LONDON

HYDE PARK & KENSINGTON

HYDE PARK & KENSINGTON

and aeroplanes to labour-saving devices for the home, a wind tunnel and flight simulator. There's also a 450-seat **IMAX cinema**.

KENSINGTON PALACE

Dating from 1605, **Kensington Palace** (Map p80; ☎ 0870 751 5170; www.hrp.org.uk; Kensington Gardens W8; adult/child £13/6.15; ⏰ 10am-6pm Mar-Oct, to 5pm Nov-Feb; ✈ High St Kensington) was the birthplace of Queen Victoria in 1819 but is best known today as the last home of Princess Diana. Hour-long tours take you around the surprisingly small **staterooms**. A collection of Princess Di's dresses is on permanent display, along with frocks and ceremonial gowns from Queen Elizabeth and her predecessors. There's an audio tour included in the entry fee.

KENSINGTON GARDENS

Blending in with Hyde Park, these **royal gardens** (Map p80; admission free; ⏰ dawn-dusk; ✈ Queensway) are part of Kensington Palace and hence popularly associated with Princess Diana. Diana devotees can visit the **Diana, Princess of Wales Memorial Playground** (Map p80) in its northwest corner, a much more restrained royal remembrance than the over-the-top

Albert Memorial (Map p80), a lavish marble, mosaic and gold affair opposite the Royal Albert Hall, built to honour Queen Victoria's purportedly humble husband, Albert (1819–61).

The gardens also house the **Serpentine Gallery** (Map p80; ☎ 7402 6075; www.serpentinegallery.org; admission free; ⏰ 10am-6pm), one of London's edgiest contemporary-art spaces.

HYDE PARK

At 145 hectares, **Hyde Park** (Map p80; ⏰ 5.30am-midnight; ✈ Marble Arch, Hyde Park Corner or Queensway) is central London's largest open space. Henry VIII expropriated it from the Church in 1536, when it became a hunting ground and later a venue for duels, executions and horse racing. These days, it serves as an occasional concert venue and a full-time green space for fun and frolics. There's boating on the Serpentine for the energetic or, near Marble Arch, **Speaker's Corner** (Map p80) for oratorical acrobats.

A more soothing structure, the **Princess Diana Memorial Fountain** (Map p80) is a meandering stream that splits at the top, flows gently downhill and reassembles in a pool at the bottom.

LONDON

SIGHTS

MARBLE ARCH

London's grandest bedsit – with a one-room flat inside – **Marble Arch** (Map p80; ⊖ Marble Arch) was designed by John Nash in 1828 as the entrance to Buckingham Palace. It was moved here in 1851.

The infamous Tyburn Tree, a three-legged gallows, once stood nearby. It is estimated that up to 50,000 people were executed here between 1196 and 1783.

MARYLEBONE

REGENT'S PARK

A former royal hunting ground, **Regent's Park** (Map p84; ⊖ Regent's Park) was designed by John Nash early in the 19th century, although what was actually laid out is only a fraction of the celebrated architect's grand plan. Nevertheless, it's one of London's loveliest open spaces – at once lively and serene, cosmopolitan and local – with football pitches, tennis courts and a boating lake. **Queen Mary's Gardens**, towards the south of the park, is particularly pretty, with spectacular roses in summer.

LONDON ZOO

A huge amount of money has been spent to bring **London Zoo** (Map p84; ☎ 7722 3333; www.londonzoo.co.uk; Regent's Park NW1; adult/child £15.40/11.90; ☽ 10am-5.30pm Mar-Oct, to 4pm Nov-Feb; ⊖ Camden Town), established in 1828, into the modern world. It now has a swanky new £5.3-million gorilla enclosure and is involved in gorilla conservation in Gabon. Feeding times, reptile handling and the petting zoo are guaranteed winners with the kids.

WALLACE COLLECTION

Housed in a beautiful, opulent Italianate mansion, the **Wallace Collection** (Map pp52-3; ☎ 7563 9500; www.wallacecollection .org; Hertford House, Manchester Sq W1; admis-

sion free, audio guide £3; ☽ 10am-5pm; ⊖ Bond St) is a treasure trove of exquisite 18th-century French furniture, Sèvres porcelain, arms, armour and art by masters such as Rubens, Titian, Rembrandt and Gainsborough.

MADAME TUSSAUDS

With so much fabulous free stuff to do in London, it's a wonder that people still join lengthy queues to visit pricey **Madame Tussauds** (Map p84; ☎ 0870 400 3000; www .madame-tussauds.co.uk; Marylebone Rd NW1; adult/child £25/21; ☽ 9.30am-5.30pm Mon-Fri, 9am-6pm Sat & Sun; ⊖ Baker St), but in a celebrity-obsessed, camera-happy world, the opportunity to pose beside Posh and Becks is not short on appeal. The life-sized wax figures are remarkably lifelike, and are as close to the real thing as most of us will get.

Tickets are cheaper when ordered online and for entries after 5pm. Combined tickets with London Eye and London Dungeon are also available (adult/child £50/35).

NORTH LONDON

Once well outside the city limits, the former hamlets of North London have long been gobbled up by the metropolis, and yet still maintain a semblance of a village atmosphere and distinct local identity.

BRITISH LIBRARY

You need to be a 'reader' (ie member) to use the vast collection of the **library** (Map p84; ☎ 7412 7332; www.bl.uk; 96 Euston Rd NW1; admission free; ☽ to 6pm Mon & Wed-Fri, to 8pm Tue, to 5pm Sat, 11am-5pm Sun; ⊖ King's Cross St Pancras), but the Treasures gallery is open to everyone. Here you'll find Shakespeare's first folio, Leonardo da Vinci's notebooks, the lyrics to *A Hard*

Day's Night scribbled on the back of Julian Lennon's birthday card, St Thomas More's last letter to Henry VIII, Jane Austen's correspondence, religious texts from around the world, and, most importantly, the 8th-century Lindisfarne Gospels and 1215 Magna Carta.

LORD'S CRICKET GROUND
The next best thing to watching a test at **Lord's** (Map pp52-3; ☎ 7616 8595; www.lords .org; St John's Wood Rd NW8; tours adult/child £12/6; ⏰ tours 10am, noon & 2pm when there's no play; ⊖ St John's Wood) is the absorbingly anecdotal 100-minute tour of the ground and facilities. It takes in the famous (members only) Long Room and the **MCC Museum** featuring evocative memorabilia including the tiny Ashes trophy.

HAMPSTEAD HEATH
With its 320 hectares of rolling meadows and wild woodlands, **Hampstead Heath** (Map pp52-3; ☒ Gospel Oak or Hampstead Heath) is a million miles away – well, approximately four – from central London. A walk up **Parliament Hill** affords one of the most spectacular views of the city and on summer days it's popular with picnickers.

HIGHGATE CEMETERY
The **cemetery** (☎ 8340 1834; www.high gate-cemetery.org; Swain's Lane N6; ⊖ Archway) weaves a creepy kind of magic, with its Victorian symbols – shrouded urns, obelisks, upturned torches (life extinguished) and broken columns (life cut short) – eerily overgrown graves and the twisting paths on the western side.

Admission to the western side is by tour only (adult/child £5/1; 2pm weekdays, on the hour 11am to 4pm weekends). On the other, less atmospheric **eastern side** (admission £3; ⏰ 10am-5pm Mon-Fri, 11am-5pm Sat &

Sun Apr-Oct, to 4pm Nov-Mar) you can pay your respects to Karl Marx and George Eliot.

GREENWICH
Simultaneously the first and last place on earth, Greenwich (*gren-itch*) straddles the hemispheres as well as the ages. All the great architects of the Enlightenment made their mark here, leaving an extraordinary cluster of buildings that have earned 'Maritime Greenwich' its place on Unesco's World Heritage list.

Greenwich is easily reached on the DLR or via train from London Bridge. **Thames River Services** (☎ 7930 4097; www.westminster pier.co.uk) has boats departing half-hourly from Westminster Pier (single/return £7.50/9.80, one hour), or take the cheaper Thames Clippers ferry (p106).

East–west meridian line, Royal Observatory (p85)

Princess Diana Memorial Fountain (p81), Hyde Park

LONDON

SIGHTS

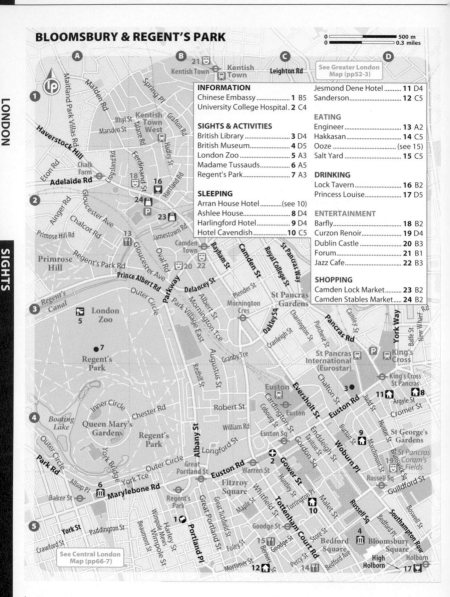

BLOOMSBURY & REGENT'S PARK

INFORMATION	
Chinese Embassy	**1** B5
University College Hospital	**2** C4

SIGHTS & ACTIVITIES	
British Library	**3** D4
British Museum	**4** D5
London Zoo	**5** A3
Madame Tussauds	**6** A5
Regent's Park	**7** A3

SLEEPING	
Arran House Hotel	(see 10)
Ashlee House	**8** D4
Harlingford Hotel	**9** D4
Hotel Cavendish	**10** C5

Jesmond Dene Hotel	**11** D4
Sanderson	**12** C5

EATING	
Engineer	**13** A2
Hakkasan	**14** C5
Ooze	(see 15)
Salt Yard	**15** C5

DRINKING	
Lock Tavern	**16** B2
Princess Louise	**17** D5

ENTERTAINMENT	
Barfly	**18** B2
Curzon Renoir	**19** D4
Dublin Castle	**20** B3
Forum	**21** B1
Jazz Cafe	**22** B3

SHOPPING	
Camden Lock Market	**23** B2
Camden Stables Market	**24** B2

See Greater London Map (pp52-3)

See Central London Map (pp66-7)

OLD ROYAL NAVAL COLLEGE

Designed by Wren, the **Old Royal Naval College** (Map pp52-3; ☎ 8269 4747; www .oldroyalnavalcollege.org; 2 Cutty Sark Gardens SE10; admission free; ☺ 10am-5pm Mon-Sat; DLR Cutty Sark) is a magnificent example of monu- mental classical architecture. Parts are now used by the University of Greenwich and Trinity College of Music, but you can visit the **chapel** and the extraordinary **Painted Hall**, which took artist Sir James Thornhill 19 years of hard graft to complete.

The complex was built on the site of the 15th-century Palace of Placentia, the birthplace of Henry VIII and Elizabeth I. This Tudor connection will be explored in **Discover Greenwich**, a new centre due to open in 2010.

NATIONAL MARITIME MUSEUM
Directly behind the old college, the **National Maritime Museum** (Map pp52-3; ☎ 8858 4422; www.nmm.ac.uk; Romney Rd SE10; admission free; ☼ 10am-5pm, last entry 4.30pm; DLR Cutty Sark) completes Greenwich's trump hand of historic buildings. The **museum** itself houses a massive collection of paraphernalia recounting Britain's seafaring history.

Behind Queen's House, idyllic **Greenwich Park** climbs up the hill, affording great views of London. It's capped by the **Royal Observatory**, which Charles II had built in 1675 to help solve the riddle of longitude. On this spot you can stand with your feet straddling the western and eastern hemispheres.

If you arrive just before lunchtime, you will see a bright-red ball climb the observatory's northeast turret at 12.58pm and drop at 1pm – as it has every day since 1833 when it was introduced for ships on the River Thames to set their clocks by.

CUTTY SARK
A famous Greenwich landmark, this **clipper** (Map pp52-3; ☎ 8858 3445; www .cuttysark.org.uk; King William Walk) was the fastest ship in the world when it was launched in 1869. Despite a fire in 2007, only a fraction of the ship was destroyed as much of its fabric had already been removed for conservation. By early 2010 it should have re-opened and be better displayed than ever – you'll even be able to walk under her. Watch the website for details.

O2
The world's largest dome (365m in diameter) opened on 1 January 2000 at a cost of £789 million as the Millennium Dome, but closed on 31 December, only hours before the third millennium began. Renamed **The O2** (off Map pp52-3; ☎ 8463 2000; www.theo2.co.uk; Peninsula Sq SE10; ⊖ North Greenwich), it's now a 20,000-seater sports and entertainment arena surrounded by shops and restaurants.

OUTSIDE CENTRAL LONDON
KEW GARDENS
In 1759 botanists began rummaging around the world for specimens they could plant in the 3-hectare plot known as the **Royal Botanic Gardens, Kew** (off Map pp52-3; ☎ 8332 5655; www.kew.org.uk; Kew Rd; adult/child £13/free; ☼ 9.30am-6.30pm Mon-Fri, to 7.30pm Sat & Sun, earlier closing in winter; ⊖ Kew Gardens). They never stopped collecting, and the gardens, which have bloomed to about 120 hectares, provide the most comprehensive botanical collection on earth (including the world's largest collection of orchids) as well as a delightful pleasure garden. It is now recognised as a Unesco World Heritage Site.

The gardens are easily reached by tube, but you might prefer to take a cruise on a riverboat from the **Westminster Passenger Services Association** (☎ 7930 2062; www.wpsa.co.uk), which runs several daily boats from April to October, departing from Westminster Pier (return adult/child £16.50/8.25, 90 minutes).

HAMPTON COURT PALACE
Built by Cardinal Thomas Wolsey in 1514 but coaxed out of him by Henry VIII just before the chancellor fell from favour, **Hampton Court Palace** (Map pp52-3; ☎ 0844-482 7777; www.hrp.org.uk/hampton

courtpalace; adult/child £13.50/6.65; ⊗ 10am-6pm Apr-Oct, to 4.30pm Nov-Mar; ⓡ Hampton Court) is England's largest and grandest Tudor structure.

Take a themed tour led by costumed historians or, if you're in a rush, visit the highlights: **Henry VIII's State Apartments**, including the Great Hall with its spectacular hammer-beamed roof; the **Tudor Kitchens**, staffed by 'servants'; and the **Wolsey Rooms**. You could easily spend a day exploring the palace and its 60 acres of riverside gardens, especially if you get lost in the 300-year-old **maze**.

Hampton Court is 13 miles southwest of central London and is easily reached by train from Waterloo. Alternatively, the riverboats that head from Westminster to Kew (p85) continue here (return adult/child £19.50/9.75, 3½ hours).

RICHMOND PARK

London's wildest **park** (off Map pp52–3) spans more than 1000 hectares and is home to all sorts of wildlife, most notably herds of red and fallow deer. It's a terrific place for bird-watching, rambling and cycling.

To get there from the Richmond tube station, turn left along George St then left at the fork that leads up Richmond Hill.

LONDON FOR CHILDREN

London has plenty of sights that parents and kids can enjoy together, and many of them are free, including the Natural History Museum (p78), Science Museum (p79) and all of the city's parks, many of which have excellent playgrounds. Pricier but popular attractions include London Dungeon (p77), London Zoo (p82), Madame Tussauds (p82), Tower of London (p73), London Aquarium (p78) and the London Eye (p77).

TOURS

One of the best ways to get yourself orientated when you first arrive in London is with a 24-hour hop-on/hop-off pass for the double-decker bus tours operated

GLENN BEANLAND

Hampton Court Palace (p85)

by the **Original London Sightseeing Tour** (☎ 8877 1722; www.theoriginaltour.com; adult/child £22/12) or the **Big Bus Company** (☎ 7233 9533; www.bigbustours.com; adult/child £24/10). The buses loop around interconnecting routes throughout the day, providing a commentary as they go, and the price includes a river cruise and three walking tours. You'll save a couple of pounds by booking online.

There are loads of walking tour operators, including **Citisights** (☎ 8806 3742; www.chr.org.uk/cswalks.htm), focusing on the academic and the literary; **London Walks** (☎ 7624 3978; www.walks.com), including Harry Potter tours, ghost walks and the ever-popular Jack The Ripper tours; and **Mystery Tours** (☎ 07957-388280; mysterywalks@hotmail.com).

Black Taxi Tours of London (☎ 7935 9363; www.blacktaxitours.co.uk; 8am-6pm £95, 6pm-midnight £100, plus £5 on weekends) takes up to five people on a two-hour spin past the major sights with a chatty cabbie as your guide.

City Cruises (☎ 7740 0400; www.city cruises.com; single/return trips from £6.40/7.80, day pass £10.50; ☽ 10am-6pm Sep-May, later Jun-Aug) operates a ferry service between Westminster, Waterloo, Tower and Greenwich piers.

FESTIVALS & EVENTS

Chinese New Year Late January or early February sees Chinatown snap, crackle and pop with fireworks, a colourful street parade and eating options aplenty.

University Boat Race (www.theboatrace .org) A posh-boy grudge match held annually since 1829 between the rowing crews of Oxford and Cambridge Universities (late March).

Chelsea Flower Show (www.rhs.org .uk/chelsea; Royal Hospital Chelsea; admission

St Paul's Cathedral (p76)

NEIL SETCHFIELD

£18-41) Held in May, the world's most renowned horticultural show attracts green fingers from near and far.

London Marathon (www.london-mara thon.co.uk) Up to half-a-million spectators watch the whippet-thin champions and often bizarrely clad amateurs take to the streets in late April.

Trooping the Colour Celebrating the Queen's official birthday (in June), this ceremonial procession of troops, marching along the Mall for their monarch's inspection, is a pageantry overload.

Wimbledon Lawn Tennis Championships (www.wimbledon.org; tickets by public ballot) Held at the end of June, the world's most splendid tennis event is

LONDON

SLEEPING

ADINA TOVY AMSEL
Performer, Notting Hill Carnival

as much about strawberries, cream and tradition as smashing balls.

Pride (www.pridelondon.org) The big event on the gay and lesbian calendar, a technicolour street parade heads through the West End in late June or early July.

Notting Hill Carnival (www.nottinghillcarnival.biz) Held over two days in August, this is Europe's largest and London's most vibrant outdoor carnival, where London's Caribbean community shows the city how to party.

SLEEPING

Take a deep breath and sit down before reading this section because no matter what your budget, London is a horribly pricey city to sleep in – one of the most expensive in the world, in fact. Anything below £80 per night for a double is pretty much 'budget'. Double rooms ranging between £80 to £150 per night are considered midrange; cheaper or more expensive options than this fall into the budget or the top-end categories respectively.

WESTMINSTER & PIMLICO

Handy to the big sights but lacking a strong sense of neighbourhood, the streets get prettier the further you stray from bustling Victoria station.

Morgan House (Map p80; ☎ 7730 2384; www.morganhouse.co.uk; 120 Ebury St SW1; s/d & tw/tr without bathroom £52/72/92, with bathroom £86/92/112; ↔ Victoria) More homely than swanky, this pleasant Georgian house offers romantic iron beds (some a little saggy), chandeliers, period fireplaces, sparkling bathrooms and a full English breakfast.

Luna & Simone Hotel (Map pp52-3; ☎ 7834 5897; www.lunasimonehotel.com; 47-49 Belgrave Rd SW1; s £45-65, d & tw/tr/q £95/115/140; ▣ wi-fi; ↔ Pimlico) The ensign of Luna (the moon) and Simone (the owner) is etched into the glass porch and this personal touch continues inside with the friendly service. The blue-and-yellow rooms aren't huge but they're clean and calming; the ones at the back are quieter.

Windermere Hotel (Map p80; ☎ 7834 5163; www.windermere-hotel.co.uk; 142-144

Warwick Way SW1; s £95-134, d £119-144, tw £126-144, f £159; wi-fi; Victoria) Chintzy but homely, this early-Victorian town house has 22 rooms, all traditionally British in decor. Lively floral curtains correspond with matching bedspreads, tartan headboards complement armchairs, and tables are draped in lace.

B&B Belgravia (Map p80; 7259 8570; www.bb-belgravia.com; 64-66 Ebury St SW1; s/d/tw/tr/q £99/115/125/145/155; wi-fi; Victoria) This small hotel's unassuming facade belies a chic, contemporary interior comprising stylish bathrooms and floor-to-ceiling dark-wood cupboards. The only design blip is the easyJet-style, orange staff uniform. Outside, the pretty courtyard garden is a suntrap.

WEST END

This is the heart of the action, so naturally accommodation comes at a price, and a hefty one at that.

Hazlitt's (Map pp66-7; 7434 1771; www.hazlittshotel.com; 6 Frith St W1; d/ste from £205/300; ; Tottenham Court Rd) Staying in this charming Georgian house (1718) is a trip back into a time when four-poster beds and claw-footed baths were the norm for gentlefolk. Each of the individually decorated 23 rooms is packed with antiques and named after a personage connected with the house.

Haymarket Hotel (Map pp66-7; 7470 4000; www.haymarkethotel.com; 1 Suffolk Pl SW1; d £250-325, ste £395-3000; wi-fi; Piccadilly Circus) The building was designed by John Nash (Buckingham Palace's main man) but the rest is Kit Kemp all the way (see boxed text, right). We love the gold loungers around the sunset-lit indoor swimming pool.

Soho Hotel (Map pp66-7; 7559 3000; www.sohohotel.com; 4 Richmond Mews W1; d £280-350, ste £385-2750; wi-fi; Oxford Circus) Hello Kitty! This Kit Kemp–designed hotel (see boxed text, below) has a giant cat sculpture in a reception that looks like a psychedelic candy store; try to refrain from licking the walls.

BLOOMSBURY & FITZROVIA

Only one step removed from the West End and crammed with Georgian townhouse conversions, these neighbourhoods are much more affordable.

Arran House Hotel (Map p84; 7636 2186; www.arranhotel-london.com; 77-79 Gower St WC1; s/d/tr/q without bathroom £50/77/95/101, with bathroom £60/100/118/122; wi-fi; Goodge St) Period features such as cornicing and fireplaces, a pretty pergola-decked back garden and a comfy lounge with PCs and TV lift this hotel from the average to the attractive. Squashed en suites or shared bathrooms are the trade-off for these reasonable rates.

Hotel Cavendish (Map p84; 7636 9079; www.hotelcavendish.com; 75 Gower St WC1E; s £85, d £105-130, tr/q £120/140; wi-fi; Goodge St) Following a complete refurbishment a few years back, bedrooms have a contemporary look, with flat-screen TVs, and all are equipped with compact en suite shower rooms (some have pretty tiles and bumper mirrors).

THE KIT KEMP CLUB

Kit Kemp's interiors purr loudly rather than whisper. She's waved her magically deranged wand over all the hotels of London's boutique Firmdale chain – including Haymarket (left), Soho (left), Knightsbridge (p91) and Number Sixteen (p91) – creating bold, playful spaces full of zany fabrics, crazy sculpture and sheer luxury.

LONDON

SLEEPING

Victoria & Albert Museum (p78)

Harlingford Hotel (Map p84; ☎ 7387 1551; www.harlingfordhotel.com; 61-63 Cartwright Gardens WC1; s/d & tw/tr/q £85/110/125/135; ☐ wi-fi; ✪ Russell Sq) This family-run hotel sports refreshing, upbeat decor such as bright-green mosaic-tiled bathrooms (with trendy sinks), fuchsia bedspreads and colourful paintings.

Sanderson (Map p84; ☎ 7300 1400; www .sandersonlondon.com; 50 Berners St W1; d £305-875, ste £611-925, apt £2500-3500; ⊠ ☐ wi-fi; ✪ Goodge St) Liberace meets Philippe Starck in an 18th-century French bordello – and that's just the reception. A 3-D space scene in the lift shuttles you into darkened corridors leading to blindingly white rooms complete with sleigh beds, oil paintings hung on the ceiling, en suites behind glass walls and pink silk curtains.

HOLBORN & CLERKENWELL
The availability of accommodation hasn't kept pace with Clerkenwell's revival, but it's still a great area to stay. The best pickings aren't exactly cheap.

Rookery (Map pp74-5; ☎ 7336 0931; www .rookeryhotel.com; Peter's Lane, Cowcross St EC1; s £175, d £210-495; ☐ wi-fi; ✪ Farringdon) Taking its name from London's notorious slums (Fagin's house in *Oliver Twist* was set a few streets west), this antique-strewn luxury hotel recreates an early-19th-century ambience with none of the attendant grime or crime.

Zetter Hotel (Map pp74-5; ☎ 7324 4444; www.thezetter.com; 86-88 Clerkenwell Rd EC1M; d £188-400; ☐ wi-fi; ✪ Farringdon) A slickly beautiful 21st-century conversion of a Victorian warehouse. The furnishings are an enticing blend of old and new, and the facilities cutting edge. You can even choose the colour of your room's lighting.

Malmaison (Map pp74-5; ☎ 7012 3700; www.malmaison.com; 18-21 Charterhouse Sq EC1; s from £205, d £225-250, ste £295-475; ☐ wi-fi; ✪ Farringdon) Given Malmaison's grand frontage onto a hidden-away square, the *Alice in Wonderland* lobby of chessboard carpet, black seats that look like pawns and supersized chairs are a quirky surprise. Once in the rooms, the look is more classic with contemporary fittings in neutral shades.

CHELSEA, KENSINGTON & KNIGHTSBRIDGE
Classy Chelsea and Kensington offer easy access to the museums and fashion retailers. It's all a bit sweetie-darling, along with the prices.

Vicarage Private Hotel (Map p80; ☎ 7229 4030; www.londonvicaragehotel.com; 10 Vicarage Gate W8; s/d/tr/q without bathroom £52/88/109/116, with bathroom £88/114/145/160;

💻 wi-fi; ⊖ **High St Kensington**) If you were staying here 15 years ago, Princess Di would have been your neighbour – you can see Kensington Palace from the doorstep. This grand Victorian town house looks onto a cul-de-sac, so you shouldn't have a problem with noise in the simply furnished rooms.

Number Sixteen (Map p80; ☎ 7589 5232; www.numbersixteenhotel.co.uk; 16 Sumner Pl SW7; s £120-165, d £200-270; 💻 wi-fi; ⊖ South Kensington) The least pricey of the Firmdale hotels (see boxed text, p89), with a lovely garden tucked away.

Knightsbridge Hotel (Map p80; ☎ 7584 6300; www.knightsbridgehotel.com; 10 Beaufort Gdn SW3; s £170-185, d £210-295, ste £345-595; 💻 wi-fi; ⊖ Knightsbridge) Another Firmdale (see boxed text, p89), this one's on a quiet, tree-lined cul-de-sac very close to Harrods. It's the most restrained of the chain.

Gore (Map p80; ☎ 7584 6601; www.gorehotel .com; 190 Queen's Gate SW7; r £187-390; 💻 wi-fi; ⊖ Gloucester Rd) A short stroll from the Royal Albert Hall, the Gore serves up British grandiosity (antiques, carved four-posters, a secret bathroom in the Tudor room) with a large slice of camp.

Levin (Map p80; ☎ 7589 6286; www .thelevinhotel.co.uk; 28 Basil St SW3; d £235-445; ⊖ Knightsbridge) As close as you can get to sleeping in Harrods, the Levin knows its market. Despite the baby-blue colour scheme, there's a subtle femininity to the decor, although it's far too elegant to be flouncey.

NOTTING HILL, BAYSWATER & PADDINGTON

Don't be fooled by Julia Roberts' and Hugh Grant's shenanigans, Notting Hill and the areas immediately north of Hyde Park are as shabby as they are chic.

New Linden Hotel (Map p80; ☎ 7221 4321; www.newlinden.co.uk; 58-60 Leinster Sq W2;

s £95, d £129-179, tr/f/ste £210/150/189; 💻 wi-fi; ⊖ Bayswater) Cramming in a fair whack of style for the price, this terrace-house hotel has interesting modern art in the rooms and carved wooden fixtures from India combined with elegant wallpaper in the guest lounge.

Hempel (Map p80; ☎ 7298 9000; www.the -hempel.co.uk; 31-35 Craven Hill Gardens; d £239-315, ste £319-1345; 💻 wi-fi; ⊖ Bayswater) As soon as you enter the expansive all-white lobby with sunken seating areas, super-modern fireplaces and dramatic ceiling-grazing flower arrangement, you know you're in for something special.

NORTH LONDON
EUSTON & KING'S CROSS

While hardly a salubrious location, King's Cross is handy to absolutely everything and has some excellent budget options.

Ashlee House (Map p84; ☎ 7833 9400; www.ashleehouse.co.uk; 261-265 Grays Inn Rd; dm £21-24, s/tw & tr £57/76; 💻 ; ⊖ King's Cross) This hostel is a cheery surprise in a gritty but central location. There's a large tube map and London scenes on the walls, green dice tables in the small lounge, bright paintwork in the compact rooms and stripy duvets on the blue bunk beds.

Jesmond Dene Hotel (Map p84; ☎ 7837 4654; www.jesmonddenehostel.co.uk; 27 Argyle St; s/d & tw/tr/q from £50/60/85/120; 💻 wi-fi; ⊖ King's Cross) A surprisingly pleasant option for a place so close to busy King's Cross station, this modest hotel has clean but small rooms, some of which share bathrooms. A full English breakfast is included in the price.

Clink (Map pp74-5; ☎ 7183 9400; www .clinkhostel.com; 78 King's Cross Rd; dm £21-28, tw with/without bathroom £70/60, d/tr 70/78; 💻 wi-fi; ⊖ King's Cross) If anyone can think of a more right-on London place to stay than the courthouse where the Clash went on

LONDON

SLEEPING

• RESTAURANT • BAR

Outdoor dining

NEIL SETCHFIELD

trial, please let us know. You can watch TV from the witness box or sleep in the cells, but the majority of the rooms are custom-built and quite comfortable.

GREENWICH

If you'd rather keep the bustle of central London at arm's length and nightclubbing is your idea of hell, Greenwich offers a villagey ambience and some great old pubs to explore.

St Alfege's (Map pp52-3; ☎ 8853 4337; www.st-alfeges.co.uk; 16 St Alfege Passage SE10; s/d £60/90; ☐ wi-fi; DLR Cutty Sark) Both the house and the host have personality plus, so much so that they were featured on TV's *Hotel Inspector* series.

WEST LONDON

Earl's Court is lively, cosmopolitan and so popular with travelling Antipodeans it's been nicknamed Kangaroo Valley. There are no real sights, but it does have inexpensive digs and an infectious holiday atmosphere.

Rushmore Hotel (Map p80; ☎ 7370 3839; www.rushmore-hotel.co.uk; 11 Trebovir Rd SW5; s £69-79, d & tw £89-99, tr/q £115/139; ☐ wi-fi; ⊖ Earl's Court) The soft pastel colours, draped fabrics and simple designs of this modest hotel create a cheery, welcoming atmosphere, heightened by the friendly family that run the joint. There's no lift, so a complimentary workout is provided for those on the upper floors. The double rooms can be tight but the twins have a bit more space.

Twenty Nevern Square (Map p80; ☎ 7565 9555; www.twentynevernsquare.co.uk; 20 Nevern Sq SW5; s £79-140, d £85-189; ☐ wi-fi; ⊖ Earl's Court) An Ottoman theme runs through this contemporary town-house hotel, where a mix of wooden furniture, luxurious fabrics and natural light helps maximise space even though the cheaper bedrooms are not particularly large.

base2stay (Map p80; ☎ 0845 262 8000; www .base2stay.com; 25 Courtfield Gardens SW5; s £93, d £107-127, tw £127; ☐ wi-fi; ⊖ Earl's Court) With smart decor, power showers, flat-screen TVs with internet access and artfully concealed kitchenettes, this boutique establishment feels like a four-star hotel without the hefty price tag.

AIRPORTS

Yotel (☎ 7100 1100; www.yotel.com; r per 4/5/6 hr £38/45/53, 7-24hr £59; 🖳 wi-fi) Heathrow (**Terminal 4**); Gatwick (**South Terminal**) The best news for early-morning flyers since coffee-vending machines, Yotel's smart 'cabins' offer pint-sized luxury: comfy beds, soft lights, internet-connected TVs, monsoon showers and fluffy towels. Swinging cats isn't recommended, but when is it ever?

EATING

Dining out in London has become so fashionable that you can hardly open a menu without banging into some celebrity chef or restaurateur. In this section, we steer you towards restaurants and cafes distinguished by their location, value for money, unique features, original settings and, of course, good food.

ST JAMES'S & MAYFAIR

Like on the Monopoly board, if you land on Mayfair you may have to sell a house (to afford to eat here).

Nobu (Map p80; ☎ 7447 4747; Metropolitan Hotel, 19 Old Park Ln W1; dishes £10-26; ⊖ Hyde Park Corner) One of London's most famous eateries, Nobu's dining room is surprisingly unremarkable but it does have nice views over Hyde Park. It's nonetheless out of this world when it comes to exquisitely prepared and presented Japanese dishes.

Tamarind (Map pp66-7; ☎ 7629 3561; 20 Queen St W1; mains £16-28; ⊖ Green Park) London's only Michelin-starred Indian restaurant serves up mouth-watering spicy classics. The set lunches are a good deal (two/three courses £17/19).

Hibiscus (Map pp66-7; ☎ 7629 2999; 29 Maddox St W1; 3-course lunch/dinner £25/60; ⊖ Oxford Circus) Claude and Claire Bosi have generated an avalanche of praise from London critics since moving their Michelin-starred restaurant from Shropshire to Mayfair. Expect adventurous French and English cuisine in an elegant dining room.

WEST END

Soho and Covent Garden are the gastronomic heart of London, with stacks of restaurants and cuisines to choose from at budgets to suit both booze hounds and theatre-goers.

Neal's Yard Salad Bar (Map pp66-7; ☎ 7836 3233; Neal's Yard WC2; mains £3-12; ⊖ Covent Garden) Occupying both sides of the courtyard, this bright-orange salad bar has waiters in black bow ties serving fresh, leafy meals and moist Brazilian cakes.

Yauatcha (Map pp66-7; ☎ 7494 8888; 15 Broadwick St W1; dishes £3-18; ⊖ Piccadilly Circus) Dim-sum restaurants don't come much cooler than this, and the menu is fantastic and Michelin-starred. Upstairs, the chilled-out teahouse serves pretty cakes.

Sacred (Map pp66-7; ☎ 7734 1415; 13 Ganton St W1; mains £4-5; 🕑 7.30am-8.30pm Mon-Fri, 9.30am-8pm Sat, 10am-7pm Sun; ⊖ Oxford Circus) The spiritual paraphernalia and blatant Kiwiana don't seem to deter the smart Carnaby St set from lounging around this eclectic cafe. It must be something to do with the excellent coffee, appealing counter food and deliciously filling cooked breakfasts (try the scrambled eggs with salmon and goats' cheese).

Mother Mash (Map pp66-7; ☎ 7494 9644; 26 Ganton St W1; mains £7; ⊖ Oxford Circus) If you've lived through a London winter, you'll know the importance of good comfort food. This Mother certainly does, offering choices of four types of mashed potato, eight varieties of sausage (including a vegetarian version), six choices of pie and five types of gravy (including the traditional, parsley-based East End 'liquor').

Sarastro (Map pp66-7; ☎ 7836 0101; 126 Drury Ln WC2; mains £8-16; ❹ Covent Garden) This Turkish-influenced restaurant is gaudy, kitsch and loads of fun. The opera theme – with balcony tables, gold everywhere (even the ceiling), crushed velvet and myriad lamps – is totally over the top.

Spiga (Map pp66-7; ☎ 7734 3444; 84-86 Wardour St W1; mains £9-18; ❹ Piccadilly Circus) With Italian movie posters on the walls, warm, colourful decor and a tasty menu of pastas, pizzas, fish and meat dishes, this popular restaurant is a winner.

Kettners (Map pp66-7; ☎ 7734 6112; 29 Romilly St W1; mains £9-20; ❹ Leicester Sq) Founded in 1867 (no, that's not a typo), Kettners has served the likes of Oscar Wilde and Edward VIII. Nowadays it dishes up pizza and burgers, which you can wash down with champagne while soaking in the gently fading grandeur and tinkling piano.

National Gallery Dining Rooms (Map pp66-7; ☎ 7747 2525; Sainsbury Wing, National Gallery, Trafalgar Sq WC2; 2 courses £25; ☺ lunch daily, dinner Fri; ❹ Charing Cross) It's fitting that Oliver Peyton's acclaimed restaurant should celebrate British food (such as smoked haddock, traditional Suffolk cob chicken and 'Farmer Shep's aged sirloin'), being in the National Gallery and overlooking Trafalgar Sq.

BLOOMSBURY & FITZROVIA

Tucked away behind busy Tottenham Court Rd, Fitzrovia's Charlotte and Goodge Sts form one of central London's most vibrant eating precincts.

Salt Yard (Map p84; ☎ 7637 0657; 54 Goodge St W1; tapas £5-8; ❹ Goodge St) Named after the place where cold meats are cured, this softly lit joint serves delicious Spanish and Italian tapas. Try the roasted chicken leg with gnocchi, wild garlic and sorrel, or flex your palate with courgette flowers stuffed with cheese and drizzled with honey.

Ooze (Map p84; ☎ 7436 9444; 62 Goodge St W1; mains £7-15; ❹ Goodge St) The humble risotto gets its moment on the catwalk in this breezy Italian restaurant. There are a handful of grills on the menu, but it's the 16 varieties of oozy, but still slightly crunchy, risotto that take centre stage.

Hakkasan (Map p84; ☎ 7907 1888; 8 Hanway Pl W1; mains £10-60; ❹ Tottenham Court Rd) Hidden down a lane like all fashionable haunts need to be, the first Chinese restaurant to get a Michelin star combines celebrity status, a stunning design, persuasive cocktails and incredibly sophisticated Chinese food.

HOLBORN & CLERKENWELL

Similarly hidden away, Clerkenwell's gems are well worth digging for. Pedestrianised Exmouth Market is a good place to start.

Little Bay (Map pp74-5; ☎ 7278 1234; 171 Farringdon Rd EC1; mains before/after 7pm £6/8; ❹ Farringdon) The crushed-velvet ceiling, handmade twisted lamps that improve around the room (as the artist got better) and elaborately painted bar and tables showing nymphs frolicking is bonkers but fun. The hearty food is very good value.

Bleeding Heart Restaurant & Bistro (Map pp74-5; ☎ 7242 8238; Bleeding Heart Yard EC1; bistro £8-16, restaurant £13-25; ❹ Farringdon) Locals have taken this place, tucked in the corner of Bleeding Heart Yard, to their hearts. Choose from formal dining in the downstairs restaurant or more relaxed meals in the buzzy bistro – wherever, the French food is divine.

Great Queen Street (Map pp66-7; ☎ 7242 0622; 32 Great Queen St WC2; mains £10-14; ☺ lunch

Tue-Sat, dinner Mon-Sat; ⊖ Holborn) There's no tiara on this Great Queen, her claret-coloured walls and mismatched wooden chairs suggesting cosiness and informality. But the food's still the best of British, including brawn, lamb that melts in the mouth and Arbroath smokie (a whole smoked fish with creamy sauce).

Smiths of Smithfield (Map pp74-5; ☎ 7251 7950; 67-77 Charterhouse St EC1; mains 1st fl £11-17, top fl £17-29; ⊖ Farringdon) This converted meat-packing warehouse endeavours to be all things to all people and succeeds. Hit the ground-floor bar for a beer, follow the silver-clad ducts and wooden beams upstairs to a relaxed dining space, or continue up for two more floors of feasting, each slightly smarter and pricier than the last.

HOXTON, SHOREDITCH & SPITALFIELDS

From the hit-and-miss Bangladeshi restaurants of Brick Lane to the Vietnamese strip on Kingsland Rd, and the Jewish, Spanish, French, Italian and Greek eateries in between, the East End's cuisine is as multicultural as its residents.

Song Que (Map pp52-3; ☎ 7613 3222; 134 Kingsland Rd E2; mains £5-7; ⊖ Old St) If you arrive after 7.30pm, expect to queue as this humble eatery has already had its cover blown as one of the best Vietnamese in London. There's never much time to admire the institutional-green walls, fake lobsters and bizarre horse portrait, as you'll be shunted out shortly after your last bite.

Hoxton Apprentice (Map pp74-5; ☎ 7749 2828; 16 Hoxton Sq N1; mains £9-17; ⊖ Old St) Similar in concept to Fifteen (right), both professionals and apprentices work the kitchen in this restaurant, housed appropriately enough in a former Victorian primary school.

Gourmet olives at a market stall

ORIEN HARVEY

Fifteen (Map pp74-5; ☎ 0871-330 1515; www.fifteen.net; 15 Westland Pl N1; breakfast £2-8.50, trattoria £9-18, restaurant £22-24; ⊖ Old St) It can only be a matter of time before TV chef Jamie Oliver becomes Sir Jamie. His culinary philanthropy started at Fifteen, set up to give unemployed young people a shot at a career. The Italian food is beyond excellent and, surprisingly, even those on limited budgets can afford a visit.

SOUTH OF THE RIVER THAMES

You'll find plenty of touristy eateries on the riverside between Westminster and Tower Bridges, making the most of the constant foot traffic and iconic London views.

LONDON

EATING

Konditor & Cook (Map pp74-5; ☎ 7407 5100; 10 Stoney St SE1; snacks £2-5; ⊖ London Bridge) The original location of arguably the best bakery in London, it serves excellent muffins, sweets, bread and coffee. There's only one table but everything is yours to take away. There's another four branches, including one at 30 St Mary Axe (Map pp74–5).

Bermondsey Kitchen (Map pp52-3; ☎ 7407 5719; 194 Bermondsey St SE1; mains £10-15; ⊖ London Bridge) Smart but informal, this place sits somewhere between a restaurant and a gastropub, serving cocktails and tapas all day. They do an outrageously tasty bouillabaisse, lunch specials under £10 and excellent brunch on the weekends.

Garrison (Map pp74-5; ☎ 7089 9355; 99-101 Bermondsey St SE1; mains £12-15; ☷ breakfast, lunch & dinner; ⊖ London Bridge) This may be a gastropub but the ambience is actually more French country kitchen than London boozer, with soft colours and baskets of fresh vegetables proudly displayed.

Delfina (Map pp74-5; ☎ 7357 0244; 50 Bermondsey St SE1; mains £13-16; ☷ lunch Mon-Fri, dinner Fri; ⊖ London Bridge) This restaurant-cum-art-gallery, in a converted Victorian chocolate factory, serves delicious modern cuisine with an Asian twist to a backdrop of contemporary canvases.

Magdalen (Map pp74-5; ☎ 7403 1342; 152 Tooley St SE1; mains £15-20; ☷ lunch Mon-Fri, dinner Mon-Sat; ⊖ London Bridge) Roasting up the best of the critters that walk, hop, flap and splash around these fair isles, Magdalen isn't the place to bring a vegetarian or a weight-conscious waif on a date. Love that pork crackling!

Oxo Tower Brasserie (Map pp74-5; ☎ 7803 3888; Barge House St SE1; 2 courses £20; ⊖ Waterloo) The spectacular views are the big drawcard, so skip the restaurant and head for the slightly less extravagantly priced brasserie, or if you're not hungry, the bar. Italian with a twist is the focus of the very proficient kitchen.

CHELSEA, KENSINGTON & KNIGHTSBRIDGE

These highbrow neighbourhoods harbour some of London's very best (and priciest) restaurants.

Jakob's (Map p80; ☎ 7581 9292; 20 Gloucester Rd SW7; mains £4-10; ⊖ Gloucester Rd) A charismatic cafe-delicatessen serving a mixture of Armenian, Persian and Mediterranean dishes including salads, falafel and quiches.

Made in Italy (Map p80; ☎ 7352 1880; 249 King's Rd SW3; pizza £5-13, mains £15-19; ⊖ Sloane Sq) Pizza is served by the tasty quarter-metre at this traditional trattoria. Sit on the Chelsea roof terrace and dream of Napoli.

Tom's Kitchen (Map p80; ☎ 7349 0202; 27 Cale St SW3; breakfast £2-11, lunch 2-courses £14, mains £17-22; ☷ breakfast Mon-Fri, lunch & dinner daily; ⊖ South Kensington) Tom Aikens is the notorious kitchen firebrand who is gradually taking over Chelsea; around the corner you will find his Michelin-starred, mortgage-your-mother eponymous restaurant and his blinged-up fish diner. This excellent, informal British-French restaurant sits between those two: dinners can be pricey but a delicious breakfast or lunch needn't break the bank.

Boxwood Cafe (Map p80; ☎ 7235 1010; Berkeley Hotel, Wilton Pl SW1; mains £16-31; ⊖ Knightsbridge) A New York–style cafe set up by superchef Gordon Ramsay, in a valiant attempt to kick back with young folk and make fine dining in London 'a little bit more relaxed'.

Gordon Ramsay (Map p80; ☎ 7352 4441; www.gordonramsay.com; 68 Royal Hospital Rd SW3; set lunch/dinner £40/90; ⊖ Sloane Sq)

Left: Roast beef and Yorkshire pudding; Right: George Inn (p99)

LEFT: NEIL SETCHFIELD; RIGHT: JONATHAN SMITH

One of Britain's finest restaurants and the only one in the capital with three Michelin stars. The food is, of course, blissful and perfect for a luxurious treat. The only quibble is that you don't get time to linger. Bookings are made in specific eat-it-and-beat-it time slots and, if you have seen the chef on TV, you won't argue.

NORTH LONDON
Allow at least an evening to explore Islington's Upper St, along with the lanes leading off it.

Breakfast Club (Map pp74–5; ☎ 7226 5454; 31 Camden Passage N1; mains £5–9; ☯ 8am-10pm Mon-Fri, 9.30am-10pm Sat & Sun; ⊖ Angel) Eighties survivors will immediately clock this place and, with dishes like *Hungry Like The Wolf* (the big breakfast) and *When Haloumi Met Salad,* they'll feel right at home. There's another branch at 33 D'Arblay St, W1 (Map pp66–7).

S&M Cafe (Map pp74–5; ☎ 7359 5361; 4/6 Essex Rd N1; mains £6–10; ☯ breakfast, lunch & dinner daily; ⊖ Angel) The S&M refers to sausages and mash in this cool diner (featured in the movie *Quadrophenia*) that won't give your wallet a spanking. There's a range of sausages, mashes and gravies.

Konstam at the Prince Albert (Map pp74–5; ☎ 7833 5040; 2 Acton St WC1; mains £11–17; ☯ closed Sun; ⊖ King's Cross) As London a restaurant as you can get, since Chef Oliver Rowe sources all but a few of his ingredients from within the tube map.

Duke of Cambridge (Map pp74–5; ☎ 7359 3066; 30 St Peter's St N1; mains £12–17; ⊖ Angel) Pioneers in bringing sustainability to the table, this tucked-away gastropub serves only organic food, wine and beer, fish from sustainable sources and locally sourced fruit, vegetables and meat.

Engineer (Map p84; ☎ 7722 0950; 65 Gloucester Ave NW1; mains £13–17; ⊖ Chalk Farm) One of London's original gastropubs, serving up consistently good international cuisine to hip north Londoners. The courtyard garden is a real treat on balmy summer nights.

LONDON

DRINKING

NEIL SETCHFIELD

Princess Louise

DRINKING

As long as there's been a city, Londoners have loved to drink. The pub is the focus of social life and there's always one near at hand.

Coach & Horses (Map pp66-7; ☎ 7437 5920; 29 Greek St W1; ⊖ Leicester Sq) This Soho institution has been patronised by Sigmund Freud, Francis Bacon, Dylan Thomas, Peter Cooke and Peter O'Toole.

Gordon's Wine Bar (Map pp66-7; ☎ 7930 1408; 47 Villiers St WC2; ⊖ Charing Cross) What's not to love about this cavernous wine cellar lit by candles and practically unchanged over the last 100 years?

Lamb & Flag (Map pp66-7; ☎ 7497 9504; 33 Rose St WC2; ⊖ Covent Garden) Everyone's Covent Garden 'find', this popular historic pub is often jammed. It was built in 1623 and formerly called the 'Bucket of Blood'.

Queen Mary (Map pp66-7; ☎ 7240 9404; Waterloo Pier WC2; ⊖ Embankment) Climb aboard this steamer for a welcoming pub-like atmosphere with great views of the London Eye and the South Bank.

Jerusalem Tavern (Map pp74-5; ☎ 7490 4281; 55 Britton St; ⊖ Farringdon) Pick a wood-panelled cubbyhole to park yourself in at this gorgeous former 18th-century coffee shop-turned-inn, and choose from a selection of St Peter's beers such as cinnamon and apple, grapefruit or, if you're not feeling fruity, creamy ale or bitter.

Princess Louise (Map p84; ☎ 7405 8816; 208 High Holborn WC1; ⊖ Holborn) This late-19th-century Victorian boozer is arguably London's most beautiful pub. Spectacularly decorated with fine tiles, etched mirrors, plasterwork and a gorgeous central horseshoe bar, it gets packed with the after-work crowd.

Commercial Tavern (Map pp74-5; ☎ 7247 1888; 142 Commercial St E1; ⊖ Liverpool St) The zany decor's a thing of wonder in this reformed East End boozer. Check out the walls coated in buttons and jigsaw-puzzle pieces.

Ten Bells (Map pp74-5; ☎ 7366 1721; cnr Commercial & Fournier Sts E1; ⊖ Liverpool St) The most famous Jack the Ripper pub, Ten Bells was patronised by his last victim before her grisly end, and possibly by the slayer himself.

George Inn (Map pp74-5; ☎ 7407 2056; Talbot Yard, 77 Borough High St SE1; ⊖ London Bridge or Borough) Tucked away in a cobbled courtyard is London's last surviving galleried coaching inn, dating from 1677 and now belonging to the National Trust.

Lock Tavern (Map p84; 35 Chalk Farm Rd NW1; ⊖ Camden Town) The archetypal Camden pub, the Lock has both a rooftop terrace and a beer garden and attracts an interesting crowd with its mix of ready conviviality, pleasant surrounds and regular live music.

ENTERTAINMENT

For a comprehensive list of what to do on any given night, check out *Time Out*. The listings in the free tube papers are also good.

THEATRE

London is a world capital for theatre and there's a lot more than mammoth musicals to tempt you into the West End. The term 'West End' – as with Broadway – generally refers to the big-money productions like musicals, but also includes such heavyweights as the **Royal Court Theatre** (Map p80; ☎ 7565 5000; www.royalcourttheatre.com; Sloane Sq SW1; ⊖ Sloane Sq), the patron of new British writing; the **National Theatre** (Map pp66-7; ☎ 7452 3000; www.nationaltheatre .org.uk; South Bank SE1; ⊖ Waterloo), which has cheaper tickets for both classics and new plays from some of the world's best companies; and the **Royal Shakespeare Company** (RSC; ☎ 0870 609 1110; www.rsc.org .uk), with productions of the Bard's classics and other quality stuff. Kevin Spacey continues his run as artistic director (and occasional performer) at the **Old Vic** (Map pp74-5; ☎ 0870-060 6628; www.oldvictheatre.com; The Cut SE1; ⊖ Waterloo).

On performance days, you can buy half-price tickets for West End productions (cash only) from the official **Leicester Square Half-Price Ticket Booth** (Map pp66-7; ◷ 10am-7pm Mon-Sat, noon-3pm Sun; Leicester Sq; ⊖ Leicester Sq), on the south side of Leicester Sq.

Off West End – where you'll generally find the most original works – includes venues such as the **Almeida** (Map pp52-3; ☎ 7359 4404; www.almeida.co.uk; Almeida St N1; ⊖ Highbury & Islington), **Battersea Arts Centre** (Map pp52-3; ☎ 7223 2223; www.bac .org.uk; Lavender Hill SW11; ⊖ Clapham Junction) and the **Young Vic** (Map pp74-5; ☎ 7922 2920; www.youngvic.org; 66 The Cut SE1; ⊖ Waterloo).

LIVE MUSIC
ROCK & JAZZ
Big-name gigs sell out quickly, so check www.seetickets.com before you travel.

Barfly (Map p84; ☎ 0844-847 2424; www.bar flyclub.com; 49 Chalk Farm Rd NW1; ⊖ Chalk Farm) Pleasantly grungy, and the place to see the best new bands. The same crew run a couple of other joints around town.

Brixton Academy (Map pp52-3; ☎ 0844-477 2000; www.brixton-academy.co.uk; 211 Stockwell Rd SW9; ⊖ Brixton) This Grade-II listed art-deco venue is always winning awards for 'best live venue' (something to do with the artfully sloped floor, perhaps) and hosts big-name acts in a relatively intimate setting (5000 capacity).

Dublin Castle (Map p84; ☎ 7485 1773; www.thedublincastle.com; 94 Parkway NW1; ⊖ Camden Town) There's live punk or alternative music most nights in this pub's back room.

Forum (Map p84; ☎ 0844-847 2405; www .kentishtownforum.com; 9-17 Highgate Rd NW5; ⊖ Kentish Town) A grand old theatre and one of London's best large venues.

Jazz Cafe (Map p84; ☎ 7485 6834; 5 Parkway NW1; ↔ Camden Town) Jazz is just one part of the picture at this intimate club that stages a full roster of rock, pop, hip hop and dance, including some famous names.

Ronnie Scott's (Map pp66-7; ☎ 7439 0747; www.ronniescotts.co.uk; 47 Frith St W1; ↔ Leicester Sq) London's legendary jazz club has been pulling in the hep cats since 1959.

Shepherd's Bush Empire (Map pp52-3; ☎ 8354 3300; www.shepherds-bush-empire .co.uk; Shepherd's Bush Green W12; ↔ Shepherd's Bush) A slightly dishevelled, midsize theatre that plays host to some terrific bands.

CLASSICAL

Barbican Centre (Map pp74-5; ☎ 0845 120 7500; www.barbican.org.uk; Silk St EC2; ↔ Barbican) This hulking complex has a full program of film, music, theatre, art and dance including loads of concerts from the London Symphony Orchestra, which is based here.

Southbank Centre (Map pp66-7; ☎ 0871-663 2509; www.southbankcentre .co.uk; South Bank; ↔ Waterloo) Home to the London Philharmonic Orchestra, London Sinfonietta and the Philharmonia Orchestra, among others, this centre includes three premier venues: the **Royal Festival Hall** (Map pp66-7) and the smaller **Queen Elizabeth Hall** (Map pp66-7) and **Purcell Room** (Map pp66-7), which host classical, opera, jazz and choral music.

Royal Albert Hall (Map p80; ☎ 7589 8212; www.royalalberthall.com; Kensington Gore SW7; ↔ South Kensington) A splendid circular Victorian arena that hosts classical concerts and the occasional contemporary act, but is best known as the venue for the Proms.

OPERA & DANCE

Royal Opera House (Map pp66-7; ☎ 7304 4000; www.royaloperahouse.org; Royal Opera House, Bow St WC2; tickets £5-190; ↔ Covent Garden) The gleaming Royal Opera House has been attracting a younger audience since its £213-million millennium redevelopment. The Royal Ballet, Britain's premier classical ballet company, is also based here.

Sadler's Wells (Map pp74-5; ☎ 0844-412 4300; www.sadlers-wells.com; Rosebery Ave EC1; tickets £10-49; ↔ Angel) A glittering modern venue that was in fact first established in the 17th century, Sadler's Wells has been given much credit for bringing modern dance to the mainstream.

COMEDY

99 Club (☎ 7739 5706; www.the99club.co.uk; admission £10-25) Not quite the famous 100 Club, this virtual venue takes over various bars around town from Tuesday to Sunday night, with four rival clones on Saturday.

Comedy Cafe (Map pp74-5; ☎ 7739 5706; www.comedycafe.co.uk; 66-68 Rivington St EC2; admission free-£15; ↔ Old St) Have dinner and watch some comedy; take to the stage on Wednesday if you're brave/foolhardy/ drunk.

Comedy Store (Map pp66-7; ☎ 7839 6642; www.thecomedystore.co.uk; 1A Oxendon St SW1; admission £13-18; ↔ Piccadilly Circus) One of London's first comedy clubs, featuring the capital's most famous improvisers, the Comedy Store Players, on Wednesday and Sunday.

Soho Theatre (Map pp66-7; ☎ 7478 0100; www.sohotheatre.com; 21 Dean St W1; ↔ Tottenham Court Rd) Where grown-up comedians graduate to once they start pulling the crowds.

CINEMAS

Glitzy premieres usually take place in one of the mega multiplexes in Leicester Sq.

Liberty
PHILIP GAME

For less mainstream movies try **Curzon Cinemas** (☎ 0870 756 4621; www.curzoncinemas.com; tickets £8-12) Mayfair (Map pp66-7; 38 Curzon St W1; ⊖ Green Park); Soho (Map pp66-7; 99 Shaftesbury Ave W1; ⊖ Leicester Sq); Renoir (Map p84; Brunswick Sq WC1; ⊖ Russell Sq); Chelsea (Map p80; 206 Kings Rd SW3; ⊖ Sloane Sq).

BFI Southbank (Map pp66-7; ☎ 7928 3232; Belvedere Rd SE1; tickets £9; ⊖ Waterloo) A film-lover's fantasy, it screens some 2000 flicks a year, ranging from classics to foreign art house.

BFI IMAX (Map pp66-7; ☎ 0870-787 2525; www.bfi.org.uk/imax; Waterloo Rd SE1; tickets £13; ⊖ Waterloo) Watch 3-D movies and cinema releases on the UK's biggest screen: 20m high (nearly five double-decker buses) and 26m wide.

SHOPPING

From world-famous department stores to quirky backstreet retail revelations, London is a mecca for shoppers with an eye for style and a card to exercise.

DEPARTMENT STORES

Harrods (Map p80; ☎ 7730 1234; 87 Brompton Rd SW1; ⊖ Knightsbridge) An overpriced theme park for fans of Britannia, Harrods is always crowded with slow tourists.

Harvey Nichols (Map p80; ☎ 7235 5000; 109-125 Knightsbridge SW1; ⊖ Knightsbridge) London's temple of high fashion, jewellery and perfume.

Fortnum & Mason (Map pp66-7; ☎ 7734 8040; 181 Piccadilly W1; ⊖ Piccadilly Circus) The byword for quality and service from a bygone era, steeped in 300 years of tradition. It is especially noted for its old-world, ground-floor food hall, where Britain's elite come for their cornflakes and bananas.

Liberty (Map pp66-7; ☎ 7734 1234; 214-220 Regent St W1; ⊖ Oxford Circus) An irresistible blend of contemporary styles and indulgent pampering in a mock-Tudor fantasyland of carved dark wood.

Selfridges (Map pp52-3; ☎ 0870 837 7377; 400 Oxford St W1; ⊖ Bond St) The funkiest and most vital of London's one-stop shops, where fashion runs the gamut from street

LONDON

SHOPPING

NEIL SETCHFIELD

Borough Market

to formal. The food hall is unparalleled and the cosmetics hall the largest in Europe.

MARKETS

London has more than 350 markets selling everything from antiques and curios to flowers and fish. Here are some of our favourites.

Borough Market (Map pp74-5; cnr Borough High & Stoney Sts SE1; ⏰ 11am-5pm Thu, noon-6pm Fri, 9am-4pm Sat; ⊖ London Bridge) A farmers market sometimes called London's Larder, it has been here in some form since the 13th century.

Brick Lane Market (Map pp74-5; Brick Lane E1; ⏰ early-2pm Sun; ⊖ Liverpool St) This is an East End pearler, a sprawling bazaar featuring everything from fruit and vegies to paintings and bric-a-brac.

Camden Market (⏰ 10am-5.30pm; ⊖ Camden Town) London's most famous market is actually a series of markets spread along Camden High St and Chalk Farm Rd. It's been quieter since the major fire in 2008, but the **Lock** (Map p84) and **Stables** (Map p84) markets are still the place for punk

fashion, cheap food, hippy shit and a whole lotta craziness.

Camden Passage Market (Map pp74-5; Camden Passage N1; ⏰ 10am-2pm Wed, to 5pm Sat; ⊖ Angel) Get your fill of antiques and trinkets galore. Not in Camden (despite the name).

Greenwich Market (Map pp52-3; College Approach SE10; ⏰ 11am-7pm Wed, 10am-5pm Thu & Fri, 10am-5.30pm Sat & Sun; DLR Cutty Sark) Rummage through antiques, vintage clothing and collectibles on weekdays, arts and crafts on weekends, or just chow down in the food section.

Portobello Road Market (Map p80; Portobello Rd W10; ⏰ 8am-6.30pm Mon-Wed, Fri & Sat, to 1pm Thu; ⊖ Ladbroke Grove) One of London's most famous (and crowded) street markets. New and vintage clothes are its main attraction, with antiques found at its south end and food at the north.

Spitalfields Market (Map pp74-5; 105a Commercial St E1; ⏰ 10am-4pm Mon-Fri, 9am-5pm Sun; ⊖ Liverpool St) It's housed in a Victorian warehouse but the market's been here since 1638. Thursdays are devoted to antiques and Fridays to fashion and art, but Sunday's the big day.

GETTING THERE & AWAY

London is the major gateway to England, so further transport information can be found in the main Transport section (p394).

AIR

For information on flying to/from London see p394.

BUS

Most long-distance coaches leave London from **Victoria Coach Station** (Map p80; ☎ 7824 0000; 164 Buckingham Palace Rd SW1; ✆ Victoria), a lovely art-deco building. The arrivals terminal is in a separate building across Elizabeth St from the main coach station.

CAR

See p397 for reservation numbers of the main car-hire firms, all of which have airport and various city locations.

TRAIN

London's main-line terminals are all linked by the tube and each serves a different destination.

Charing Cross (Map pp66-7) Canterbury.
Euston (Map p84) Manchester, Liverpool, Carlisle, Glasgow.
King's Cross (Map p84) Cambridge, Hull, York, Newcastle, Scotland.
Liverpool Street (Map pp74-5) Stansted airport, Cambridge.
London Bridge (Map pp74-5) Gatwick airport, Brighton.
Marylebone (Map pp52-3) Birmingham.
Paddington (Map pp52-3) Heathrow airport, Oxford, Bath, Bristol, Exeter, Plymouth, Cardiff.

St Pancras (Map p84) Gatwick and Luton airports, Brighton, Nottingham, Sheffield, Leicester, Leeds, Paris.
Victoria (Map p80) Gatwick airport, Brighton, Canterbury.
Waterloo (Map pp66-7) Windsor, Winchester, Exeter, Plymouth.

GETTING AROUND
TO/FROM THE AIRPORTS
HEATHROW

Transport connections to Heathrow are excellent. The Piccadilly line is accessible from every terminal (£4, one hour to central London, departing from Heathrow every five minutes from around 5am to 11.30pm).

The fastest and the easiest way to central London is the **Heathrow Express** (☎ 0845 600 1515; www.heathrowexpress.co.uk),

NEIL SETCHFIELD

Canary Wharf Underground station

an ultramodern train to Paddington station (one way/return £14.50/28, 15 minutes, every 15 minutes 5.10am to 11.25pm). You can purchase tickets on board (£2 extra), online or from self-service machines (cash and credit cards accepted) at both stations.

A black cab to the centre of London will cost you between £40 and £70, a minicab around £35.

GATWICK

There are **National Rail** (www.national rail.co.uk) services from Gatwick's South Terminal to Victoria (£9.50, 37 minutes), running every 15 minutes during the day and hourly through the night. Other trains head to St Pancras (£8.90, 63 minutes), stopping at London Bridge, City Thameslink, Blackfriars and Farringdon. If you're racing to make a flight, the **Gatwick Express** (☎ 0845 850 1530; www .gatwickexpress.co.uk) departs Victoria every 15 minutes from 5.50am to 12.35am (one way/return £18/31, 30 minutes, first/last train 4.35am/1.35am).

Prices start very low, depending on when you book, for the **EasyBus** (www .easybus.co.uk) minibus service between Gatwick and Victoria (return from £11, allow 1½ hours, every 30 minutes from 3am to 1am). You'll be charged extra if you have more than one carry-on and one check-in bag.

Gatwick's taxi partner, **Checker Cars** (www.checkercars.co.uk), has a counter in each terminal. Fares are quoted and paid in advance (about £83 for the 65-minute ride to Central London). A black cab costs similar, a minicab around £55.

STANSTED

The **Stansted Express** (☎ 0845 600 7245; www.stanstedexpress.com) connects with Liverpool St station (one way/return £17/26, 46 minutes, departing every 15 minutes from 5.10am to 10.55pm, first/last train 4.40am/11.25pm).

LONDON'S OYSTER DIET

To get the most out of London, you need to be able to jump on and off public transport like a local, not scramble to buy a ticket each time at hefty rates. The best and cheapest way to do this is with an Oyster card, a reusable smartcard on which you can load either a season ticket (weekly/monthly £24.20/93) or pre-paid credit. The card itself is free with a season ticket, otherwise it's £3.

London is divided into six concentric transport zones, although almost all of the places covered in this book are in Zones 1 and 2. An Oyster bus trip costs 90p as opposed to £2, while a Zone 1 tube journey is £1.50 as opposed to £4. Even better, in any single day your fares will be capped at the equivalent of the Oyster day-pass rate for the zones you've travelled in (Zones 1 and 2 peak/off-peak £6.30/4.80).

Assuming you'll avoid the tube during peak hours (before 9.30am), this ready reckoner gives the cheapest options for your length of stay:
- one-four days: non-Oyster off-peak daily (£5.30 per day)
- five-25 days: Oyster weeklies topped up with pre-pay for any remaining days
- 26-31 days: monthly

Black cab (p106)

JAMES BRAUND

As with Gatwick, **EasyBus** (www.easy bus.co.uk) has services between Stansted, Baker St and Victoria (return from £13, allow 1¾ hours, every 30 minutes from 3am to 1.05am). The **Airbus A6** (☎ 0870 580 8080; www.nationalexpress.com) links with Victoria coach station (one way/return £10/16, allow 1¾ hours, departing at least every 30 minutes).

A black cab to/from central London costs about £100, a minicab around £55.

LONDON CITY
The Docklands Light Railway (DLR) connects London City Airport to the tube, taking 22 minutes to reach Bank station (£4). A black taxi costs around £25 to/from central London.

LUTON
There are regular **National Rail** (www .nationalrail.co.uk) services from St Pancras (£14, 28 to 48 minutes) to Luton Airport Parkway station, where a shuttle bus (£1) will get you to the airport within 10 minutes. **EasyBus** (www.easybus.co.uk) mini-

buses head from Victoria and Baker St to Luton (return from £12, allow 1¼ hours, departing every 30 minutes). A black taxi costs around £95 to/from central London, minicabs around £55.

CAR
Driving in London is a nightmare: traffic is heavy, parking is either impossible or expensive and wheel-clampers keep busy. If you drive into central London from 7am to 6pm on a weekday, you'll need to pay an £8 per day congestion charge (visit www.tfl .gov.uk/roadusers/congestioncharging/to register) or face a hefty fine. If you're hiring a car to continue your trip, take the tube to Heathrow and pick it up from there.

PUBLIC TRANSPORT
Although locals love to complain about it, London's public transport is excellent, with tubes, trains, buses and boats conspiring to get you anywhere you need to go. **Transport for London** (TFL; www .tfl.gov.uk) is the glue that hinges the network together.

LONDON UNDERGROUND, DLR & OVERGROUND

'The tube', as it's universally known, extends its subterranean tentacles throughout London and into the surrounding counties, with services running every few minutes from 5.30am to roughly 12.30am (from 7am on Sunday). Tickets (or Oyster card top-ups) can be purchased from counters or machines at the entrance to each station using either cash or credit card. See also boxed text, p104. Also included within the network are the driverless Docklands Light Railway (DLR), and the train lines shown on tube maps as 'Overground'. The DLR links the City to Docklands, Greenwich and London City Airport.

BOAT

Thames Clippers (☎ 0871-781 5049; www .thamesclippers.com) runs regular commuter services between Embankment, Waterloo, Bankside, London Bridge, Tower, Canary Wharf, Greenwich and Woolwich piers (adult £2.50 to £6.50, child £1.25 to £3.25), from 7am to 12.30pm (from 9am weekends). Another service runs from Putney to Blackfriars during the morning and evening rush hours.

Leisure services include the Tate-to-Tate boat (see boxed text, above), Westminster-to-Greenwich services (p83) and a loop route taking in Westminster, Embankment, Festival, Bankside, London Bridge and St Katherine's piers (day pass adult/child £7.80/3.70, May to September). For boats to Kew Gardens and Hampton Court Palace, see p85.

BUS

Travelling round London by double-decker bus is an enjoyable way to get a feel for the city, but it's usually more difficult and slower than the tube.

TATE-A-TATE

To get between London's Tate galleries in style, the **Tate Boat** – which sports a Damien Hirst dot painting – will whisk you between the two, stopping en route at the London Eye. Services run 10am to 6pm daily at 40-minute intervals. A River Roamer hop-on hop-off ticket (purchased on board) costs £8, single tickets £4.

Buses run regularly during the day, while less-frequent night buses (prefixed with the letter 'N') wheel into action when the tube stops. Single-journey bus tickets (valid for two hours) cost £2 (90p on Oyster, capped at £3 per day); cash day passes are £3.50 and books of six tickets are £6. At stops with yellow signs, you have to buy your ticket from the automatic machine *before* boarding. Buses stop on request, so clearly signal the driver with an outstretched arm.

TAXI

London's famous black cabs are available for hire when the yellow light above the windscreen is lit. Fares are metered, with flag fall at £2.20 and the additional rate dependent on time of day, distance travelled and taxi speed. A 1-mile trip will cost between £4.40 and £8. To order a black cab by phone, try **Dial-a-Cab** (☎ 7253 5000); you must pay by credit card and will be charged a premium.

Licensed minicabs operate out of agencies (most busy areas have a walk-in office with drivers waiting); they are a cheaper alternative to black cabs and quote a fare for the trip in advance. To find a local minicab firm, visit www.tfl.gov.uk/tfl/getting around/findaride.

SOUTHERN ENGLAND

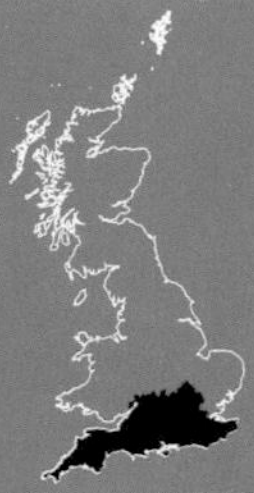

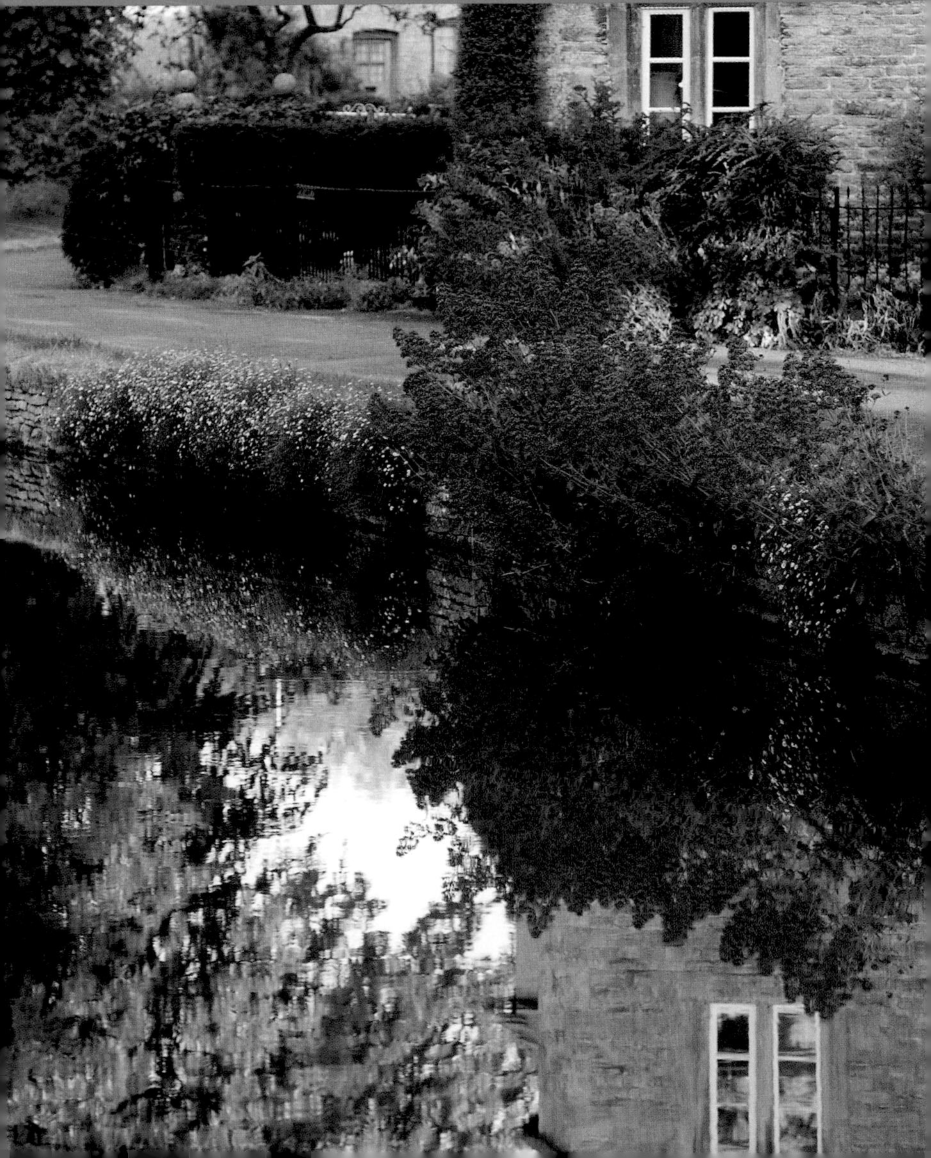

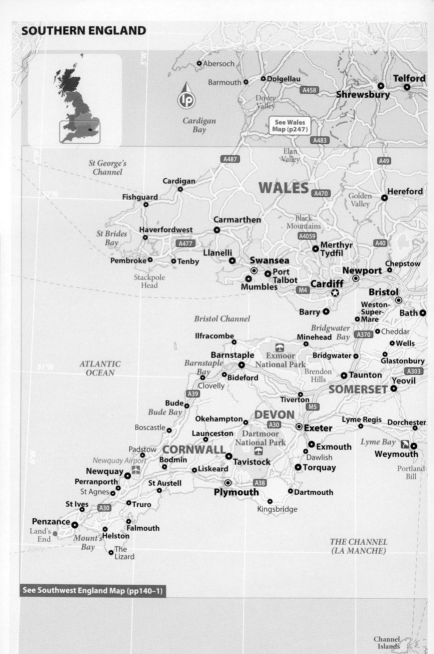

SOUTHERN ENGLAND

See Wales Map (p247)

See Southwest England Map (pp140–1)

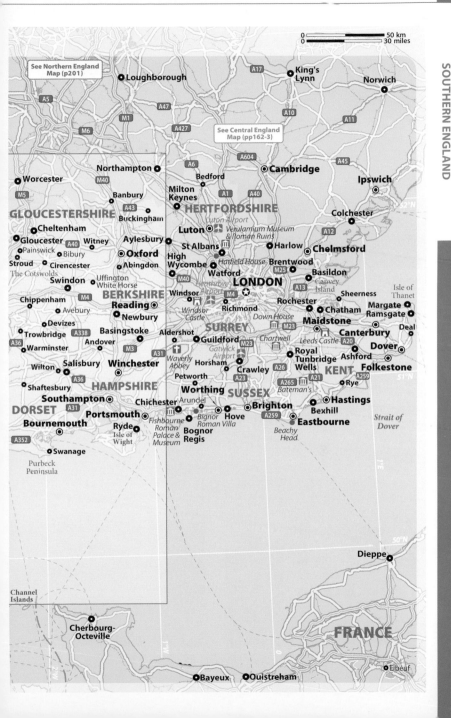

0   50 km
0   30 miles

See Northern England
Map (p201)

Loughborough

A17

King's
Lynn

Norwich

A5

A47

M1

M6

A427

See Central England
Map (pp162-3)

A10

A11

Northampton

A6

Bedford

A604

Cambridge

A45

Ipswich

Worcester

M40

Banbury

Milton
Keynes

A1

A40

HERTFORDSHIRE

Colchester

M5

A43

Buckingham

GLOUCESTERSHIRE

Cheltenham

Luton Airport

Venulamium Museum
& Roman Ruins

A12

Gloucester

A40

Witney

Aylesbury

Luton

Painswick

Bibury

Oxford

St Albans

Harlow

Chelmsford

Stroud

Cirencester

Abingdon

High
Wycombe

Hatfield House

Brentwood

The Cotswolds

Uffington
White Horse

Swindon

BERKSHIRE

Watford

LONDON

M25

Basildon

Canvey
Island

Chippenham

M4

Windsor

A13

Sheerness

Isle of
Thanet

Avebury

Reading

Richmond

Heathrow
Airport

M4

Rochester

Margate

Devizes

Newbury

Windsor
Castle

Down House

Chatham

Ramsgate

Trowbridge

A338

Basingstoke

Aldershot

SURREY

Maidstone

Deal

A36

Warminster

Andover

M3

Guildford

Gatwick
Airport

M23

Chartwell

Leeds Castle

A20

Canterbury

Dover

Salisbury

Winchester

A31

Waverly
Abbey

Horsham

Crawley

Royal
Tunbridge
Wells

Ashford

Folkestone

Wilton

A36

HAMPSHIRE

Petworth

A23

A26

Bateman's

KENT

A259

Shaftesbury

Worthing

SUSSEX

A265

A21

Rye

Southampton

Chichester

Arundel

Brighton

Hastings

DORSET

A31

Portsmouth

Bignor
Roman Villa

Hove

Bexhill

Bournemouth

Ryde

Fishbourne
Roman
Palace &
Museum

Bognor
Regis

Beachy
Head

Eastbourne

Strait of
Dover

A352

Isle of
Wight

A259

Swanage

Purbeck
Peninsula

Channel
Islands

Dieppe

Cherbourg-
Octeville

FRANCE

Elbeuf

Bayeux

Ouistreham

SOUTHERN ENGLAND HIGHLIGHTS

1 STONEHENGE & AROUND

BY PAT SHELLEY OF SALISBURY GUIDED TOURS
I've been running guided tours of the Stonehenge area for the last three years. It has become a full-time passion – for me, nowhere sums up the magic and mystery of ancient Britain better than Stonehenge.

↘ PAT SHELLEY'S DON'T MISS LIST

❶ INSIDE THE CIRCLE
Access to Stonehenge is restricted, and many visitors simply turn up and snap a few photos through the fence. It's really worth taking the audio tour or, better still, a **special access tour** (p143) which allows you to actually see inside the circle. Places are very limited; book well ahead!

❷ THE CURSUS & THE AVENUE
The best route to the circle is the path ancient people used. Walk northeast along the bridleway from the main carpark towards the Cursus, the long earthwork that runs in an east–west line. Turn right towards the Avenue, an ancient path perfectly aligned with the summer solstice. Watching Stonehenge looming up on the horizon ahead is an unforgettable experience.

❸ WOODHENGE
Nearly 2 miles northeast of Stonehenge, Woodhenge consists of concentric circles once marked by wooden poles (now replaced by concrete posts). Woodhenge is clearly linked

Clockwise from top: Avebury (p148); Salisbury Cathedral (p144); Old Sarum (p148); Stonehenge (p143)

SOUTHERN ENGLAND

SOUTHERN ENGLAND HIGHLIGHTS

to Stonehenge, although its function remains uncertain.

❹ AVEBURY
This is Britain's largest **stone circle** (p148). Many of the stones are missing, and there's a road right through the middle of it – but in terms of sheer scale it's hard not to be impressed. Other monuments in the area include Silbury Hill and West Kennet Long Barrow.

❺ SALISBURY CATHEDRAL
Salisbury's best-known landmark is un-doubtedly the great **cathedral** (p144), boasting the tallest spire in Britain. Just outside Salisbury are the remains of the city's original cathedral, **Old Sarum** (p148), abandoned in the 14th century.

❶ Stonehenge
❷ The Cursus & the Avenue
❸ Woodhenge
❹ Avebury
❺ Salisbury Cathedral

0 — 6 km
0 — 3 miles

↘ THINGS YOU NEED TO KNOW
Best time to visit Early or late in the day **How long will I need?** At least half a day to explore the whole Stonehenge area **Photo op** Isn't it obvious? **For full details on Stonehenge, see p143**

SOUTHERN ENGLAND HIGHLIGHTS

2

↘ EDEN PROJECT

Record producer turned eco-champion Tim Smit has turned an old claypit near St Austell in Cornwall into the space-age **Eden Project** (p157). Three massive biomes – the world's largest – recreate a diverse range of natural habitats, from the tropical rainforest to the dry desert, while the rest of the site explores all the hot-topic issues surrounding climate change, sustainability and environmental protection.

3

↘ ROYAL CRESCENT, BATH

Bath (p145) is often described as Britain's most beautiful city – little wonder the whole place has been designated as a World Heritage Site. In the 18th century two pioneering architects (John Woods Snr and Jnr) transformed Bath from a sleepy spa town into one of the triumphs of the Georgian Age. The jewel in the city's crown is the magnificent **Royal Crescent** (p147).

⬈ BRIGHTON

Only an hour's train ride from central London, buzzy Brighton (p122) is a small town with a big heart, full of quirky shops, funky cafes and an unmistakably alternative atmosphere. The Prince Regent, who later became King George IV, certainly let the sea air go to his head – his pimped-up Pavilion (p122) wouldn't look out of place in St Petersburg.

⬊ WINDSOR CASTLE

There's pomp and ceremony aplenty at the Queen's weekend getaway, Windsor Castle (p137). It's been used as a royal residence since the days of William the Conqueror, and has been lavishly restored to its full aristocratic splendour since it was badly damaged in a fire in 1992. Don't forget to catch the ceremonial Changing of the Guard.

⬊ OXFORD

Orderly Oxford (p127) is long acknowledged as the nation's foremost seat of learning (unless you happen to be in Cambridge, that is). The city of dreaming spires is an essential stop if you're visiting southern England – you'll need at least a couple of days to soak up the sights.

2 NEIL SETCHFIELD; 3 DENNIS JOHNSON; 4 DAVID TOMLINSON; 5 PHILIP GAME; 6 ADINA TOVY AMSEL

2 Eden Project (p157); 3 Royal Crescent (p147), Bath; 4 Royal Pavilion (p122), Bath; 5 Changing of the Guard, Windsor Castle (p137); 6 Radcliffe Camera (p129), Oxford

SOUTHERN ENGLAND'S BEST...

⤷ LANDMARKS

- **Canterbury Cathedral** (p119) A real showstopper.
- **Uffington White Horse** (p133) Admire this ancient charger.
- **Stonehenge** (p143) The world's most famous circle.
- **Cerne Giant** (p148) This chalk figure certainly isn't shy.
- **St Michael's Mount** (p158) Cornwall's Mont St-Michel.

⤷ COUNTRY HOUSES

- **Stourhead** (p144) Princely Palladian splendour.
- **Longleat** (p144) Stately home turned safari park.
- **Chartwell** (p121) Churchill's country retreat.
- **Hatfield House** (p137) Jacobean grandiosity.
- **Lanhydrock** (p156) Elegant estate in the Cornish countryside.

⤷ URBAN ESCAPES

- **New Forest** (p142) Wonderful woodland.
- **The Cotswolds** (p133) Chocolate box villages and quiet market towns.
- **Exmoor** (p159) Spot Exmoor ponies and red deer.
- **Cheddar Gorge** (p151) Explore these subterranean caverns.
- **Isles of Scilly** (p159) The Cornish Caribbean?

⤷ PLACES WITH A VIEW

- **White Cliffs of Dover** (p121) There'll be bluebirds over...
- **Dartmoor** (p159) Unspoilt moorland dotted with granite tors.
- **Salisbury Plain** (p143) One of England's greatest landscapes.
- **Winchester Cathedral's tower** (p139) Views to the Isle of Wight on a clear day.
- **Land's End** (p158) Where the British mainland runs out of steam.

LEFT: GLENN BEANLAND; RIGHT: HOLGER LEUE

Left: Sudeley Castle (p134), the Cotswolds; Right: Fishbourne Roman Palace & Museum (p126)

THINGS YOU NEED TO KNOW

⟱ VITAL STATISTICS

- Population 7.51 million
- Area 609 sq miles

⟱ AREAS IN A NUTSHELL

- Sussex (p121) Commuters and urban escapees favour London's backyard.
- Berkshire (p137) Stately monuments aplenty.
- Wiltshire (p142) Littered with ancient landmarks.
- Somerset (p150) Sleepy rural county; the spiritual home of scrumpy.
- Devon (p152) The epitome of green and pleasant England.
- Cornwall (p154) Beaches and cliffs characterise the wild west.

⟱ ADVANCE PLANNING

- Two months before Get your accommodation planning done early, especially in Oxford, Brighton and the southwest.
- Two weeks before It doesn't hurt to book as early as possible for major sights including Windsor Castle, Longleat, Stourhead, Blenheim Palace and Bath's Roman Baths.
- One week before Cross your fingers and hope the sun shines.

⟱ RESOURCES

- South West Tourist Board (www.visitsouthwest.com)
- Tourism South East (www.visitsoutheastengland.com) Official website for south and southeast England.
- Visit Cornwall (www.visitcornwall.com)
- Visit Kent (www.visitkent.co.uk)
- Visit Somerset (www.visitsomerset.co.uk)
- Visit Surrey (www.visitsurrey.com)
- Visit Sussex (www.visitsussex.org)

⟱ GETTING AROUND

- Bus Many different companies and complicated timetables make bus travel tougher than it should be.
- Train The Great Western line is still going strong.
- Car Convenient, but you won't escape a traffic jam or two.

⟱ BE FOREWARNED

- High season The southwest counties (especially Devon and Cornwall) are prime holiday areas. You might find July and August not as relaxing as you might have hoped.
- Bath Summer crowds are just a fact of life in Bath. Spring and autumn are much less hectic.
- Minor roads Many of the southwest's minor roads are narrow, windy and tricky to navigate. GPS becomes notoriously unreliable the further off the beaten track you go.

SOUTHERN ENGLAND ITINERARIES

ENGLISH ICONS Three Days

This whistle-stop trip takes in three of England's great national institutions, beginning with **(1) Windsor Castle** (p137), where the Queen and Prince Philip like to while away their time when they're not staying at one of their other little country getaways. Nearby is arguably the most exclusive school in England, **(2) Eton** (p138); pupils here still dress in traditional top hat and tails, and in order to secure a place it's normally necessary to sign your offspring up several decades in advance. Then it's over to **(3) Oxford** (p127), another notoriously selective academic institution – even if you don't quite make the intellectual grade, it's still worth spending a couple of days here soaking up the unforgettable architecture and collegial atmosphere.

CITY TO CITY Five Days

For this urban-themed itinerary we've strung together some of southern England's key cities. Begin in **(1) Brighton** (p122), where the seaside air and alternative ambience feels a world away from the hustle and bustle of London; you'll probably need a couple of days to cover the **Royal Pavilion** (p122), browse the shops and cafes (p124) and perhaps make a day trip to **(2) Arundel Castle** (p126) or **Bignor Roman Villa** (p126) in Sussex.

On day three travel west to either **(3) Winchester** (p139) or **(4) Salisbury** (p144), both stately cities centred around their soaring cathedrals; if you fancy sticking around, Salisbury also makes a great base for venturing further into Wiltshire or taking a day trip to **Stonehenge** (p143).

Last up is **(5) Bath** (p145), where you could easily while away a couple of days visiting the **Roman baths** (p145), the **abbey** (p146) and relaxing in the fantastic **Thermae Bath Spa** (p149). For out-and-out luxury, a night in the **Queensberry Hotel** (p149) and a meal at the **Olive Tree** (p149) certainly won't disappoint.

SOUTHERN BELLES One Week

For our final route we've concentrated on some of southern England's greatest manmade wonders, ranging from fantastic cathedrals to stone circles and cliff-top theatres. **(1) Canterbury Cathedral** (p119) is the obvious place to start – if you've only got time to visit one of England's ecclesiastical buildings, this is definitely the one to choose. From Canterbury skirt round the edge of London to **(2) Blenheim Palace** (p133), whose fabulous landscaped grounds were laid out by the Duke of Marlborough and much later provided Winston Churchill

with a rather posh childhood playground. From here it's an easy drive to the (3) Uffington White Horse (p133) and the stone circles of (4) Avebury (p148) and Stonehenge (p143), with an optional stop to admire (5) Salisbury Cathedral's fantastic spire (p144). (6) Bath's (p145) Georgian architecture is a must, especially to see the city's smartest address on the Royal Crescent (p147), while nearby (7) Exeter (p152) boasts one of the loveliest cathedral closes in southern England. Cross the border into Celtic Cornwall, whose best-known modern-day landmarks are the futuristic biomes of the (8) Eden Project (p157) – apparently they're even visible from space. Finish this adventure all the way out west with a performance at the cliff-top (9) Minack Theatre (p158) – if there's a more dramatic place to stage a play, we haven't found it yet.

DISCOVER SOUTHERN ENGLAND

For many people, the southern counties are the essence of England: a pastoral patchwork of thatched cottages, market towns and historic castles, where stone circles loom on the plains and chalk horses gallop across the hills. There's no doubt that this is one of the nation's most historic corners – some of the most crucial battles in English history have been fought on southern soil, and the elegant cities of Bath, Salisbury, Oxford and Windsor are crammed with more heritage per square foot than anywhere in the British Isles.

But the south is far from a dry and dusty textbook. Many of the cities have a distinctively youthful kick, while gastropubs, bistros and boutique B&Bs are springing up all along the coastline and groundbreaking initiatives such as the Eden Project are flying the flag for a more sustainable future. Throw in mile upon mile of glorious coastline, Britain's most beautiful beaches and a host of ancient monuments, and you've got a region that deserves some serious exploring.

SOUTHEAST ENGLAND

This corner of England is both blessed and cursed by its proximity to London. The well-off counties of Kent, East and West Sussex and Surrey are among the most popular parts of Britain to live and visit, home to commuter hubs and business communities as well as huge crowds of visitors when the weather gets sunny. Yet the region is also peppered with picturesque villages, meandering country lanes and out-of-the way country pubs, enveloped in manicured farmland and rolling chalk downs.

GETTING THERE & AROUND

The southeast is easily explored by train or bus, and many attractions can be visited in a day trip from London. Contact the **National Traveline** (☎ 0871 200 2233; www.travelinesoutheast.org.uk) for comprehensive information on public transport in the region.

BUS

Explorer tickets (adult/child £6.40/4.50) provide day-long unlimited travel on most buses throughout the region; buy them at bus stations or on your first bus.

Stagecoach Coastline (www.stagecoach bus.com) serves the coastline, East Kent and East Sussex areas. Travellers can buy an unlimited day (£7) or week (£18) ticket.

TRAIN

If you're based in London but day-tripping around the southeast, the BritRail London Plus Pass allows unlimited regional rail travel for two days in eight (£102), four days in eight (£164), or seven days in fifteen (£197) and must be purchased outside the UK; see p400 for more on train passes.

You can secure 33% discounts on most rail fares over £10 in the southeast by purchasing a **Network Railcard** (☎ 08457 225 225; www.railcard.co.uk/network/network.htm; per yr £20). Children under 15 can save 60%, but a minimum £1 fare applies.

KENT

Kent isn't described as the garden of England for nothing. Inside its sea-lined borders you'll find a clipped landscape of gentle hills, lush farmland, cultivated country estates and fruitful orchards.

CANTERBURY

The Church of England could not have a more imposing mother church than the extraordinary early Gothic **Canterbury Cathedral** (☎ 01227-762862; www.canterbury -cathedral.org; adult/concession £7/5.50; ☉ 9am-6.30pm Mon-Sat Easter-Sep, 9am-4.30pm Mon-Sat Oct-Easter, plus 12.30-2.30pm & 4.30-5.30pm Sun year-round), the centrepiece of the city's World Heritage Site and repository of over 1400 years of Christian history. The spot in the northwest transept where Archbishop Thomas Becket met his grisly end has been drawing pilgrims for over 800 years.

The wealth of detail in the cathedral is immense and unrelenting, so it's well worth joining a one-hour **tour** (adult/ child £5/3; ☉ 10.30am, noon & 2.30pm Mon-Fri, 10.30am, noon & 1.30pm Sat Apr-Sep, noon & 2pm Mon-Sat Oct-Mar), or you can take a 30-minute self-guided **audio tour** (adult/child £3.95/1.95). There is an additional charge to take photographs.

An integral but often overlooked part of the Canterbury World Heritage Site, **St Augustine's Abbey** (EH; ☎ 01227-767345; adult/child £4.20/2.10; ☉ 10am-6pm daily Jul & Aug, 11am-5pm Sat & Sun Sep-Mar, 10am-5pm Wed-Sun Apr-Jun) was founded in AD 597, marking the rebirth of Christianity in southern England. Later requisitioned as a royal palace, it was to fall into disrepair and now only stumpy foundations remain.

SLEEPING

Canterbury Cathedral Lodge (☎ 01227-865350; www.canterburycathedrallodge.org; Canterbury Cathedral precincts; r from £79; ☐ wi-fi) The position of this modern, circular lodge is unbeatable. It's right opposite the cathedral within the precinct itself. The clean, modern rooms – done out in white and blond wood – have excellent facilities but what really makes this place are the views.

VERONICA GARBUTT

Canterbury Cathedral

Abode Canterbury (☎ 01227-766266; www.abodehotels.co.uk; 30-33 High St; s/d from £89/109) The only boutique hotel in town, rooms here are graded from 'comfortable' to 'fabulous' and for the most part they live up to their names, and they come with little features such as handmade beds, cashmere throws, velour bathrobes, beautiful modern bathrooms and little tuck boxes of locally produced snacks.

EATING

Karl's (☎ 01227-764380; 43 St Peter's St; snacks £3-7; ⊗ 9am-6pm Mon-Sat) The walls of this bright little deli are crammed with fine cheeses, artisan breads and pastries, coffee beans and food-friendly wines.

Tiny Tim's Tearoom (☎ 01227-450793; 34 St Margaret's St; mains £7-13; ⊗ 9.30-5pm Tue-Sat, 10.30am-4pm Sun) Not a hint of chintz in this English tearoom, it's pure 1930s elegance. Come in to enjoy big breakfasts full of Kent ingredients, or tiers of cakes, crumpets and sandwiches for high tea.

our pick **Goods Shed** (☎ 01227-459153; Station Rd West; lunch £8-12, dinner £10-16; ⊗ market 10am-7pm Tue-Sat, to 4pm Sun, restaurant lunch & dinner Tue-Sun) Farmers market, food hall and fabulous restaurant all rolled into one, this converted station warehouse by the railway is a hit with everyone from self-caterers to sit-down gourmets.

GETTING THERE & AWAY

Canterbury is 58 miles from London and 15 miles from Margate and Dover.

BUS

The bus station is just within the city walls on St George's Lane. There are frequent buses to London Victoria (£12.70, two hours, hourly) and services to Dover (£5.20, 35 minutes, hourly). There are also buses to Margate (53 minutes, three per hour), Broadstairs (one hour, twice hourly), Ramsgate (80 minutes, twice hourly) and Whitstable (30 minutes, every 15 minutes).

TRAIN

There are two train stations: Canterbury East, accessible from London Victoria;

Canterbury pub life

ORIEN HARVEY

and Canterbury West, accessible from London's Charing Cross and Waterloo East stations. London-bound trains leave frequently (£20.90, 1½ hours, two to three hourly), as do Canterbury East to Dover Priory trains (£6.70, 16 to 28 minutes, every 30 minutes).

THE WHITE CLIFFS

Immortalised in song, film and literature, these iconic cliffs are embedded in the national consciousness, acting as a big, white 'Welcome Home' sign to generations of travellers and soldiers. The cliffs rise 100m high and extend for 10 miles on either side of Dover, but it is the 6-mile stretch east of town – properly known as the Langdon Cliffs – that particularly captivates visitors' imaginations.

The cliffs are 2 miles east of Dover along Castle Hill Rd and the A258 road to Deal or off the A2 past the Eastern Docks. Buses 113 and 90/1 from Dover stop near the main entrance.

DOWN HOUSE

Charles Darwin's home from 1842 until his death in 1882, **Down House** (EH; ☎ 01689-869119; adult/5-14yr £7.20/3.60; ⏰ 11am-5pm daily Jul & Aug, 11am-5pm Wed-Sun Mar-Jun, Sep & Oct, closed Nov-Feb) witnessed the development of Darwin's theory of evolution by natural selection. The house and gardens have been restored to look much as they would have in Darwin's time, including Darwin's study, where he undertook much of his reading and writing; the drawing room, where he tried out some of his indoor experiments; and the gardens and greenhouse, where some of his outdoor experiments are recreated.

Down House is in Luxted Rd, Downe, off the A21. Take bus 146 from Bromley North or Bromley South railway station, or service R8 from Orpington.

CHARTWELL

The home of Sir Winston Churchill from 1924 until his death in 1965, **Chartwell** (☎ 01732-868 381; Westerham; adult/child £11.20/5.60, garden & studio only £5.60/2.80; ⏰ 11am-5pm Wed-Sun Apr-Jun, Sep & Oct, Tue-Sun Jul & Aug), 6 miles east of Sevenoaks, offers a breathtakingly intimate insight into the life of England's famous cigar-chomping bombast. This 19th-century house and its rambling grounds have been preserved much as Winnie left them, full of books, pictures, maps and personal mementos. Churchill was also a prolific painter and his daubings are scattered throughout the house and fill the garden studio.

LEEDS CASTLE

This immense moated pile is, for many, the world's most romantic **castle** (☎ 01622-765 400; www.leeds-castle.com; adult/4-15yr/senior & student £15/9.50/12.50; ⏰ 10.30am-6pm Apr-Oct, to 4pm Nov-Mar), and it's certainly one of the most visited in Britain. While it looks formidable enough from the outside – a hefty structure balancing on two islands amid a large lake and sprawling estate – it's actually known as something of a 'ladies castle'. This stems from the fact that in its over 1000 years of history, it has been home to a who's who of medieval queens, most famously Henry VIII's first wife, Catherine of Aragon. The castle was transformed from fortress to lavish palace over the centuries, and its last owner, the high-society hostess Lady Baillie, used it as a princely family home and party pad to entertain the likes of Errol Flynn, Douglas Fairbanks and JFK.

SUSSEX

Home to lush countryside, medieval villages and gorgeous coastline, this lovely corner of the country is besieged by

SOUTHERN ENGLAND

SOUTHEAST ENGLAND

Royal Pavilion

ADINA TOVY AMSEL

weekending Londoners whenever the weather is fine. Brighton, a highlight of a visit here, offers vibrant nightlife, offbeat shopping and shingly shores.

BATEMAN'S

It was love at first sight when Rudyard Kipling, author of *The Jungle Book,* set eyes on **Bateman's** (NT; ☎ 01435-882302; adult/child £7.20/3.60; ☯ 11am-5pm Sat-Wed mid-Mar–Oct), the glorious little 1634 Jacobean mansion he would call home for the last 34 years of his life, and where he would draw inspiration for the *Just So Stories* and other vivid tales. Everything is pretty much just as the writer left it after his death in 1936, down to the blotting paper on his study desk.

Bateman's is about half a mile south of the town of Burwash along the A259.

BRIGHTON & HOVE
pop 247, 817

Brighton and Hove is the most vibrant seaside resort in England and a high point of any visit to the region. It's a thriving, cosmopolitan city with a Bohemian spirit; home to an exuberant gay community, a dynamic student population and a healthy number of ageing and new-age hippies, as well as traditional candyfloss fun.

INFORMATION
INTERNET RESOURCES
Brighton City Guide (www.brighton.co.uk)
visitbrighton.com (www.visitbrighton.com)

TOURIST INFORMATION
Tourist office (☎ 0906-711 2255; www.visit brighton.com; Royal Pavilion Shop, Royal Pavilion; ☯ 9.30am-5.30pm daily) Overworked staff and a 50p-per-minute telephone line provide local information. You may find the website and on-site 24-hour-accessible computer more helpful.

SIGHTS
ROYAL PAVILION
An absolute must of a visit to Brighton is the **Royal Pavilion** (☎ 01273-290900; www .royalpavilion.org.uk; adult/under 15yr £8.50/5.10; ☯ 10am-4.30pm Oct-Mar, 9.30am-5pm Apr-Sep), the glittering, exotic party-pad-cum-palace of Prince George, later Prince Regent then King George IV. The flamboyant Indian-style domes and Moorish minarets outside are only a prelude to the palace's lavish oriental-themed interior, where no colour is deemed too strong, dragons swoop and snarl from gilt-smothered ceilings, gem-encrusted snakes slither down pillars, and crystal chandeliers seem ordered by the ton.

SOUTHERN ENGLAND

BRIGHTON & HOVE

BRIGHTON & HOVE

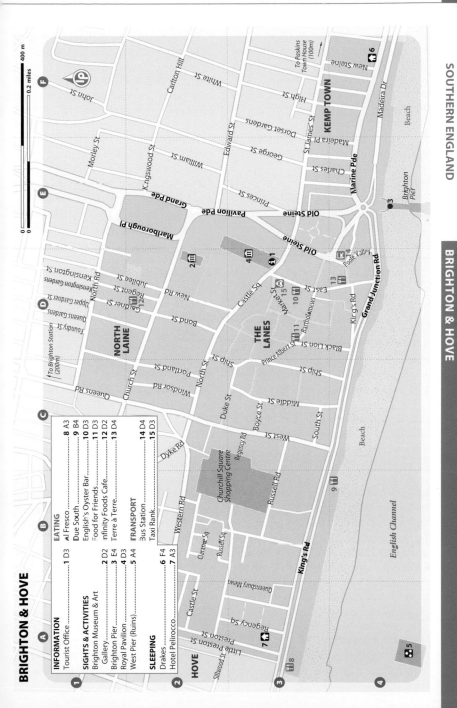

INFORMATION
Tourist Office...................................**1** D3

SIGHTS & ACTIVITIES
Brighton Museum & Art
  Gallery.......................................**2** D2
Brighton Pier................................**3** E4
Royal Pavilion..............................**4** D3
West Pier (Ruins).........................**5** A4

SLEEPING
Drakes..**6** F4
Hotel Pelirocco.............................**7** A3

EATING
Al Fresco.......................................**8** A3
Due South....................................**9** B4
English's Oyster Bar....................**10** D3
Food for Friends..........................**11** D3
Infinity Foods Cafe.....................**12** D2
Terre à Terre................................**13** D4

TRANSPORT
Bus Station..................................**14** D4
Taxi Rank.....................................**15** D3

BRIGHTON MUSEUM & ART GALLERY

Set in the Royal Pavilion's renovated stable block, this **museum and art gallery** (☎ 01273-290 900; Royal Pavilion Gardens; admission free; ✆ 10am-7pm Tue, to 5pm Wed-Sat, 2-5pm Sun) has a glittering collection of 20th-century art and design, including a crimson Salvador Dali sofa modelled on Mae West's lips.

BRIGHTON PIER

This grand old centenarian **pier** (Palace Pier; www.brightonpier.co.uk; admission free), full of glorious gaudiness, is the place to come to experience the tackier side of Brighton. Look west and you'll see the sad remains of the **West Pier** (www.westpier.co.uk), a skeletal iron hulk that attracts flocks of birds at sunset. It's a sad end for a Victorian marvel upon which the likes of Charlie Chaplin and Stan Laurel once performed.

TOURS

Brighton Walks (☎ 01273-888596; www.brightonwalks.com; adult/child £6/3.50) A huge variety of standard and offbeat themes including a Murder Walk and a Rich & Famous tour. Show up for prescheduled walks or contact to book.

City Sightseeing (www.city-sightseeing.co.uk; adult/child £7/3; ✆ tours every 30 min late May-late Sep) Has open-top, hop-on hop-off bus tours that leave from Grand Junction Rd near Brighton Pier and take you around the main sights.

Tourist Tracks (www.tourist-tracks.com) Has MP3 audio guides downloadable from their website (£5) or available on a preloaded MP3 player at the tourist office (£6 per half-day).

FESTIVALS & EVENTS

There's always something fun going on in Brighton, from **Gay Pride** (www.brightonpride.org) in late July to food and drink festivals.

The showpiece is May's three-week-long **Brighton Festival** (☎ 01273-709709; www.brighton-festival.org.uk), the biggest arts festival in Britain after Edinburgh, attracting theatre, dance, music and comedy performers from around the globe.

SLEEPING

Despite a glut of hotels in Brighton, prices are relatively high and you'd be wise to book well ahead for summer weekends and for the Brighton Festival in May.

Paskins Town House (☎ 01273-601203; www.paskins.co.uk; 18/19 Charlotte St; d from £90; ▣ wi-fi) An environmentally friendly B&B spread between two elegant town houses. It prides itself on using ecofriendly products such as recycled toilet paper, low-energy bulbs and biodegradable cleaning materials.

Hotel Pelirocco (☎ 01273-327055; www.hotelpelirocco.co.uk; 10 Regency Sq; s £50-65, d £90-140, suite £300; ▣ wi-fi) There's a range of individually designed rooms, some by artists, some by big-name sponsors, from a basic single done up like a boxing ring, to the Motown room, full of gold satin, LPs and a vintage record player, to the playroom suite with a 3m circular bed, mirrored ceiling and pole-dancing area.

Drakes (☎ 01273-696934; www.drakesofbrighton.com; 43-44 Marine Pde; r £100-325; ▣ wi-fi) Drakes oozes understated class: a stylish, minimalist boutique hotel that eschews the need to shout its existence from the rooftops. Feature rooms have giant free-standing tubs set in front of full-length bay windows with stunning views out to sea. It also has one of Brighton's best restaurants, Gingerman.

EATING

Infinity Foods Cafe (☎ 01273-670743; 50 Gardner St; mains £5-8; ✆ 9.30am-5pm Mon-Sat) The sister establishment of Infinity Foods

Sussex seaside

HOLGER LEUE

wholefoods shop, a Brighton institution, serves a wide variety of vegetarian and organic food, with many vegan and wheat- or gluten-free options including tofu burgers, meze plates and falafel.

Food for Friends (☎ 01273-202310; www .foodforfriends.com; 17a Prince Albert St; mains £8-13; ☺ lunch & dinner) This airy, glass-sided restaurant attracts the attention of passers-by as much as it does the loyalty of its customers, with an ever-inventive choice of vegetarian and vegan food.

Al Fresco (☎ 01273-206532; The Milkmaid Pavilion, Kings Rd Arches; mains £9-20; ☺ noon-midnight) Al Fresco sits a mere 100m from the West Pier, a curved-glass structure with a huge, staggered outdoor terrace and amazing views up and down the seafront and out to sea. The pizzas, pastas and Italian meat dishes make a tasty accompaniment to the views.

our pick **Terre à Terre** (☎ 01273-729051; 71 East St; mains £10-15; ☺ noon-10.30pm Tue-Fri, to 11pm Sat, to 10pm Sun) Even staunch meat-eaters will come out raving about this legendary vegetarian restaurant. Terre à Terre offers a sublime dining experience, from the vibrant, modern space, to the entertaining menus, to the delicious, inventive dishes full of rich robust flavours.

English's Oyster Bar (☎ 01273-327980; www.englishs.co.uk; 29-31 East St; mains £10-29; ☺ lunch & dinner) A 60-year institution, this Brightonian seafood paradise dishes up everything from oysters to lobster to Dover sole. It's converted from fishermen's cottages, with echoes of the elegant Edwardian era inside and buzzing alfresco dining on the pedestrian square outside.

Due South (☎ 01273-821218; www.due south.co.uk; 139 Kings Rd Arches; mains £14-20; ☺ lunch & dinner Mon-Sat, lunch Sun) Sheltered under a cavernous Victorian arch on the seafront, with a curvaceous front window and small bamboo-screened terrace on the promenade, this refined, yet relaxed, restaurant specialises in dishes cooked with the best environmentally sustainable and seasonal Sussex produce.

GETTING THERE & AWAY

BUS

National Express (☎ 08705-808080; www.nationalexpress.com) coaches leave for London Victoria (£10.90, 80 minutes, hourly), and there are regular coach links to all London airports.

Buses 28, 29 and 29A go to Lewes (£2.80, 35 minutes), bus 12 to Eastbourne (£3, 80 minutes), and bus 700 to Chichester (£3, 80 minutes) and Arundel (two hours).

TRAIN

There are two hourly services to London Victoria (£19, 50 to 70 minutes) and two to London Bridge (50 minutes to 1¼ hours). For £2 on top of the rail fare, you can get a PlusBus ticket that gives unlimited travel on Brighton & Hove buses for the day. There's one direct service to Portsmouth (£14.50, 1½ hours, hourly), twice-hourly services to Chichester, Eastbourne and Hastings, and links to Canterbury and Dover.

ARUNDEL

Originally built in the 11th century, all that's left of the first **Arundel Castle** (☎ 01903-882173; www.arundelcastle.org; adult/under 16yr/student & senior £13/7.50/10.50; ☺ 11am-5pm Tue-Sun Easter-Oct), are the modest remains of its keep at its core. Thoroughly ruined during the English Civil War, most of what you see today is the result of passionate reconstruction by the eighth, 11th and 15th dukes of Norfolk between 1718 and 1900. The current duke still lives in part of the castle. Highlights include the atmospheric keep, the massive Great Hall and the library, which has paintings by Gainsborough and Holbein.

Trains run to London Victoria (£20.50, 1½ hours, twice hourly), and to Chichester (20 minutes, twice hourly); change at

Ford or Barnham. There are also links to Brighton (£7.80, one hour 20 minutes, twice hourly); change at Ford or Barnham.

BIGNOR ROMAN VILLA

Discovered in 1811 by a farmer ploughing his fields, **Bignor** (☎ 01903-869259; www.bignorromanvilla.co.uk; adult/child £4.35/1.85; ☺ 10am-6pm Jun-Sep, to 5pm May & Oct, Tue-Sun Mar & Apr) was built around AD 190. The wonderful mosaic floors include vivid scenes of chunky-thighed gladiators, a beautiful Venus whose eyes seem to follow you about the room and an impressive 24m-long gallery design.

While Bignor is well worth the trip, it's a devil of a place to reach without your own wheels. It's located 6 miles north of Arundel off the A29.

FISHBOURNE ROMAN PALACE & MUSEUM

Anyone mad about mosaics should head straight for **Fishbourne Palace** (☎ 01243-785 859; www.sussexpast.co.uk; Salthill Rd; adult/child £7/3.70; ☺ 10am-5pm Mar-Jul, Sep & Oct, to 6pm Aug, to 4pm Nov-Feb), the largest known Roman residence in Britain. Happened upon by labourers in the 1960s, it's thought that this once-luxurious mansion was built around AD 75 for a Romanised local king.

Fishbourne Palace is 1.5 miles west of Chichester, just off the A259.

PETWORTH

On the outskirts of its namesake village, the imposing 17th-century stately home, **Petworth House** (NT; ☎ 01798-342207; adult/child £9.50/4.80; ☺ 11am-5pm Sat-Wed Apr-Oct), has an extraordinary art collection, the National Trust's finest. JMW Turner was a regular visitor and the house is still home to the largest collection of his paintings outside London's Tate Gallery. There are also many paintings by Van Dyck, Reynolds, Gainsborough, Titian, Bosch and William Blake.

The surrounding **Petworth Park** (**adult/child £3.80/1.90;** ⏰ **8am-sunset**) is the highlight – the fulfilment of Lancelot 'Capability' Brown's romantic natural-landscape theory.

Petworth is 12 miles northeast of Chichester off the A285.

OXFORDSHIRE

A well-bred, well-preened kind of place, Oxfordshire is a region of old money, academic achievement and genteel living. Dominated by its world-famous university, and renowned for its brilliant minds, the county town is a major highlight with over 1500 listed buildings, a choice of excellent museums and an air of refined sophistication.

GETTING THERE & AROUND

The main train stations are in Oxford and Banbury and have frequent connections to London Paddington and Euston, Hereford, Birmingham, Bristol and Scotland.

The main bus operators are the **Oxford Bus Company** (☎ **01865-785400; www.oxford bus.co.uk**) and **Stagecoach** (☎ **01865-772250; www.stagecoachbus.com/oxfordshire**).

OXFORD

pop 134,248

An air of genteel sophistication and long-held privilege hits you as soon as you arrive in Oxford. The august buildings, hushed college quads, grand libraries and gowned cyclists mark it out as a place unlike most others. Although traffic and shoppers rush along the streets, inside the hallowed walls of the city's 39 colleges a reverent hush and studious

JERRY GALEA

Arundel Castle

calm descends. It's a wonderful place to ramble; the oldest colleges date back almost 750 years and little has changed since then.

HISTORY

Oxford was a key Saxon town that grew dramatically in importance when Henry II banned Anglo-Norman students from attending the Sorbonne in 1167. The first colleges, Balliol, Merton and University, were built in the 13th century, with at least three more being added in each of the following three centuries. Newer colleges, such as Keble, were added in the 19th and 20th centuries and today there are 39 colleges catering for about 20,000 students.

OXFORD

INFORMATION

Tourist Office	1 C3

SIGHTS & ACTIVITIES

Ashmolean Museum	2 C2
Bodleian Library	3 C3
Bridge of Sighs	4 D3
Christ Church College	5 C4
Magdalen College	6 E3
Merton College	7 D4
New College	8 D3
Radcliffe Camera	9 D3

SLEEPING

Buttery Hotel	10 C3
Malmaison	11 B3
Old Parsonage Hotel	12 B1

EATING

Edamame	13 D2
Jam Factory	14 A3
Quod	15 D3

TRANSPORT

Gloucester Green Bus/Coach Station	16 B3

INFORMATION

Tourist office (☎ 01865-252200; www
.visitoxford.org; 15-16 Broad St; ⏰ 9.30am-5pm
Mon-Sat, to 6pm Thu-Sat Jul & Aug, 10am-4pm
Sun) Stocks a *Welcome to Oxford* brochure (£1), which features a walking
tour and college opening times.

SIGHTS

CHRIST CHURCH COLLEGE

The largest and grandest of all of Oxford's
colleges, **Christ Church** (☎ 01865-276492;
www.chch.ox.ac.uk; St Aldate's; adult/under 16yr
£4.90/3.90; ⏰ 9am-5pm Mon-Sat, 1-5pm Sun) is
also its most popular. The magnificent
buildings, illustrious history and latter-
day fame as a location for the Harry Potter
films have tourists coming in droves. The
college was founded in 1525 by Cardinal
Thomas Wolsey, Over the years numerous luminaries have been educated here
including Albert Einstein, philosopher
John Locke, poet WH Auden, Charles
Dodgson (Lewis Carroll) and 13 British
prime ministers.

MAGDALEN COLLEGE

Set amid 40 hectares of lawns, woodlands,
river walks and deer park, **Magdalen**
(mawd-len; ☎ 01865-276000; www.magd.ox.ac
.uk; High St; adult/under 16yr £4/3; ⏰ noon-6pm
Jul-Sep, 1pm-6pm/dusk Oct-Jun) is one of the
wealthiest and most beautiful of Oxford's
colleges. An elegant Victorian gateway
leads into a medieval chapel, with its glorious 15th-century tower, and on to the
remarkable cloisters, some of the finest in
Oxford. The strange gargoyles and carved
figures here are said to have inspired CS
Lewis' stone statues in *The Chronicles of
Narnia*.

BODLEIAN LIBRARY

Oxford's **Bodleian Library** (☎ 01865-
277224; www.bodley.ox.ac.uk; Broad St) is one
of the oldest public libraries in the world,
and one of England's three copyright libraries. It holds more than seven million
items on 118 miles of shelving and has
seating space for up to 2500 readers.

Most of the rest of the library is closed
to visitors, but **library tours** (admission £6;
⏰ tours 10.30am, 11.30am, 2pm & 3pm) allow
access to the medieval Duke Humfrey's
library, where, the library proudly boasts,
no less than five kings, 40 Nobel Prize winners, 25 British prime ministers and writers such as Oscar Wilde, CS Lewis and JRR
Tolkien studied.

RADCLIFFE CAMERA

Just south of the library is the **Radcliffe
Camera** (Radcliffe Sq; ⏰ no public access), the
quintessential Oxford landmark and one
of the city's most photographed buildings. The spectacular circular library was
built between 1737 and 1749 in grand
Palladian style, and boasts Britain's third-
largest dome. The only way to see the
library is to join an extended tour (£12),
which also explores the warren of underground tunnels and passages leading to
the library's vast book stacks. Tours take
place once a month (more often in July
and August) on Saturday at 10.30am and
last about an hour and a half. Advanced
booking is recommended.

NEW COLLEGE

From the Bodleian, stroll under the **Bridge
of Sighs**, a 1914 copy of the famous bridge
in Venice, to **New College** (☎ 01865-279555;
www.new.ox.ac.uk; Holywell St; admission Easter-
Sep £2, Oct-Easter free; ⏰ 11am-5pm Easter-Sep,
2-4pm Oct-Easter). This 14th-century college
was the first in Oxford to accept under-
graduates and is a fine example of the
glorious Perpendicular style.

MERTON COLLEGE

From the High St follow the wonderfully named Logic Lane to **Merton College** (☎ 01865-276310; www.merton.ox.ac.uk; Merton St; admission free; ☷ 2-4pm Mon-Fri, 10am-4pm Sat & Sun), one of Oxford's original three colleges. Founded in 1264, Merton was the first to adopt collegiate planning, bringing scholars and tutors together into a formal community and providing a planned residence for them. The charming 14th-century **Mob Quad** here was the first of the college quads.

ASHMOLEAN MUSEUM

A vast, rambling collection of art and antiquities is on display at the mammoth **Ashmolean** (☎ 01865-278000; www.ashmolean.org; Beaumont St; admission free; ☷ 10am-5pm Tue-Sat, noon-5pm Sun), Britain's oldest public museum. Established in 1683, it is based on the extensive collection of the remarkably well-travelled John Tradescant, gardener to Charles I, and it is housed in one of Britain's best examples of neo-Grecian architecture.

TOURS

Blackwell (☎ 01865-333606; oxford@blackwell .co.uk; 48-51 Broad St; adult/child £6.50/4; ☷ late May-Oct) Oxford's most famous bookshop runs 1½-hour tours, including a literary tour (2pm Tuesdays and 11.30am Thursdays), an 'Inklings' tour (11.45am Wednesdays) – the Inklings was an informal literary group whose members included CS Lewis and JRR Tolkien – and a town-and-gown tour (2pm Fridays).

City Sightseeing (☎ 01865-790522; www.citysightseeingoxford.com; adult/under 16yr £11.50/6; ☷ every 10-15min 9.30am-6pm Apr-Oct) Runs hop-on hop-off bus tours from the bus and train stations or any of the 20 dedicated stops around town.

Tourist office (☎ 01865-252200; www.visit oxford.org; 15-16 Broad St; ☷ 9.30am-5pm Mon-Sat, 10am-4pm Sun) Runs two-hour tours of Oxford city and colleges (adult/under 16yr £7/3.50; at 11am and 2pm year-round, also at 10.30am and 1pm during July and August), Inspector Morse tours (£7.50/4; 1.30pm Saturday), family walking tours (£5.50/3.50; 1.30pm school holidays)

New College (p129)

SEAN CAFFREY

and a selection of themed tours (adult/ child £7.50/4) that run on various dates throughout the year.

SLEEPING

Tilbury Lodge (☎ 01865-862138; www .tilburylodge.com; 5 Tilbury Lane; s £70, d £80-90; P ▣) Spacious, top-of-the-line rooms with plush, modern decor and excellent bathrooms make this stylish B&B worth the trip outside the centre of town.

our pick Orchard House (☎ 01865-249200; www.theorchardhouseoxford.co.uk; 225 Iffley Rd; s £75-85, d £85-95; P) Set in beautiful se-cluded gardens just a short walk from the city centre, this lovely arts-and-crafts-style house is a wonderful retreat from the city. The two bedrooms are sleek and stylish and very spacious, each with its own sofa and breakfast table, and the limestone bathrooms are luxuriously modern.

Buttery Hotel (☎ 01865-811950; www .thebutteryhotel.co.uk; 11-12 Broad St; s/d from £60/95; ▣) Right in the heart of the city with views over the college grounds, the Buttery is Oxford's newest hotel. Considering its location, it's a great deal, with spacious, modern rooms, decent bathrooms and the pick of the city's at-tractions on your doorstep.

Malmaison (☎ 01865-268400; www.mal maison-oxford.com; 3 Oxford Castle; d/ste from £160/245; ▣) Lock yourself up for the night in one of Oxford's most spectacular set-tings. This former Victorian prison has been converted into a sleek and slinky hotel with plush interiors, sultry lighting, dark woods and giant beds.

our pick Old Parsonage Hotel (☎ 01865-310210; www.oldparsonage-hotel.co.uk; 1 Banbury Rd; r £170-250; P ▣) Wonderfully quirky and instantly memorable, the Old Parsonage is a small boutique hotel with just the right blend of old-world charac-ter, period charm and modern luxury.

EATING

our pick Edamame (☎ 01865-246916; 15 Holywell St; sushi £2.50-3.50, mains £6-7; ⊙ lunch Wed-Sun, dinner Thu-Sat) You'll find this tiny Japanese place by looking for the queue out the door as you head down Holywell St, but it's well worth the wait. The food here is simply divine with the best rice and noodle dishes in town and sushi (Thursday night only) to die for.

Aziz (☎ 01865-794945; 228 Cowley Rd; mains £8-10) Thought by many to be Oxford's best curry house, this award-winning res-taurant attracts vegans, vegetarians and curry lovers in hordes. There's an exten-sive menu, chilled surroundings and por-tions generous enough to ensure you'll be rolling out the door.

Jam Factory (☎ 01865-244613; www.the jamfactoryoxford.com; 27 Park End St; mains £8-12) Arts centre, bar and restaurant rolled into one, the Jam Factory is a laid-back, boho kind of place, with changing exhibitions and hearty breakfasts, an excellent-value £10 two-course lunch and an understated menu of modern British dishes.

Quod (☎ 01865-202505; www.quod.co.uk; 92 High St; mains £10.50-15.50) Bright, buzz-ing and decked out with modern art and beautiful people, this designer joint dishes up Mediterranean brasserie-style food to the masses. It doesn't take reser-vations, is always heaving and, at worst, will tempt you to chill by the bar with a cocktail while you wait.

Gee's (☎ 01865-553540; www.gees-restau rant.co.uk; 61 Banbury Rd; mains £15-21.50) Set in a Victorian conservatory, this top-notch place is a sibling of Quod's but much more conservative. Popular with the vis-iting parents of university students, the food is modern British and European and the setting stunning, but it's all a little stiff.

GETTING THERE & AWAY

BUS

Oxford's main bus/coach station is at **Gloucester Green**, in the heart of the city. Competition on the Oxford–London route is fierce, with two companies running buses (£15 return, four per hour) at peak times. Services run all through the night and take about 90 minutes to reach central London:

Oxford Espress (☎ 01865-785400; www.oxfordbus.co.uk)

Oxford Tube (☎ 01865-772250; www.oxfordtube.com)

The Heathrow Express (£18, 70 minutes) runs half-hourly 4am to 10pm and at midnight and 2am, while the Gatwick Express (£22, two hours) runs hourly 5.15am to 8.15pm and every two hours 10pm to 4am.

National Express has five direct buses to Birmingham (£11, two hours), and one service to Bath (£9.50, two hours) and Bristol (£13.80, 2¾ hours). All these destinations are easier to reach by train.

Stagecoach serves most of the small towns in Oxfordshire and runs the X5 service to Cambridge (£9, 3½ hours) roughly every half-hour.

CAR & MOTORCYCLE

Thanks to a complicated one-way system and a shortage of parking spaces, driving and parking in Oxford is a nightmare. Drivers are strongly advised to use the five Park & Ride car parks on major routes leading in to town. Three car parks are free to use, the others cost £1. The return bus journey to town (10 to 15 minutes, every 10 minutes) costs £2.50.

TRAIN

There are half-hourly services to London Paddington (£22.50, one hour) and roughly hourly trains to Birmingham (£22, 1¼ hours), Worcester (£29, 1½ hours) and Hereford (£17.40, two hours). Hourly services also run to Bath (£19.60, 1¼ hours) and Bristol (£21.40, 1½ hours), but require a change at Didcot Parkway.

GLENN BEANLAND

Blenheim Palace

BLENHEIM PALACE

One of England's greatest stately homes, **Blenheim Palace** (☎ 08700 602080; www.blenheimpalace.com; adult/under 16yr £16.50/10, park & garden only £9.50/4.80; ⏰ palace 10.30am-5.30pm daily mid-Feb–Oct, Wed-Sun Nov–mid-Dec, park open year-round) is a monumental baroque fantasy designed by Sir John Vanbrugh and Nicholas Hawksmoor between 1705 and 1722. The land and funds to build the house were granted to John Churchill, Duke of Marlborough, by a grateful Queen Anne after his decisive victory at the Battle of Blenheim. Now a Unesco World Heritage Site, Blenheim (*blen*-num) is home to the 11th duke and duchess.

Inside, the house is stuffed with statues, tapestries, ostentatious furniture and giant oil paintings in elaborate gilt frames. Highlights include the **Great Hall**, a vast space topped by 20m-high ceilings adorned with images of the first duke in battle; the opulent **Saloon**, the grandest and most important public room; the three **state rooms** with their plush decor and priceless **china cabinets**; and the magnificent 55m **Long Library**.

From the library, you can access the **Churchill Exhibition**, which is dedicated to the life, work and writings of Sir Winston, who was born at Blenheim in 1874.

UFFINGTON WHITE HORSE

One of England's oldest chalk carvings, the **Uffington White Horse** is a stylised image cut into a hillside almost 3000 years ago. This huge figure measures 114m long and 49m wide but is best seen from a distance, or, if you're lucky enough, from the air, because of the stylised lines of perspective.

THE COTSWOLDS

Glorious honey-coloured villages riddled with beautiful old mansions, thatched cottages, atmospheric churches and rickety almshouses draw crowds of tourists to the Cotswolds, a region of lush rolling hills that grew wealthy during a boom in the medieval wool trade. This is prime tourist territory, however, and the most popular villages can be besieged in summer.

ORIENTATION & INFORMATION

For information on attractions, accommodation and events:
Cotswolds (www.the-cotswolds.org)
Cotswolds Tourism (www.cotswolds.com)
Oxfordshire Cotswolds (www.oxfordshirecotswolds.org)

GETTING AROUND

Public transport through the Cotswolds is fairly limited, with bus services running to and from major hubs only, and train services just skimming the northern and southern borders. For help planning an itinerary pick up the *Explore the Cotswolds* brochures at local tourist offices.

CHIPPING CAMPDEN

pop 1943

A truly unspoiled gem in an area full of achingly pretty villages, Chipping Campden is a glorious reminder of life in the Cotswolds in medieval times.

The town's most obvious sight is the wonderful 17th-century **Market Hall** with its multiple gables and elaborate timber roof. Further on, at the western end of the High St, is the 15th-century **St James'**, one of the great wool churches of the Cotswolds. The surviving **Court Barn** (☎ 01386-841951; www.courtbarn.org.uk; Church St; adult/child under 16yr £3.75/free; ⏰ 10.30am-

5.30pm Tue-Sat, 11.30am-5.30pm Sun Apr-Sep, 11am-4pm Tue-Sat, 11.30am-4pm Sun Oct-Mar) is now a museum of craft and design featuring work from the Arts and Crafts Movement.

About 4 miles northeast of Chipping Campden, **Hidcote Manor Garden** (NT; ☎ 01386-438333; Hidcote Bartrim; adult/under 18yr £8.50/4.25; ☽ 10am-5pm Sat-Wed mid-Mar–Oct, plus 10am-5pm Fri Jul & Aug) is one of the finest examples of arts and crafts landscaping in Britain.

SLEEPING & EATING

Eight Bells (☎ 01386-840371; www.eightbells inn.co.uk; Church St; s £55-85, d £85-125) Dripping with old-world character and charm, but also decidedly modern, this 14th-century inn has a range of sleek, comfy rooms and a well-respected restaurant serving a British and Continental menu (mains £11 to £12) in rustic settings.

ourpick Cotswold House Hotel (☎ 01386-840330; www.cotswoldhouse.com; The Square; r £150-650; P ⌨) If you're after a spot of luxury, look no further than this chic Regency town house turned boutique hotel. You can dine in style at Juliana's (two-/three-course set dinner £39.50/49.50) or take a more informal approach at Hick's Brasserie (mains £9 to £18).

GETTING THERE & AROUND

Between them, buses 21 and 22 run almost hourly to Stratford-upon-Avon or Moreton-in-Marsh. Bus 21 also stops in Broadway. There are no Sunday services.

WINCHCOMBE

pop 3682

Winchcombe is a sleepy Cotswold town, very much a working, living place with butchers, bakers and small independent shops giving it a very lived-in, authentic feel. The town's main attraction is magnificent **Sudeley Castle** (☎ 01242-602308; www .sudeleycastle.co.uk; adult/under 15yr £7.20/4.20; ☽ 10.30am-5pm Sun-Thu mid-Mar–Oct), once a favoured retreat of Tudor and Stuart monarchs.

ourpick 5 North St (☎ 01242-604566; 5 North St; 2/3-course lunch £20.50/24.50, 3-course dinner £33-43; ☽ lunch Wed-Sat, dinner Tue-Sun)

BARBARA VAN ZANTEN

Hidcote Manor Garden

The top spot to eat for miles around, this Michelin-starred restaurant has no airs and graces, just beautifully prepared food in down-to-earth surroundings.

GETTING THERE & AWAY
Bus 606 runs from Broadway (65 minutes, four daily Monday to Saturday) to Cheltenham via Winchcombe.

CIRENCESTER
pop 15,861

Refreshingly unpretentious, with narrow, winding streets and graceful town houses, charming Cirencester is an affluent, elegant kind of place. The lovely market square is surrounded by wonderful 18th-century and Victorian architecture, and the nearby streets showcase a harmonious medley of buildings from various eras.

Under the Romans, Cirencester was second only to London in terms of size and importance and, although little of this period remains, you can still see the grassed-over ruins of one of the largest amphitheatres in the country.

Standing elegantly on the Market Sq, cathedral-like **St John's** (suggested donation £3; 🕙 10am-5pm) is one of England's largest parish churches. An outstanding Perpendicular-style tower with wild flying buttresses dominates the exterior, but it is the majestic three-storey south porch that is the real highlight.

Innovative displays and computer reconstructions bring one of Britain's largest collections of Roman artefacts to life at the **Corinium Museum** (☎ 01285-655611; www .cotswolds.gov.uk/museum; Park St; adult/under 16yr £3.95/2; 🕙 10am-5pm Mon-Sat, 2-5pm Sun).

SLEEPING & EATING
Old Brewhouse (☎ 01285-656099; www .theoldbrewhouse.com; 7 London Rd; s £50-55, d £65-70; P) Set in a charming 17th-century town house, this lovely B&B has bright, pretty rooms with cast-iron beds and subtle, country-style florals or patchwork quilts.

No 12 (☎ 01285-640232; ww.no12cirencester .co.uk; 12 Park St; d £85) This Georgian town house right in the centre of town has gloriously unfussy rooms kitted out with a tasteful mix of antiques and modern furnishings.

Jesse's Bistro (☎ 01285-641497; Blackjack St; mains £12.50-21.50; 🕙 lunch Mon-Sat, dinner Tue-Sat) Hidden away in a cobbled stable yard with its own fishmonger and cheese shop, Jesse's is a great little place with flagstone floors, wrought-iron chairs and mosaic tables.

GETTING THERE & AWAY
National Express buses run roughly hourly from Cirencester to London (£17, 2½ hours) and to Cheltenham Spa (30 minutes) and Gloucester (one hour). Stagecoach bus 51 also runs to Cheltenham Monday to Saturday (40 minutes, hourly). Bus 852 goes to Gloucester (four daily Monday to Saturday).

BIBURY
pop 623

Once described by William Morris as 'the most beautiful village in England', Bibury is another Cotswold gem with a cluster of gorgeous riverside cottages and tangle of narrow streets flanked by wayward stone buildings. It's an impossibly quaint place whose main attraction is **Arlington Row**, a stunning sweep of cottages now thought to be the most photographed street in Britain.

Buses 860, 863, 865, 866 and 869 pass through Bibury en route to Cirencester at least once daily from Monday to Saturday (20 minutes).

PAINSWICK

pop 1666

One of the most beautiful and unspoilt towns in the Cotswolds, hilltop Painswick is an absolute gem. The village centres on **St Mary's Church**, a fine, Perpendicular wool church surrounded by table-top tombs and 99 clipped yew trees. Sliding downhill beside and behind the church is a series of gorgeous streetscapes. Look out for **Bisley St**, the original main drag, which was superseded by the now ancient-looking New St in medieval times.

Just a mile north of town, the ostentatious **Painswick Rococo Garden** (☎ 01452-813204; www.rococogarden.co.uk; adult/under 16yr £5.50/2.75; ☽ 11am-5pm Jan-Oct) is the area's biggest attraction.

Village house, the Cotswolds (p133)

SLEEPING & EATING

St Michaels (☎ 01452-814555; www.stmichaels restaurant.co.uk; Victoria St; d £80; 2/3-course dinner £28/32.50; ☽ lunch & dinner Wed-Sat, dinner Sun; ☐) The three rooms at St Michaels are a handsome mix of luxurious fabrics, exposed stone work, rustic furniture and carved woods.

Cardynham House (☎ 01452-814006; www.cardynham.co.uk; The Cross; s £65-85 d £80-185) The individually decorated rooms at 15th-century Cardynham House offer four-poster beds, heavy-patterned fabrics and buckets of character. Downstairs, the **Bistro** (mains £11.50-16.50; ☽ lunch Tue-Sun, dinner Tue-Sat) serves modern British cuisine.

GETTING THERE & AROUND

Bus 46 connects Cheltenham (30 minutes) with Painswick hourly Monday to Saturday. Bus 256 connects Painswick to Gloucester twice daily on Wednesday and Saturday.

GLOUCESTERSHIRE

Gloucestershire has a languid charm that makes a welcome break from the crowds of the Cotswolds.

FOREST OF DEAN

An ancient woodland with a unique, almost magical character, the Forest of Dean is the oldest oak forest in England and a wonderfully scenic place to walk, cycle or paddle. The forest was designated England's first National Forest Park in 1938.

The **tourist office** (☎ 01594-812388; www.visitforestofdean.co.uk; High St, Coleford; ☽ 10am-5pm Mon-Sat Apr-Sep, plus 10am-2pm Sun Jul & Aug, 10am-4pm Mon-Fri Oct-Mar, plus 10am-2pm Sat Oct, Feb & Mar) stocks walking and cycling guides and also offers a free accommodation booking service.

From Gloucester, bus 31 (one hour, half-hourly) runs to Coleford and there are trains to Lydney (20 minutes, hourly). The **Dean Forest Railway** (☎ 01594-845840; www.deanforestrailway.co.uk) runs steam trains from Lydney to Parkend (day ticket adult/under 16 years £9/5) on selected days from March to December.

HERTFORDSHIRE

This sleepy county is a pastoral home to swathes of London commuters, and is little-visited by tourists.

VERULAMIUM MUSEUM & ROMAN RUINS

A fantastic exposé of everyday life under the Romans, the **Verulamium Museum** (☎ 01727-751810; www.stalbansmuseums.org.uk; St Michael's St; adult/child £3.30/2; ☼ 10am-5.30pm Mon-Sat, 2-5.30pm Sun) is home to a large collection of arrowheads, glassware and grave goods. Its centrepiece is the **Mosaic Room**, where five superb mosaic floors, uncovered between 1930 and 1955, are laid out.

Across the busy A4147 are the grassy foundations of a **Roman theatre** (☎ 01727-835035; www.romantheatre.co.uk; adult/child £2/1; ☼ 10am-5pm Mar-Oct, to 4pm Nov-Feb), which once seated 2000 spectators.

HATFIELD HOUSE

For over 400 years, **Hatfield House** (☎ 01707-287010; house & garden adult/child £10/4.50, park only £2.50/1.50; ☼ noon-4pm Wed-Sun & public holidays, gardens 11am-5.30pm Easter-Sep) has been home to the Cecils, one of England's most influential political families. This magnificent Jacobean mansion was built between 1607 and 1611 for Robert Cecil, first earl of Salisbury and secretary of state to both Elizabeth I and James I, and is awash with grandiose portraits, tapestries, furnishings and armour.

BERKSHIRE

Posh and prosperous Berkshire is littered with handsome villages, historic houses and exquisitely maintained villages, and acts as a country retreat for some of London's most influential figures. The Queen's favourite weekend getaway, Windsor Castle, is here, as is one of the world's most prestigious schools, Eton.

WINDSOR & ETON

pop 30,568

The largest and oldest occupied fortress in the world, **Windsor Castle** (☎ 020-7766 7304; www.royalcollection.org.uk; adult/child £15/8.50; ☼ 9.45am-4pm Mar-Oct, to 3pm Nov-Feb) is a majestic vision of battlements and towers used for state occasions and as the Queen's weekend retreat.

William the Conqueror first established a royal residence in Windsor in 1070 when he built a motte and bailey here, the only naturally defendable spot in the Thames valley. Since then successive monarchs have rebuilt, remodelled and refurbished the castle complex to create the massive and sumptuous palace that stands here today. The castle largely escaped the bombings of WWII, but in 1992 a devastating fire tore through the building destroying or damaging more than 100 rooms. By chance, the most important treasures were in storage at the time, and with skilled craftsmanship and painstaking restoration, the rooms were returned to their former glory.

A fabulous spectacle of pomp, with loud commands, whispered conversations, triumphant tunes from a military band and plenty of shuffling and stamping of feet, the **changing of the guard** (☼ 11am Mon-Sat Apr-Jun, alternate days Jul-Mar) draws the crowds to the castle gates each day.

ETON COLLEGE

Cross the bridge over the River Thames to Eton and you'll enter another world, one where old-school values and traditions seem to ooze from the very walls. The streets here are surprisingly hushed as you make your way down to the most enduring and most illustrious symbol of England's class system, **Eton College** (☎ 01753-671177; www.etoncollege .com; adult/child £4.20/3.45, tours £5.50/4.50; ☽ 10.30am-4.30pm Mar & Apr, Jul-Sep [school holidays], 2-4.30pm term time, guided tours 2.15pm & 3.15pm).

Those who have studied here include 19 prime ministers, countless princes, kings and maharajahs, famous explorers, authors and economists, among them the Duke of Wellington, Princes William and Harry, George Orwell, Ian Fleming, Aldous Huxley, Sir Ranulph Fiennes and John Maynard Keynes.

Tours take in the **chapel** (which you can see from Windsor Castle), the **cloisters**, the **Museum of Eton Life**, the **lower school** and the **school yard**. *Chariots of Fire, The Madness of King George, Mrs Brown* and *Shakespeare in Love* are just some of the classics that have been filmed here.

LEGOLAND WINDSOR

A fun-filled theme park of white-knuckle rides, **Legoland** (☎ 08705 040404; www .legoland.co.uk; adult/child 3-15yr £34/26; ☽ hours vary) is more about the thrills of scaring yourself silly than the joys of building your own make-believe castle from the eponymous bricks. The professionals have already done this for you, with almost 40-million Lego bricks transformed into some of the world's greatest landmarks.

The Legoland shuttle bus departs from High St and Thames St from 10am, with the last bus returning 30 minutes after the park has closed.

SOUTHWEST ENGLAND

Southwest England offers up, on one verdant, sea-fringed platter, the pick of Britain's cities, coast and countryside. Stretching west from Hampshire to the soaring cliffs and golden sands of Cornwall, the region takes in Dorset's chocolate box-pretty villages, Wiltshire's prehistoric sites, Bath's exquisite Georgian cityscape, hippie-chic Somerset and Devon's beguiling blend of moors and shores.

GETTING AROUND

It is perfectly possible to get around the southwest using public transport, but services to some of the more remote areas are limited; using your own wheels gives you more flexibility. **Traveline South West** (☎ 0871 200 22 33; www.travelinesw.com) can answer regionwide questions about bus and train routes (calls cost 10p per minute).

BUS

The region's bus network is fairly comprehensive, but becomes increasingly patchy the further you move away from the main towns; Dartmoor and west Cornwall can be particularly tricky to negotiate.

First Travel (☎ timetables 0871 200 22 33, customer service 0870 010 6022; www.firstgroup .com) The region's largest bus company. The FirstDay Southwest ticket (adult/child £7/5.20) is valid for one day on most First buses in Devon, Cornwall, Bristol, Somerset and Dorset.

PlusBus (www.plusbus.info) Allows you to add local bus travel to your train ticket. Participating cities include Bath, Bristol, Taunton and Weymouth. Tickets cost from £2 to £3 per day and can be bought at railway stations.

Annual procession at Windsor Castle (p137)

Stagecoach (☎ timetables 0871 200 22 33, customer service 0845 121 0190) A key provider in Hampshire. A one-day Explorer Ticket costs £7/4 per adult/child.

Wilts & Dorset (☎ 01202-673555; www .wdbus.co.uk) One-day Explorer tickets (adult/child £7/4) cover transport on most Wilts & Dorset buses and some other companies.

CAR & MOTORCYCLE
The M5 runs past Bath and Bristol, becomes the A38 at Exeter and continues on into Cornwall. Another main route is the A303, which cuts west across Salisbury Plain past Stonehenge on its way towards Exeter and Plymouth, before joining the A38 into Cornwall.

TRAIN
A key train line to the southwest follows the historic Great Western Railway route to Bristol, from where there are regular links to London Paddington, as well as services north to Scotland via Birmingham.

The **Freedom of the SouthWest Rover pass** (adult/child £95/45) allows eight days' unlimited travel over 15 days in an area that includes Salisbury, Bath, Bristol and Weymouth.

HAMPSHIRE
Hampshire is the historic heart of the ancient kingdom of Wessex, a Dark Age territory that at its height stretched from Kent through Dorset, Wiltshire, Somerset, Bath and Devon to Cornwall.

WINCHESTER
pop 41,420
Calm, collegiate Winchester is a mellow must-see for all visitors to the region. Almost 1000 years of history are crammed into Winchester's superb **cathedral** (☎ 01962-857200; www.winchester -cathedral.org.uk; adult/child £5/free, combined admission & tower tour £8; ⊙ 8.30am-6pm Mon-Sat, to 5.30pm Sun), which is not only the city's star attraction but one of southern England's most awe-inspiring buildings. The interior contains one of the longest

SOUTHWEST ENGLAND

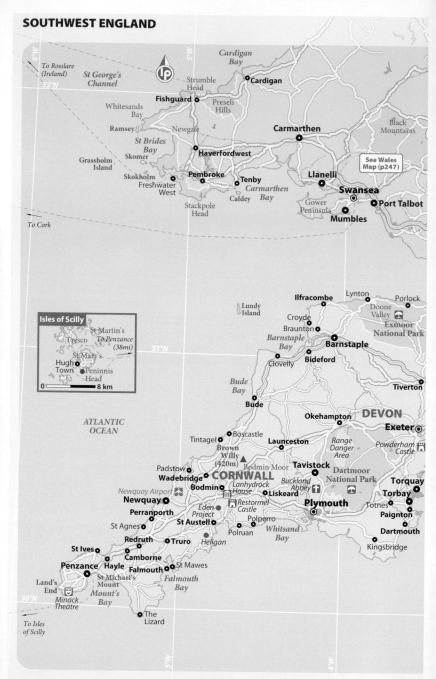

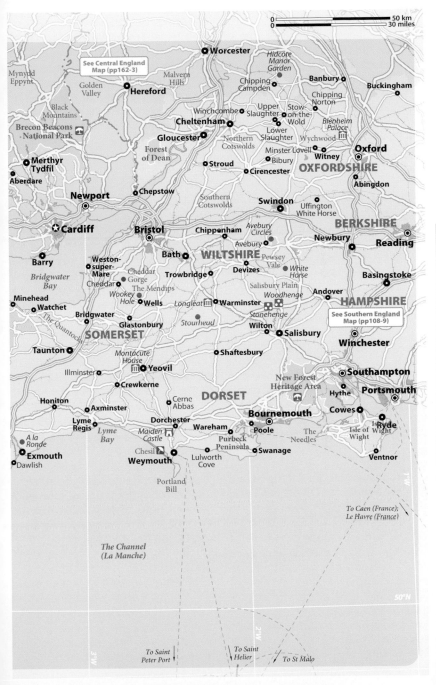

50 km
30 miles

Mynydd
Eppynt

See Central England
Map (pp162-3)

Worcester

Hidcote
Manor
Garden

Malvern
Hills

Chipping
Campden

Banbury

Buckingham

Golden
Valley

Hereford

Winchcombe

Upper
Slaughter

Stow-
on-the-
Wold

Chipping
Norton

Black
Mountains

Cheltenham

Lower
Slaughter

Blenheim
Palace

Brecon Beacons
National Park

Gloucester

Northern
Cotswolds

Minster Lovell

Wychwood

Witney

Oxford

Forest
of Dean

Stroud

Bibury

OXFORDSHIRE

Merthyr
Tydfil

Cirencester

Abingdon

Aberdare

Chepstow

Southern
Cotswolds

Swindon

Uffington
White Horse

BERKSHIRE

Newport

Bristol

Chippenham

Avebury
Circles

Newbury

Reading

Cardiff

Avebury

Bath

WILTSHIRE

Pewsey
Vale

Barry

Weston-
super-
Mare

Cheddar
Gorge

Trowbridge

Devizes

White
Horse

Basingstoke

Bridgwater
Bay

Cheddar

The Mendips

Salisbury Plain

Woodhenge

Andover

HAMPSHIRE

Minehead

Wookey
Hole

Wells

Longleat

Warminster

See Southern England
Map (pp108-9)

Watchet

Stonehenge

Winchester

The Quantocks

Bridgwater

Glastonbury

Stourhead

Wilton

Salisbury

SOMERSET

Taunton

Montacute
House

Yeovil

New Forest
Heritage Area

Southampton

Illminster

Crewkerne

Shaftesbury

Hythe

Portsmouth

Honiton

Axminster

Cerne
Abbas

DORSET

Cowes

Lyme
Regis

Lyme
Bay

Dorchester

Wareham

Bournemouth

Isle of
Wight

Ryde

A la
Ronde

Maiden
Castle

Poole

The
Needles

Ventnor

Exmouth

Chesil

Purbeck
Peninsula

Swanage

Dawlish

Weymouth

Lulworth
Cove

Portland
Bill

To Caen (France);
Le Havre (France)

The Channel
(La Manche)

50°N

To Saint
Peter Port

To Saint
Helier

To St Malo

medieval naves (164m) in Europe, and a fascinating jumble of features from all eras. You can also see the grave of one of England's best-loved authors, Jane Austen.

Cathedral body **tours** (free; ☽ hourly 10am-3pm Mon-Sat) last one hour. There are also **tower and roof tours** (£5; ☽ 2.15pm Mon-Fri, 11.30am & 2.15pm Sat Jun-Sep, 2.15pm Wed, 11.30am & 2.15pm Sat Oct-May) up narrow stairwells and with views as far as the Isle of Wight.

The fantastical, crumbling remains of early-12th-century **Wolvesey Castle** (EH; ☎ 023-9237 8291; admission free; ☽ 10am-5pm Apr-Sep) still huddle in the protective embrace of the city's walls, despite the building having been largely demolished in the 1680s.

ourpick **Wykeham Arms** (☎ 01962-853834; www.accommodating-inns.co.uk; 75 Kingsgate St; s £90-100, d £105-150) At 250-odd years old, the Wykeham is bursting with history – it used to be a brothel and also put up Nelson for a night (some say the two events coincided). Creaking, winding stairs lead to the cosy, traditionally styled bedrooms above the pub, while the posher rooms (over the converted post office, opposite) look out onto a pocked-sized courtyard garden.

Hotel du Vin (☎ 01962-841414; www.hotelduvin.com; Southgate St; r £135-205; ℗ ▢ wi-fi) Tucked in behind a red-brick facade and gleaming white porticoes, this oh-so-chic hotel boasts ultracool minimalist furniture, ornate chaises lounges and opulent stand-alone baths. The bistro delivers Georgian elegance and modern versions of English and French classics (mains £16).

Brasserie Blanc (☎ 01962-810870; 19 Jewry St; mains £13; ☽ lunch & dinner) Get a taste of French home cooking, Raymond (Blanc) style, at this super-sleek chain.

GETTING THERE & AWAY

Winchester is 65 miles west of London and 14 miles north of Southampton. National Express has several direct buses to London Victoria bus station (£13, 2¼ hours).

Trains leave every 20 minutes from London Waterloo (£24, one hour) and Southampton (15 to 23 minutes) and hourly from Portsmouth (£8.60, one hour). There are also fast links to the Midlands.

NEW FOREST

With typical, accidental, English irony, the New Forest is anything but new. This ancient swathe of wild heath and woodland has a unique history and archaic traditions that date to 1079, when William the Conqueror designated it a royal hunting preserve. Verderers, or commoners, still have ancient grazing rights on 130 sq km of the forest; its incarnation as a national park is much more modern – it was only awarded that protective status in 2005. For more information, go to www.thenewforest.co.uk.

The **New Forest Tour Bus** (☎ 023-8061 8233; www.thenewforesttour.info; adult/child £9/4.50; ☽ tours hourly 10am-4pm late-May-Aug) is a two-hour hop-on hop-off bus service that passes through Lyndhurst's main car park, Brockenhurst Station, Lymington and Beaulieu; buses also have cycle trailers.

A **Wilts & Dorset** (www.wdbus.co.uk) Network Ticket offers unlimited travel on main bus lines in the region (one/seven days £7.50/20).

WILTSHIRE

In Wiltshire you get the very best of ancient England. This verdant landscape is rich with the reminders of ritual and is littered with more ancient barrows, processional avenues and mysterious stone rings than anywhere else in Britain.

ANDERS BLOMQVIST

Stonehenge

⬏ STONEHENGE

Stonehenge is Britain's most iconic archaeological site. This compelling ring of monolithic stones has been attracting a steady stream of pilgrims, poets and philosophers for the last 5000 years.

Despite the constant flow of traffic from the main road beside the monument, and the huge numbers of visitors who traipse around the perimeter on a daily basis, Stonehenge still manages to be a mystical, ethereal place – a haunting echo from Britain's forgotten past, and a reminder of the people who once walked the many ceremonial avenues across Salisbury Plain. Even more intriguingly, it's still one of Britain's great archaeological mysteries: despite countless theories about what the site was used for, ranging from a sacrificial centre to a celestial timepiece, in truth, no one really knows what drove prehistoric Britons to expend so much time and effort on its construction.

You can't stroll around the centre of the site during normal opening hours, but unforgettable evening and early-morning **Stone Circle Access Visits** (☎ 01722-343834; adult/child £13/6) can be arranged. Each visit only takes up to 26 people, so you'll need to book well in advance.

The **Stonehenge Tour** (☎ 01722-336855; return adult/child £11/5) leaves Salisbury's railway and bus stations half-hourly in June and August, and hourly between September and May.

Several companies offer organised tours:

Salisbury Guided Tours (☎ 01722-337960; www.salisburyguidedtours.com)
Wessex Tourist Guides (☎ 01980-623463)

Things you need to know: EH/NT; ☎ 01980-624715; adult/child £6.50/3.30; ⏱ 9am-7pm Jun & Aug, 9.30am-6pm mid-Mar–May & Sep–mid-Oct, 9.30am-4pm mid-Oct–mid-Mar

INFORMATION

The **Visit Wiltshire** (www.visitwiltshire.co.uk) website is a good source of information.

GETTING AROUND

BUS

First (☎ 0871 200 22 33; www.firstgroup.com) Serves the far west of the county.

Wilts & Dorset Buses (☎ 01722-336855; www.wdbus.co.uk) Covers most destinations; its Explorer ticket is valid for a day (adult/child £7.50/4.50).

TRAIN

Rail lines run from London to Salisbury and beyond to Exeter and Plymouth, branching off north to Bradford-on-Avon, Bath and Bristol, but most of the smaller towns and villages aren't served by trains.

SALISBURY

pop 43,335

Britain is a nation endowed with countless stunning churches, but few can match the grandeur and sheer spectacle of **Salisbury Cathedral** (☎ 01722-555120; www.salisburycathedral.org.uk; requested donation adult/child £5/3; ☼ 7.15am-6.15pm Sep-May, to 7.15pm Jun-Aug). Built between 1220 and 1258, the cathedral bears all the hallmarks of the early English Gothic style, with an elaborate exterior decorated with pointed arches and flying buttresses, and a sombre, austere interior designed to keep its congregation suitably pious.

Beyond the highly decorative **West Front**, a small passageway leads into the 70m-long nave, lined with handsome pillars of Purbeck stone. In the north aisle look out for a fascinating **clock** dating from 1386, probably the oldest working timepiece in the world. The splendid **spire**, the tallest in Britain, was added in the mid-14th century.

There are 1½-hour tower **tours** (adult/child £5.50/4.50; ☼ 2.15pm year-round, plus 11.15am Mar-Oct & Dec, plus 3.15pm Apr-Sep, plus 5pm mid-Jun–mid-Aug), which climb up 332 vertigo-inducing steps to the base of the spire.

GETTING THERE & AWAY

BUS

There's a daily coach to Bath (£8.80, 1½ hours) and Bristol (£8.80, two hours). Buses X4 and X5 travel direct to Bath (two hours, hourly Monday to Saturday). Tour buses leave Salisbury for Stonehenge regularly; see p143.

TRAIN

Trains run half-hourly from London Waterloo (£27.60, 1½ hours) and hourly on to Exeter (£25.70, two hours) and the southwest. Another line runs from Portsmouth (£14.40, 1½ hours, hourly) via Southampton (£7.20, 30 minutes), with connections to Bath (£8, one hour, hourly) and Bristol (£9.50, 1¼ hours, hourly).

STOURHEAD

Overflowing with vistas, temples and follies, **Stourhead** (NT; ☎ 01747-841152; Stourton; house or garden adult/child £6.30/3.80, house & garden £10.50/5.80; ☼ house 11.30am-4.30pm Fri-Tue mid-Mar–Oct, garden 9am-7pm or sunset year round) is landscape gardening at its finest. The Palladian house has some fine Chippendale furniture and paintings by Claude and Gaspard Poussin, but it's a sideshow to the magnificent 18th-century gardens, which spread out across the valley.

Stourhead is off the B3092, 8 miles south of Frome (in Somerset).

LONGLEAT

Half ancestral mansion, half safari park, **Longleat** (☎ 01985-844400; www.longleat.co.uk; house & grounds adult/child £10/6, safari park

£11/8, all-inclusive passport £22/16; ⊗ house 10am-5pm year round, safari park 10am-4pm Apr-Nov, other attractions 11am-5pm Apr-Nov) became the first stately home in England to open its doors to the public, in 1946. Britain's first safari park opened on the estate in 1966, and soon Capability Brown's landscaped grounds had been transformed into an amazing drive-through zoo, populated by a menagerie of animals more at home in an African wilderness than the fields of Wiltshire.

Longleat is just off the A362, 3 miles from both Frome and Warminster.

BATH

pop 90,144

If you only explore one English city outside London, make it Bath. Here you'll find one of the finest Roman bathhouses in the world, extensive, exquisite Regency architecture and a chic new spa that lets you swim alfresco in a heated rooftop pool after a mud wrap and full body massage. With its grand Georgian terraces, Palladian parades and lofty town houses, Bath boasts so many listed buildings that the whole city has been named a World Heritage Site by Unesco.

HISTORY

The Romans established the town of Aquae Sulis in AD 44 and built the extensive thermal baths complex, and a temple to the goddess Sulis-Minerva. During the early 18th century Richard 'Beau' Nash (an influential socialite and dandy) and Ralph Allen made Bath's bathing complexes the centre of fashionable society. Allen employed the two John Woods (father and son) to create the glorious buildings you see today.

INFORMATION

Tourist office (☎ 0906 711 2000, per min 50p; www.visitbath.co.uk; Abbey Churchyard; ⊗ 9.30am-5pm Mon-Sat, 10am-4pm Sun)

SIGHTS

BATHS

Ever since the Romans arrived in Bath, life in the city has revolved around the three natural springs that bubble up near the abbey. In typically ostentatious style, the Romans constructed a glorious complex of bathhouses above these thermal waters, to take advantage of their natural temperature – a constant 46°C.

The 2000-year-old baths now form one of the best-preserved ancient Roman spas in the world. The **Roman Baths Museum** (☎ 01225-477785; www.romanbaths.co.uk; Abbey

Sunny day in the park, Bath

THOMAS WINZ

BATH

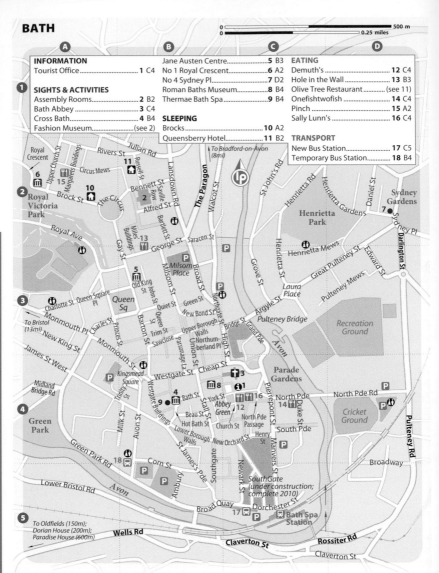

0 — 500 m
0 — 0.25 miles

INFORMATION	
Tourist Office	1 C4

SIGHTS & ACTIVITIES	
Assembly Rooms	2 B2
Bath Abbey	3 C4
Cross Bath	4 B4
Fashion Museum	(see 2)
Jane Austen Centre	5 B3
No 1 Royal Crescent	6 A2
No 4 Sydney Pl	7 D2
Roman Baths Museum	8 B4
Thermae Bath Spa	9 B4

SLEEPING	
Brocks	10 A2
Queensberry Hotel	11 B2

EATING	
Demuth's	12 C4
Hole in the Wall	13 B3
Olive Tree Restaurant	(see 11)
Onefishtwofish	14 C4
Pinch	15 A2
Sally Lunn's	16 C4

TRANSPORT	
New Bus Station	17 C5
Temporary Bus Station	18 B4

Churchyard; adult/child £11/6.80, incl Fashion Museum £14/8.30; 9am-6pm Mar-Jun, Sep & Oct, 9am-10pm Jul & Aug, 9.30am-5.30pm Nov-Feb) gets very, very busy in summer; you can usually dodge the worst crowds by visiting early on a midweek morning, or by avoiding July and August.

BATH ABBEY

Edgar, the first king of united England, was crowned in a church in Abbey Courtyard in 973, but the present **Bath Abbey** (01225-422462; www.bathabbey.org; requested donation £2.50; 9am-6pm Mon-Sat

Easter-Oct, to 4.30pm Nov-Easter, plus 1-2.30pm & 4.30-5.30pm Sun year-round) was built between 1499 and 1616, making it the last great medieval church raised in England. The nave's wonderful fan vaulting was erected in the 19th century.

ROYAL CRESCENT

The crowning glory of Georgian Bath and the city's most prestigious address is Royal Crescent, a semicircular terrace of majestic houses overlooking a private lawn and the green sweep of Royal Victoria Park. Designed by John Wood the Younger (1728–82) and built between 1767 and 1775, the houses would have originally been rented for the season by wealthy socialites.

For a glimpse into the splendour and razzle-dazzle of Georgian life, head for **No 1 Royal Crescent** (☎ 01225-428126; www.bath-preservation-trust.org.uk; adult/child £5/2.50; ⏱ 10.30am-5pm Tue-Sun Feb-Oct, to 4pm Nov), which contains an astonishing amount of period furniture. Only materials available during the 18th century were used in its refurbishment, so it's about as authentically Georgian as you can get; the same can't be said for the endearingly hammy staff dressed in period costume.

ASSEMBLY ROOMS & FASHION MUSEUM

Opened in 1771, the city's glorious **Assembly Rooms** (☎ 01225-477789; Bennett St; admission free; ⏱ 11am-6pm Mar-Oct, to 5pm Nov-Feb) were where fashionable Bath socialites once gathered to waltz, play cards and listen to the latest chamber music. Highlights include the card room, tearoom and the truly splendid ballroom, all of which are lit by their original 18th-century chandeliers.

In the basement, the **Fashion Museum** (☎ 01225-477173; www.fashionmuseum.co.uk;

adult/child £7/5, incl Roman Baths Museum £14/8.30; ⏱ 10.30am-5pm Mar-Oct, to 4pm Nov-Feb) displays costumes worn from the 16th to late-20th centuries, including some alarming crinolines that would have forced women to approach doorways side on.

JANE AUSTEN CENTRE

Bath is known to many as a location in Jane Austen's novels. *Persuasion* and *Northanger Abbey* were both largely set in the city; the writer visited it many times and lived here from 1801 to 1806 (a plaque marks one of her former houses at **No 4 Sydney Pl**, opposite the Holburne Museum). The author's connections with the city are explored at the **Jane Austen Centre** (☎ 01225-443000; www.janeausten.co.uk; 40 Gay St; adult/child £6.50/3.50; ⏱ hours vary), where displays also include period costume and contemporary prints of Bath.

SLEEPING

Bath gets incredibly busy. If you can, avoid weekends, when room prices can rise dramatically.

Oldfields (☎ 01225-317984; www.oldfields.co.uk; 102 Wells Rd; s £49-99, d £65-135, f from £85; Ⓟ) This has to be one of the best deals in Bath: spacious rooms and soft beds for comfort; brass bedsteads and antique chairs for character; and Laura Ashley fabrics and Molton Brown bath-stuffs for luxury. It's all wrapped up in a lemon-coloured stone house with views over Bath's rooftops.

Paradise House (☎ 01225-317723; www.paradise-house.co.uk; 88 Holloway; s £60-115, d £65-170; Ⓟ) If the tourist crowds become too much for you, beat a retreat to this chimney-crowned villa and its charming walled garden.

MICAH WRIGHT

Avebury

⟲ IF YOU LIKE...

If you're a sucker for ancient sites, here are a few other suggestions to ponder...

- **Maiden Castle (EH; admission free; ⊙ 24hr)** The largest Iron Age hill fort in Britain, encircling 120 acres (the equivalent of 50 football pitches). Maiden Castle is 0.9 miles southwest of Dorchester.
- **Avebury** While tour buses usually head for Stonehenge, prehistoric purists make for the massive ring of stones at Avebury – the largest stone circle in the world, with a diameter of about 348m.
- **Cerne Giant** Nude, full frontal and notoriously well endowed, this chalk figure is revealed in all his glory on a hill on the edge of town. Some claim he's Roman but the first historical reference actually dates from 1694.
- **Glastonbury Abbey (☎ 01458-832267; www.glastonburyabbey.com; Magdalene St; adult/child £5/3; ⊙ 9.30am-6pm or dusk Sep-May, from 9am Jun-Aug)** Famous for its annual music festival, hippie-central Glastonbury is also home to the ruins of an abbey supposedly founded by Joseph of Arimathea. Nearby is Glastonbury Tor, rumoured to be King Arthur's last resting place.
- **Old Sarum** You can still just about make out the remains of Salisbury's original cathedral on this hilltop just outside town.

Dorian House (☎ 01225-426336; www.dorianhouse.co.uk; 1 Upper Oldfield Park; s £65-78, d £80-155; P ⌨ wi-fi) Owned by a cellist with the London Symphony Orchestra, this chic B&B is a symphony of sumptuous style. The marble bathrooms, scattered antiques, elaborate floor tiles and plush throws all chime together perfectly, with never a duff note.

Brocks (☎ 01225-338374; www.brocksguesthouse.com; 32 Brock St; d £87-125) Part of the Georgian terrace linking the Circus and the Royal Crescent, Brocks nestles in the heart of elegant Bath. Teddy bears sit in lemon, cream and blue rooms – the ones to the rear have views of yet more classy architecture and the leafy hills beyond.

our pick Queensberry Hotel (☎ 01225-447928; www.thequeensberry.co.uk; 4 Russell St; s £95-300, d £105-425; P) One to save your pennies for – this boutique barnstormer is sexy, swanky and super. It's hidden away in four town houses, where modern fabrics, muted colour schemes and funky throws meet polished wardrobes, feature fireplaces and Zen-tinged furniture.

EATING

Sally Lunn's (☎ 01225-461634; 4 North Parade Passage; lunch mains £5-6, dinner mains from £8; ☾ lunch & dinner) People have been taking afternoon tea here since the 1680s, and it's still high on many a tourist to-do list. The atmosphere – quintessential English chintz – makes it a genteel spot to devour the trademark Sally Lunn's bun.

Demuth's (☎ 01225-446059; 2 North Parade Passage; mains £11.50-16; ☾ lunch & dinner) Having made Bath's vegetarians smile for more than 20 years, Demuth's still delights. Imaginative, superbly flavoured seasonal fare includes asparagus tart, spinach and chickpea curry, and a 'vitality salad'.

Onefishtwofish (☎ 01225-330236; 10A North Pde; mains £13-18; ☾ dinner Tue-Sun) Tables are crammed in under a barrel-brick roof, full of twinkly light in this cosy cellar restaurant. Seafood is shipped in from Devon ports, and chefs cook up everything from wonton salmon to Marseillaise bouillabaisse.

our pick Pinch (☎ 01225-421251; 11 Margarets Bldgs; 2-course lunch £10, dinner mains £14-20; ☾ lunch & dinner Wed-Sat) Pinch brings the flavours of Bordeaux, Burgundy and the Left Bank to Bath; many Brits will dearly wish there were more snug eateries like this over here.

Olive Tree Restaurant (☎ 01225-447928; 4 Russell St; lunch/dinner mains £14/18; ☾ lunch Tue-Sun, dinner daily) Break out the glad-rags –

> ## BATH'S REBIRTH
>
> Larking about in the Roman Baths might be off the agenda, but thankfully you can still sample the city's curative waters at **Thermae Bath Spa** (☎ 0844 888 0844; www.thermae bathspa.com; Hot Bath St; New Royal Bath spa session per 2hr/4hr/day £22/32/52, spa packages from £65; ☾ New Royal Bath 9am-10pm). Here the old **Cross Bath**, incorporated into an ultramodern shell of local stone and plate glass, is now the setting for a variety of luxurious spa packages.

the Queensberry Hotel's (left) restaurant is a posh, pricey extravaganza of boutique British cuisine.

Hole in the Wall (☎ 01225-425242; 16 George St; mains £15-20; ☾ lunch & dinner Mon-Sat) This long-standing favourite with Bath's gourmands takes you on a cook's tour through Anglo-French flavours – braised pork with Puy lentils, or Chew Magna lamb with potato fondant.

GETTING THERE & AWAY
BUS
Buses X39 and 339 (55 minutes, several per hour) and 332 (50 minutes, hourly, seven on Sunday) run to Bristol. Other useful services include X71 and X72 to Devizes (one hour, hourly Monday to Saturday, six on Sunday) and 173 and 773 to Wells (1¼ hours, hourly Monday to Saturday, seven on Sunday).

TRAIN
There are trains to London Paddington (£60.50, 1½ hours, half-hourly) and Cardiff (£14.90, 1¼ hours, four hourly), and several each hour to Bristol (£5.50, 11 minutes), from where you can connect with

Cox's Cave, Cheddar Gorge

HOLGER LEUE

the main-line trains to northern England and the southwest.

Trains travel approximately hourly to Oxford (£17.20, 1½ hours, change at Didcot Parkway), Weymouth (£12.60, two hours) and Dorchester West (£12.30, 1¾ hours); and Portsmouth (£29, 2½ hours) hourly via Salisbury (£13, one hour).

SOMERSET

Sleepy Somerset provides the type of pleasing pastoral wanderings that are reminiscent of a simpler, calmer, kinder world. The cloistered calm of the cathedral city of Wells acts as a springboard for the spectacular limestone caves and gorges around Cheddar, while hippie haven Glastonbury adds an ancient abbey, mud-drenched festival and masses of Arthurian myth.

GETTING AROUND

Most buses in Somerset are operated by **First** (☎ 0845 606 4446; www.firstgroup.com), supplemented by a few smaller operators. For timetables and general travel infor-

mation contact **Traveline South West** (☎ 0871 200 22 33; www.travelinesw.com). Key train services link Bath, Bristol, Bridgwater, Taunton and Weston-Super-Mare.

WELLS

pop 10,406

This tiny, picturesque metropolis is England's smallest city, and only qualifies for the 'city' title thanks to a magnificent medieval cathedral, which sits in the centre beside the grand Bishop's Palace. Set in a marvellous medieval close, the **Cathedral Church of St Andrew** (☎ 01749-674483; www.wellscathedral.org.uk; Chain Gate, Cathedral Green; requested donation adult/child £5.50/2.50; 7am-7pm Apr-Sep, 7am-dusk Oct-Mar) was built in stages between 1180 and 1508. The building incorporates several Gothic styles, but its most famous asset is the wonderful **west front**, an immense sculpture gallery decorated with more than 300 figures, built in the 13th century and restored to its original splendour in 1986.

Inside, the most striking feature is the pair of **scissor arches** separating the nave from the choir, designed to counter the subsidence of the central tower. High up in the north transept is a wonderful **mechanical clock** dating from 1392 – the second-oldest surviving in England after the one at Salisbury Cathedral (p144).

ourpick Beryl (☎ 01749-678738; www .beryl-wells. co.uk; Hawkers Lane; s £65-75, d £85-120; **P**) A mile from the city centre, this tree-shaded, gabled Victorian mansion is set in 13 acres of private parkland and boasts the kind of luxurious accommodation you'd normally find at double (or triple) the price.

Old Spot (☎ 01749-689099; 12 Sadler St; 2/3 courses £18.50/21.50; ⏲ lunch Wed-Sun, dinner Tue-Sat) Worn floorboards, a tiled and mirrored bar and very comfy chairs set the scene at this superstylish restaurant. The menu is imaginative, too: flavour favourites include black pudding salad, cod with garlic purée, and warm apple and almond pud.

GETTING THERE & AROUND

The bus station is south of Cuthbert St, on Princes Rd.

Bus 173 runs from Bath to Wells (1¼ hours, hourly, seven on Sunday). Bus 376 travels to Wells from Bristol (one hour, hourly) before continuing on to Glastonbury (15 minutes) and Street (25 minutes). Bus 126 runs to Cheddar (25 minutes) hourly Monday to Saturday and every two hours on Sunday. There's no train station in Wells.

WOOKEY HOLE

On the southern edge of the Mendips, the River Axe has carved out a series of deep caverns collectively known as **Wookey Hole** (☎ 01749-672243; www.wookey.co.uk; adult/child/family £15/10/45; ⏲ 10am-5pm Apr-Oct, 10.30am-4pm Nov-Mar). The caves are littered with dramatic natural features, including a subterranean lake and some fascinating stalagmites and stalactites (one of which is supposedly the legendary Witch of Wookey Hole, who was turned to stone by a local priest).

Bus 670 runs from Wells (10 minutes, nine daily, four on Sunday).

CHEDDAR GORGE

If Wookey Hole is a little too touristy for your tastes, then you'd better brace yourself for **Cheddar Gorge Caves** (☎ 01934-742343; www.cheddarcaves.co.uk; Explorer Ticket adult/child £15/9.50; ⏲ 10am-5.30pm Jul & Aug, 10.30am-5pm Sep-Jun), a spectacular series of limestone caverns that are always jammed with visitors throughout the summer months.

NEIL SETCHFIELD

Cathedral and gardens, Wells

SOUTHERN ENGLAND

SOUTHWEST ENGLAND

Although the network extends deep into the surrounding rock, only a few are open to the public; the most impressive are Cox's Cave and Gough's Cave, both decorated with an amazing gallery of stalactites and stalagmites, and subtly lit to bring out the spectrum of colours in the limestone rock. Outside the caves, the 274 steps of **Jacob's Ladder** lead up to an impressive panorama of the surrounding countryside; on a clear day you can see all the way to Glastonbury Tor and Exmoor.

Bus 126 runs to Wells (25 minutes) hourly Monday to Saturday and every two hours on Sunday.

DEVON

If counties were capable of emotions, those in the rest of England would envy Devon. It's all to do with a rippling landscape studded with prehistoric sites, historic homes, vibrant cities, ancient villages, intimate coves and wild, wild moors.

INFORMATION

Discover Devon (☎ 0870 608 5531; www .discoverdevon.com) Has plenty of useful information.

GETTING AROUND

Traveline South West (☎ 0871 200 2233; www.travelinesw.com) can answer timetable questions. Tourist offices stock timetables, the *Devon Bus Map* and the *Discovery Guide to Dartmoor*. **First** (☎ timetables 0871 200 2233, customer services 0845 600 1420; www.firstgroup.com) is the key bus operator in north, south and east Devon, and Dartmoor.

EXETER

Magnificent in warm, honey-coloured stone, Exeter's **Cathedral Church of St Peter** (☎ 01392-255573; www.exeter-cath edral.org.uk; Cathedral Cl; suggested donation £4; ⏰ 9.30am-6.30pm Mon-Fri, 9am-5pm Sat, 7.30am-6.30pm Sun) is framed by lawns and wonky half-timbered buildings – a quintessentially English scene often peopled

LEFT: IAN CONNELLAN; RIGHT: GLENN BEANLAND

Left: Cycling, New Forest (p142); Right: Fishing boats, Padstow (p155)

by picnickers snacking to the sound of the bells. Above the **Great West Front** scores of weather-worn figures line an image screen that was originally brightly painted – now it forms the largest collection of 14th-century sculpture in England. Free 45-minute guided tours run at 11am and 2.30pm Monday to Friday, 11am on Saturday and 4pm on Sunday, April to October.

Exeter's medieval, vaulted **passages** (☎ 01392-665887; Paris St; adult/child £5/3.50; ☿ 9.30am-5.30pm Mon-Sat, 10.30am-4pm Sun Jun-Sep, 11.30am-5.30pm Tue-Fri, 9.30am-5.30pm Sat & 11.30am-4pm Sun Oct-May) were built to house pipes bringing fresh water to the city. Guides lead you on a scramble through the network regaling you with tales of ghosts, escape routes and cholera. The last tour is an hour before closing.

SLEEPING

ourpick **Raffles** (☎ 01392-270200; www.raffles-exeter.co.uk; 11 Blackall Rd; s/d/f £38/68/78; **P**) Creaking with antiques and oozing atmosphere, this late-Victorian B&B is a lovely blend of old woods and tasteful modern fabrics.

ourpick **Hotel Barcelona** (☎ 01392-281000; www.aliashotels.com; Magdalen St; s £105, d £125-145; **P** ▣) The fabulous revamp of this former eye hospital has more wit than a festival full of comedians. The building's medical past features alongside ultra-arty twists: plush deep-green carpets slice across the original hospital flooring, while the hospital lift still ferries guests up and down.

Abode at the Royal Clarence Hotel (☎ 01392-319955; www.abodehotels.co.uk/exeter; Cathedral Yard; r £125-250) Georgian grandeur meets minimalist chic in these, the poshest rooms in town, where wonky floors and stained glass blend with pared-down furniture and neutral tones.

EATING

Cafe Paradiso (☎ 01392-281000; Magdalen St; mains lunch £4-9, dinner £11-28; ☿ lunch & dinner) Set in a futuristic glass-sided circus top, Hotel Barcelona's funky restaurant is dotted with Rothko-esque artwork and (intriguingly) painted white bicycles.

Michael Caines (☎ 01392-223638; www.michaelcaines.com; Cathedral Yard; mains £24; ☿ breakfast, lunch & dinner) Housed in the Royal Clarence and run by a locally famous Michelin-starred chef, the food here is a complex fusion of Westcountry ingredients and full-bodied French flavours. Top tips are the monkfish with red wine butter or the Devon lamb with ratatouille. There's a bargain two-course lunch (£14.50) and a seven-course tasting menu (£58).

GETTING THERE & AWAY

AIR

Scheduled services connect **Exeter International Airport** (☎ 01392-367433; www.exeter-airport.co.uk) with cities in Europe and the UK, including Glasgow, Manchester and Newcastle, as well as the Channel Islands and the Isles of Scilly.

BUS

Bus X38 goes to Plymouth (£6, 1¼ hours, hourly). Bus X9 runs to Bude (£5.50, three hours, five daily, two on Sunday) via Okehampton.

TRAIN

Trains link Exeter St David's to London Paddington (£58, 2¾ hours, hourly), Bristol (£20, 1¼ hours, half-hourly) and Penzance (£15, three hours, hourly). Main-line trains run to Plymouth (£6.90, one hour, two or three per hour); a branch line also shuttles to Torquay (£6, 45 minutes, hourly) and Paignton (£6.30, 50 minutes). Frequent trains go to Totnes (£8.50, 45 minutes).

POWDERHAM CASTLE

The historic home of the Earl of Devon, **Powderham** (☎ 01626-890243; www.pow derham.co.uk; adult/child £8.50/6.50; ⏰ 10am-5.30pm Easter-Oct, closed Sat) is a stately but still friendly place, built in 1391, damaged in the Civil War and remodelled in the Victorian era. A visit takes in a fine wood-panelled Great Hall, park land with 650 deer and a glimpse of life 'below stairs' in the kitchen.

Powderham is on the River Exe near Kenton, 8 miles south of Exeter. Bus 2 runs from Exeter (20 minutes, every 15 minutes Monday to Saturday, every 30 minutes Sunday).

A LA RONDE

A La Ronde (NT; ☎ 01395-265514; Summer Lane, Exmouth; adult/child £5.40/2.70; ⏰ 11am-5pm Sat-Wed late Mar-Oct) is a DIY job with a difference. This delightfully quirky 16-sided cottage was built in 1796 for two spinster cousins to display a mass of curiosities acquired on a 10-year European grand tour. Its glass alcoves, low lintels and tiny doorways mean it's like clambering through a doll's house – highlights are a delicate feather frieze in the drawing room and a gallery smothered with a thousand seashells. The house is 10 miles south of Exeter, near Exmouth; bus 57 runs close by.

BUCKLAND ABBEY

Stately **Buckland Abbey** (NT; ☎ 01822-853607; Yelverton; adult/child £7/3.50; ⏰ 10.30am-5.30pm Fri-Wed mid-Mar–Oct, 2-5pm Sat & Sun Nov–mid-Mar) was originally a Cistercian monastery and 13th-century abbey church, but was transformed into a family residence by Sir Richard Grenville before being purchased in 1581 by his cousin and nautical rival Sir Francis Drake. Buckland Abbey is 11 miles north of Plymouth.

CLOVELLY

pop 452

Clovelly is picture-postcard pretty. Its white cottages cascade down cliffs to meet a curving crab claw of a harbour, which is lined with lobster pots and set against a deep blue sea. Clovelly's cobbled streets are so steep cars can't negotiate them, so supplies are still brought in by sledge – you'll see these big bread baskets on runners leaning outside people's homes.

Entry to the privately owned village is via the **visitor centre** (☎ 01237-431781; adult/child £5.50/3.50). Land Rovers ferry visitors up and down the slope for £2 from Easter to October. Bus 319 runs five times daily to Bideford (40 minutes) and Barnstaple (one hour).

CORNWALL

If you were creating a perfect holiday haven from scratch, you'd probably come up with Cornwall. This rugged wedge of rock offers impossibly pretty beaches, improbably quaint villages and impressively craggy cliffs.

ORIENTATION & INFORMATION

Visit Cornwall (☎ 01872-322900; www .visitcornwall.co.uk) has information on everything from Cornish cuisine to events, accommodation and adventure sports.

GETTING AROUND

Most of Cornwall's main bus, train and ferry timetables are collected into one handy brochure (available free from bus stations and tourist offices). **Traveline South West** (☎ 0871 200 2233; www.travelinesw.com) can also answer timetable queries.

BUS

The main bus operator in Cornwall is **First** (☎ timetables 0871 200 2233, customer services 0845 600 1420; www.firstgroup.com). A FirstDay ticket (adult/child £7/5.20) offers unlimited travel on the network for 24 hours.

TRAIN

Key routes from London, Bristol and the north pass through Exeter, Plymouth, Liskeard, Truro and Camborne en route to Penzance; there are also branch lines to St Ives, Falmouth, Newquay and Looe.

The **Devon and Cornwall Rover** allows unlimited travel across the counties. Three days' travel in one week costs £40; eight days' travel in 15 costs £60. You can buy it at most main train stations.

The **Freedom of the South West Rover pass** (adult £95) allows eight days' travel in 15 days in an area west of (and including) Salisbury, Bath, Bristol and Weymouth.

TINTAGEL

pop 1822

The spectre of King Arthur looms large over the village of Tintagel and its spectacular cliff-top **castle** (EH; ☎ 01840-770328; adult/child £4.70/2.40; ☽ 10am-6pm Apr-Sep, 10am-5pm Oct, 10am-4pm Nov-Mar). Though the present-day ruins mostly date from the 13th century, archaeological digs have revealed the foundations of a much earlier fortress, fuelling speculation that the legendary king may indeed have been born at the castle as local fable claims.

PADSTOW

pop 3162

If anywhere symbolises Cornwall's culinary renaissance it's Padstow. Decades ago this was an industrious fishing village where the day's catch was battered and served up in newspaper. Today it's seared, braised or chargrilled, garnished with wasabi and dished up in some of the poshest restaurants this side of the Tamar. The transformation is largely due to one man, celebrity chef Rick Stein,

BARBARA VAN ZANTEN
Cottages and cobbled lanes, Clovelly

whose property portfolio now includes three eateries, three shops, six places to stay and even (with glorious irony) a fish-and-chip outlet.

Much favoured by directors of costume dramas, the stately manor house of **Prideaux Place** (☎ 01841-532411; admission £7, grounds only £2; ☽ 12.30-4pm Sun-Thu Easter-mid-Apr & mid-May Sep) above the village was built by the Prideaux-Brune family (who still reside here), purportedly descendants of William the Conqueror.

SLEEPING

Treverbyn House (☎ 01841-532855; www .treverbynhouse.com; Station Rd; d from £75) Harry Potter would feel at home at this charming villa of five colour-coded rooms – it's even got a turret hideaway. Pine beds, pocket-sprung mattresses, stunning views and a choice of three breakfasts make this a top Padstow choice.

Ballaminers House (☎ 01841-540933; www.ballaminershouse.co.uk; Little Petherick; tw/ d £70/85; P) Two miles south of Padstow, this smart stone farmhouse blends old-world atmosphere and modern elegance. Calming rooms are dotted with Balinese furniture and antique chests, and boast sweeping views of the surrounding fields.

EATING

Rick Stein's Cafe (☎ 01841-532700; Middle St; mains £8.50-15; ⊗ closed Sun) Stripped-down versions of Stein's Seafood Restaurant fare are on offer at this continental backstreet cafe-bistro. It's buzzy and busy, with a faint seaside feel.

Pescadou (☎ 01841-532359; South Quay; mains £14-18; ⊗ lunch & dinner) Mr Stein isn't the only one around town who can turn out top-notch seafood, as this brightly toned brasserie next to the Old Custom House pub proves.

ourpick **Seafood Restaurant** (☎ 01841-532700; www.rickstein.com; Riverside; mains £18-45; ⊗ lunch & dinner) The place that kick-started the Stein empire, and still the best of the bunch. You'll need friends in high places to get a table, but this is one eatery that lives up to the hype.

GETTING THERE & AWAY

Bus 555 goes to Bodmin Parkway (50 minutes, hourly, six on summer Sundays) via Wadebridge. Bus 554 travels to St Columb Major, with connecting buses to Truro (1¼ hours, five daily Monday to Saturday), while bus 556 serves Newquay (1¼ hours, seven daily Monday to Saturday, five on summer Sundays).

LANHYDROCK HOUSE

Lanhydrock (NT; ☎ 01208-265950; adult/ child £9/4.50, gardens only £5/2.50; ⊗ house 11am-5.30pm Tue-Sun mid-Mar–Sep, to 5pm Oct, gardens 10am-6pm year round) is reminiscent of the classic 'upstairs-downstairs' film *Gosford Park*. Set in 900 acres of sweeping grounds above the River Fowey, parts date from the 17th century but the property was extensively rebuilt after a fire in 1881, creating the quintessential Victorian county house. Highlights include the gentlemen's smoking room (complete with old Etonian photos, moose heads and tigerskin rugs), the children's toy-strewn nursery, and the huge original kitchens.

Lanhydrock is 2.5 miles southeast of Bodmin; you'll need your own transport to get here.

THE LOST GARDENS OF HELIGAN

Before he dreamt up the Eden Project, ex-record producer Tim Smit was best known for rediscovering the lost gardens of **Heligan** (☎ 01726-845100; www.heligan .com; Pentewan; adult/child £8.50/5; ⊗ 10am-6pm Mar-Oct, 10am-5pm Nov- Feb). Formal terraces, flower gardens, a working kitchen garden and a thrilling jungle walk through the 'Lost Valley' are just some of Heligan's secrets.

The Lost Gardens of Heligan are 1.5 miles from Mevagissey and 7 miles from St Austell. Bus 526 (30 minutes, six daily, three on Sunday) links Heligan with Mevagissey and St Austell train station.

FALMOUTH
pop 20775

Falmouth is a pleasing blend of bustling port, holiday resort and mildly alternative student town. Flanked by the third deepest natural harbour in the world, its

GLENN BEANLAND

Eden Project biomes

THE EDEN PROJECT

If any one thing is emblematic of Cornwall's regeneration, it is the Eden Project. Ten years ago the site was a dusty, exhausted clay pit, a symbol of the county's industrial decline. Now it's home to the largest plant-filled greenhouses in the world and is effectively a superb, monumental education project about how much people depend on the natural world. Tropical, temperate and desert environments have been recreated inside the massive biomes, so a single visit carries you from the steaming rainforests of South America to the dry deserts of North Africa.

It's impressive and immensely popular: crowds (and queues) can be large, so avoid peak times. Eden is about 3 miles northeast of St Austell. Shuttle buses run from St Austell, Newquay and Truro: check times with **Traveline South West** (☎ 0871 200 22 33; www.travelinesw.com). Alternatively, if you arrive by bike or on foot, you'll get £3 off the admission price.

Things you need to know: ☎ 01726-811911; www.edenproject.com; Bodelva; adult/child £15/5; ⏱ 10am-6pm Apr-Oct, 10am-4.30pm Nov-Mar

---

fortunes were made in the 18th and 19th centuries when clippers, trading vessels and mail packets from across the world stopped off to unload their cargoes.

The **National Maritime Museum** (☎ 01326-313388; www.nmmc.co.uk; Discovery Quay; adult/child £7.95/5.25; ⏱ 10am-5pm) houses one of the largest maritime collections in the UK, second only to its sister museum in Greenwich in London.

Perched on a promontory overlooking Falmouth harbour, **Pendennis Castle** (EH; ☎ 01326-316594; adult/child £5.50/2.80; ⏱ 10am-6pm Jul-Aug, 10am-5pm Apr-Jun & Sep, 10am-4pm Oct-Mar, closes 4pm Sat year round) provides an evocative taste of its 460-year-old history. Highlights include a superbly atmospheric Tudor gun deck (complete with cannon flashes, smoke and shouted commands), a WWI guard house and a remarkable re-creation of a WWII-observation post.

GETTING THERE & AWAY

Falmouth is at the end of the branch train line from Truro (£3.50, 20 minutes, every two hours). Buses 89/90 run to Truro (1¼ hours, half-hourly Monday to Saturday) and on to Newquay.

ST MICHAEL'S MOUNT

Looming up from the waters of Mount's Bay, the island abbey of **St Michael's Mount** (NT; ☎ 01736-710507; **adult/child £6.60/3;** ⏲ **10.30am-5pm Sun-Fri Mar-Oct**) is one of Cornwall's iconic landmarks. Set on a collection of craggy cliffs and con-nected to the mainland by a cobbled causeway that's submerged by the rising tide, there's been a monastery here since at least the 5th century.

Highlights include the rococo Gothic drawing room, the original armoury, the 14th-century priory church and its sub-tropical **gardens** (**adult/child £3/1**) which teeter dramatically above the sea. You can

walk across the causeway at low tide, or catch a ferry at high tide in the summer.

Bus 2 passes Marazion as it travels from Penzance to Falmouth (half hourly Monday to Saturday, six on Sunday).

MINACK THEATRE

At the **Minack** (☎ 01736-810181; www.minack .com; **tickets from £8.50**) the actors are con-stantly upstaged by the setting. Carved directly into the steep cliffs overlooking Porthcurno Bay, this alfresco amphi-theatre is the legacy of Rowena Cade, an indomitable local woman who came up with the idea in the 1930s, helped with the construction for 20 years and oversaw the theatre until her death in 1983.

The Minack is above beautiful Porthcurno beach, 3 miles from Land's End and 9 miles from Penzance. Bus 1A from Penzance to Land's End stops at Porthcurno, Monday to Saturday.

LAND'S END

At the most westerly point of main-land England, the coal-black cliffs,

STEPHEN SAKS

Padstow (p155)

heather-covered headlands and booming Atlantic surf at Land's End should steal the show. Unfortunately the tawdry **Legendary Land's End** (☎ 0870 458 0099; www.landsend-landmark.co.uk; adult/child £11/7; ☻ 10am-5pm summer, 10am-3pm winter) theme park does rather get in the way. On a clear day the Isles of Scilly are visible, 28 miles out to sea.

Land's End is 9 miles from Penzance (and 886 miles from John O'Groats). Buses 1 and 1A travel from Penzance (one hour, seven to 10 daily Monday to Saturday). Bus 300 heads to St Ives (one hour 20 minutes, four daily May to October).

ST IVES
pop 9870

Sitting on the fringes of a glittering arc-shaped bay, St Ives was once one of Cornwall's busiest pilchard-fishing harbours, but it's better known now as the centre of the county's arts scene. Turner sketched the town in 1811 and by the 1930s the sculptor Barbara Hepworth and the abstract painters Peter Lanyon and Ben Nicholson had set up camp. In the 1960s and '70s St Ives' artistic avant-garde included Terry Frost, Patrick Heron and Roger Hilton.

The work of many of these local artists features at the stunning **Tate St Ives** (☎ 01736-796226; www.tate.org.uk/stives; Porthmeor Beach; adult/18yr & under £5.75/free, joint ticket with Barbara Hepworth museum £8.75/free; ☻ 10am-5pm Mar-Oct, 10am-4pm Tue-Sun Nov-Feb) gallery, which hovers like a white concrete curl above Porthmeor Beach.

BARBARA HEPWORTH MUSEUM & SCULPTURE GARDEN

Barbara Hepworth (1903–75) was one of the leading abstract sculptors of the 20th century, and a key figure in the St Ives art scene; fittingly her former studio has

HOLGER LEUE
Dartmoor

◄ IF YOU LIKE...

If you're a sucker for Land's End, try these wild ideas…

- **Dartmoor** (www.discoverdartmoor .co.uk) Dartmoor's blustery moors and granite hills (called tors) are a haven for bikers, hikers and horse-riders.
- **Exmoor** (www.visitexmoor.co.uk) Some of England's largest red deer herds live on Exmoor.
- **Jurassic Coast** (www.jurassiccoast .com) The rust-red cliffs along southern Dorset's coastline are a favourite for fossil-hunters.
- **Bodmin Moor** (www.bodminmoor .co.uk) This ancient moorland occupies a hefty chunk of central Cornwall.
- **Isles of Scilly** (www.simplyscilly .co.uk) This isolated island archipelago sits 28 miles west of Land's End.
- **Forest of Dean** (www.visitforestof dean.co.uk) One of the nation's oldest oak woodlands.

been transformed into a moving archive and **museum** (☎ 01736-796226; www.tate .org.uk/stives; Barnoon Hill; adult/18yr & under £4.75/free, joint ticket with Tate St Ives £8.75/free; ☻ 10am-5pm daily Mar-Oct, 10am-4pm Tue-Sun Nov-Feb).

GLENN BEANLAND
Land's End (p158)

SLEEPING

Organic Panda (☎ 01736-793890; www
.organicpanda.co.uk; 1 Pednolver Tce; d £80-120;
P 🖳 wi-fi) Sleep with a clear conscience
(and in style) at this super-sleek B&B,
which is run along all-organic lines.

ourpick Primrose Valley (☎ 01736-
794939; www.primroseonline.co.uk; Porthminster
Beach; d £105-155, ste £175-225; P) One of St
Ives' secret gems, this swish guesthouse-
cum-boutique hotel has ecofriendly
credentials and a real eye for interior
design. All the rooms have character-
istic quirks – some boast blonde wood,
leather armchairs and exposed brick,
while others delight with sea blues,

Philippe Starck lights and mosaic-lined
bathrooms.

Blue Hayes (☎ 01736-797129; www
.blue-hayes.co.uk; Trelyon Ave; r £160-190; P)
Another boutique beauty, Blue Hayes
boasts five luxurious cream-coloured
suites (including one with its own private roof patio), body-jet showers and a
balustraded breakfast terrace overlooking the bay.

EATING

Blas Burgerworks (☎ 01736-797272; The
Warren; burgers £5-9; 🕒 dinner Tue-Sun) The
humble burger becomes a work of art
at this fab diner where creations range
from beetburgers in sunflower baps to
black-bean burgers laced with lashings
of chilli sauce.

St Andrews St Bistro (☎ 01736-797074;
16 Andrews St; mains £9-15; 🕒 dinner) A hectic
heap of North African rugs and oddball
furniture covers this eatery where mod-
ern-British fare meets African and Middle
Eastern cuisine. Artisan bread, lentil cur-
ries, grilled fish and spicy casseroles all
feature on the menu.

ourpick Alba (☎ 01736-797222; Old Lifeboat
House; mains £15-20; 🕒 lunch & dinner) The
award-winning Alba is a byword for sophisticated seafood in a stylish, open-
plan setting. Try the Provençale fish soup,
whisky-cured salmon or lobster pasta.

GETTING THERE & AWAY

Buses 17/17A/17B travel to Penzance (30
minutes) regularly; the circular bus 300
stops at Land's End en route. St Ives is
on a scenic branch train line from St Erth
(£2.50, 20 minutes, hourly), which is on
the main London–Penzance line.

CENTRAL ENGLAND

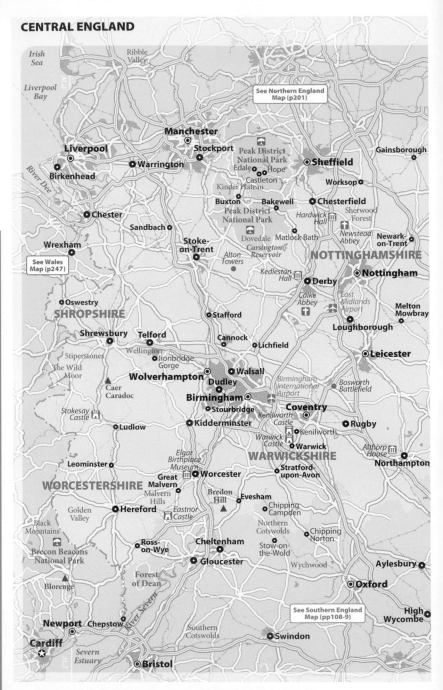

Irish Sea

Liverpool Bay

Ribble Valley

See Northern England Map (p201)

Manchester

Stockport

Warrington

Liverpool

Birkenhead

River Dee

Chester

Sandbach

Wrexham

See Wales Map (p247)

Oswestry

SHROPSHIRE

Shrewsbury

Stiperstones

The Wild Moor

Caer Caradoc

Stokesay Castle

Ludlow

Leominster

WORCESTERSHIRE

Golden Valley

Black Mountains

Brecon Beacons National Park

Blorenge

Newport

Cardiff

Severn Estuary

Chepstow

River Severn

Southern Cotswolds

Bristol

Peak District National Park

Edale   Hope

Castleton

Kinder Plateau

Buxton   Bakewell

Peak District National Park

Dovedale   Matlock Bath

Carsington Reservoir

Alton Towers

Stoke-on-Trent

Kedleston Hall

Stafford

Cannock

Telford

Wellington

Ironbridge Gorge

Wolverhampton   Walsall

Dudley

Birmingham

Stourbridge

Kidderminster

Elgar Birthplace Museum

Great Malvern   Worcester

Malvern Hills

Eastnor Castle

Bredon Hill

Hereford

Ross-on-Wye

Forest of Dean

Gloucester

Cheltenham

Evesham

Chipping Campden

Northern Cotswolds

Stow-on-the-Wold

Chipping Norton

Wychwood

Lichfield

Birmingham International Airport

Bosworth Battlefield

Kenilworth Castle

Kenilworth

Warwick Castle   Warwick

WARWICKSHIRE

Stratford-upon-Avon

Coventry

Rugby

Athorp House

Northampton

Aylesbury

Oxford

High Wycombe

Sheffield   Gainsborough

Worksop

Chesterfield

Hardwick Hall

Sherwood Forest

Newstead Abbey

Newark-on-Trent

NOTTINGHAMSHIRE

Derby   Nottingham

Calke Abbey

East Midlands Airport

Loughborough

Melton Mowbray

Leicester

Swindon

See Southern England Map (pp108-9)

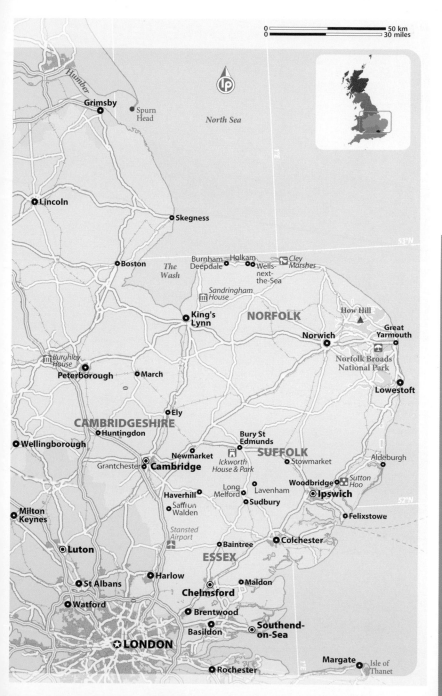

0 — 50 km
0 — 30 miles

Humber

Grimsby

Spurn Head

North Sea

Lincoln

Skegness

Boston

The Wash

Burnham Deepdale

Holkam

Wells-next-the-Sea

Cley Marshes

Sandringham House

King's Lynn

NORFOLK

How Hill

Norwich

Great Yarmouth

Norfolk Broads National Park

Lowestoft

Burghley House

Peterborough

March

Ely

CAMBRIDGESHIRE

Huntingdon

Wellingborough

Newmarket

Grantchester

Cambridge

Bury St Edmunds

Ickworth House & Park

SUFFOLK

Stowmarket

Aldeburgh

Woodbridge

Sutton Hoo

Long Melford

Lavenham

Ipswich

Haverhill

Saffron Walden

Sudbury

Felixstowe

Stansted Airport

Baintree

Colchester

ESSEX

Luton

Harlow

Maldon

Milton Keynes

St Albans

Chelmsford

Watford

Brentwood

Southend-on-Sea

Basildon

LONDON

Margate

Isle of Thanet

Rochester

CENTRAL ENGLAND

CENTRAL ENGLAND HIGHLIGHTS

CENTRAL ENGLAND HIGHLIGHTS

1 STRATFORD-UPON-AVON

BY PETER SHOREY, ACTOR AT THE ROYAL SHAKESPEARE COMPANY

It's an amazingly exciting time to be working at the Royal Shakespeare Company (RSC), with two of our main performance spaces (the Royal Shakespeare Theatre and the Swan Theatre) being rebuilt in time for 2010. There's something very special about performing Shakespeare's plays in his own home town.

➤ PETER SHOREY'S DON'T MISS LIST

❶ A SHAKESPEARE PLAY
Of course I'd say this, but you can't begin to understand Shakespeare until you've seen his plays performed. One of the joys of the RSC (p181), temporarily calling the Courtyard Theatre home, is the experience we've built up over the last 50 years; employing a permanent company of actors allows us to explore Shakespeare in a truly unique way.

❷ HOLY TRINITY CHURCH
Stratford's awash with Shakespeare sights – tasteful and tacky – but the most moving of all is his simple grave in the church of Holy Trinity (p179). You can also see his baptism and burial records, as well as a carved bust that's supposedly one of his best likenesses.

❸ DIRTY DUCK
This gorgeous riverside pub (p180) is my favourite place for a pint in Stratford. It's officially called *The Black Swan*, but has been given a new name by the actors. There's a lovely courtyard where you'll often find RSC types post-performance.

Clockwise from top: Swan Theatre (p181); Boating on the Avon; Model gliders, Malvern Hills (p182); Shakespeare's grave, Holy Trinity Church (p179)

CLOCKWISE FROM TOP: GLENN BEANLAND; GLENN BEANLAND; JON DAVISON; KEVIN WHITE / ALAMY

❹ MALVERN HILLS

When I was a youngster I could see the Malvern Hills (p182) from my bedroom window. Whenever I want to escape from the hustle and bustle of Stratford, the Malverns are where I head first. There's a real edge of wildness about them and the views are out of this world.

❺ WALKING BY THE AVON

Stratford is surrounded by lovely countryside. There's a really nice walk along the river that passes two of the town's oldest bridges, Clopton and Trinity, and links up with a disused railway track that's now been converted into a public greenway. Perfect for picnicking.

❶ Courtyard Theatre
❷ Holy Trinity Church
❸ Dirty Duck
❹ Malvern Hills
❺ The Avon

0 — 100 m
0 — 0.05 miles

Bridge St
Canal Basin
Sheep St
Waterside
Scholar's La
Chapel La
Church St
Avon
Bull St
Old Town
Southern La
College La
Mill La
Ryland St

↘ THINGS YOU NEED TO KNOW

Transport Traffic can be hellish in high summer – try and arrive by public transport **Top tip** A combined ticket covers five of the big Shakespeare sites **Photo op** Standing outside Shakespeare's Birthplace (p179) or Anne Hathaway's Cottage (p179) **For full details on the RSC, see p181**

CENTRAL ENGLAND HIGHLIGHTS

CAMBRIDGE

Along with arch-rival Oxford, the scholarly city of **Cambridge** (p188) has been educating the nation's intellectual elite for nigh on nine centuries. Many of the university's famous colleges are open to the public: don't miss the chance to peek inside the chapel of **King's College** (p189) or stage your own re-enactment of *Chariots of Fire* in the courtyard of **Trinity College** (p189).

IRONBRIDGE GORGE

A couple of centuries ago, the Midlands was the thumping engine-room of England's Industrial Revolution. While the smokestacks and slag-heaps are largely a thing of the past, you can still get a flavour of the nation's industrial heritage in the Unesco-listed **Ironbridge Gorge** (p184). Ten fascinating museums explore everything from china-making and iron-smelting to pipe manufacture.

4

⬈ PEAK DISTRICT

Wilderness is hard to come by in England these days, but if it's big skies and sweeping vistas that light your candle, the Peak District (p174) is definitely the place. Generations of walkers have stalked these windswept hills in search of solitude and inspiration – the views are magnificent even if you're not the energetic type.

5

⬈ CHATSWORTH

If it's country-house splendour you're looking for, the stately setting of Chatsworth (p176) is tough to top. Surrounded by 25 sq miles of landscaped grounds, the ancestral seat of the dukes of Devonshire is one of the nation's great architectural treasures, famous for its artworks, priceless antiques and frescoed ceilings.

6

⬈ NORFOLK BROADS

Nature-lovers and birdwatchers alike make a beeline for the Norfolk Broads (p197), a 125-mile stretch of reed-fringed canals and misty fens right in the heart of Norfolk. Some of England's rarest birds, butterflies and animals can be spotted amongst the wild meadows, bogs, marshes and lakes.

2 DAVID TOMLINSON; 3 TOM MACKIE / ALAMY; 4 DAVID ELSE; 5 GLENN BEANLAND; 6 HOLMES GARDEN PHOTOS / ALAMY

2 King's College Chapel (p189) and punts on the river; 3 Iron Bridge (p185); 4 Froggatt Edge, Peak District (p174); 5 Chatsworth (p176); 6 Norfolk Broads (p197)

CENTRAL ENGLAND'S BEST...

CASTLES & CATHEDRALS

- **Warwick Castle** (p177) The region's finest medieval fortress.
- **Kenilworth Castle** (p177) Less crowded than its Warwickshire neighbour.
- **Ely Cathedral** (p193) One of England's loveliest.
- **Ludlow Castle** (p187) Riddled with secret passageways.

STATELY HOMES

- **Chatsworth** (p176) Central England's architectural jewel.
- **Hardwick Hall** (p175) Bask in the Elizabethan extravagance.
- **Calke Abbey** (p178) Secret corridors and stags' heads.
- **Burghley House** (p178) This flamboyant home is a darling of the silver screen.
- **Sandringham** (p198) The Queen's modest country getaway.

NATURE SPOTS

- **Malvern Hills** (p182) Where Elgar headed for inspiration.
- **Peak District** (p174) The region's much-loved national park.
- **Sherwood Forest** (p174) Where Robin Hood ruled the roost.
- **Cley Marshes** (p197) Top for twitchers.
- **Holkham Beach** (p198) Three miles of coastal splendour.

COUNTRY TOWNS

- **Ludlow** (p187) The foodies' fave.
- **Buxton** (p174) The Midlands' answer to Bath.
- **Shrewsbury** (p183) The jewel in Shropshire's crown.
- **Lavenham** (p195) Crammed with medieval atmosphere.
- **Aldeburgh** (p196) Norfolk's prettiest coastal town.

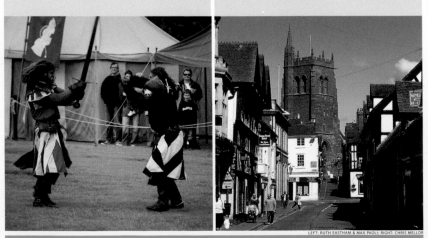

Left: Mock sword fight, Warwick Castle (p177); Right: Shrewsbury (p183)

THINGS YOU NEED TO KNOW

⟍ VITAL STATISTICS

- Area 17,015 sq miles
- Population 13 million
- Best time to go Avoid July and August if you possibly can

⟍ AREAS IN A NUTSHELL

- Shropshire (p183) England's old industrial heartland.
- Peak District (p174) The nation's most-visited national park.
- Cambridgeshire (p188) Architecture and academia in abundance.
- Warwickshire (p177) Shakespeare's old stomping ground.
- Suffolk (p195) Quaint and quintessentially English.
- Norfolk (p197) Where coast and countryside collide.
- Nottinghamshire (p173) Trace the tales of DH Lawrence and Robin Hood.
- Worcestershire (p181) From the Malvern Hills to the Midlands.

⟍ ADVANCE PLANNING

- Two months before Sort hotel bookings and RSC (p180) tickets.
- One month before Arrange your train tickets and car hire.
- Two weeks before Check opening times and ticket availability for key sights, especially Chatsworth (p176), Warwickshire (p177) and the main Shakespeare sights around Stratford-upon-Avon (p177).

⟍ RESOURCES

- Heart of England (☎ 01905-761100; www.visitheartofengland.com)
- East Midlands Tourism (www.enjoyenglandseastmidlands.com)
- East of England (☎ 01284-727470; www.visiteastofengland.com)
- Peak District (www.visitpeakdistrict.com)
- Go Leicestershire (www.goleicestershire.com)
- Visit Nottinghamshire (www.visitnottingham.com)
- Shakespeare Country (www.shakespeare-country.co.uk)
- Visit Cambridge (www.visitcambridge.org)

⟍ GETTING AROUND

- Bus can be patchy in rural areas.
- Train connections between the major towns are good.
- Car is by far the easiest way of getting around but the main motorways can get clogged up around the larger cities.

⟍ BE FOREWARNED

- Major Sights Popular areas including Stratford-upon-Avon, Warwick, Cambridge and the Peak District get seriously busy in summer.
- RSC Tickets for major productions are often sold out months in advance.
- Cambridge Many colleges are closed for the Easter term and summer exams.

CENTRAL ENGLAND ITINERARIES

EASTERN EXPLORER Three Days

This short three-day stint provides the perfect wind-down if you've been spending a few days exploring the stressful big city. Start out in soothing **Suffolk** (p195) with an easy day exploring **(1) Ickworth House** (p178) and the gorgeous little villages of **(2) Long Melford** (p195) and **(3) Lavenham** (p195). Overnight at the **Lavenham Priory**, before heading out towards the coast on day two to visit the Anglo-Saxon burial site at **(4) Sutton Hoo** (p195), followed by an afternoon exploring **(5) Aldeburgh** (p196), one of Suffolk's most appealing seaside towns (and the former home of composer Benjamin Britten). Day three is dedicated to **(6) Norfolk**, where you can soak up the sea air along the coast around the **(7) Cley Marshes** (p197) and **(8) Holkham** (p198), or spot rare wading birds around the **Norfolk Broads** (p197).

AN ARCHITECTURAL TOUR Five Days

Kick off in stately **(1) Cambridge** (p188), with its many colleges and bridges. Take day trips to **(2) Ickworth House** (p178), **(3) Peterborough Cathedral** (p194) and **(4) Burghley House** (p178), before heading north to visit HM The Queen's country estate at **(5) Sandringham** (p198). Detour via **(6) Lincoln Cathedral** (p194) en route to Byron's former home, **(7) Newstead Abbey** (p173), and take your pick from the area's many other country houses, such as **(8) Hardwick Hall** (p175) and **(9) Calke Abbey** (p178). As always, we've saved the best till last: the Duke of Devonshire's magnificent home of **(10) Chatsworth** (p176) makes a fittingly extravagant end to your architectural adventure.

FOOTSTEPS OF HISTORY One Week

This trip through time takes in some of the region's most historic sights. Start in the historic kingdom of East Anglia, with a visit to the Anglo-Saxon burial mound of **(1) Sutton Hoo** (p195). Spin forward a few centuries to the Gothic glory of **(2) Ely Cathedral** (p193), one of the oldest in East Anglia, before moving forward a century to the foundation of the first college of **(3) Cambridge University** (p189) in 1284. Then it's on to **(4) Stratford-upon-Avon** (p177), the birthplace of England's national poet, Will Shakespeare. Take time to visit the many museums and houses associated with the Bard, and don't miss a performance at the **RSC** (Royal Shakespeare Company, p181). Nearby are the imposing medieval castles of **(5) Warwick** (p177) and **(6) Kenilworth** (p177) and the crucial battlefield of **(7) Bosworth** (p173), where the Wars of the Roses came to a bloody end in 1485.

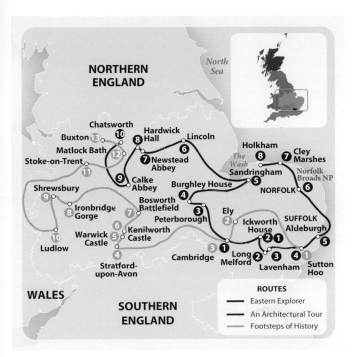

A different period of English history plays out to the west along **(8) Ironbridge Gorge** (p184), where a fascinating series of museums explore the history of England's Industrial Revolution. You'll need a full day to do the site justice, especially if you visit the lovingly recreated Victorian village of **Blist's Hill** (p186). The delightful market town of **(9) Shrewsbury** (p183) and its medieval abbey makes an appealing base, but foodies might prefer the old strategic stronghold of **(10) Ludlow** (p187). Further north, you'll find the hallowed home of English pottery in **(11) Stoke-on-Trent** (p181), while Georgian grandeur awaits in the genteel spa towns of **(12) Matlock Bath**, a popular town 2 miles south of Matlock, and **(13) Buxton** (p174).

DISCOVER CENTRAL ENGLAND

Sprawling from the Welsh Marches all the way to the windswept Peak District, the Midlands is one of Britain's most overlooked regions. The towns and factories of the Midlands served as the crucible of Britain's Industrial Revolution, and while many people may write the area off as a cultural wasteland, it's actually crammed with fascinating sights – including the history-packed castles of Warwick and Kenilworth, the World Heritage–listed industrial complex of Ironbridge Gorge and, of course, Bill Shakespeare's birthplace in Stratford-upon-Avon.

By contrast, East Anglia is a more established stop along the tourist trail. The fascinating Saxon burial site of Sutton Hoo draws its fair share of visitors, but for most people it's the stunning cathedrals of Ely and Peterborough and the stately colleges of Cambridge which are the region's main draw. If time allows, don't overlook Suffolk and Norfolk's starkly scenic coastline, where you'll discover shingly beaches sitting side-by-side with some of England's most quintessential candy-floss towns.

THE MIDLANDS & THE MARCHES

Those who aren't in the know may write off the Midlands as an industrial and cultural wasteland. But while the region does have more than its fair share of bleak industrial settlements, it also has important castles at Kenilworth and Warwick; dazzling cathedrals at Lichfield and Lincoln; Stratford-upon-Avon, a pilgrimage site for Shakespeare-lovers; and some of Britain's most beautiful countryside.

GETTING THERE & AROUND

Rail networks are extensive in the Midlands, but less so in the rural Marches, where they're only good for major towns. Useful train operators:

London Midland (www.londonmidland .com) Operates a train service throughout the Midlands and has excellent connections with London.

Wrexham and Shropshire (www.wrex hamandshropshire.co.uk) Operates a direct train service from Shropshire to London Marylebone.

The main bus operators:

Arriva (☎ 0844 800 4411; www.arrivabus .co.uk) An Arriva Go Anywhere ticket gives one day of unlimited travel.

First Travel (☎ 0800 587 7381; www.first group.com) A FirstDay Wyvern ticket (adult/child £5.50/3.80) offers the same deal on the First network in Worcestershire, Herefordshire and adjoining counties.

Stagecoach (☎ 01788-535555; www.stage coachbus.com; Dayrider Gold tickets adult/child £6.50/4.50)

Travel West Midlands (www.travelwm .co.uk)

NOTTINGHAMSHIRE

Nottinghamshire is awash with myth and storytelling. Home to outlaw Robin Hood and his band of thieves, it's also the birthplace of provocative writer DH Lawrence and played host to hedonist poet Lord Byron.

NEWSTEAD ABBEY

With its attractive gardens, evocative lakeside ruins and notable connections with Romantic poet Lord Byron (1788–1824), whose country pile it was, Newstead Abbey (☎ 01623-455900; www.newsteadabbey.org.uk; adult/child £7/4, gardens only £3/2; ☯ house noon-5pm Apr-Sep, garden 9am-dusk) houses some interesting Byron memorabilia, from pistols to manuscripts, and you can have a peek at his old living quarters. Many of the rooms are recreated in convincing period styles.

The house is 12 miles north of Nottingham, off the A60.

DH LAWRENCE SITES

The DH Lawrence Birthplace Museum (☎ 01773-717353; 8A Victoria St, Eastwood; admission Mon-Fri free, Sat & Sun £2; ☯ 10am-5pm Apr-Oct, to 4pm Nov-Mar), former home of the

BOSWORTH BATTLEFIELD

Sixteen miles southwest of Leicester, off the A447, the Battlefield Heritage Centre (☎ 01455-290429; bosworthbattlefield.com; admission £3.25; ☯ 11am-5pm Apr-Oct) features an interactive exhibition about the Wars of the Roses and the battle that ended it – the Battle of Bosworth. This is one of the most important battle sites in England, where Richard III was defeated by the future Henry VII in 1485.

controversial Nottingham author (1885–1930), has been reconstructed as it would have been in his childhood, with period furnishings.

Down the road, the Durban House Heritage Centre (☎ 01773-717353; Mansfield Rd; admission Mon-Fri free, Sat & Sun £2; ☯ 10am-5pm Apr-Oct, to 4pm Nov-Mar) sheds light on the background to Lawrence's books by recreating the life of the mining

MICAH WRIGHT

Archery practice, Sherwood Forest (p174)

community at the turn of the 20th century. A combined ticket for Durben House and the DH Lawrence Birthplace Museum costs £3.50.

Eastwood is about 10 miles northwest of the city.

SHERWOOD FOREST COUNTRY PARK

You'll have to put in some effort to lose yourself like an outlaw: today's Sherwood Forest can be incredibly crowded, especially in summer. Stray off the main circuit, though, and you can still find peaceful (and beautiful) spots. The **Sherwood Forest Visitor Centre** (☎ 01623-824490; www.sherwoodforest.org.uk; admission free, parking £3; ⏰ 10am-5.30pm Apr-Oct, to 4.30pm Nov-Mar) houses 'Robyn Hode's Sherwode', a deeply naff exhibition of wooden cut-outs, murals and life-size figures describing the lifestyles of bandits, kings, peasants and friars. One of the most popular attractions is the **Major Oak**, a 1-mile walk from the visitors centre and supposedly once a hiding place for Mr Hood; these days it seems to be on its last legs. The **Robin Hood Festival** is a massive medieval re-enactment that takes place here every August.

PEAK DISTRICT

One of the most beautiful parts of the country, the Peak District National Park crams in pretty villages, wild moorland, grand houses, deep, dark limestone caves and the southernmost hills of the Pennines. This is one of England's best-loved national parks (it's the busiest in Europe, and the world's second busiest after Mt Fuji), but don't be put off by its popularity.

The Peak District is one of the most popular walking areas in England, crossed by a vast network of footpaths and tracks.

The Peak's most famous walking trail is the **Pennine Way**, with its southern end at Edale and its northern end over 250 miles away in Scotland.

For general information, the free *Peak District* newspaper and the official park website at www.peakdistrict.org cover transport, activities, local events, guided walks and so on.

BUXTON

With its grand Georgian architecture, central crescent, flourishing parks and thermal waters, Buxton invites comparisons to Bath. It was the Romans who discovered the area's natural warm-water springs, but the town's glory days came in the 18th century when 'taking the waters' was highly fashionable.

Buxton's gorgeously restored **Opera House** (☎ 0845 127 2190; www.buxtonopera house.org.uk; Water St) enjoys a full program of drama, dance, concerts and comedy as well as staging some renowned festivals and events. Next to the Opera House is the **Pavilion**, an impressive palace of glass and cast iron built in 1871 and overlooking the impeccably manicured **Pavilion Gardens**.

The **Pump Room**, which dispensed Buxton's spring water for nearly a century, now hosts temporary art exhibitions. Just outside is **St Ann's Well**, a fountain from which Buxton's famous thermal waters still flow – and where a regular procession of tourists queue to fill plastic bottles and slake their thirst with the liquid's 'curative' power.

SLEEPING

our pick **Roseleigh Hotel** (☎ 01298-24904; www.roseleighhotel.co.uk; 19 Broad Walk; s/d incl breakfast from £33/70; P wi-fi) This gorgeous family-run B&B in a spacious old terraced house has lovingly decorated

JOHN BORTHWICK

Hardwick Hall

⬛ HARDWICK HALL

This Elizabethan hall should rank high on your list of must-see stately homes. It was home to the 16th century's second-most-powerful woman, Elizabeth, countess of Shrewsbury – known to all as Bess of Hardwick.

Bess's fourth husband died in 1590, leaving her with a huge pile of cash to play with, and she had Hardwick Hall built using the designs of eminent architect Robert Smythson. Glass was a status symbol, so she went all out on the windows; as a contemporary ditty quipped, 'Hardwick Hall – more glass than wall'. Also magnificent are the High Great Chamber and Long Gallery.

Next door is Bess's first house, Hardwick Old Hall (EH; adult/child £4/2, joint ticket £11/5; ☒ 11am-6pm Mon & Wed-Sun Apr-Sep, to 5pm Oct), now a romantic ruin. Also fascinating are the formal gardens, and the hall sits in the great expanse of Hardwick Park with short and long walking trails leading across fields and through woods. Ask at the ticket office for details.

Hardwick Hall is 10 miles southeast of Chesterfield, just off the M1.

Things you need to know: NT; ☎ 01246-850430; adult/child £9.50/4.75; ☒ noon-4.30pm Wed, Thu, Sat & Sun Mar-Oct, 11am-3pm Sat & Sun Dec

rooms, many with fine views out onto the ducks paddling in the picturesque Pavilion Gardens lake.

Old Hall Hotel (☎ 01298-22841; www .oldhallhotel buxton.co.uk; the Square; s/d incl breakfast £65/100 ⌨ wi-fi) There is a tale to go with every creak of the floorboards at this genial, history-soaked establishment,

supposedly the oldest hotel in England. Mary, Queen of Scots, was held here from 1576 to 1578, and the wood-panelled corridors and rooms are as well appointed and as elegant as they must have been in her day.

GLENN BEANLAND

Chatsworth and its gardens

▲ CHATSWORTH

Known as the 'Palace of the Peak', this vast edifice has been occupied by the dukes of Devonshire for centuries. The original house was started in 1551 by the inimitable Bess of Hardwick; a little later came Chatsworth's most famous guest, Mary, Queen of Scots. She was imprisoned here on and off between 1570 and 1581 at the behest of Elizabeth I, under the guard of Bess's fourth husband, the Earl of Shrewsbury. The Scots bedrooms (adult/child incl the house £12/5), nine Regency rooms named after the imprisoned queen, are sometimes open to the public.

The house sits in 25 sq miles of gardens (adult/child £7/4), home to a fountain so high it can be seen from miles away in the hills of the Dark Peak, and several bold, modern sculptures, of which the Duke and Duchess of Devonshire are keen collectors.

Chatsworth is 3 miles northeast of Bakewell. If you're driving, it's £2 to park. Buses 170 and 218 go direct from Bakewell to Chatsworth (15 minutes, several daily). On Sunday, bus 215 also runs to Chatsworth.

Things you need to know: ☎ 01246-582204; www.chatsworth.org; adult/child £11/6; ⊗ 11am-5.30pm Mar-Dec

EATING & DRINKING

Columbine Restaurant (☎ 01298-78752; Hall Bank; mains £11-13; ⊗ 7-10pm Mon & Wed-Sat) Perched on the slope leading down to the Crescent, this excellent understated restaurant is top choice among Buxtonites in the know.

Place (☎ 01298-214565; www.theplacebuxton .co.uk; 9-11 Market St; mains £11-14; ⊗ dinner Tue & Wed, lunch & dinner Thu-Sat, lunch Sun) Lively, trendy modern restaurant serving light lunches and sandwiches as well as more expensive modern European cooking.

ourpick **Project X** (☎ 01298-77079; The Old Court House, George St; ⊗ 8am-midnight)

The lavender walls, bright artwork, fairy lights, stacks of cookbooks and separate Moroccan-style nook make for an eclectic, cosy space that attracts local Buxton hipsters as well as tea-sipping grannies.

GETTING THERE & AWAY
Buxton is well served by public transport. The best place to get the bus is Market Sq, where services go to Derby (1½ hours, twice hourly), Chesterfield (1¼ hours, several daily) and Sheffield (65 minutes, every 30 minutes). Trains run to and from Manchester (50 minutes, hourly).

WARWICKSHIRE
Warwickshire could have been just another picturesque English county of rolling hills and market towns were it not for the birth of a rather well-known wordsmith. Stratford-upon-Avon is one of the country's most visited areas outside London, attracting Shakespeare-hungry tourists from around the world.

WARWICK CASTLE
Incredibly well-preserved medieval Warwick Castle (☎ 0870 442 2000; www .warwick-castle.co.uk; adult/child £18/11; ☼ 10am-6pm Apr-Sep, to 5pm Oct-Mar; Ⓟ) is an absolute stunner. Part of the Tussauds Group, it is prone to commercialism, crowds and cheesiness, of which the deeply naff Warwick Ghosts 'Alive' experience (entry £2.75) is a prime example. With eerily lifelike waxwork-populated private apartments, sumptuous interiors, ramparts, armour displays, dungeons (with torture chamber), gorgeous landscaped gardens and a 19th-century power-generating mill house, there's more than enough to see.

KENILWORTH CASTLE
Red-sandstone Kenilworth Castle (EH; ☎ 01926-852078; adult/child £6.20/3.10; ☼ 10am-5pm Mar-Oct, 10am-4pm Nov-Feb) isn't as popular as its commercial neighbour in Warwick, but is arguably more rewarding, and the dramatic ruins are brought to life through an excellent audio tour. A number of powerful men, including John of Gaunt, Simon de Montfort and Robert Dudley (favourite of Elizabeth I), held sway here. Following the Civil War siege, the castle's vast lake was drained in 1644, and it fell into disrepair.

STRATFORD-UPON-AVON
Few towns are so dominated by one man's legacy as Stratford is by William Shakespeare, who was born here in 1564. Be prepared to fight the tourist masses for breathing space in the historic buildings associated with England's most famous wordsmith – especially during summer and on most weekends.

INFORMATION
Tourist office (☎ 0870 160 7930; www .shakespeare -country.co.uk; Bridgefoot; ☼ 9am-5.30pm Mon-Sat, 10am-4pm Sun Apr-Oct, 9am-5pm Mon-Sat, 10am-3pm Sun Nov-Mar)

SIGHTS
The Shakespeare Birthplace Trust (☎ 01789-204016; www.shakespeare.org.uk; adult/child all 5 properties £15/7.50, 3 in-town houses £9/4.50; ☼ generally 9am-5pm Mon-Sat, 10am-5pm Sun Jun-Aug, hours vary rest of year) manages five buildings associated with Shakespeare. Three of the houses are central, one is an easy walk away, and the fifth a drive or bike ride out; a combination ticket costs about half as much as the individual admission fees combined.

GLENN BEANLAND

Burghley House

➘ IF YOU LIKE…

Fallen for Chatsworth (p176)? Then you might want to consider these other stately homes…

- **Althorp House** (☎ 01604-770107; www.althorp.com; adult/child £12.50/6, plus access to upstairs of house £2.50; ⊙ 11am-5pm Jul & Aug, last entry 4pm) Pronounced *altrup*, this country house was the ancestral home and last resting place of Diana, Princess of Wales, who is commemorated in a memorial and museum.

- **Haddon Hall** (☎ 01629-812855; www.haddonhall.co.uk; adult/child £9/5; ⊙ noon-5pm, last admission 4pm Sat-Mon Apr & Oct, daily May-Sep) Highlights include the Chapel, and the Banqueting Hall, virtually unchanged since the days of Henry VIII.

- **Attingham Park** (NT; ☎ 01743-708123; house & grounds adult/child £7.40/3.70, grounds only £4.20/2.20; ⊙ house 1-5pm Thu-Tue mid-Mar-Oct, grounds 10am-dusk Thu-Tue mid-Mar-Oct) Highlights of Shropshire's finest stately home include a picture gallery by John Nash and two wings decorated with lavish Regency interiors.

- **Ickworth House** (NT; ☎ 01284-735270; www.nationaltrust.org/ickworth; adult/child house & park £8.30/3.30, park only £4.20/1.10; ⊙ house 1-5pm Fri-Tue mid-Mar-Sep, to 4.30pm Oct, park 8am-8pm year-round) The whimsical creation of fourth Earl of Bristol and Bishop of Derry, Frederick Hervey (1730-1803), contains paintings by Titian, Gainsborough and Velasquez. There's also a lovely Italian garden and a country park designed by Capability Brown.

- **Burghley House** (☎ 01780-752451; www.burghley.co.uk; adult/child incl sculpture garden £10.90/5.40; ⊙ 11am-5pm Sat-Thu Easter-Oct) The flamboyant home of the Cecil family was built by Queen Elizabeth's adviser William Cecil. These days it's a filmic favourite, and recently featured in *The Da Vinci Code* and *Elizabeth: The Golden Age*.

- **Calke Abbey** (NT; ☎ 01332-863822; adult/child £9/4; ⊙ 12.30-5pm Sat-Wed Apr-Oct) Built around 1703, this eclectic estate has been left much as it was in the late 1800s, complete with secret corridors, underground tunnels and rooms crammed with ancient furniture, animal heads and piles of bric-a-brac.

The number-one Shakespeare attraction, **Shakespeare's Birthplace** (Henley St), has olde-worlde charm hidden behind a modern exterior. It's been a tourist hot spot for three centuries (though there's no conclusive evidence Will was born here). Family rooms have been recreated in the style of Shakespeare's time, and in short performances throughout the day some of Shakespeare's most famous characters come to life. Tickets include admission to the adjacent **Shakespeare Exhibition**, where well-devised displays chart the life of Stratford's most famous son.

When Shakespeare retired, he bought a handsome home at New Pl on the corner of Chapel St and Chapel Lane. He died there in April 1616 and the house was demolished in 1759. An attractive Elizabethan **knot garden** now occupies part of the grounds. Displays in the adjacent **Nash's House**, where Shakespeare's granddaughter Elizabeth lived, describe the town's history and contain a collection of 17th-century oak furniture and tapestries.

Shakespeare's daughter Susanna married respected doctor John Hall, and their fine Elizabethan town house, **Hall's Croft** (☎ 01789-292107), stands near Holy Trinity Church.

Before marrying Shakespeare, Anne Hathaway lived in Shottery, a mile west of the centre, in a pretty thatched farmhouse now known as **Anne Hathaway's Cottage** (☎ 01789-292100). As well as contemporary furniture, there's an orchard and **Shakespeare Tree Garden**, with examples of all the trees mentioned in Shakespeare's plays.

Mary Arden was Shakespeare's mother, and a **house** (☎ 01789-293455) at Wilmcote, 3 miles west of Stratford, was her childhood home. Mary Arden's house is now home to the **Shakespeare Countryside Museum**.

Holy Trinity Church (☎ 01789-266316; Old Town; admission to church free, Shakespeare's grave adult/child £1.50/50p; ☺ 8.30am-6pm Mon-Sat & 12.30-5pm Sun Apr-Oct, 9am-4pm Mon-Sat & 12.30-5pm Sun Nov-Mar), where Shakespeare is buried, is thought to be the most visited parish church in England. In the chancel are photocopies of Shakespeare's baptism and burial records, the graves of Will and his wife, and a bust created seven years after Shakespeare's death but before his wife's and therefore assumed to be a good likeness.

TOURS

Two-hour **guided walks** (☎ 01789-292478; adult/child £5/2; ☺ 11am Mon-Wed, 2pm Thu-Sun) depart from Waterside, opposite Sheep St.

SLEEPING

Moonraker House (☎ 01789-268774; www.moonrakerhouse.com; 40 Alcester Rd; s/d incl breakfast from £47/70; P 🖳) Pristine to the point of fussy, the rooms behind the whitewashed facade of this memorable B&B are frilly, almost feminine affairs, and have a Shakespeare theme.

White Sails (☎ 01789-264326; www.white-sails.co.uk; 85 Evesham Rd; r from £95; P 🖳 wi-fi) This gorgeous, intimate guesthouse has four plush, individually furnished rooms with flat-screen TVs, climate control and glamorous modern bathrooms.

Shakespeare Hotel (☎ 0870 400 8182; www.mercure.com; Chapel St; s/d £135/150; P 🖳) A labyrinth of rooms enchants guests at this classic Tudor hotel. The pick of the rooms are those named after Shakespeare's plays.

EATING

Vintner Wine Bar (☎ 01789-297259; 5 Sheep St; mains £7-13; ☺ 9.30am-10pm Mon-Fri, to 9.30pm Sun) This quirky space is full of

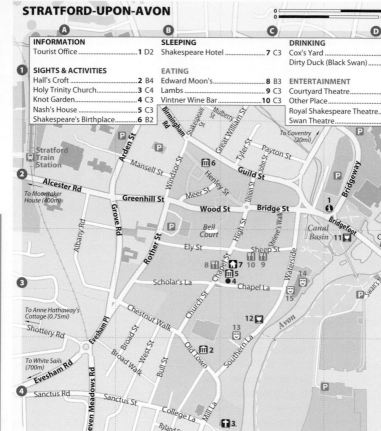

STRATFORD-UPON-AVON

INFORMATION		SLEEPING		DRINKING	
Tourist Office	1 D2	Shakespeare Hotel	7 C3	Cox's Yard	11 D3
				Dirty Duck (Black Swan)	12 C3
SIGHTS & ACTIVITIES		EATING			
Hall's Croft	2 B4	Edward Moon's	8 B3	ENTERTAINMENT	
Holy Trinity Church	3 C4	Lambs	9 C3	Courtyard Theatre	13 C3
Knot Garden	4 C3	Vintner Wine Bar	10 C3	Other Place	(see 13)
Nash's House	5 C3			Royal Shakespeare Theatre	14 C3
Shakespeare's Birthplace	6 B2			Swan Theatre	15 C3

beams, exposed brick, tucked-away spaces and low ceilings to bang your head on.

Lambs (☎ 01789-292554; 12 Sheep St; mains £11-18; ⏱ noon-2pm daily, plus 5-10pm Mon-Sat, 6-9.30pm Sun) The classiest joint in town – from the imposing manor-house door to the aristocratic interior, to the delectable cuisine (pan-fried calves' liver £16) and a fancy wine list.

Edward Moon's (☎ 01789-267069; 9 Chapel St; mains £11-17; ⏱ lunch & dinner) Edward Moon was an itinerant cook who worked in the colonial service and loved English food spiced with local ingredients. His phi-losophy inspires the food at this charming, glass-fronted brasserie.

DRINKING

Dirty Duck (☎ 01789-297312; Waterside) Officially called the 'Black Swan', this enchanting riverside alehouse should be on your list of must-visit pubs in Stratford. It's a favourite postperformance thespian watering hole, and has a roll-call of former regulars (Olivier, Attenborough etc) that reads like an actors' *Who's Who*.

Cox's Yard (☎ 01789-404600; Bridgefoot) Large riverside complex with a pub, cafe and music venue. It's a lovely place to enjoy a coffee, drink or a full-blown meal while watching the swans glide past.

ENTERTAINMENT

Royal Shakespeare Company (RSC; ☎ 0844 800 1110; www.rsc.org.uk; tickets £8-38; ☺ 9.30am-8pm Mon-Sat) Seeing a RSC production is a must. Major stars have trod the boards here and productions are of very high standard. At the time of writing, the main Royal Shakespeare Theatre was closed for extensive renovations and was due to reopen in 2010. The adjoining Swan Theatre is also closed during this time. In the meantime, performances take place in the striking temporary Courtyard Theatre by the Other Place.

GETTING THERE & AWAY

Chiltern Railways offers direct services to London Marylebone (2¼ hours).

In July and August, the **Shakespeare Express steam train** (☎ 0121-708 4960; www.vintagetrains.co.uk) operates between Birmingham Snow Hill and Stratford stations (adult/child £10/5, return £20/10, one hour, twice Sunday only).

STOKE-ON-TRENT

Stoke-on-Trent is Staffordshire's industrial heart, and is famed for its pottery production. The recently expanded **Wedgwood Visitor Centre** (☎ 0870 606 1759; www.thewedgwoodvisitorcentre.com; Barlaston; Mon-Fri £8.25, Sat & Sun £6.25; ☺ 9am-5pm Mon-Fri, 10am-5pm Sat & Sun), set in 81 hectares of attractive parkland, offers an absorbing look at the bone-china production process. Tours take in an extensive collection of historic pieces, and you can watch artisans calmly painting their designs onto china.

The **Potteries Museum & Art Gallery** (☎ 01782-232323; Bethesda St, Hanley; admission

Anne Hathaway's Cottage (p179)

ANN CECIL

free; ☺ 10am-5pm Mon-Sat & 2-5pm Sun Mar-Oct, 10am-4pm Mon-Sat & 1-4pm Sun Nov-Feb) covers the history of the Potteries and houses an impressively extensive ceramics display as well as a fine-art collection (Picasso, Degas).

Trains run to Stafford (20 minutes, every 30 minutes) and London (1¾ hours, hourly).

WORCESTERSHIRE

Serene Worcestershire's southern and western fringes burst with lush countryside, stunning walking trails and attractive riverside market towns, though the northern and eastern plains blend into the West Midlands, and have little to offer to visitors.

ELGAR BIRTHPLACE MUSEUM

England's greatest classical composer, Edward Elgar, receives due pomp and circumstance at the **Elgar Birthplace Museum** (☎ 01905-333224; www.elgarmuseum.org; Lower Broadheath; adult/child £6/2; ☷ 11am-5pm), partly housed in the humble cottage in which he was born in 1857, 3 miles west of Worcester. You can browse through an engrossing collection of the walrus-mustachioed composer's possessions, which range from his gramophone and musical manuscripts to endearing doodlings in the morning paper.

GREAT MALVERN

pop 35,558

This well-to-do Victorian spa town tumbles prettily down the slopes of the gorgeous **Malvern Hills**, which soar upwards from the flat Worcestershire plains.

In June the town goes music-mad in the biannual **Elgar Festival** (☎ 01684-892277; www.elgar-festival.com) to celebrate the life and works of the composer who lived nearby at Malvern Link.

The 11th-century **Great Malvern Priory** (☎ 01684-561020; www.greatmalvernpriory.org.uk; Church St; suggested donation £3; ☷ 9am-6.30pm Apr-Oct, 9am-4.30pm Nov-Mar) is packed with remarkable features: it's lined with clumsy Norman pillars and hides a delightfully bizarre collection of 14th-century misericords under the tip-up seats of the monks' stalls.

The jack-in-the-box Malvern Hills, which pop up dramatically out of the innocently low Severn plains on the boundary between Worcestershire and Herefordshire, are made up of 18 named peaks; highest of the bunch being Worcester Beacon at 419m. The hills are criss-crossed by more than 100 miles of paths; trail guides (£1.75) are available at the tourist office.

SLEEPING

Bredon House Hotel (☎ 01684-566990; www.bredonhouse.co.uk; 34 Worcester Rd; s/d from £45/70; ☐ ☐) A short saunter from the centre, this genteel family- and pet-friendly Victorian hotel has superb views and courteous service.

Treherne House (☎ 01684-572445; www.trehernehouse.co.uk; 53 Guarlford Rd; r from £90; ☐) This fine old gentleman's residence-turned-boutique B&B has sumptuous bedrooms with a hint of French reproduction styling and to-die-for food.

EATING

St Ann's Well Cafe (☎ 01684-560285; St Ann's Well; piece of cake £2; ☷ lunch daily Apr-Sep, Sat & Sun only Oct-Mar) The best of Malvern's many cafes is in a handsome early-19th-century villa, a steep 99-step ascent from town.

Pepper and Oz (☎ 01684-562676; 23 Abbey Rd; mains £7-18.50; ☷ lunch & dinner Tue-Sat) Right by the museum, this brasserie has a lovely alfresco terrace and photography gallery, and serves solid classics such as butch Herefordshire steaks. There's a decent wine list and it also does good-value pretheatre menus.

GETTING THERE & AROUND

There are twice-hourly trains to Worcester (12 to 18 minutes) and every half-hour to Hereford (£6.50, 30 minutes). National Express runs one bus daily to London (£21.10, 3½ hours) via Worcester (20 minutes). Bus 44 connects Worcester (30 minutes, hourly) with Great Malvern.

Handy for walkers, bus 244 – otherwise known as the 'Malvern Hills Hopper' – runs a hop-on, hop-off service (five daily weekends and bank holidays mid-April to October).

RIGHT: RUTH EASTHAM & MAX PAOLI; LEFT: NEIL SETCHFIELD

Left: Warwick Castle (p177); Right: Pottery painting, Stoke-on-Trent (p181)

SHROPSHIRE

Dreamily beautiful and sparsely populated, Shropshire ripples over the River Severn from the Welsh border to Birmingham. The lovely Tudor town of Shrewsbury is the county capital, and nestled nearby is the remarkable World Heritage Site of Ironbridge Gorge. At the county's base you'll find foodie-magnet Ludlow, with its handsome castle and epicurean ways.

INFORMATION

For online county information:

North Shropshire (www.northshropshire .co.uk)

Secret Shropshire (www.secretshropshire .org.uk)

Shropshire Tourism (www.shropshiretour ism.info)

Virtual Shropshire (www.virtual-shrop shire.co.uk)

Visit South Shropshire (www.visitsouth shropshire.co.uk)

GETTING AROUND

You can hop on handy rail services from Shrewsbury to Church Stretton, Craven Arms and Ludlow. The invaluable *Shropshire Bus & Train Map,* available free from tourist offices, shows public-transport routes. Call **Traveline** (☎ 0870 200 2233; www.traveline.org.uk) with queries.

SHREWSBURY

pop 67,126

The higgledy-piggledy mass of medieval streets in the heart of Shropshire's most picturesque town doesn't take long to work its magic. Ancient passageways wind their way between crooked Tudor buildings; dusky-red sandstone warms an ancient abbey and castle, and elegant parks tumble down to the River Severn.

Most famous as a setting for the monastic whodunits the *Chronicles of Brother Cadfael* by Ellis Peters, the lovely red-sandstone **Shrewsbury Abbey** (☎ 01743-232723; www.shrewsburyabbey.com; Abbey Foregate; donation adult/child £2/1; ⏱ 10am-4.30pm Mon-Sat,

11.30am-2.30pm Sun) is what remains of a large Benedictine monastery founded in 1083, its outbuildings mostly lost and its flanks unceremoniously chopped.

SLEEPING

164 B&B (☎ 01743-367750; www.164bedandbreakfast.co.uk; 164 Abbey Foregate; s/d £35/54, with bathroom £45/58; **P** 🖵 wi-fi) Despite the age of the building you won't find any chintz or faux-Tudor interiors here. This B&B celebrates its lovely 16th-century timber frame with bright colours, contemporary fabrics and a quirky mix of artwork.

Mad Jack's (☎ 01743-358870; www.madjacksuk.com; 15 St Mary's St; s/d from £65/75) The foot-sinking cream carpets, leather furniture and soft fur throws of this guesthouse's four smart rooms blend in perfectly with the quirks of the old building.

Lion Hotel (☎ 01753 353 107; www.thelionhotelshrewsbury.co.uk; Wyle Cop; s/d from £76/92; **P**) A cowardly lion presides over the doorway of this grand old coaching inn. The most famous hotel in town, it has hosted many a luminary through its 400-year history.

EATING

Good Life Wholefood Restaurant (☎ 01743-350455; Barracks Passage; mains £3.50-7; 🕙 lunch Mon-Sat) Healthy, freshly prepared vegetarian food is the name of the game in this cute little refuge off Wyle Cop. Favourites include quiches, nut loaf and slightly less health-conscious cakes and desserts.

Mad Jack's (☎ 01743-358870; www.madjacksuk.com; 15 St Mary's St; mains £11-16; 🕙 10am-10pm) Posh cafe, restaurant and bar that's passionate about local produce. Breakfasts, light lunches, afternoon tea and dinners are served in a bright, elegant dining room or a lovely plant-filled courtyard.

Drapers Hall (☎ 01743-344679; St Mary's Pl; mains £12-17.50; 🕙 lunch & dinner) Award-wining, Anglo-French haute cuisine is divided between dark oak-panelled rooms decked out in sumptuous fabrics and antique screens.

GETTING THERE & AROUND

BUS

National Express has two direct buses to London (£17.80, 4½ hours) and two to Birmingham (£5.70, 1½ hours). Bus 96 serves Ironbridge (30 minutes) every two hours Monday to Saturday. Bus 435 travels to Ludlow (1¼ hours) via Church Stretton (45 minutes) eight times daily, and bus 553 heads to Bishop's Castle (one hour) 10 times daily.

TRAIN

There are five direct daily services between Shrewsbury and London Marylebone (£33, 3½ hours) on the Wrexham and Shropshire line. Trains run twice-hourly to Ludlow (£8.40, 30 minutes) during the week and hourly at weekends.

IRONBRIDGE GORGE

Winding your way through the woods, hills and villages of this peaceful river gorge, it can be hard to imagine the trailblazing events that took place here some 300 years ago. But it was this sleepy enclave that gave birth to the Industrial Revolution, when three generations of the pioneering Darby family set about transforming their industrial processes and in so doing irreversibly changed the world.

Now written into history books as the birthplace of the Industrial Revolution, Ironbridge is a World Heritage Site and the Marches' top attraction.

NICHOLAS REUSS

Iron Bridge

ORIENTATION & INFORMATION

The **tourist office** (☎ 01952-884391; www .visitironbridge.co.uk; Tollhouse; ⏰ 10am-5pm) is by the bridge.

SIGHTS & ACTIVITIES

The great-value **passport ticket** (adult/child £15/10) that allows year-round entry to all of the sites can be bought at any of the museums or the tourist office. The museums open from 10am to 5pm unless stated otherwise.

MUSEUM OF THE GORGE

A good way to begin your visit is the **Museum of the Gorge** (The Wharfage; adult/child £3/2.50), which offers an overview of the site. Housed in a Gothic warehouse by the river, it's filled with touch screens, fun exhibits and details of the horrific consequences of pollution and environmental hazards at the cutting edge of industry (Abraham I and III both died at 39).

COALBROOKDALE MUSEUM OF IRON & DARBY HOUSES

What was once the Coalbrookdale iron foundry, where pioneering Abraham Darby first smelted iron ore with coke, now houses the **Coalbrookdale Museum of Iron** (adult/child £5.95/4.25). The early industrial settlement that surrounds the site has also happily survived, with workers' cottages, chapels, church and graveyard undisturbed. Just up the hill are the beautifully restored 18th-century **Darby Houses** (☎ 01952-433522; adult/child £4/2.50; ⏰ Apr-Oct), which housed generations of the industrial bigwigs in gracious but modest Quaker comfort.

IRON BRIDGE & TOLLHOUSE

The flamboyant arching **Iron Bridge** that gives the area its name was a symbol of the iron industry's success; a triumph of engineering that left contemporaries flabbergasted by its apparent flimsiness. The **tollhouse** (admission free; ⏰ 10am-5pm) houses an exhibition on the bridge's history.

BLISTS HILL VICTORIAN TOWN

To travel back to 19th-century Britain, hear the pounding of steam hammers and the clip-clop of horse hooves, or tip your hat to a cycling bobby, head to the vast open-air Victorian theme park, **Blists Hill** (☎ 01952-433522; Legges Way, Madeley; adult/child £10.50/7.50; ☺ 10am-5pm). This ambitious project does a good job of reconstructing an entire village, encompassing everything from a working foundry to a bank, where you can exchange your cash for shillings to use on-site.

COALPORT CHINA MUSEUM & TAR TUNNEL

When iron-making moved elsewhere, Coalport china slowed the region's decline and the restored works now house an absorbing **Coalport China Museum** (adult/child £6/4.25) tracing the region's glory days as a manufacturer of elaborate pottery and crockery.

A short stroll along the canal brings you to the 200-year-old **Tar Tunnel** (adult/child £2/1.50; ☺ Apr-Sep), dug as a water-supply channel but halted abruptly when natural bitumen unexpectedly started trickling treacle-like from its walls. You can still don a hard hat and stoop in deep enough to see the black stuff ooze.

JACKFIELD TILE MUSEUM

A kaleidoscopic collection of Victorian tiles, faience and ceramics can be found at the **Jackfield Tile Museum** (adult/child £6/4.25), displayed through a series of gas-lit period-style galleries reconstructing lustrous tiled interiors of everything from pubs to churches, tube stations and remarkably fancy toilets.

BROSELEY PIPEWORKS

Sucking on tobacco was the height of gentlemanly fashion in the late 17th and early 18th centuries, and the **Broseley Pipeworks** (adult/child £4/2.50; ☺ 1-5pm mid-May–Sep), once Britain's most prolific pipe manufacturer, charts the history of the industry. It's a mile-long walk to get here, signposted from the bridge.

ENGINUITY

Championing Ironbridge's spirit of brains before brawn, the fabulous interactive design and technology centre **Enginuity** (adult/child £6.25/5.25) invites you to move a steam engine with the flick of a wrist, X-ray everyday objects, power up a vacuum cleaner with self-generated electricity and basically dive head first into a vast range of hands-on, brains-on challenges, games and gadgets that explore design and engineering in modern life.

DAVID TOMLINSON

Shopfront, Ludlow

GETTING THERE & AWAY

The nearest train station is 6 miles away at Telford. Bus 96 runs every two hours (Monday to Saturday) between Shrewsbury (40 minutes) and Telford (15 to 20 minutes) via Ironbridge, stopping near the Museum of the Gorge. Bus 9 runs from Bridgnorth (30 minutes, four daily).

GETTING AROUND

The Gorge Connect bus connects nine of the museums every half-hour on weekends and bank holidays only. It costs 50p per journey, or there's a Day Rover pass (£2.50/1.50 per adult/child). The service is free to museum-passport holders.

LUDLOW

pop 9548

Fanning out from the rambling ruins of a fine Norman castle, beautiful Ludlow's muddle of narrow streets, flanked by half-timbered Jacobean and elegant Georgian buildings, is a magnet for foodies from miles around.

Ludlow's helpful **tourist office** (☎ 01584-875053; www.ludlow.org.uk; Castle Sq; ⏰ 10am-5pm) is in the 19th-century assembly rooms.

SIGHTS & ACTIVITIES

The town's finest attraction is **Ludlow Castle** (☎ 01584-873355; www.ludlowcastle.com; Castle Sq; adult/child/senior & student £4.50/2.50/4; ⏰ 10am-7pm Aug, to 5pm Apr-Jul & Sep, 10am-4pm Oct-Mar, weekends only Dec & Jan), which sits in an ideal defensive location atop a cliff above a crook in the river. One of a line of fortifications built along the Marches to ward off the marauding Welsh, it is full of secret passageways, ruined rooms, tucked-away nooks and mysterious stairwells.

The town's busy calendar peaks with the **Ludlow Festival** (☎ 01584-872150; www.ludlowfestival.co.uk), a fortnight of theatre and music in June and July that uses the castle as its dramatic backdrop. The renowned **Ludlow Marches Food & Drink Festival** (☎ 01584-873957; www.foodfestival.co.uk) is one of Britain's best, and takes place over a long weekend in September.

SLEEPING

Feathers Hotel (☎ 01584-875261; www.feathersatludlow.co.uk; Bull Ring; s/d from £75/95; Ⓟ) Three storeys of stunning black-and-white timber-framed facade serve to introduce this famous Jacobean inn. Not all rooms are in the wonderfully atmospheric original building, so make sure you're getting the real deal when booking.

Degreys (☎ 01584-872764; www.degreys.co.uk; 73 Lower Broad St; r £75-140) Set in an Elizabethan town house at Ludlow's heart, this classy B&B has nine luxurious rooms with low ceilings, beams, leaded windows and solid oak beds.

EATING

Ludlow Food Centre (☎ 01584-856000; Bromfield; mains £5-8; ⏰ 9.30am-5.30pm Mon-Sat, 10.30am-4.30pm Sun) Wonderful food shop selling fresh baked bread and cakes, cheese, local meats, ciders, fresh pies and quiches ripe for a picnic. Two miles northwest of Ludlow, just off the A49.

La Bécasse (☎ 01584-872325; www.labecasse.co.uk; 17 Corve St; 2-course lunch £20, 6-course gourmand menu £55; ⏰ dinner Tue-Sat, lunch Wed-Sun) Artfully presented modern French cuisine bursting with inventive flavour fusions – the spectacular tasting menu is enough to make you weak at the knees.

Mr Underhill's (☎ 01584-874431; www.mr-underhills.co.uk; Dinham Weir; 6-course set menu £45-55; ⏰ dinner Wed-Sun) Ludlow's only Michelin-starred restaurant is set in a converted corn mill that dips its toes in

St John's College, Cambridge University

DAVID TOMLINSON

the river. It also offers stylish rooms (singles £120, doubles £140 to £190, suites £235 to £290).

GETTING THERE & AROUND

Trains go twice-hourly to Shrewsbury (£8.40, 30 minutes) and Hereford (£6.40, 25 minutes), and hourly to Church Stretton (16 minutes). Slower buses go to Shrewsbury (bus 435, 1½ hours, five daily) and to nearby towns.

EAST ANGLIA

Perched on the back end of Britain, East Anglia is characterised by its flat, sprawling landscape where vast fenlands sweep gently out to the sea. This is a country of big skies, mysterious marshes and stunning sunsets, but the counties of Cambridgeshire, Suffolk, Norfolk and Essex feature far more than lush farmland and sparking waters. Hidden between the meandering rivers and gentle hills are magnificent cities, achingly pretty villages and mile upon mile of sweeping, sandy beach.

CAMBRIDGESHIRE

The beautiful university town of Cambridge is famous for its august old buildings, gowned cyclists, wobbly punters and glorious chapels, but beyond the breathtaking city and its brilliant minds, lies a county of vast open landscapes, epic sunsets and unsullied horizons.

CAMBRIDGE

Renowned worldwide for its academic prowess, Cambridge is a grand old dame of a city, dripping with ancient architecture, soaked in history and tradition and in many ways oblivious to the passing of time. The first Cambridge college, Peterhouse, was founded in 1284. The collegiate system is still intact today and unique to Oxford and Cambridge.

INFORMATION

Tourist office (☎ 0871 266 8006; www.visit cambridge.org; Wheeler St; ☯ 10am-5.30pm Mon-Fri, 10am-5pm Sat year-round, plus 11am-3pm Sun Apr-Sep) You can pick up a guide

to the Cambridge colleges (£3.99) here or a leaflet (£1.20) outlining a city walk.
Visit Cambridge (www.visitcambridge.org) The official tourism site for the city.

SIGHTS

CAMBRIDGE UNIVERSITY

Cambridge University comprises 31 colleges; five of these – King's, Queen's, Clare, Trinity and St John's – charge tourists admission. Most colleges close to visitors for the Easter term and all are closed for exams from mid-May to mid-June.

Chances are you will already have seen it on a thousand postcards, tea towels and choral CDs before you catch your first glimpse of the grandiose **King's College Chapel** (☎ 01223-331212; www.kings.cam .ac.uk/chapel; King's Pde; adult/concession £5/3.50; ☺ during term 9.30am-3.30pm Mon-Fri, 9.30am-3.15pm Sat, 1.15pm-2.30pm Sun, outside academic terms 9.30am-4.30pm Mon-Sat, 10am-5pm Sun), but still it awes. It's one of the most extraordinary examples of Gothic architecture in England, and was begun in 1446 as an act of piety by Henry VI and finished by Henry VIII around 1516.

The largest of Cambridge's colleges, **Trinity College** (☎ 01223-338400; www.trin .cam.ac.uk; Trinity St; adult/child £2.50/1 Mar-Oct; ☺ Library noon-2pm Mon-Fri, Hall 3-5pm, Chapel 10am-5pm), is entered through an impressive Tudor gateway first created in 1546. As you enter the **Great Court**, scholastic humour gives way to wonderment, for it is the largest of its kind in the world. The square is also the scene of the run made famous by the film *Chariots of Fire* – 350m in 43 seconds (the time it takes the clock to strike 12). Although many students attempt it, Harold Abrahams (the hero of the film) never actually did, and the run wasn't even filmed here.

Known locally as Caius (pronounced keys), **Gonville and Caius College**

(☎ 01223-332400; www.cai.cam.ac.uk; Trinity St) is of particular interest thanks to its three fascinating gates: Virtue, Humility and Honour. They symbolise the progress of the good student, since the third gate (the *Porta Honoris*, a fabulous domed and sundial-sided confection) leads to the Senate House and thus graduation.

After King's College, **St John's College** (☎ 01223-338600; www.joh.cam.ac.uk; St John's St; adult/child £2.80/1.70; ☺ 10am-5pm Mon-Fri, 9.30am-5pm Sat & Sun Mar-Oct, Sat & Sun only Nov-Feb) is one of the city's most photogenic colleges, and is also the second-biggest after Trinity. Founded in 1511, it sprawls along both banks of the river, joined by the Bridge of Sighs, a masterpiece of stone tracery.

Over 500 years old and a grand old institution, **Christ's College** (☎ 01223-334900; www.christs.cam.ac.uk; St Andrew's St; ☺ 9am-dusk) is worth visiting if only for its gleaming Great Gate emblazoned with heraldic carvings of spotted Beaufort yale (antelope-like creatures), Tudor roses and portcullis. A stout oak door leads into First Court, which has an unusual circular lawn, magnolias and wisteria creepers.

Entry to the illustrious **Corpus Christi College** (☎ 01223-338000; www.corpus.cam .ac.uk; Trumpington St) is via the so-called New Court that dates back a mere 200 years. To your right is the door to the Parker Library, which holds the finest collection of Anglo-Saxon manuscripts in the world. Look out for the fascinating sundial and plaque to playwright and past student Christopher Marlowe (1564–93), author of *Dr Faustus* and *Tamburlaine*.

Tranquil 15th-century **Jesus College** (☎ 01223-339339; www.jesus.cam.ac.uk; Jesus Lane), was once a nunnery before its founder, Bishop Alcock, expelled the nuns for misbehaving. Highlights include a Norman arched gallery, a 13th-century chancel and art-nouveau features by

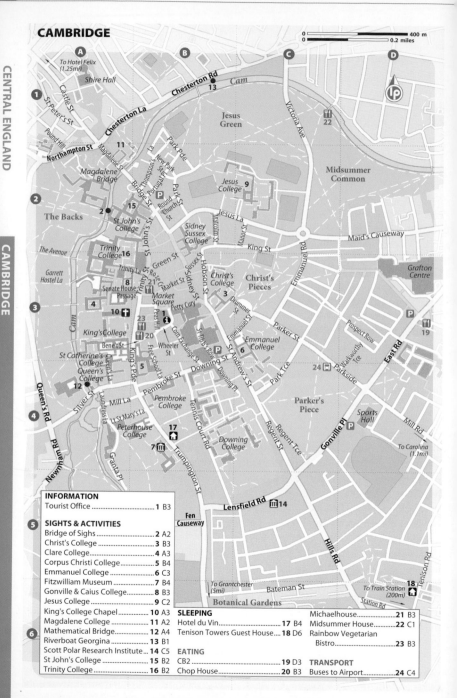

CAMBRIDGE

INFORMATION		
Tourist Office	1	B3

SIGHTS & ACTIVITIES		
Bridge of Sighs	2	A2
Christ's College	3	B3
Clare College	4	A3
Corpus Christi College	5	B4
Emmanuel College	6	C3
Fitzwilliam Museum	7	B4
Gonville & Caius College	8	B3
Jesus College	9	C2
King's College Chapel	10	A3
Magdalene College	11	A2
Mathematical Bridge	12	A4
Riverboat Georgina	13	B1
Scott Polar Research Institute	14	C5
St John's College	15	B2
Trinity College	16	B2

SLEEPING		
Hotel du Vin	17	B4
Tenison Towers Guest House	18	D6

EATING		
CB2	19	D3
Chop House	20	B3

Michaelhouse	21	B3
Midsummer House	22	C1
Rainbow Vegetarian Bistro	23	B3

TRANSPORT		
Buses to Airport	24	C4

King's College Chapel (p189), Cambridge University

JON DAVISON

Pugin, William Morris (ceilings), Burne-Jones (stained glass) and Madox Brown.

Originally a Benedictine hostel, riverside **Magdalene College** (☎ 01223-332100; www.magd.cam.ac.uk; Magdalene St) has the dubious honour of being the last college to allow women students; when they were finally admitted in 1988, male students wore black armbands and flew the college flag at half-mast. Its greatest asset is the Pepys Library, housing the magnificent collection of books the famous mid-17th-century diarist bequeathed to his old college.

The 16th-century **Emmanuel College** (☎ 01223-334200; www.emma.cam.ac.uk; St Andrew's St) is famous for its exquisite chapel designed by Sir Christopher Wren. Here too is a plaque commemorating John Harvard (BA 1632) a scholar here who later settled in New England and left his money to found his namesake university in the Massachusetts town of Cambridge.

THE BACKS

Behind the grandiose facades, stately courts and manicured lawns of the city's central colleges lies a series of gardens and parklands butting up against the river.

The oldest crossing is at **Clare College**, built in 1639 and ornamented with decorative balls. The fanciful **Bridge of Sighs** (built in 1831) at St John's is best observed from the stylish bridge designed by Wren just to the south. Most curious of all though is the flimsy looking wooden construction joining the two halves of Queen's College. Known as the **Mathematical Bridge**, it was first built in 1749 and – despite what unscrupulous guides may tell you – it wasn't the handiwork of Sir Isaac Newton (he died in 1727), originally built without nails, or taken apart by students who then couldn't figure out how to put it back together.

FITZWILLIAM MUSEUM

Fondly dubbed 'the Fitz' by locals, this colossal neoclassical pile was one of the first public **art museums** (☎ 01223-332900; www.fitzmuseum.cam.ac.uk; Trumpington St; admission free; ☻ 10am-5pm Tue-Sat, noon-5pm Sun) in Britain, built to house the fabulous treasures that the seventh Viscount Fitzwilliam had bequeathed to his old university. An unabashedly over-the-top building, it sets out to mirror its contents in an ostentatious jumble of styles that mixes mosaic with marble, Greek with Egyptian and more.

SCOTT POLAR RESEARCH INSTITUTE

For anyone interested in polar exploration or history the **Scott Polar Research Institute** (☎ 01223-336540; www.spri.cam.ac.uk/museum; Lensfield Rd; admission free; ⏲ 11am-1pm & 2-4pm Tue-Fri, noon-4pm Sat) has a fantastic collection of artefacts, journals, paintings, photographs, clothing, equipment and maps in its museum.

TOURS

City Sightseeing (☎ 01223-423578; www.city-sightseeing.com; adult/child £10/5; ⏲ 10am-4pm) Hop-on hop-off tour buses running every 20 to 30 minutes with 21 stops around town.

Riverboat Georgina (☎ 01223-307694; www.georgina.co.uk; per person £16-24) Two-hour cruises from the river at Jesus Lock including a cream tea or boatman's lunch.

Walking tours (☎ 01223-457574; tours@cambridge.gov.uk; tickets incl entry to King's/St John's Colleges adult/under 12yr £10/5; ⏲ tours 11.30pm & 1.30pm, with extra tours at 10.30am & 2.30pm Jul & Aug)

SLEEPING

Carolina (☎ 01223-247015; www.carolinaguesthouse.co.uk; 138 Perne Rd; s/d from £30/55; Ⓟ ▣ wi-fi) This lovely, bright B&B is a homely place with cosy rooms decked out in pale blue colour schemes, crisp linens and rustic wooden furniture. It's a 30-minute walk from the city centre but right on a regular bus route.

Tenison Towers Guest House (☎ 01223-363924; www.cambridgecitytenisontowers.com; 148 Tenison Rd; s/d £35/60) This exceptionally friendly and homely B&B is really handy if you're arriving by train, but well worth seeking out whatever way you arrive in town. The rooms are bright and simple with pale colours and fresh flowers and the aroma of freshly baked muffins greets you on arrival.

Hotel du Vin (☎ 01223-227330; www.hotelduvin.com; Trumpington St; d from £140; ▣ wi-fi) This boutique hotel chain really knows how to do things right. Its Cambridge offering has all the usual trademarks from quirky but incredibly stylish rooms with monsoon showers and luxurious Egyptian-cotton sheets to the atmospheric vaulted cellar bar and the French-style bistro (mains £12.75 to £22.75).

Hotel Felix (☎ 01223-277977; www.hotelfelix.co.uk; Whitehouse Lane, Huntingdon Rd; s/d incl breakfast from £145/180; Ⓟ ▣) This luxurious boutique hotel occupies a lovely grey-brick Victorian villa in landscaped grounds a mile from the city centre. Its 52 rooms embody designer chic with minimalist style but lots of comfort.

EATING

Michaelhouse (☎ 01223-309167; Trinity St; mains £3.55-6.35; ⏲ 9.30am-5pm Mon-Sat) You can sup fair-trade coffee and nibble focaccia among soaring medieval arches or else take a pew within reach of the altar at this stylishly converted church, which still has a working chancel.

CB2 (☎ 01223-508503; 5-7 Norfolk St; mains £4-13; ⏲ noon-midnight) Internet cafe, bistro, music venue and cinema all rolled into one, this lively place dishes up a great range of rustic global cuisine in a relaxed and friendly atmosphere.

Rainbow Vegetarian Bistro (☎ 01223-321551; www.rainbowcafe.co.uk; 9a King's Pde; mains £8.50-9.50; ⏲ 10am-10pm Tue-Sat) First-rate vegetarian food and a pious glow emanate from this snug subterranean gem, accessed down a narrow passageway off King's Pde.

Chop House (☎ 01223-359506; 1 King's Pde; mains £9-15; ☺ 11am-10.30pm Mon-Fri, to 11pm Sat, 10am-10.30pm Sun) If you're craving sausage and mash, a sizzling steak, suet pudding, fish pie or potted ham look no further.

Midsummer House (☎ 01223-369299; www.midsummerhouse.co.uk; Midsummer Common; set lunch £30, 3-course dinner £60; ☺ lunch Wed-Sun, dinner Tue-Sat) For sheer gastronomic delight this sophisticated place serves up what is possibly the best food in East Anglia. With two Michelin stars and a host of rave reviews from famous foodies, it's *the* place to go for a special occasion.

GETTING THERE & AWAY

Cambridge is well served by trains, though not so well by bus. Trains run at least every 30 minutes from London's King's Cross and Liverpool St stations (£17.90, 45 minutes to 1¼ hours). There are also three trains per hour to Ely (£3.30, 15 min-

utes) and hourly connections to Bury St Edmunds (£7.60, 44 minutes) and King's Lynn (£8.30, 48 minutes).

From Parkside, Parker's Piece there are regular buses to Stansted airport (£10.50, 55 minutes), Heathrow (£26, 2½ to three hours) and Gatwick (£30.50, 3¾ hours) airports, while a Luton (£13, 1½ hours) service runs every two hours.

ELY

pop 15,102

A small but charming city steeped in history and dominated by a jaw-dropping cathedral, Ely (ee-lee) makes an excellent day trip from Cambridge.

Dominating the town and visible across the flat fenland for vast distances, the stunning silhouette of **Ely Cathedral** (☎ 01353-667735; www.cathedral.ely.anglican.org; adult/child under 16yr/concession £5.50/free/4.70; ☺ 7am-7pm Easter-Aug, 7.30am-6pm Mon-Sat, 7.30am-5pm Sun Sep-Easter) is locally dubbed the 'Ship of the Fens'. The cathedral is renowned for its entrancing ceilings and the masterly 14th-century octagon and

WAYNE WALTON

Riverside walk, Ely

CENTRAL ENGLAND

EAST ANGLIA

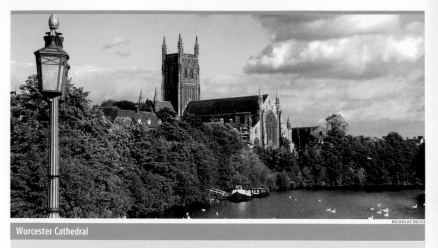

NICHOLAS REUSS

Worcester Cathedral

⬎ IF YOU LIKE...

If you've been smitten by Ely Cathedral (p193), factor in time for some of central England's other ecclesiastical marvels.

- **Peterborough Cathedral** (☎ 01733-355300; www.peterborough-cathedral.org.uk; requested donation £3; ✹ 9am-5.15pm Mon-Fri, to 5pm Sat, noon-5pm Sun) Few cathedrals can rival the instant 'wow' factor of Peterborough, with its elaborate Gothic west front, three-storeyed Norman nave and breathtaking 13th-century timber ceiling.
- **Hereford Cathedral** (☎ 01432-374200; www.herefordcathedral.org; 5 College Cloisters; suggested donation £4; ✹ 7.30am-Evensong) This harbours two ancient treasures: the magnificent 13th-century Mappa Mundi, a large calfskin vellum map depicting a world map as imagined by the era's scholars, and the world's largest surviving chained library, hooked to its shelves by a cascade of long shackles.
- **Worcester Cathedral** (☎ 01905-732900; www.worcestercathedral.org.uk; suggested donation £3; ✹ 7.30am-6pm) Encapsulates an assortment of styles and eras – the atmospheric Norman crypt is the largest in England. Other highlights include a striking 13th-century Lady Chapel and a lovely 12th-century circular chapterhouse. The cathedral's most notorious inhabitant, King John, is buried in the choir.
- **Lincoln Cathedral** (☎ 01522-544544; www.lincolncathedral.com; adult/under 16yr £4/1; ✹ 7.15am-8pm Mon-Fri, to 6pm Sat & Sun Jun-Aug, 7.15am-6pm Mon-Sat, to 5pm Sun Sep-May) Lincoln's three great towers dominate the city; one is the third-highest in England at 81m.

lantern towers, which soar upwards in shimmering colours.

Near the entrance a stained-glass museum (☎ 01353-660347; www.stainedglassmu

seum.com; adult/child £3.50/2.50; ✹ 10.30am-5pm Mon-Fri, to 5.30pm Sat, to 6pm Sun Easter-Oct, to 5pm Nov-Easter) tells the history of decorated glasswork from the 14th century onwards. Joint admission to the cathedral and museum is £8 for adults and £6.50 for children.

Ely is on the A10, 15 miles northeast of Cambridge. The easiest way to get to Ely from Cambridge is by train (15 minutes, every 20 minutes). There are also twice-hourly trains to Peterborough (£8.10, 35 minutes) and Norwich (£13.50, one hour), and hourly services to King's Lynn (£5.40, 30 minutes).

SUFFOLK

Littered with picturesque villages seemingly lost in time, and quaint seaside resorts that have doggedly refused to sell their souls to tourism, this charming county makes a delightfully tranquil destination. You can whet your appetite for the region further through the websites www.visitsuffolkattractions.co.uk and www.visit-suffolk.org.uk.

SUTTON HOO

Somehow missed by plundering grave robbers and left undisturbed for 1300 years, the hull of an enormous Anglo-Saxon ship was discovered here in 1939, buried under a mound of earth. The ship was the final resting place of Raedwald, King of East Anglia until AD 625, and was stuffed with a fabulous wealth of Saxon riches.

Many of the original finds and a full-scale reconstruction of his ship and burial chamber can be seen in the visitors centre (NT; ☎ 01394-389700; www.nationaltrust.org.uk/sutton hoo; Woodbridge; adult/child £6.20/3.20; ☉ 10.30am-5pm daily Jul & Aug, Wed-Sun mid-Mar–Jun, Sep & Oct, Sat & Sun 11am-4pm Nov–mid-Mar).

LONG MELFORD

pop 3675

Strung out along a winding road, the village of Long Melford is home to a clutch of historic buildings and two impressive country piles. From outside, the romantic Elizabethan mansion of Melford Hall (NT; ☎ 01787-376395; www.nationaltrust.org.uk/mel fordhall; adult/child £5.80/2.90; ☉ 1.30-5pm Wed-Sun May-Sep, 1.30-5pm Sat & Sun Apr & Oct) little seems changed since it entertained the queen in 1578. Inside, there's a panelled banqueting hall, much Regency and Victorian finery and a display on Beatrix Potter, who was related to the Parker family who owned the house from 1786 to 1960.

There's a noticeably different atmosphere at Long Melford's other red-brick Elizabethan mansion, Kentwell Hall (☎ 01787-310207; www.kentwell.co.uk; adult/child £8.50/5.50; ☉ 11am-5pm Apr-Sep). Despite being full of Tudor pomp and centuries-old ghost stories, it is still used as a private home and has a wonderfully lived-in feel.

LAVENHAM

Many of Lavenham's most enchanting buildings cluster along High St, Water St and around Market Pl, which is dominated by the early-16th-century guildhall (NT; ☎ 01787-247646; www.nationaltrust.org.uk/laven ham; adult/child £4/1.65; ☉ 11am-5pm Apr-Oct, 11am-4pm Sat & Sun Nov, 11am-4pm Wed-Sun Mar), a superb example of a close-studded, timber-framed building. It is now a local-history museum with displays on the wool trade, and in its tranquil garden you can see dye plants that produced the typical medieval colours.

ourpick Lavenham Priory (☎ 01787-247404; www.lavenhampriory.co.uk; Water St; s/d from £75/100; P) A rare treat, this sumptuously restored 15th-century B&B steals your heart as soon as you walk in the door. Every room oozes Elizabethan charm with cavernous fireplaces, leaded windows and exquisite period features.

JON DAVISON

Tudor-style house, Lavenham (p195)

Swan Hotel (☎ 01787-247477; www.theswan atlavenham.co.uk; High St; s £75-85, d £115-280; P) A warren of stunning timber-framed 15th-century buildings now shelters one of the region's best-known hotels. Rooms are suitably spectacular, some with immense fireplaces, colossal beams and magnificent four-posters.

Great House (☎ 01787-247431; www.great house.co.uk; Market Pl; s £85-120, d £85-180; 🖳 wi-fi) Chic design blends with 15th-century character at this much-loved restaurant with rooms in the centre of town. The acclaimed French restaurant (three-course lunch/dinner £16.95/26.95) serves classic French dishes with a modern flourish.

GETTING THERE & AWAY

Chambers Buses connects Lavenham with Bury St Edmunds (30 minutes) hourly until 6pm Monday to Saturday (no service on Sunday). The nearest train station is Sudbury.

ALDEBURGH

pop 2790

One of the region's most charming coastal towns, the small fishing and boat-building village of Aldeburgh has an understated appeal that attracts visitors back year after year. Ramshackle fishing huts sell fresh-from-the-nets catch, handsome pastel-coloured houses, independent shops and art galleries line the High St, and a sweeping shingle beach stretches along the shore offering tranquil big-sky views.

Composer Benjamin Britten and lesser-known poet George Crabbe both lived and worked here; Britten founded East Anglia's primary arts and music festival, the **Aldeburgh Festival** (☎ 01728-687110; www.aldeburgh.co.uk), which takes place in June and has been going for over 60 years. Britten's legacy is commemorated by Maggi Hambling's wonderful *Scallop* sculpture, a short stroll left along the seashore.

Aldeburgh's other photogenic gem is the intricately carved and timber-framed **Moot Hall** (☎ 01728-454666; www.aldeburgh museum.ork.uk; adult/child £1/free; 🕙 2.30-5pm Sat & Sun Apr, 2.30-5pm daily May, Sep & Oct, noon-5pm Jun-Aug), which now houses a local-history museum.

SLEEPING & EATING

our pick **Ocean House** (☎ 01728-452094; www.oceanhousealdeburgh.co.uk; 25 Crag Path; s/d £70/90) Right on the seafront and with only the sound of the waves to lull you to sleep at night, this beautiful Victorian guesthouse has cosy, period-styled rooms.

Dunan House (☎ 01728-452486; www .dunanhouse.co.uk; 41 Park Rd; r incl breakfast £75-85) Set well back off the street in lovely gardens, this charming B&B has a range of individually styled rooms mixing contemporary and traditional elements to surprisingly good effect.

Regatta Restaurant (☎ 01728-452011; www.regattaaldeburgh.com; 171 High St; mains £8.50-13.50; ☻ noon-2pm & 6-10pm) Good ol' English seaside food is given star treatment at this sleek, contemporary restaurant where local fish is the main attraction.

NORFOLK

Big skies, sweeping beaches, windswept marshes, meandering inland waterways and pretty flint houses make up the county of Norfolk, a handsome rural getaway which is home to a thriving regional capital.

NORFOLK BROADS

A mesh of navigable slow-moving rivers, freshwater lakes, wild water meadows, fens, bogs and saltwater marshes make up the Norfolk Broads, a 125-mile stretch of lock-free waterways and the county's most beautiful attraction. The Broads is home to some of the UK's rarest plants and animals and are protected as a national park, with flourishing nature reserves and bird sanctuaries attracting gangs of birdwatchers.

Details on scores of conservation centres and birdwatching hides can be found through the **Broads Authority** (☎ 01603-610734; www.broads-authority.gov.uk). There's more information on Norfolk Broads at www.norfolkbroads.com and the RSPB at www.rspb.org.uk.

You can hire boats from **Blakes** (☎ 0870 2202 498; www.blakes.co.uk) and **Hoseasons** (☎ 01502-502588; www.hoseasons.co.uk) among others. Depending on boat size, facilities and season, a boat for two to four people costs around £450 to £850 for a week including fuel and insurance.

Alternatively, **Broads Tours** (www.broads .co.uk) Wroxham (☎ 01603-782207; The Bridge); Potter Heigham (☎ 01692-670711; Broads Haven) runs 1½-hour pleasure trips (adult/child £6.50/5) from April to October.

CLEY MARSHES

One of England's premier birdwatching sites, Cley (pronounced Cly) Marshes is a mecca for twitchers with over 300 species of bird recorded here. There's

NEIL SETCHFIELD

Shingle beach, Aldeburgh

Holkham beach

ROBERT ESTALL PHOTO AGENCY / ALAMY

a **visitors centre** (☎ 01263-740008; www .norfolkwildlifetrust.org.uk; adult/child £3.75/free; ⏱ 10am-5pm Apr-Oct, to 4pm Nov-Mar) built on high ground and a series of hides hidden amid the golden reedbeds.

HOLKHAM

The main draw here is **Holkham Hall** (☎ 01328-710227; www.holkham.co.uk; hall & museum adult/child £10/5; ⏱ noon-5pm Sun-Thu Easter & Jun-Sep), a grand Palladian mansion set in a vast deer park designed by Capability Brown. The slightly industrial-looking brick mansion is the ancestral seat of the Earls of Leicester and has a sumptu-ous interior, dripping with gilt, tapestries, fine furniture and family history.

For many, Holkham's true delight is not the stately home but the pristine 3-mile **beach** that meanders along the shore. Regularly voted one of England's best, it's a popular spot with walkers but the vast expanse of sand swallows people up and gives a real sense of isolation with giant skies stretching overhead. The only place to park for access to the beach is Lady Anne's Drive (parking £3.50).

SANDRINGHAM HOUSE

Royalists and those bemused by the English sovereigns will have plenty to mull over at this, the Queen's country **estate** (☎ 01553-612908; www.sandringhamestate.co.uk; adult/child 5-15yr £9/5, gardens & museum only £6/3.50; ⏱ 11am-4.45pm late-Mar-Oct unless royal family is in residence) set in 25 hectares of landscaped gardens and lakes, and open to the hoi polloi when the court is not at home.

Queen Victoria bought the estate in 1862 for her son, the Prince of Wales (later Edward VII), but he promptly had it overhauled in the style later named Edwardian. Visitors can shuffle around the house's ground-floor rooms, regularly used by the royal family, then head out to the old stables, which house a **museum** filled with diverse royal memorabilia including the superb vintage royal car collection. There are guided tours of the gardens on Friday and Saturday at 11am and 2pm.

Sandringham is 6 miles northeast of King's Lynn off the B1440. First Eastern Counties bus 411 or Coastliner run here from the King's Lynn bus station (24 minutes, every 15 minutes).

NORTHERN ENGLAND

York Minster (p225)

LAWRENCE WORCESTER

NORTHERN ENGLAND

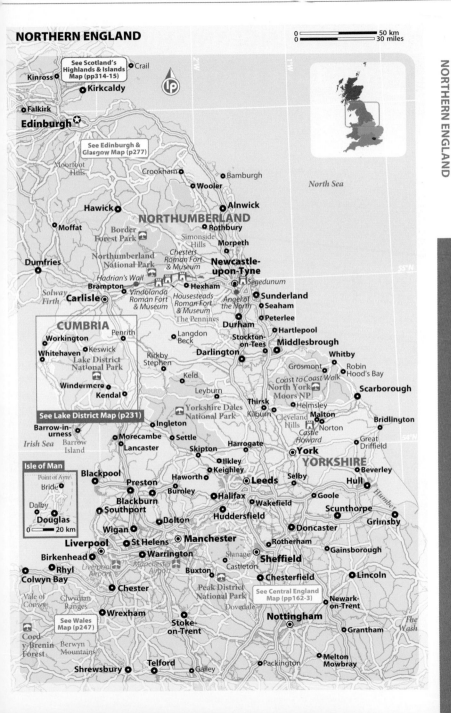

0 — 50 km
0 — 30 miles

See Scotland's Highlands & Islands Map (pp314–15)

Kinross
Crail
Kirkcaldy
Falkirk
Edinburgh

See Edinburgh & Glasgow Map (p277)

Moorfoot Hills
Crookham
Bamburgh
Wooler
North Sea
Hawick
Alnwick
Moffat
NORTHUMBERLAND
Rothbury
Border Forest Park
Simonside Hills
Morpeth
Northumberland National Park
Chesters Roman Fort & Museum
Newcastle-upon-Tyne
Dumfries
Hadrian's Wall
Segedunum
Brampton
Hexham
Sunderland
Carlisle
Vindolanda Roman Fort & Museum
Housesteads Roman Fort & Museum
Angel of the North
Seaham
Solway Firth
The Pennines
Peterlee
CUMBRIA
Penrith
Langdon Beck
Durham
Hartlepool
Workington
Keswick
Stockton-on-Tees
Middlesbrough
Whitehaven
Lake District National Park
Kirkby Stephen
Darlington
Grosmont
Whitby
Robin Hood's Bay
Windermere
Keld
Coast to Coast Walk
Kendal
Leyburn
North York Moors NP
Scarborough
Thirsk
Helmsley
Barrow-in-urness
Yorkshire Dales National Park
Kilburn
Cleveland Hills
Malton
Bridlington
Ingleton
Castle Howard
Norton
Irish Sea
Barrow Island
Morecambe
Settle
Harrogate
York
Great Driffield
Isle of Man
Lancaster
Skipton
See Lake District Map (p231)
Ilkley
Beverley
Point of Ayre
Blackpool
Keighley
Leeds
Selby
Hull
Bride
Preston
Haworth
Dalby
Burnley
Halifax
Goole
Douglas
Blackburn
Wakefield
Scunthorpe
0 — 20 km
Southport
Huddersfield
Grimsby
Wigan
Bolton
Doncaster
Liverpool
St Helens
Manchester
Rotherham
Gainsborough
Birkenhead
Warrington
Stanage
Sheffield
Rhyl
Liverpool Airport
Manchester Airport
Castleton
Colwyn Bay
Buxton
Chesterfield
Lincoln
Chester
Peak District National Park
See Central England Map (pp162–3)
Newark-on-Trent
Vale of Conwy
Clwydian Ranges
Wrexham
Dovedale
The Wash
Coed y-Brenin Forest
See Wales Map (p247)
Berwyn Mountains
Stoke-on-Trent
Nottingham
Grantham
Shrewsbury
Telford
Gailey
Packington
Melton Mowbray

NORTHERN ENGLAND HIGHLIGHTS

1 THE LAKE DISTRICT

BY SALLY ROBINSON OF THE WORDSWORTH TRUST

The Lake District is unlike anywhere else in Britain. Wordsworth, Coleridge and the other Romantic poets all came here for poetic inspiration, and it's not hard to see why – the fells, lakes and fields have a truly magical quality. I couldn't think of any place I'd rather live!

⬊ SALLY ROBINSON'S DON'T MISS LIST

❶ DOVE COTTAGE
You absolutely mustn't miss a visit to this **cottage** (p233), the first house in the Lake District occupied by the grown-up William Wordsworth. He wrote some of his most famous poetry here and it's pretty much as he left it. The guided tours are really entertaining. Next door is the **Wordsworth Museum**.

❷ RYDAL MOUNT
Just up the road you can visit one of Wordsworth's other **houses** (p233).

He rented it for 37 years with his wife, sister and children. Just below the house is the famous daffodil field which Wordsworth planted in memory of his eldest daughter Dora, who died of tuberculosis.

❸ FELL WALKING
There are enough hills to fill a lifetime of walking, but my favourite is **Helm Crag**. Known locally as the 'Lion and the Lamb' after two distinctive rocks at the summit, it's a steep walk up from Grasmere but the views are worth it!

Clockwise from top: Grasmere (p232); Keswick (p235); Derwent Water (p235); Dove Cottage (p233)

❹ GRASMERE GINGERBREAD

Along with its Romantic connections, Grasmere is also famous for its **gingerbread** (p234), which has been made to a secret recipe in the village for almost 150 years. It's quite different to the gingerbread you might have tasted elsewhere – sticky, crumbly and crunchy all at the same time. Delicious!

❺ KESWICK

This busy town a short drive north of Grasmere is one of my favourite places in the Lake District. It's full of nice shops, restaurants and cafes, and sits beside one of the loveliest of all the lakes, Derwent Water. Everyone should make time for a cruise on the **Keswick Launch** (p235)!

❶ Dove Cottage
❷ Rydal Mount
❸ Helm Crag
❹ Grasmere
❺ Keswick

↘ THINGS YOU NEED TO KNOW

Best time to visit Any time but summer (crowds are at their worst) **Public transport** Local buses are a great way to travel round the Lake District **Parking** Make sure you don't leave any valuables on display in your car **For more on the Lake District, see p228**

NORTHERN ENGLAND HIGHLIGHTS

2 NEWCASTLE-GATESHEAD

BY MARK O'KANE, MEMBER OF THE BALTIC VISITOR CREW

I was actually born in Liverpool, but I've lived in Newcastle since I was six, so I suppose I'm just about considered a local these days! The city's had a new lease of life over the last decade, and it's been fantastic to see the way it's changed.

↘ MARK O'KANE'S DON'T MISS LIST

❶ THE BALTIC

Twenty years ago you'd never have found a world-class **gallery** (p237) like this in Newcastle, but since it was opened it's become one of the city's best-loved landmarks. The artworks are obviously fantastic, but for me the highlight is the spectacular view across the city.

❷ OUSEBURN

This is my tip for the city's coolest corner. It's a real oasis of creativity, with lots of interesting artists' workshops, cafes and bars. It's also where you'll find two of my favourite pubs: the **Free Trade Inn** and the **Cumberland Arms** (p239).

❸ GREAT NORTH MUSEUM

This **museum** (p237) has just had a major makeover, and its collections include everything from Greek sculpture to artefacts from Hadrian's Wall. My favourite exhibit is a budgerigar (now stuffed) called Sparkie Williams, who became quite a celebrity in the late 1950s thanks to his extensive vocabulary.

Clockwise from top: Tyne Bridge (p236); Secret garden, Alnwick (p244); Quayside; *Angel of the North* (p240)

CLOCKWISE FROM TOP: CHRIS MELLOR; PAWEL LIBERA /PHOTOLIBRARY; DOUG MCKINLAY; DAVID ELSE

❹ QUAYSIDE

This was quite a rough area when I was a young 'un, but it's been smartened up quite a bit these days, and it's now a great place for an afternoon wander. It's best-known for its bridges, including the old **Tyne Bridge** and the new **Millennium Bridge** (p236).

❺ ALNWICK GARDENS

I love Northumberland for its wildness and solitude, and one of my favourite places is this **garden** (p244). It's one of northern England's loveliest, and has featured in lots of films including *Elizabeth*, *Harry Potter* and *King Arthur*. On a sunny day there's no better spot.

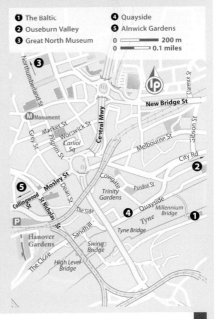

❶ The Baltic
❷ Ouseburn Valley
❸ Great North Museum
❹ Quayside
❺ Alnwick Gardens

0 — 200 m
0 — 0.1 miles

⬦ THINGS YOU NEED TO KNOW

Top photo spot Standing by the Tyne Bridges or beside the *Angel of the North* **Public transport** Newcastle has an excellent underground Metro system **For more on Newcastle, see p235**

NORTHERN ENGLAND HIGHLIGHTS

3

⬂ HADRIAN'S WALL

This awesome engineering project stretches for 117km across the north of England, and was built by the Roman Emperor Hadrian to defend against cross-border raids from the troublesome Picts. Several of the original garrison forts are still standing, including wonderful examples at **Vindolanda** (p241), **Chesters** (p241) and **Housesteads** (p243).

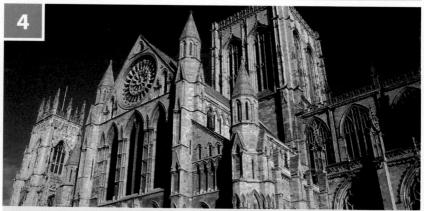

4

⬃ YORK

No visit to the north would be complete without some time in **York** (p225), one of Britain's oldest and loveliest provincial cities. Its most obvious landmark is the marvellous **minster** (p225), a triumph of medieval architecture, and nearby you can trace the remains of the old **city walls** (p225), explore the tangle of alleyways known as the **Shambles** (p226), or retrace Viking history at **Jorvik** (p226).

5 ◥ CASTLE HOWARD

If you're looking for Britain's quintessential country estate, you'd be wise to start your search at Castle Howard (p230). This palatial edifice was designed by the architect Sir John Vanbrugh for the third earl of Carlisle in the early 18th century, and it set the Baroque benchmark for everyone else to follow.

6 ◥ IMPERIAL WAR MUSEUM NORTH

Like many of northern England's cities, Manchester has enjoyed a new lease of life in recent years. One of its most interesting new additions is this striking war museum (p213), designed in typically imaginative style by the American architect Daniel Liebeskind. Its southern sister (p78) is in London.

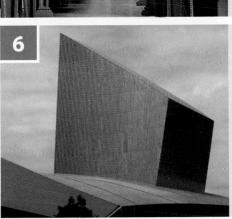

7 ◥ HAWORTH

The bleakly beautiful landscape of the Pennines is inextricably linked with the three Brontë sisters, who were born and raised in the village of Haworth (p223). Their former home has now been turned into a museum devoted to their life and work, and features lots of fascinating furniture and personal possessions associated with the sisters.

3 MANFRED GOTTSCHALK; 4 GLENN BEANLAND; 5 JOE CORNISH/PHOTOLIBRARY; 6 NEIL SETCHFIELD; 7 VERONICA GARBUTT

3 Hadrian's Wall (p240); 4 York Minster (p225); 5 Castle Howard (p230); 6 Northern facade, Imperial War Museum North (p213); 7 Brontë Parsonage Museum (p224), Haworth

NORTHERN ENGLAND'S BEST...

↘ BEAUTY SPOTS

- **Yorkshire Dales** (p224) The heart of God's Own Country.
- **Northumberland** (p243) Britain's wildest corner.
- **The Lake District** (p228) Where Wordsworth found inspiration.
- **The Pennines** (p243) England's last wilderness.
- **Hadrian's Wall** (p240) The Romans' spectacular engineering project.

↘ URBAN EXPERIENCES

- Taking in the famous **Tyne Bridges** (p236).
- Ticking off Liverpool's landmarks situated along **Albert Dock** (p218).
- Delving into the delights of **York** (p225), northern England's most bewitching town.
- Exploring Newcastle's funkiest suburb, **Ouseburn** (p235).

↘ CULTURAL DESTINATIONS

- **Angel of the North** (p240) Antony Gormley's winged statue has become a British landmark.
- **Sage Gateshead** (p239) Catch the classics at this fabulous concert hall.
- **Durham Cathedral** (p242) Ecclesiastical extravagance.
- **Tate Liverpool** (p218) The northern version of Britain's top artistic institution.

↘ BOUTIQUE HOTELS

- **Hope Street Hotel** (p221) Old architecture meets modern minimalism here.
- **Greystreethotel** (p238) Designer lines in downtown Newcastle.
- **Lowry** (p215) The one to beat in Manchester.
- **Malmaison** (p238) Northern outpost of the boutique chain.

LEFT: NEIL SETCHFIELD; RIGHT: CHRIS MELLOR

Left: Salford Quays, Manchester (p212); Right: Yorkshire Dales National Park (p224)

THINGS YOU NEED TO KNOW

⬧ VITAL STATISTICS

- **Area** 17,380 sq miles
- **Population** 14.7 million
- **Best time to go** Summer or autumn

⬧ AREAS IN A NUTSHELL

- **Newcastle** (p235) The north's hippest city.
- **Liverpool** (p217) There's much more to Liverpool than the Beatles.
- **Manchester** (p212) Britain's second city? You decide.
- **Yorkshire** (p223) Grandeur and greenery.
- **Cumbria and the Lake District** (p228) Stalk the fells and feed yourself silly.
- **Northumberland** (p243) The very edge of England.

⬧ ADVANCE PLANNING

- **Two months before** Book hotels, especially in popular areas such as the Lake District, York and the Yorkshire Dales.
- **One month before** Consider booking tickets for big-ticket sights such as Castle Howard (p230) and Hill Top (p234). Investigate train tickets for the best deals.
- **Two weeks before** Check out the weather forecast. Then ignore it.

⬧ RESOURCES

- **Visit Manchester** (www.visitmanchester.com) The official city site.
- **Virtual Manchester** (www.manchester.com) Restaurants, pubs, clubs.
- **Liverpool Magazine** (www.liverpool.com) Insiders' guide to the city.
- **Visit Liverpool** (www.visitliverpool.com) The official city site.
- **Discover England's Northwest** (www.visitnorthwest.com)
- **Lake District** (www.lake-district.gov.uk) Official online portal for the Lakes.
- **Northumberland National Park** (www.northumberland-national-park.org.uk) Get the online lowdown on this wild corner of England.
- **Yorkshire** (www.visityorkshire.com) Typically efficient site covering everything from attractions to accommodation.

⬧ GETTING AROUND

- **Bus** Good bus networks cover most of the north, but it's a slow way of exploring.
- **Train** Lots of links between the big cities, plus several scenic regional lines.
- **Car** You'll regret taking a car into the big three cities. Use public transport instead.

⬧ BE FOREWARNED

- **Crowds** Be prepared for summer crowds and traffic jams, especially in the Yorkshire Dales and the Lake District.
- **Weather** Statistically speaking, the north is colder and wetter than most of the rest of England. Come prepared.
- **Football** is practically a religion in Newcastle, Liverpool and Manchester, and the cities can get rowdy on match days.

NORTHERN ENGLAND ITINERARIES

YORK & AROUND Three Days

Seeing much of northern England in three days is a tall order, but if there's one place you really mustn't miss, it's **(1) York** (p225). It's one of England's comeliest cities, crammed with jaw-dropping architecture and fascinating sights, so you'll probably need a couple of days to do it justice. At the very least, you'll want to do the **minster** (p225), the **Shambles** (p226), the **city walls** (p225) and **Jorvik** (p226), while the kids will want to check out some interactive archaeology at **Dig** (p226). If you're planning on staying overnight, **Mount Royale** (p228) and **Elliotts B&B** (p226) both make lovely bases, while **Melton's** (p228) and **J Baker's** (p228) are our current top tips for supper.

Day three leaves time for exploring further afield: you could strike out for the hilltop trails and scenic grandeur of the **(2) Yorkshire Dales** (p224), or perhaps devote a day to the stately surroundings of **(3) Castle Howard** (p230), arguably the most impressive country estate in northern England.

URBAN ESSENTIALS Five Days

This five-day route factors in a day at northern England's three buzziest cities, interspersed with a couple of cultural detours en route. We begin in **(1) Newcastle-upon-Tyne** (p235), which has sloughed off the post-industrial blues and now boasts some of the finest cultural institutions in northern England, including the **Baltic** (p237), the **Sage** (p239) and the **Great North Museum** (p237). The action's just as exciting after-dark: Ouseburn and Jesmond are both awash with funky bars and brasseries. Devote a day to Antony Gormley's marvellous **(2) Angel of the North** (p240) and **(3) Durham Cathedral** (p242).

On day three head into **(4) Manchester** (p212) for visits to the **Imperial War Museum North** (p213), the **Lowry** (p213) and the **Museum of Science & Industry** (p212). Football fanatics won't want to miss a pilgrimage to Man Utd's home ground at **Old Trafford** (p213).

With two days left, you might feel the need to linger for another day in Manchester, or spend both days exploring the historic waterfront and lively nightlife of **(5) Liverpool** (p217). The Beatles will be likely to feature on your sightseeing list, and you should at least make time for the **Beatles Story** (p218), a Beatles-themed **tour** (p220) and a visit to the **Cavern** (p222). But don't get too hung up on the Fab Four; Liverpool's other attractions include the **Walker Art Gallery** (p217), the **Merseyside Maritime Museum** (p218) and the fantastic **Tate Liverpool** (p218).

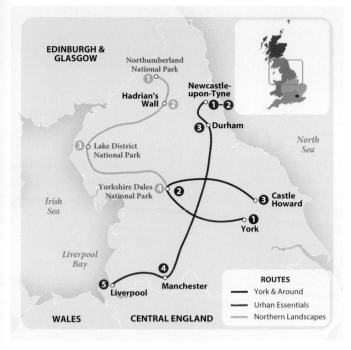

NORTHERN LANDSCAPES One Week

The north of England is one of the country's most stunning regions, and this itinerary explores some of the area's mustn't-miss landscapes. Start smack bang beside the Scottish border in (1) Northumberland National Park (p243), famous for its big open skies, windlashed coast and romantic ruins, including the remains of the great ancient Lego project known as (2) Hadrian's Wall (p240). Trace the wall west before veering off into (3) Cumbria and The Lake District (p228) with its distinctive humpback fells, babbling brooks and mile upon mile of drystone walls. Several of the lakes offer scenic cruises, Including Derwent Water (p235), Ullswater (p235) and Windermere (p230). Last up is the (4) Yorkshire Dales (p224), whose hills, dales and sweeping views have proved an irresistible lure for generations of hikers.

DISCOVER NORTHERN ENGLAND

It's grim up north, so the old saying goes, but since the collapse of heavy industries such as coal mining and iron smelting, many of the region's smog-blackened cities have turned a corner, smartened up their act and reinvented themselves as centres of commerce and culture. Liverpool's finally stepped out of the shadow of the Fab Four and served a stint as Europe's Capital of Culture, while nearby Manchester is awash with cutting-edge museums and galleries. But it's in Newcastle where the change has been most obvious: with its blinking bridges, gleaming concert halls and funky nightlife, not to mention a rather famous winged sculpture by Antony Gormley, this is definitely a city on the up.

Beyond the big cities, England's landscape takes centre stage in the flagship national parks of the Yorkshire Dales, Northumberland and the Lake District, while the stunning city of York combines Viking heritage and a famous minster with one of Britain's most atmospheric medieval centres.

MANCHESTER

pop 394,270

Ask a Mancunian to name Britain's second city and there's a pretty good chance they'll say 'London,' such is the confidence in their native town. Few cities in Europe have embraced change so enthusiastically; it's where much of the best music of the last couple of decades came from; and it has both the world's best-supported football team and, as of 2008, the world's richest one too.

INFORMATION

Tourist office (☎ 0871 222 8223; www.visit manchester.com; Town Hall Extension, St Peter's Sq; ☼ 10am-5.15pm Mon-Sat, 10am-4.30pm Sun)

SIGHTS & ACTIVITIES

MANCHESTER ART GALLERY

A superb collection of British art and a hefty number of European masters are on display at the city's top **gallery** (☎ 0161-235 8888; www.manchestergalleries.org; Mosley St; admission free; ☼ 10am-5pm Tue-Sun). The older wing, designed by Charles Barry (of Houses of Parliament fame) in 1834, has an impressive collection that includes 37 Turner watercolours, as well as the country's best collection of Pre-Raphaelite art. The newer gallery features a permanent collection of 20th-century British art starring Lucien Freud, Francis Bacon, Stanley Spencer, Henry Moore and David Hockney.

MUSEUM OF SCIENCE & INDUSTRY (MOSI)

The city's largest **museum** (☎ 0161-832 1830; www.msim.org.uk; Liverpool Rd; admission free, charge for special exhibitions; ☼ 10am-5pm) comprises 2.8 hectares in the heart of 19th-century industrial Manchester. If there's anything you want to know about the Industrial (and post-Industrial) Revolution and Manchester's key role in it, you'll find the answers among the collection of steam engines and locomotives, factory machinery from the mills, and the excellent exhibition telling the story of Manchester from the sewers up.

IMPERIAL WAR MUSEUM NORTH

War museums generally appeal to those with a fascination for military hardware and battle strategy (toy soldiers optional), but Daniel Libeskind's visually stunning **Imperial War Museum North** (☎ 0161-836 4000; www.iwm.org.uk/north; Trafford Wharf Rd; admission free; 🕑 10am-6pm Mar-Oct, 10am-5pm Nov-Feb) takes a radically different approach. Although the audiovisuals and displays are quite compelling, the extraordinary aluminium-clad building itself is a huge part of the attraction, and the exhibition spaces are genuinely breathtaking. Libeskind designed three distinct structures (or shards) that represent the three main theatres of war: air, land and sea.

LOWRY

Looking more like a shiny steel ship than an arts centre, the **Lowry** (☎ 0161-876 2020; www.thelowry.com; Pier 8, Salford Quays; 🕑 11am-8pm Tue-Fri, 10am-8pm Sat, 11am-6pm Sun & Mon) is the quays' most notable success. The complex is home to more than 300 paintings and drawings by northern England's favourite artist, LS Lowry (1887–1976), who was born in nearby Stretford.

OLD TRAFFORD (MANCHESTER UNITED MUSEUM & TOUR)

Here's a paradox: the world's most famous and supported football club, beloved of fans from Bangkok to Buenos Aires, is the most hated club in England and has a smaller fan base in Manchester than its far less successful cross-town rival, Manchester City. United fans snigger and dismiss this as small-minded jealousy, while treating the **Old Trafford stadium** (www.manutd.com; Sir Matt Busby Way; 🕑 9.30am-5pm) like holy ground and the stars who play there like minor deities.

We strongly recommend that you take the **tour** (☎ 0870 442 1994; adult/child £12/8; 🕑 every 10min 9.40am-4.30pm except match days), which includes a seat in the stands, a stop in the changing rooms, a peek at the players' lounge (from which the manager is banned unless invited by the players) and a walk down the tunnel to the pitchside dugout, which is as close to ecstasy as many of the club's fans will ever get.

DAVID TOMLINSON

Old Trafford stadium

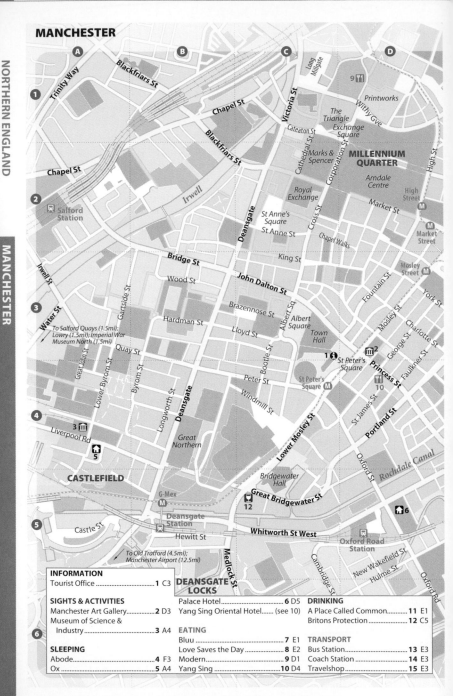

MANCHESTER

SLEEPING

Ox (☎ 0161-839 7740; www.theox.co.uk; 71 Liverpool Rd; d/tr from £55/75) Not quite your traditional B&B (breakfast is extra), but an excellent choice, nonetheless: nine ox-blood-red rooms with tidy amenities above a fine gastropub in the heart of Castlefield. It's the best deal in town for the location.

Palace Hotel (☎ 0161-288 1111; www.principal-hotels.com; Oxford St; r from £80) An elegant refurbishment of one of Manchester's most magnificent Victorian palaces has resulted in a pretty special boutique hotel, combining the grandeur of the public areas with the modern look of the bedrooms.

Abode (☎ 0161-247 7744; www.abodehotels.co.uk; 107 Piccadilly St; r from £80; 🖳) Modern British style is the catchword at this converted textile factory, which has successfully combined the original fittings with 61 spanking-new bedrooms divided into four categories of ever-increasing luxury: Comfortable, Desirable, Enviable and Fabulous, the last being five seriously swanky top-floor suites.

ourpick **Yang Sing Oriental Hotel** (☎ 0161-920 9651; www.yangsingoriental.com; 36 Princess St; r/ste from £179/239; 🖳) Japanese silk duvets and pillows; beautiful bespoke Asian furnishings; a complimentary minibar; and your choice of five separate room aromas (which you can select when booking) – just some of the extravagant offerings at this exquisitely elegant new hotel, which has already raised the hospitality bar by several notches.

Lowry (☎ 0161-827 4000; www.rfhotels.com; 50 Dearman's Pl, Chapel Wharf; s/d from £350/385) Simply dripping with designer luxury and five-star comfort, Manchester's top hotel has fabulous rooms with enormous beds, ergonomically designed furniture, walk-in wardrobes, and bathrooms finished with Italian porcelain tiles and glass mosaic.

EATING

Love Saves the Day (☎ 0161-832 0777; Tib St; lunch £6; ☺ 8am-7pm Mon-Wed, to 9pm Thu, to 8pm Fri, 10-6pm Sat, 10am-4pm Sun) The Northern Quarter's most popular cafe is a New York–style deli, small supermarket and sit-down eatery in one large, airy room.

Al Bilal (☎ 0161-257 0006; 87-89 Wilmslow Rd; mains £7-14; ☺ lunch & dinner Sun-Fri) It's a given that you cannot leave Manchester without tucking into a curry along Wilmslow Rd, which is as famous as Bradford or Birmingham for its Indian cuisine.

Yang Sing (☎ 0161-236 2200; 34 Princess St; mains £9-16; ☺ lunch & dinner) A serious contender for best Chinese restaurant in England, Yang Sing attracts diners from all over with its Cantonese cuisine.

Bluu (☎ 0161-839 7740; www.bluu.co.uk; Unit 1, Smithfield Market, Thomas St; 3-course lunch £15, dinner mains £10-15; ☺ lunch & dinner) It's a chain cafe-bar, but Manchester's version has retained its kudos thanks to its location, look and clientele – a steady stream of hipsters who appreciate its aforementioned strengths and menu, which offers an inventive choice of British and Continental dishes using only the freshest ingredients.

ourpick **Modern** (☎ 0161-605 8282; Urbis, Cathedral Gardens, Corporation Street; 2-/3-course lunch £13/16, dinner mains £11-21; ☺ lunch & dinner) Top fare on top of the world, or an excellent meal atop Manchester's most distinctive landmark, Urbis, is one of the city's most enjoyable dining experiences.

DRINKING

A Place Called Common (☎ 0161-832 9245; www.aplacecalledcommon.co.uk; 39-41 Edge St; ☺ noon-midnight Mon-Wed, to 1am Thu, to 2am Fri & Sat, 2pm-midnight Sun) Common by name but great by nature, this is a terrific boozer favoured by an unpretentious crowd who like the changing artwork on the walls and the DJs who play nightly.

ourpick **Britons Protection** (☎ 0161-236 5895; 50 Great Bridgewater St; mains around £7) Whisky – 200 different kinds of it – is the beverage of choice at this liver-threatening, proper English pub that also does Tudor-style meals (boar, venison and the like). An old-fashioned boozer; no fancy stuff.

GETTING THERE & AWAY
AIR

Manchester Airport (☎ 0161-489 3000; www.manchesterairport.co.uk), south of the city, is the largest airport outside London and is served by 17 locations throughout Britain.

BUS

National Express (☎ 08717 81 81 81; www.nationalexpress.com) serves most major cities almost hourly from Chorlton St coach station in the city centre. Destinations include Liverpool (£5, 1¼ hours, hourly), Leeds (£7.60, one hour, hourly) and London (£23, 3¾ hours, hourly).

TRAIN

Manchester Piccadilly (east of the Gay Village) is the main station for trains to and from the rest of the country, although Victoria station (north of Urbis) serves Halifax and Bradford. The two stations are linked by Metrolink. Trains head to Blackpool (£12.20, 1¼ hours, half-hourly), Liverpool Lime St (£8.80, 45 minutes, half-hourly), Newcastle (£41.20, three hours, six daily) and London (£115, three hours, seven daily).

GETTING AROUND
TO/FROM THE AIRPORT

The airport is 12 miles south of the city. A train to or from Victoria station costs £3.80, and a coach is £3.20. A taxi is nearly four times as much in light traffic.

PUBLIC TRANSPORT

The excellent public-transport system can be used with a variety of **Day saver tickets** (bus £3, bus & train £3.80, bus & Metrolink £4.50, train & Metrolink £5, bus, train & Metrolink £6). For inquiries about local transport, including night buses, contact **Travelshop** (☎ 0161-228 7811; www.gmpte.com; 9 Portland St, Piccadilly Gardens; ☼ 8am-8pm).

LIVERPOOL

pop 469,020

Desperate for the kind of recognition given to its neighbour and rival Manchester, Liverpool took to its role as European Capital of Culture for 2008 with fervour. The title itself may not have amounted to much more than an appearance at the launch by Ringo Starr, and a year-long program of events that would have probably happened anyway, but the city grabbed the opportunity to remake and reshape itself with both hands…and still hasn't let go.

INFORMATION

The tourist office has three branches in the city. It also has an **accommodation hotline** (☎ 0845 601 1125; ☼ 9am-5.30pm Mon-Fri, 10am-4pm Sat).

08 Place tourist office (☎ 0151-233 2008; Whitechapel; ☼ 9am-8pm Mon-Sat, 11am-4pm Sun Apr-Sep, 9am-6pm Mon-Sat, 11am-4pm Sun Oct-Mar) Tourist office main branch.

Albert Dock tourist office (☎ 0151-478 4599) Anchor Courtyard (☼ 10am-6pm); Merseyside Maritime Museum (☼ 10am-6pm)

SIGHTS

The wonderful Albert Dock is the city's biggest tourist attraction, and the key to understanding the city's history, but the city centre is where you'll find most of Liverpool's real day-to-day life.

Sculpture, the Lowry (p213)

NEIL SETCHFIELD

CITY CENTRE
ST GEORGE'S HALL

Arguably Liverpool's most impressive building, **St George's Hall** (☎ 0151-707 2391; William Brown St; admission free; ☼ 10am-5pm Tue-Sat, 1-5pm Sun) was built in 1854 and restored in recent years to the tune of £27 million – it finally reopened in 2007. Curiously, it was built as law courts *and* a concert hall – presumably a judge could pass sentence and then relax to a string quartet. Tours (£5) of the hall are run in conjunction with the tourist office; check for times.

WALKER ART GALLERY

Touted as the 'National Gallery of the North', the city's foremost **gallery** (☎ 0151-478 4199; www.liverpoolmuseums.org.uk/walker; William Brown St; admission free; ☼ 10am-5pm) is the national gallery for northern England, housing an outstanding collection of art dating from the 14th century. Its strong suits are Pre-Raphaelite art, modern British art, and sculpture – not to mention the rotating exhibits of contemporary expression.

WORLD MUSEUM LIVERPOOL

Natural history, science and technology are the themes of this sprawling **museum** (☎ 0151-478 4399; www.liverpoolmuseums.org .uk/wml; William Brown St; admission free; ☺ 10am-5pm), where exhibits range from birds of prey to space exploration.

LIVERPOOL CATHEDRAL

At Hope St's southern end stands the life work of Sir Giles Gilbert Scott (1880–1960), the neo-Gothic **Liverpool Cathedral** (☎ 0151-709 6271; www.liverpoolcathedral .uk; Hope St; ☺ 8am-6pm). Sir Giles' other contributions to the world were the red telephone box, and the power station in London that is now home to the Tate Modern. The central bell is the world's third-largest (with the world's highest and heaviest peal), while the organ, with its 9765 pipes, is probably the world's largest operational model.

There are terrific views of Liverpool from the top of the cathedral's 101m **tower** (☎ 0151-702 7217; adult/child £4.25/3, combined tower & Great Space tour adult/child £6.75/5; ☺ 10am-5pm Mon-Sat, noon-2.30pm Sun).

ALBERT DOCK

Liverpool's biggest tourist attraction is **Albert Dock** (☎ 0151-708 8854; www.albert dock.com; admission free), 2¾ hectares of water ringed by enormous cast-iron columns and impressive five-storey warehouses; these make up the country's largest collection of protected buildings and are a World Heritage Site.

MERSEYSIDE MARITIME MUSEUM

The story of one of the world's great ports is the theme of this excellent **museum** (☎ 0151-478 4499; www.liverpoolmuse ums.org.uk/maritime; Albert Dock; admission free; ☺ 10am-5pm) and, believe us, it's a graphic and compelling page-turner. One of the many great exhibits is Emigration to a New World, which tells the story of nine million emigrants and their efforts to get to North America and Australia; the walk-through model of a typical ship shows just how tough conditions on board really were.

INTERNATIONAL SLAVERY MUSEUM

Museums are, by their very nature, like a still of the past, but the extraordinary **International Slavery Museum** (☎ 0151-478 4499; www.liverpoolmuseums.org.uk/ism; Albert Dock; admission free; ☺ 10am-5pm) resonates very much in the present. It reveals slavery's unimaginable horrors – including Liverpool's own role in the triangular slave trade – in a clear and uncompromising manner.

TATE LIVERPOOL

Touted as the home of modern art in the north, this **gallery** (☎ 0151-702 7400; www .tate.org.uk/liverpool; Albert Dock; admission free, special exhibitions adult/child from £5/4; ☺ 10am-5.50pm daily Jun-Aug, 10am-5.50pm Tue-Sun Sep-May) features a substantial checklist of 20th-century artists across its four floors, as well as touring exhibitions from the mother ship on London's Bankside.

BEATLES STORY

Liverpool's most popular **museum** (☎ 0151-709 1963; www.beatlesstory.com; Albert Dock; adult/child £12.50/6.50; ☺ 9am-7pm) won't illuminate any dark, juicy corners in the turbulent history of the world's most famous foursome – there's ne'er a mention of internal discord, drugs, Yoko Ono or the Frog

LIVERPOOL

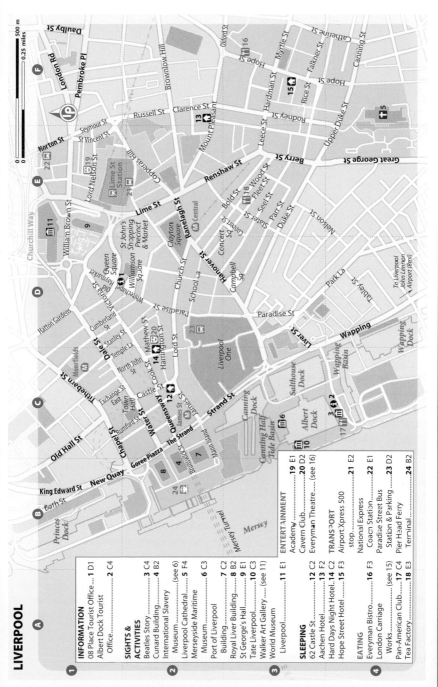

INFORMATION
08 Place Tourist Office.....**1** D1
Albert Dock Tourist
  Office........................**2** C4

SIGHTS &
ACTIVITIES
Beatles Story.................**3** C4
Cunard Building.............**4** B2
International Slavery
  Museum..................(see 6)
Liverpool Cathedral.........**5** F4
Merseyside Maritime
  Museum.....................**6** C3
Port of Liverpool
  Building.....................**7** C2
Royal Liver Building........**8** B2
St George's Hall............**9** E1
Tate Liverpool..............**10** C3
Walker Art Gallery........(see 11)
World Museum
  Liverpool..................**11** E1

SLEEPING
62 Castle St................**12** C2
Aachen Hotel...............**13** F2
Hard Days Night Hotel...**14** C2
Hope Street Hotel.........**15** F3

EATING
Everyman Bistro...........**16** F3
London Carriage
  Works...................(see 15)
Pan-American Club.......**17** C4
Tea Factory................**18** E3

ENTERTAINMENT
Academy.....................**19** E1
Cavern Club................**20** D2
Everyman Theatre.....(see 16)

TRANSPORT
Airport Xpress 500
  stop........................**21** E2
National Express
  Coach Station.............**22** E1
Paradise Street Bus
  Station & Parking.......**23** D2
Pier Head Ferry
  Terminal...................**24** B2

Albert Dock

GLENN BEANLAND

Song – but there's plenty of genuine memorabilia to keep a Beatles fan happy.

NORTH OF ALBERT DOCK

The area to the north of Albert Dock is known as **Pier Head**, after a stone pier built in the 1760s. This is still the departure point for ferries across the River Mersey (see p222), and was, for millions of migrants, their final contact with European soil.

Their story – and that of the city in general – will be told in the enormous **Museum of Liverpool**, being built at the time of research on an area known as Mann Island and not slated to open until 2011. Until its opening, this part of the dock will continue to be dominated by a trio of Edwardian buildings known as the 'Three Graces', dating from the days when Liverpool's star was still ascending. The southernmost, with the dome mimicking St Paul's Cathedral, is the **Port of Liverpool Building**, completed in 1907. Next to it is the **Cunard Building**, in the style of an Italian palazzo, once HQ to the Cunard Steamship Line. Finally, the **Royal Liver Building** (pronounced *lie*-ver) was opened in 1911 as the head office of the Royal Liver Friendly Society. It's crowned by Liverpool's symbol, the famous 5.5m copper Liver Bird.

TOURS

Liverpool Beatles Tour (☎ 0151-281 7738; www.beatlestours.co.uk; tours £45-80) Your own personalised tour of every bit of minutiae associated with the Beatles, from cradle to grave. Pick-ups are arranged upon booking.

Magical Mystery Tour (☎ 0151-709 3285; www.cavernclub.org; per person £13; ⊙ 2.30pm year round, plus noon Sat Jul & Aug) This two-hour tour takes in all Beatles-related landmarks – their birthplaces, childhood homes, schools and places such as Penny Lane and Strawberry Field – before finishing up in the Cavern Club (which isn't the original). Departs from outside the tourist office at the 08 Place.

Yellow Duckmarine Tour (☎ 0151-708 7799; www.theyellowduckmarine.co.uk; adult/

child/family £12/10/34; ❤ from 11am) Take to the dock waters in a WWII amphibious vehicle after a quickie tour of the city centre's main points of interest. Departs from Albert Dock, near the Beatles Story.

SLEEPING

Aachen Hotel (☎ 0151-709 3477; www.aachen hotel.co.uk; 89-91 Mt Pleasant; s/d from £50/70) This funky listed building is a perennial favourite, with a mix of rooms (some with attached bathroom, some shared). The decor is strictly late '70s to early '80s – lots of flower patterns and crazy colour schemes – but it's all part of the welcoming, offbeat atmosphere.

our pick **Hope Street Hotel** (☎ 0151-709 3000; www.hopestreethotel.co.uk; 40 Hope St; r/ste from £115/180) Luxurious Liverpool's pre-eminent flag-waver is this stunning boutique hotel, on the city's most elegant street. The building's original features – heavy wooden beams, cast-iron columns and plenty of exposed brickwork – have been incorporated into a contemporary design inspired by the style of a 16th-century Venetian palazzo.

Hard Days Night Hotel (☎ 0151-236 1964; www.harddaysnighthotel.com; Central Bldgs, North John St; r £120-160, ste from £180) You don't have to be a fan to stay here, but it helps: unquestionably luxurious, the 110 ultramodern, fully equipped rooms come with a specially commissioned piece of artwork by Shannon, who has made a career out of drawing John, Paul, George and Ringo.

62 Castle St (☎ 0151-702 7898; www .62castlest.com; 62 Castle St; s/d from £150/180; P 🖵) As exclusive a boutique hotel as you'll find anywhere, this wonderful new property successfully blends the traditional Victorian features of the building with a sexy, contemporary style.

EATING

Everyman Bistro (☎ 0151-708 9545; www. everyman.co.uk; 13 Hope St; mains £5-8; ❤ noon-2am Mon-Fri, 11am-2am Sat, 7-10.30pm Sun) Out-of-work actors and other creative types on a budget make this great cafe-restaurant (located beneath the Everyman Theatre) their second home – with good reason. Great tucker and a terrific atmosphere.

Tea Factory (☎ 0151-708 7008; 79 Wood St; mains £7-12; ❤ 11am-late) Who knew that cod 'n' chips could be so…cool? The wide-ranging menu covers all bases from typical Brit to funky finger food such as international tapas, but it's the room, darling, that makes this place so popular.

Pan-American Club (☎ 0151-709 7097; Britannia Pavilion, Albert Dock; mains £13-24; ❤ 11am-2am) A truly beautiful warehouse conversion has created this top-class restaurant and bar, easily one of the best dining addresses in town.

London Carriage Works (☎ 0151-705 2222; www.tlcw.co.uk; 40 Hope St; 2-/3-course meals £35/45; ❤ 8am-10pm Mon-Sat, 8am-8pm Sun) Liverpool's dining revolution is being led by Paul Askew's award-winning restaurant. Its followers are the fashionistas, socceristas and other members of the style brigade who share the large, open space that is the dining room – actually more of a bright glass box divided only by a series of sculpted glass shards.

ENTERTAINMENT

The schedule is pretty full these days, whether it's excellent fringe theatre, a performance by the superb Philharmonic or an all-day rock concert. For all information, consult the *Liverpool Echo*.

THEATRE

Everyman Theatre (☎ 0151-709 4776; 13 Hope St) This is one of England's most famous repertory theatres, and it's an avid

Relaxing outdoors, York (p225)

NEIL SETCHFIELD

supporter of local talent, which has included the likes of Alan Bleasdale.

LIVE MUSIC

Academy (☎ 0151-794 6868; **Liverpool University, 11-13 Hotham St**) This is the best venue to see major touring bands.

Cavern Club (☎ 0151-236 1965; **8-10 Mathew St**) The 'world's most famous club' is not the original basement venue where the Fab Four began their careers, but it's a fairly faithful reconstruction. There's usually a good selection of local bands, and look out for all-day gigs.

GETTING THERE & AWAY
AIR
Liverpool John Lennon Airport (☎ 0870 750 8484; www.liverpooljohnlennonairport.co.uk)

serves a variety of international destinations including Amsterdam, Barcelona, Dublin and Paris, as well as destinations in the UK (Belfast, London and the Isle of Man).

BUS
The **National Express Coach Station** (☎ 08705 808080; **Norton St**) is situated 300m north of Lime St station. There are services to/from most major towns, including Manchester (£5, 1¼ hours, hourly), London (£24, five to six hours, seven daily), Birmingham (£10.20, 2¾ hours, five daily) and Newcastle (£20.50, 6½ hours, three daily).

TRAIN
Liverpool's main station is Lime St. It has hourly services to almost everywhere, including Chester (£4.45, 45 minutes), London (£61.60, 3¼ hours), Manchester (£8.80, 45 minutes) and Wigan (£4.60, 50 minutes).

GETTING AROUND
TO/FROM THE AIRPORT
The airport is 8 miles south of the centre. **Arriva Airlink** (**per person £1.70**; ☼ 6am-11pm) buses 80A and 180 depart from Paradise St station, and **Airportxpress 500** (**per person £2.50**; ☼ 5.15am-12.15am) buses leave from outside Lime St station. Buses from both stations take half an hour and run every 20 minutes. A taxi to the city centre should cost no more than £15.

BOAT
The famous cross-Mersey **ferry** (**adult/child £1.35/1.05**) for Woodside and Seacombe departs from Pier Head Ferry Terminal, next to the Royal Liver Building (to the north of Albert Dock).

PUBLIC TRANSPORT

Local public transport is coordinated by **Merseytravel** (☎ 0151-236 7676; www.merseytravel.gov.uk). Highly recommended is the **Saveaway ticket** (adult/child £3.70/1.90), which allows for one day's off-peak travel on all bus, train and ferry services throughout Merseyside. Tickets are available at shops and post offices throughout the city. Paradise St bus station is in the city centre.

MERSEYRAIL

Merseyrail (☎ 0151-702 2071; www.merseyrail.org) is an extensive suburban rail service linking Liverpool with the Greater Merseyside area. There are four stops in the city centre: Lime St, Central (handy for Ropewalks), James St (close to Albert Dock) and Moorfields.

YORKSHIRE

With a population as big as Scotland's, and an area half the size of Belgium, Yorkshire is almost a country in itself. It even has its own flag (a white rose on a blue background), its own distinctive dialect (known as 'Tyke'), and its own official celebration (Yorkshire Day, 1 August). Needless to say, while Yorkshire folk are proud to be English, they're even prouder to be natives of 'God's Own Country', as they (only half-jokingly) refer to their home patch.

The **Yorkshire Tourist Board** (www.yorkshire.com; 312 Tadcaster Rd, York, YO24 1GS) has plenty of general leaflets and brochures – postal and email enquiries only.

ACTIVITIES

Yorkshire's varied landscape of wild hills, tranquil valleys, high moors and spectacular coastline offers plenty of opportunities for outdoor activities. See www.outdoor yorkshire.com for more details.

GETTING THERE & AROUND

The major north-south transport routes – the M1 and A1 motorways and the main London to Edinburgh railway line – run through the middle of Yorkshire, serving the key cities of Sheffield, Leeds and York.

Traveline Yorkshire (☎ 0871 200 2233; www.yorkshiretravel.net) provides public-transport information for the whole of Yorkshire.

BUS

Bus transport around Yorkshire is frequent and efficient, especially between major towns. Services are more sporadic in the national parks but still adequate for reaching most places, particularly in the summer months (June to September).

TRAIN

The main line between London and Edinburgh runs through Yorkshire, with at least 10 trains a day calling at York and Doncaster, where you can change trains for other Yorkshire destinations.

GETTING AROUND

The Metro is West Yorkshire's highly efficient train and bus network. For transport information call **Metroline** (☎ 0113-245 7676; www.wymetro.com). The excellent Day Rover (£5 for train or bus, £6 train and bus) tickets are good for travel on buses and trains after 9.30am on weekdays and all day at weekends.

HAWORTH
pop 6100

It seems that only Shakespeare himself is held in higher esteem than the beloved Brontë sisters – Emily, Anne and Charlotte; at least, judging by the 8 million visitors a year who trudge up the hill from the train station to pay their respects at the

Yorkshire Dales National Park

GLENN VAN DER KNIJFF

handsome parsonage where the literary classics *Jane Eyre* and *Wuthering Heights* were born.

Your first stop should be **Haworth Parish Church** (admission free), a lovely old place of worship built in the late 19th century on the site of the 'old' church that the Brontë sisters knew, which was demolished in 1879. In the surrounding churchyard, gravestones are covered in moss or thrust to one side by gnarled tree roots, giving the place a tremendous feeling of age.

Set in a pretty garden overlooking the church and graveyard, the **Brontë Parsonage Museum** (☎ 01535-642323; www .bronte.info; admission £6; ☯ 10am-5.30pm Apr-Sep, 11am-5pm Oct-Mar) is where the Brontë family lived from 1820 till 1861. The rooms are meticulously furnished and decorated exactly as they were in the Brontë era, with many personal possessions on display.

GETTING THERE & AWAY

From Leeds, the easiest approach to Haworth is via Keighley, which is on the Metro rail network. Bus 500 runs from Keighley bus station to Haworth (15 minutes, hourly) and continues to Todmorden and Hebden Bridge. However, the most interesting way to get from Keighley to Haworth is via the Keighley & Worth Valley Railway.

YORKSHIRE DALES NATIONAL PARK

The Yorkshire Dales – named from the old Norse word *dalr*, meaning 'valleys' – is the central jewel in the necklace of three national parks strung across the neck of northern England, with the dramatic fells of the Lake District to the west and the brooding heaths of the North York Moors to the east.

The Dales have been protected as a national park since the 1950s, assuring their status as a walker's and cyclist's paradise. Two of England's most famous long-distance routes cross the Dales. The Pennine Way (p243) goes through the rugged western half of the park. The **Coast to Coast Walk** passes through Swaledale in the northern Dales. Another long-distance possibility is the **Dales Way** (www.dalesway.org.uk), which begins in Ilkley, follows the River Wharfe through the heart of the Dales, and finishes at Bowness-on-Windermere in the Lake District.

YORK

pop 181,100

Nowhere in northern England says 'medieval' quite like York, a city of extraordinary cultural and historical wealth that has lost little of its preindustrial lustre. Its medieval spider's web of narrow streets is enclosed by a magnificent circuit of 13th-century walls. At its heart lies the immense, awe-inspiring minster, one of the most beautiful Gothic cathedrals in the world.

INFORMATION

York Visitor Centre (☎ 01904-550099; www.visityork.org; De Grey Rooms, Exhibition Sq; ☯ 9am-6pm Mon-Sat & 10am-5pm Sun Apr-Sep, 9am-5pm Mon-Sat & 10am-4pm Sun Oct-Mar) There's another branch at the train station (same hours).

SIGHTS

YORK MINSTER

Not content with being Yorkshire's most important historic building, the awe-inspiring **York Minster** (☎ 01904-557200; www.yorkminster.org; adult/child minster only £5.50/free, all areas £9.50/3; ☯ minster 9am-5pm Mon-Sat & noon-3.45pm Sun Apr-Oct, 9.30am-5pm Mon-Sat & noon-3.45pm Sun Nov-Mar) is also the largest medieval cathedral in all of Northern Europe.

The present minster, built mainly between 1220 and 1480, manages to encompass all the major stages of Gothic architectural development. The transepts (1220 to 1255) were built in Early English style; the octagonal chapter house (1260

THE SETTLE-CARLISLE LINE

The Settle-Carlisle Line (SCL), built between 1869 and 1875, offers one of England's most scenic railway journeys. The 72-mile line's construction was one of the great engineering achievements of the Victorian era: 5000 navvies armed with picks and shovels built 325 bridges, 21 viaducts and blasted 14 tunnels in horrific conditions – nearly 200 of them died in the process.

Trains run between Leeds and Carlisle via Settle about eight times a day. The entire journey takes two hours and 40 minutes and costs £22/27 for a single/day return; from Settle to Carlisle is 1¾ hours and £16/18. Various hop-on-hop-off passes for one or three days are also available. Contact **National Rail Enquiries** (☎ 08457 484950) or click on to www.settle-carlisle.co.uk.

---

to 1290) and the nave (1291 to 1340) in the Decorated style; and the west towers, west front and central, or lantern, tower (1470 to 1472) in Perpendicular style. At the heart of the minster is the massive **tower** (adult/child £4/2; ☯ 9.30am-5pm Mon-Sat & 12.30-5pm Sun Apr-Oct, from 10am Nov-Mar), which is well worth climbing for the unparalleled views of York.

CITY WALLS

If the weather's good, don't miss the chance to walk the **City Walls** (admission free; ☯ 8am-dusk), which follow the line of the original Roman walls – it gives a whole new perspective on the city. The full circuit is 4.5 miles (allow 1½ to two hours); if you're pushed for time, the short stretch from Bootham Bar to Monk Bar is worth doing for the views of the minster.

SHAMBLES

The narrow, cobbled lane known as the Shambles (www.yorkshambles.com), lined with 15th-century Tudor buildings that overhang so much they seem to meet above your head, is the most visited street in Europe. Quaint and picturesque it most certainly is, and it hints at what a medieval street may have looked like – if it was overrun with people told they had to buy a tacky souvenir and be back on the tour bus in 15 minutes. It takes its name from the Saxon word *shamel*, meaning 'slaughterhouse' – in 1862 there were 26 butcher shops on this one street.

JORVIK

Interactive multimedia exhibits aimed at 'bringing history to life' often achieve just the opposite, but the much-hyped Jorvik (☎ 01904-543403; www.vikingjorvik.com; Coppergate; adult/child £8.50/6, Jorvik & Dig combined £11.25/8.50; ☯ 10am-5pm Apr-Oct, 10am-4pm Nov-Mar) – the most visited attraction in town after the minster – manages to pull it off with admirable aplomb. It's a smells-and-all reconstruction of the Viking settlement that was unearthed here during excavations in the late 1970s, brought to you courtesy of a 'time-car' monorail that transports you through 9th-century Jorvik (the Viking name for York).

You can cut time spent waiting in the queue by booking your tickets online and choosing the time you want to visit – it only costs £1 extra.

DIG

Under the same management as Jorvik, Dig (☎ 01904-543403; www.digyork.co.uk; St Saviour's Church, St Saviourgate; adult/child £5.50/5, Dig & Jorvik £11.25/8.50; ☯ 10am-5pm) cashes

in on the popularity of archaeology programs on TV by giving you the chance to be an 'archaeological detective', unearthing the 'secrets' of York's distant past as well as learning something of the archaeologist's world – what they do, how they do it and so on.

NATIONAL RAILWAY MUSEUM

York's National Railway Museum (☎ 0844 815 3139; www.nrm.org.uk; Leeman Rd; admission free; ☯ 10am-6pm daily, closed 24-26 Dec) – the biggest in the world, with more than 100 locomotives – is so well presented and full of fascinating stuff that it's interesting even to folk whose eyes don't mist over at the thought of a 4-6-2 A1 Pacific class chuffing into a tunnel.

TOURS

Breadcrumbs Trail (☎ 01904-610676; Collage Corner, 2 Norman Ct) Explore York by following the Hansel-and-Gretel-type trails laid out in the book – a novel and excellent way to keep the kids entertained.

Ghost Hunt of York (☎ 01904-608700; www.ghosthunt.co.uk; adult/child £5/3; ☯ tours 7.30pm) Award-winning and highly entertaining 75-minute tour laced with authentic ghost stories; the kids just love this one. Begins at the Shambles, no need to book.

Yorkwalk (☎ 01904-622303; www.yorkwalk .co.uk; adult/child £5.50/2.50) Offers a series of two-hour themed walks on an ever-growing list of themes.

SLEEPING

Elliotts B&B (☎ 01904-623333; www.elliotts hotel.co.uk; 2 Sycamore Pl; s/d from £38/75; ⓟ ▯) A beautifully converted 'gentleman's residence', Elliotts leans towards the boutique end of the guesthouse market with stylish and elegant rooms, and hi-tech touches such as flat-screen TVs and free wi-fi.

23 St Mary's (☎ 01904-622738; www.23st marys.co.uk; 23 St Mary's; s £45-55, d £70-90; P 🖳) A smart and stately town house with nine chintzy, country house-style rooms, some with hand-painted furniture for that rustic look, while others are decorated with antiques, lace and polished mahogany.

Dairy Guesthouse (☎ 01904-639367; www.dairyguesthouse.co.uk; 3 Scarcroft Rd; s/d from £55/75; P) A lovely Victorian home that has retained many of its original features,

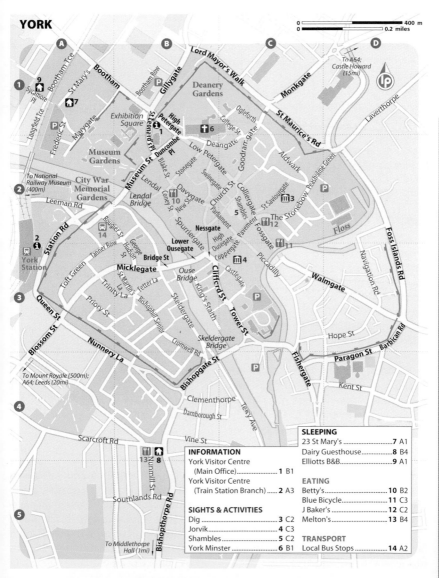

YORK

INFORMATION	
York Visitor Centre	
(Main Office)......................	**1** B1
York Visitor Centre	
(Train Station Branch)	**2** A3

SIGHTS & ACTIVITIES	
Dig	**3** C2
Jorvik	**4** C3
Shambles	**5** C2
York Minster	**6** B1

SLEEPING	
23 St Mary's	**7** A1
Dairy Guesthouse...............	**8** B4
Elliotts B&B........................	**9** A1

EATING	
Betty's	**10** B2
Blue Bicycle........................	**11** C3
J Baker's	**12** C2
Melton's	**13** B4

TRANSPORT	
Local Bus Stops	**14** A2

including pine doors, stained glass and cast-iron fireplaces, but the real treat is the flower- and plant-filled courtyard that leads to the cottage-style rooms. Minimum two-night stay at weekends.

Mount Royale (☎ 01904-628856; www .mountroyale.co.uk; The Mount; r £100-210; P) A grand, early-19th-century listed building that has been converted into a superb luxury hotel, complete with a solarium, beauty spa and outdoor heated tub and swimming pool.

Middlethorpe Hall (☎ 01904-641241; www.middlethorpe.com; Bishopsthorpe Rd; s/d from £130/190; P ▣) York's top spot is this breathtaking 17th-century country house set in 20 acres of parkland that was once the home of diarist Lady Mary Wortley Montagu.

EATING

Betty's (☎ 01904-659142; www.bettys.co.uk; St Helen's Sq; mains £6-11, afternoon tea £15; ☺ 9am-9pm) Afternoon tea, old-school style, with white-aproned waitresses, linen tablecloths and a teapot collection ranged along the walls. House speciality is the Yorkshire Fat Rascal – a huge fruit scone smothered in melted butter.

Melton's (☎ 01904-634341; www.meltonsres taurant.co.uk; 7 Scarcroft Rd; mains £15-18; ☺ lunch Tue-Sat, dinner Mon-Sat) Foodies come from far and wide to dine in one of Yorkshire's best restaurants. It tends to specialise in fish dishes but doesn't go far wrong with practically everything else, from sea trout with sorrel to marinaded wild boar.

Blue Bicycle (☎ 01904-673990; www.the bluebicycle.com; 34 Fossgate; mains £15-22; ☺ lunch & dinner) French food at its finest – the occasional anti-*foie gras* protester outside the door gives a clue as to the menu – served in a romantic candle-lit room makes for a top-notch dining experience.

ourpick J Baker's (☎ 01904-622688; www .jbakers.co.uk; 7 Fossgate; 2-/3-course dinner £23/27.50; ☺ lunch & dinner) Superstar chef Jeff Baker left Leeds' Pool Court and his Michelin star to pursue his own vision of Modern British cuisine here.

GETTING THERE & AWAY
BUS

For timetable information call **Traveline Yorkshire** (☎ 0871 200 2233; www.yorkshire travel.net), or check the computerised 24-hour information points at the train station and Rougier St. All local and regional buses stop on Rougier St, about 200m northeast of the train station.

There are National Express coaches to London (£24, 5¼ hours, four daily), Birmingham (£25, 3¼ hours, one daily) and Newcastle (£14, 2¾ hours, four daily).

TRAIN

York is a major railway hub with frequent direct services to Birmingham (£40, 2¼ hours), Newcastle (£25, one hour), Leeds (£10, 25 minutes), London's King's Cross (£103, two hours), Manchester (£20, 1½ hours) and Scarborough (£12, 50 minutes).

CUMBRIA & THE LAKE DISTRICT

Ever since William Wordsworth and his Romantic chums ventured into the hills in search of poetic inspiration in the late 18th century, this part of England has been a byword for natural grandeur, although in many ways the Cumbrian landscape, with its glacier-etched valleys, ridges and peaks, is closer to the rugged panoramas of the Scottish Highlands than the green and pleasant vistas of England. The region's distinctive jade-green hills (locally

Lake District National Park

known as 'fells') have been a favoured haunt for generations of peak-baggers, trail trekkers and view junkies.

Brockhole National Park Visitor Centre (☎ 015394-46601; www.lake-district.gov .uk; ☺ 10am-5pm Easter-Oct) The Lake District's flagship visitor centre is 3 miles north of Windermere on the A591, with a teashop, adventure playground and gardens.

GETTING THERE & AWAY
BUS
National Express coaches run direct from London and Glasgow to Windermere, Carlisle and Kendal; count on seven hours between London Victoria and Windermere.

TRAIN
Carlisle is on the main Virgin West Coast line from London Euston–Manchester–Glasgow, with trains running roughly hourly from both north and south. To get to the Lake District, you need to change at Oxenholme, from where regular trains travel west into Kendal and Windermere.

There are at least three direct trains from Windermere and Kendal south to Lancaster, Manchester and Manchester Airport.

GETTING AROUND
Traveline (☎ 0871 200 22 33; www.travel inenortheast.info) provides travel information. Tourist offices stock the free *Getting Around Cumbria* booklet, with timetables for buses, trains and ferries.

BUS
The main operator is **Stagecoach** (www .stagecoachbus.com). The North West Explorer ticket (one/four/seven days £9.50/21/30) gives unlimited travel on services in Cumbria and Lancashire. Twenty-four-hour Dayrider tickets can be purchased from the bus driver. Useful buses include the 555 and 556 (Lakeslink) between Lancaster and Carlisle, which stop at all the main towns; bus 505 (Coniston Rambler), linking Kendal, Windermere, Ambleside and Coniston; and the X4/X5

Castle Howard

JOE CORNISH/ PHOTOLIBRARY.COM

↘ CASTLE HOWARD

Stately homes may be two a penny in England, but you'll have to try pretty damn hard to find one as breathtakingly stately as Castle Howard, a work of theatrical grandeur and audacity set in the rolling Howardian Hills. This is one of the world's most beautiful buildings, instantly recognisable from its starring role in *Brideshead Revisited* – which has done its popularity no end of good since the TV series first aired in the early 1980s.

Castle Howard is 15 miles northeast of York, off the A64. There are several organised tours from York – check with the tourist office for up-to-date schedules.

Things you need to know: ☎ 01653-648333; www.castlehoward.co.uk; adult/child house & grounds £10.50/6.50, grounds only £8/5; ⊙ house 11am-4.30pm, grounds 10am-4.30pm Mar-Oct & 1st three weeks of Dec

CAR

Driving in the Lake District can be a headache, especially on holiday weekends; you might find it easier to leave the car wherever you're staying and get around using local buses instead.

WINDERMERE & BOWNESS

pop 8432

Of all England's lakes, none carries the cachet of regal Windermere. Stretching for 10.5 silvery miles from Ambleside to Newby Bridge, it's been a centre for Lakeland tourism since the first steam trains chugged into town in 1847 (much to the chagrin of the local gentry, including William Wordsworth). The town itself is split into two: Windermere, 1.5 miles uphill from the lake, and bustling Bowness, where a bevy of boat trips, ice-cream booths and frilly teashops jostle for space around the shoreline.

The first passenger ferry was launched back in 1845, and **Windermere Lake Cruises** (☎ 015395-31188; www.windermere-lakecruises.co.uk) keeps the tradition alive. Cruises allow you to jump off at one of the ferry landings (Waterhead/Ambleside, Wray Castle, Brockhole, Bowness, Ferry Landing, Fell Foot Ferry and Lakeside) and catch a later boat back.

Classic standard-gauge steam trains puff their way along the vintage **Lakeside & Haverthwaite Railway** (☎ 015395-31594; www.lakesiderailway.co.uk; Haverthwaite Station; adult/5-15yr/family £5.40/2.70/14.80; ⊙ mid-Mar–Oct) from Haverthwaite, near Ulverston, to Newby Bridge and Lakeside.

SLEEPING

Applegarth Hotel (☎ 015394-43206; www.lakesapplegarth.co.uk; College Rd; s £55-60, d £96-156; Ⓟ) Polished wood panels, antique lamps and stained glass conjure a staid

from Penrith to Workington via Troutbeck, Keswick and Cockermouth.

The **Cross-Lakes Shuttle** (9 or 10 possible returns daily; ⊙ mid-Mar–Oct) allows you to cross from Windermere to Coniston using a combination of buses and boats; a return from Bowness to Coniston and back costs £16.60/9 per adult/child.

Victorian vibe; cheaper rooms are bland, but the pricier ones feature four-posters and fell views.

Coach House (☎ 015394-44494; www.lake districtbandb.com; Lake Rd; d £60-80; P) Citrus yellows meet candy pinks and sky blues at this off-the-wall number, converted from a Victorian stables.

Oakbank House (☎ 015394-43386; www .oakbankhousehotel.co.uk; Helm Rd; d £82-88; P) The pick of the Bowness B&Bs, inside a slate-topped house along Helm Rd. Lake views throughout, plus access to a nearby country club.

Gilpin Lodge (☎ 015394-88818; www .gilpinlodge.co.uk; Crook Rd; r £135-155, ste £170-195; P) This much-lauded country-house hotel reposes in 8 private hectares 2 miles from the lakeshore.

EATING & DRINKING

Lucy 4 at the Porthole (☎ 015394-42793; 3 Ash St; mains £10-20; ☺ dinner Wed-Mon) The homely old Porthole has been overhauled courtesy of the Lake District's culinary trendsetter Lucy Nicholson (founder of Lucy's on a Plate and several other Ambleside eateries).

LAKE DISTRICT

Jericho's (☎ 015394-42522; www.jerichos.co.uk; Waverley Hotel, College Rd; mains £14-18; ✆ dinner Tue-Sun) Tuck into sophisticated dishes – Gressingham duck, Scotch beef and baked portobello mushroom – in refined new surroundings on the ground floor of the Waverley Hotel.

GETTING THERE & AWAY

Windermere is the only town inside the national park accessible by train. It's on the branch line to Kendal and Oxenholme (£4, 30 minutes, 14 to 16 Monday to Saturday, 10 on Sunday), with regular connections to Manchester (£25.50, two hours, hourly) and London Euston (£123.50, four hours, eight to 10 daily Monday to Saturday, six on Sunday), and north to Glasgow (£35.50, hourly, two to 2½ hours) or Edinburgh (£35.50, 14 to 18 daily, two to three hours).

AMBLESIDE

pop 3382

Sheltering at Windermere's northerly end among a dramatic cluster of fells, Ambleside is one of the Lake District's main walking bases. Ambleside's best-known landmark is **Bridge House**, which spans the tumbling brook of **Stock Ghyll** downhill from Market Cross. Nearby at the **Armitt Museum** (☎ 015394-31212; www.armitt.com; Rydal Rd; adult £2.50; ✆ 10am-5pm), artefacts include a lock of John Ruskin's hair, a collection of botanical watercolours by Beatrix Potter, and prints by the pharmacist-turned-photographer Herbert Bell.

SLEEPING & EATING

Easedale Lodge (☎ 015394-32112; www.easedaleambleside.co.uk; Compston Rd; d £70-96) Twisted willow, zingy cushions and wrought-iron bed frames decorate this immaculate guesthouse.

Cote How Organic Guest House (☎ 015394-32765; www.bedbreakfastlakedistrict.com; Rydal, near Ambleside; s £98-£108, d £110-120; P ✆ wi-fi) You won't find a greener place in the Lakes than this ecofriendly cottage. Food is 100% local and organic, power's sourced from a green supplier, and there's a 5% discount if you hang up your car keys, too.

Waterhead Hotel (☎ 08458-504503; waterhead@elhmail.co.uk; r £106-256; P ✆) This swish town house hotel has been revamped with all the boutique trappings: ice-white walls, wall-mounted TVs, mountain-sized beds, contemporary fabrics and oodles of leather, stripped wood and slate.

Lucy's on a Plate (☎ 015394-31191; www.lucysofambleside.co.uk; Church St; lunch £6-12, dinner £15-25; ✆ 10am-9pm) Lucy's started life in 1989 as a specialist grocery, but over the last decade it's mushroomed into a full-blown gastronomic empire. This hugger-mugger bistro is Lucy's original outpost: laidback and informal, with a handwritten intro courtesy of the great lady and offbeat dishes veering from 'fruity porker' to 'fell-walker filler'.

Glass House (☎ 015394-32137; Rydal Rd; lunch £8-14, dinner £13-19; ✆ lunch & dinner) Housed in a converted watermill, this ritzy restaurant is the town's top table. Asian, Med and French flavours are underpinned by top-quality local ingredients – Herdwick lamb, Lakeland chicken, and fish from the north-coast ports.

GRASMERE

pop 1458

Even without its Romantic connections, gorgeous Grasmere would still be one of the Lakes' biggest draws. It's one of the prettiest of the Lakeland hamlets, huddled at the base of a sweeping valley dotted with woods, pastures and slate-

Lake Ullswater, Lake District National Park

coloured hills, but most of the thousands of trippers come in search of its famous former residents: opium-eating Thomas de Quincey, unruly Coleridge and grand old man William Wordsworth.

First stop is **Dove Cottage** (☎ 015394-35544; www.wordsworth.org.uk; adult/child £7.50/4.50; ⏰ 9.30am-5.30pm), where Wordsworth penned some of his great early poems and kick-started the Romantic movement. Next door is the **Wordsworth Museum & Art Gallery**, which houses a fascinating collection of letters, portraits and manuscripts relating to the Romantic movement, and regularly hosts events and poetry readings.

While most people flock to poky Dove Cottage in search of William Wordsworth, those in the know head for **Rydal Mount** (☎ 015394-33002; www.rydalmount.co.uk; adult/5-15yr £5.50/2, gardens only £3; ⏰ 9.30am-5pm daily Mar-Oct, 10am-4pm Wed-Mon Nov & Feb), the Wordsworth family home from 1813 to his death in 1850. Below the house is **Dora's Field**, which Wordsworth planted with daffodils in memory of his eldest daugh-

ter, who succumbed to tuberculosis in 1847. The house is 1.5 miles northwest of Ambleside, off the A591.

SLEEPING & EATING

Lancrigg (☎ 015394-35317; www.lancrigg.co.uk; Easedale; r £140-210; P) Originally the home of Arctic adventurer John Richardson, Lancrigg now touts itself as the Lakes' only 100% vegetarian hotel. All the rooms have individual quirks: Whittington is lodged in the attic and reached via a private staircase, Franklin has Middle Eastern rugs and a four-poster, while Richardson has a plasterwork ceiling and claw-foot bath screened by lace curtains.

ourpick Moss Grove Hotel · Organic (☎ 015394-35251; www.mossgrove.com; r £225-325; P 💻 wi-fi) If you're going to splash out in Grasmere, this ecofriendly beauty is the place to do it. Bedrooms are massive and minimal, with bespoke wallpapers, duckdown duvets, Bose hi-fis and fantastic underfloor-heated bathrooms; and the buffet breakfast overflows with organic and Fairtrade treats.

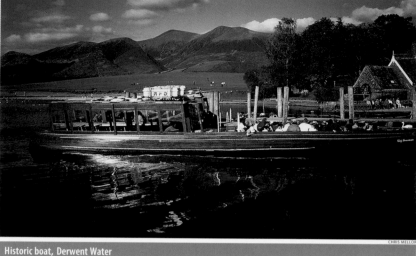

Historic boat, Derwent Water

CHRIS MELLOR

Sarah Nelson's Gingerbread Shop
(☎ 015394-35428; www.grasmeregingerbread
.co.uk; Church Stile; 12 pieces of gingerbread £3.50;
⊕ 9.15am-5.30pm Mon-Sat, 12.30-5pm Sun) Sarah
Nelson's legendary gingerbread has been
produced to the same secret recipe for the
last 150 years, and is still served by ladies
in frilly pinnies and starched bonnets.

our pick **Jumble Room** (☎ 015394-35188;
Langdale Rd; mains £13-23; ⊕ lunch & dinner Wed-
Sun) You won't find a warmer welcome
anywhere in Cumbria than at this boho
bistro, run by an energetic husband-and-
wife team with a dyed-in-the-wool dedi-
cation to Lakeland produce.

HILL TOP

Ground zero for Potterites is the picture-postcard farmhouse of **Hill Top**
(NT; ☎ 015394-36269; adult/child £5.80/2.90;
⊕ 10.30am-4.30pm Sat-Thu, garden 10.30am-
5pm mid-Mar–Oct, 10am-4pm Nov-Feb, weekends
only early Mar), where Beatrix wrote and il-
lustrated many of her famous tales. The
house features in *Samuel Whiskers*, *Tom
Kitten* and *Jemima Puddleduck*, while the

garden appeared in *Peter Rabbit*, and the
cast-iron kitchen range graced many of
Potter's underground burrows. Entry is
by timed ticket, and the queues can be
seriously daunting during the summer
holidays.

Hill Top is situated 2 miles south of
Hawkshead.

WASDALE

The valley of Wasdale is as close as you'll
get to true wilderness in the Lake District.
Surrounded by a brooding circle of scree-
scattered peaks, including the summits
of Scaféll Pike and Great Gable, it's a
world away from the bustling quays of
Windermere: the only signs of human
habitation are a couple of cottages and
a sturdy inn, dwarfed by the green-grey
arc of **Wastwater**, England's deepest
lake. Little wonder that Wasdale recently
topped a television poll to find Britain's
favourite view: you won't find a grander
spot this side of the Scottish highlands.

KESWICK

pop 5257

Ask many people for their picture-perfect image of a Lakeland town, and chances are they'll come up with something close to Keswick. This sturdy slate town is nestled alongside one of the region's most idyllic lakes, Derwent Water, a silvery curve studded by wooded islands and criss-crossed by puttering cruise boats.

You can catch a cruise across Derwent Water with the **Keswick Launch Company** (☎ 017687-72263; www.keswick-launch.co.uk). Boats call at seven landing stages: Ashness Gate, Lodore Falls, High Brandlehow, Low Brandlehow, Hawse End, Nichol End and back to Keswick. Boats leave every hour (adult/child £8.50/4.25, 50 minutes). There are at least six daily boats from mid-March to mid-November, with extra sailings in summer, plus a twilight cruise at 7.30pm (adult/child £9/4.50, one hour, July and August). Only two boats run from mid-November to mid-March.

Oakthwaite House (☎ 017687-72398; www.oakthwaite-keswick.co.uk; 35 Helvellyn St; d £58-68) Just four rooms at this upper-crust guesthouse, but all scream achingly good taste. Digital TVs, power showers, white linen and cool shades throughout, with a cosy dormer room for that attic hideaway feel, or two swanky king-size rooms if you're a sucker for fell views.

our pick **Howe Keld** (☎ 017687-72417; www.howekeld.co.uk; 5-7 The Heads; s £45, d £80-90) On the edge of Hope Park, this old workhorse has had a glamorous makeover. Gone are the chintzy wallpapers; in come luxury pocket-sprung beds, Egyptian cotton sheets and goosedown duvets, plus designer wall hangings and handmade furniture courtesy of a local joiner.

ULLSWATER & AROUND

Second only to Windermere in terms of stature, stately Ullswater stretches for 7.5 miles between Pooley Bridge and Glenridding and Patterdale in the south.

Ullswater 'Steamers' (☎ 017684-82229; www.ullswater-steamers.co.uk) set out from the Pooley Bridge jetty, stopping at Howtown and Glenridding. The company's two oldest vessels have worked on Ullswater for over a century: *Lady of the Lake* was launched in 1887, followed by *Raven* in 1889.

Up to 12 daily ferries run in summer, dropping to three in winter. Current returns from Pooley Bridge are £4.80 to Howtown, or £11.30 to Glenridding and back. Children travel half price.

NEWCASTLE-UPON-TYNE

pop 189,863

Hip, happening Newcastle will surprise the first-time visitor, especially if you've come armed with notions about hard-bitten lads and lasses going all hell-for-leather in sub-zero temperatures in a sooty, industrial landscape. There's culture, heritage and some of Britain's most elegant streets, while the absolutely brilliant and alternative Ouseburn testifies to a nightlife beyond the alco-pop shots and high-octane cheesefest favoured by so many hen and stag parties

INFORMATION

Tourist offices (www.visitnewcastlegateshead.com) Main branch (☎ 0191-277 8000; Central Arcade, Market St; ⊙ 9.30am-5.30pm Mon-Wed, Fri & Sat, to 7.30pm Thu year-round, plus 10am-4pm Sun Jun-Sep); Gateshead Library (☎ 0191-433 8420; Prince Consort Rd; ⊙ 9am-7pm Mon, Tue, Thu & Fri, to 5pm Wed, to 1pm Sat); Guildhall (☎ 0191-277 8000;

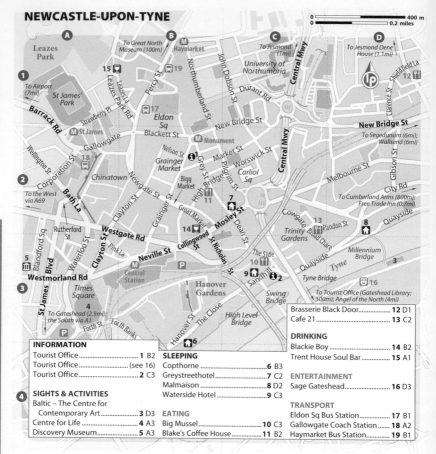

NEWCASTLE-UPON-TYNE

INFORMATION	
Tourist Office	**1** B2
Tourist Office	(see 16)
Tourist Office	**2** C3

SIGHTS & ACTIVITIES	
Baltic – The Centre for Contemporary Art	**3** D3
Centre for Life	**4** A3
Discovery Museum	**5** A3

SLEEPING	
Copthorne	**6** B3
Greystreethotel	**7** C2
Malmaison	**8** D2
Waterside Hotel	**9** C3

EATING	
Big Mussel	**10** C3
Blake's Coffee House	**11** B2

Brasserie Black Door	**12** D1
Cafe 21	**13** C2

DRINKING	
Blackie Boy	**14** B2
Trent House Soul Bar	**15** A1

ENTERTAINMENT	
Sage Gateshead	**16** D3

TRANSPORT	
Eldon Sq Bus Station	**17** B1
Gallowgate Coach Station	**18** A2
Haymarket Bus Station	**19** B1

Newcastle Quayside; 11am-6pm Mon-Fri, 9am-6pm Sat, 9am-4pm Sun); Sage Gateshead (0191-478 4222; Gateshead Quays; 9am-5pm Mon-Fri, 10am-5pm Sat, 11am-5pm Sun)

SIGHTS
TYNE BRIDGES

The most famous view in Newcastle is the cluster of Tyne bridges, and the most famous of these is the **Tyne Bridge** (1925–28), built at about the same time as (and very reminiscent of) Australia's Sydney Harbour Bridge. The quaint little **Swing Bridge** pivots in the middle to let ships through. Nearby, **High Level Bridge**, designed by Robert Stephenson, was the world's first road and railway bridge (1849). The most recent addition is the multiple-award-winning **Millennium Bridge** (aka Blinking Bridge; 2002), which opens like an eyelid to let ships pass.

CENTRE FOR LIFE

This excellent **science village** (0191-243 8210; www.life.org.uk; Scotswood Rd; adult/child £8/5.85; 10am-6pm Mon-Sat, 11am-6pm Sun, last admission 4pm) has a series of hands-on exhibits that allow you (or your kids) to discover the incredible secrets of life. The highlight is the Motion Ride, a motion simulator that, among other things, lets you 'feel' what it's like to score a goal at St James' Park and bungee jump from the Tyne Bridge.

DISCOVERY MUSEUM

Newcastle's rich history is uncovered through a fascinating series of exhibits at this excellent **museum** (☎ 0191-232 6789; www.twmuseums.org.uk; Blandford Sq; admission free; ☺ 10am-5pm Mon-Sat, 2-5pm Sun). The exhibits, spread across three floors of the former Co-operative Wholesale Society building, surround the mightily impressive 30m-long *Turbinia*, the fastest ship in the world in 1897. The different sections are all worth a look; our favourites were the self-explanatory Story of the Tyne and the interactive Science Maze.

GREAT NORTH MUSEUM

The **Great North Museum** (☎ 0191-222 8996; www.greatnorthmuseum.org) is one of the north's foremost museums of the natural sciences, archaeology, history and culture. The main exhibition hall is in the neoclassical building that once was home to the natural-history exhibits of the prestigious Hancock Museum, where new additions include a life-size model of a *Tyrannosaurus rex*. Besides the expanded contents of the Hancock, the 11 galleries also combine the contents of Newcastle University's other museums: the Greek art and archaeology of the Shefton Museum and the magnificent Museum of Antiquities, the Roman exhibits of which include an interactive model of Hadrian's Wall.

GATESHEAD

You probably didn't realise that that bit of Newcastle south of the Tyne is the 'town' of Gateshead, but local authorities are going to great lengths to put it right, even promoting the whole kit-and-caboodle-on-Tyne as 'NewcastleGateshead'.

Once a huge, dirty, yellow grain store overlooking the Tyne, **Baltic – The Centre for Contemporary Art** (☎ 0191-478 1810; www.balticmill.com; admission free; ☺ 10am-6pm Mon, Tue & Thu-Sun, to 8pm Wed) is now a huge, dirty, yellow art gallery to rival London's Tate Modern. The constantly rotating shows feature the work and installations of some of contemporary art's biggest show-stoppers.

SLEEPING
CITY CENTRE

Waterside Hotel (☎ 0191-230 0111; www.watersidehotel.com; 48-52 Sandhill, Quayside;

GRAEME HALL SNAPS / ALAMY

Grey St, Newcastle-upon-Tyne

s/d £75/80) The rooms are a tad small, but they're among the most elegant in town: lavish furnishings and heavy velvet drapes in a heritage-listed building. The location is excellent.

Copthorne (☎ 0191-222 0333; www.millenniumhotels.com; The Close, Quayside; s/d from £75/85; P ☐ wi-fi) A superb waterside location makes this modern hotel a perfect choice – especially if you pick a room overlooking the water (the Connoisseur rooms, for instance).

our pick **Greystreethotel** (☎ 0191-230 6777; www.greystreethotel.com; 2-12 Grey St; d/ste from £145/165; P) A bit of designer class along the classiest street in the city centre has been long overdue: the rooms at the Greystreethotel are gorgeous if a tad poky, all cluttered up with flat-screen TVs, big beds and handsome modern furnishings.

Malmaison (☎ 0191-245 5000; www.malmaison.com; Quayside; r from £125, ste £225-350; P ☐ wi-fi) The affectedly stylish Malmaison touch has been applied to this former warehouse with considerable success, even down to the French-speaking lifts. Big beds, sleek lighting and designer furniture flesh out the Rooms of Many Pillows. Breakfast costs £13.

JESMOND

The northeastern suburb of Jesmond is packed with budget and midrange accommodation to cater to the thousands that throng the area's bars and restaurants. Catch the Metro to Jesmond or West Jesmond, or bus 80 from near Central Station, or bus 30, 30B, 31B or 36 from Westgate Rd.

Jesmond Dene House (☎ 0191-212 3000; www.jesmonddenehouse.co.uk; Jesmond Dene Rd; s £135, d £160-200, ste £225-275; P ☐) As elegant a hotel as you'll find anywhere, this exquisite property is the perfect marriage between tradition and modern luxury.

EATING
CITY CENTRE

Blake's Coffee House (☎ 0191-261 5463; 53 Grey St; breakfast £3-4.50, sandwiches £3-4; ☼ 9am-6pm) There is nowhere better than this high-ceilinged cafe for a Sunday-morning cure on any day of the week. It's friendly, relaxed and serves up the biggest selection of coffees in town, from the gentle push of a Colombian blend to the toxic shove of Old Brown Java.

Big Mussel (☎ 0191-232 1057; www.bigmussel.co.uk; 15 The Side; mains £6-12; ☼ lunch & dinner) Mussels and other shellfish – all served with chips – are a very popular choice at this informal diner.

Cafe 21 (☎ 0191-222 0755; Trinity Gardens, Quayside; mains £14.50-22; ☼ lunch & dinner Mon-Sat) Simple but hardly plain, this elegant restaurant – all white tablecloths and smart seating – offers new interpretations of England's culinary backbone: pork and cabbage, liver and onions and a sensational Angus beef and chips.

OUSEBURN VALLEY

Brasserie Black Door (☎ 0191-260 5411; Biscuit Factory, 16 Stoddard St; mains £10-16; ☼ lunch & dinner Mon-Sat) Less of a museum restaurant and more of a restaurant in a museum, the Black Door serves up excellent modern English fare – which generally involves a twist from pretty much any other part of the world – in a bright, elegant room.

JESMOND

our pick **Jesmond Dene House** (☎ 0191-212 3000; www.jesmonddenehouse.co.uk; Jesmond Dene Rd; mains £18-22) Chef Terry Laybourne is the architect of an exquisite menu heavily influenced by the northeast: venison from County Durham, oysters from Lindisfarne and the freshest herbs plucked straight from the garden.

DRINKING
CITY CENTRE

Blackie Boy (☎ 0191-232 0730; 11 Groat Market) At first glance, this darkened old boozer looks like any old traditional pub. Look closer. The overly red lighting. The single bookcase. The large leather armchair that is rarely occupied. The signage on the toilets: 'Dick' and 'Fanny'. This place could have featured in *Twin Peaks,* which is why it's so damn popular with everyone.

ourpick **Trent House Soul Bar** (☎ 0191-261 2154; 1-2 Leazes Lane) Totally relaxed and utterly devoid of pretentiousness, it is an old-school boozer that out-cools every other bar because it isn't trying to, and because it has the best jukebox in all of England – you could spend years listening to the extraordinary collection of songs it contains.

OUSEBURN VALLEY

Free Trade Inn (☎ 0191-265 5764; St Lawrence Rd) Our favourite bar in the Ouseburn is a no nonsense boozer overlooking the Tyne that is frequented by students and long-standing patrons; it doesn't look like much but it's one of the coolest pubs in town (and the jukebox is brilliant).

Cumberland Arms (☎ 0191-265 6151; off Byker Bank, Ouseburn) Sitting on a hill at the top of the Ouseburn, this 19th-century bar has a sensational selection of ales as well as a range of Northumberland meads.

ENTERTAINMENT

Sage Gateshead (☎ 0191-443 4666; www .thesagegateshead.org; Gateshead Quays) Norman Foster's magnificent chrome-and-glass horizontal bottle is not just worth gaping at and wandering about in – it is also a superb venue to hear live music, from folk to classical orchestras.

GETTING THERE & AWAY
AIR

Newcastle International Airport (☎ 0191-286 0966; www.newcastleairport.com) is 7 miles north of the city off the A696. It has direct services to a host of UK and European cities as well as long-haul flights to Dubai.

CHRIS MELLOR

Millennium Bridge (p236)

BUS

National Express buses arrive and depart from the Gallowgate coach station. You can get to most anywhere, including London (£27, seven hours, six daily) and Manchester (£17.50, five hours, six daily). Local and regional buses leave from Haymarket or Eldon Sq bus stations. For local buses around the northeast, don't forget the excellent-value Explorer North East ticket, valid on most services for £7.

TRAIN

Newcastle is on the main rail line between London and Edinburgh. Services go to Alnmouth (for connections to Alnwick; £8.40, 30 minutes, four daily), Berwick (£23.80, 45 minutes, every two hours), Edinburgh (£42, 1½ hours, half-hourly), London King's Cross (£124.50, three hours, half-hourly) and York (£21.40, 45 minutes, every 20 minutes). There's also the scenic Tyne Valley Line west to Carlisle.

GETTING AROUND

TO/FROM THE AIRPORT & FERRY TERMINAL

The airport is linked to town by the Metro (£2.80, 20 minutes, every 15 minutes). There's a taxi rank at the terminal; it costs about £18 to the city centre.

PUBLIC TRANSPORT

There's a large bus network, but the best means of getting around is the excellent underground Metro, with fares from £1.30. The DaySaver (£4.50, £3.70 after 9am) gives unlimited Metro travel for one day, and the DayRover (adult/child £5.80/3) gives unlimited travel on all modes of transport in Tyne and Wear for one day.

AROUND NEWCASTLE

ANGEL OF THE NORTH

One of the world's most frequently viewed works of art is this extraordinary 200-tonne, rust- coloured human frame – we are, of course, referring to the Gateshead Flasher – with wings towering over the A1 (M) about 5 miles south of Newcastle; if you're driving, you just can't miss it. At 20m high and with a wingspan wider than a Boeing 767, Antony Gormley's most successful work is the country's largest sculpture. Buses 723 and 724 from Eldon Sq station, or 21, 21A and 21B from Pilgrim St, will take you there.

SEGEDUNUM

The last strong post of Hadrian's Wall was the fort of **Segedunum** (☎ 0191-295 5757; **www.twmuseums.org.uk; adult/child/concession £4/free/2.25;** ⏲ **9.30am-5.30pm Apr-Aug, 10am-5pm Sep, 10am-3.30pm Nov-Mar**), 6 miles east of Newcastle at Wallsend. Beneath the 35m tower, which you can climb for some terrific views, is an absorbing site that includes a reconstructed Roman bathhouse (with steaming pools and frescoes) and a fascinating museum that gives visitors a well-rounded picture of life during Roman times. Take the Metro to Wallsend.

HADRIAN'S WALL

What exactly have the Romans ever done for us? The aqueducts. Law and order. And this enormous wall, built between AD 122 and 128 to keep 'us' (Romans, subdued Brits) in and 'them' (hairy Pictish barbarians from Scotland) out. Hadrian's Wall, named in honour of the emperor who ordered it built, was one of Rome's greatest engineering projects, a spectacular 73-mile testament to ambition and the

Left: *Angel of the North*; Right: Walking the Pennine Way (p243), Hadrian's Wall

LEFT: DAVID ELSE; RIGHT: DAVID ELSE

practical Roman mind. The official portal for the whole of Hadrian's Wall Country is www.hadrians-wall.org, an excellent, attractive and easily navigable site.

GETTING THERE & AROUND
BUS

The AD 122 Hadrian's Wall bus (three hours, six daily June to September) is a hail-and-ride guided service that runs between Hexham (the 9.15am service starts in Wallsend) and Bowness-on-Solway. Bus 185 covers the route the rest of the year (Monday to Saturday only).

The Hadrian's Wall Rover ticket (adult/child one day £7.50/4.80, three day £15/9.60) is available from the driver or the tourist offices, where you can also get timetables.

TRAIN

The railway line between Newcastle and Carlisle (Tyne Valley Line) has stations at Corbridge, Hexham, Haydon Bridge, Bardon Mill, Haltwhistle and Brampton.

This service runs daily, but not all trains stop at all stations.

CHESTERS ROMAN FORT & MUSEUM

The best-preserved remains of a Roman cavalry fort in England are at **Chesters** (EH; ☎ 01434-681379; admission £4.50; ⏰ 9.30am-6pm Apr-Sep, 10am-4pm Oct-Mar), set among idyllic green woods and meadows and originally constructed to house a unit of troops from Asturias in northern Spain. They include part of a bridge (beautifully constructed and best appreciated from the eastern bank) across the River North Tyne, four well-preserved gatehouses, an extraordinary bathhouse and an underfloor heating system. Take bus 880 or 882 from Hexham (5.5 miles away); it is also on the route of Hadrian's Wall bus AD 122.

VINDOLANDA ROMAN FORT & MUSEUM

The extensive site of **Vindolanda** (☎ 01434-344277; www.vindolanda.com; admission £5.20, with Roman Army Museum £8; ⏰ 10am-6pm Apr-Sep, to

DAVID TOMLINSON

Durham Cathedral

↘ DURHAM CATHEDRAL

Durham's most famous building – and the main reason for visiting unless some-one you know is at university here – has earned superlative praise for so long that to add more would be redundant; the definitive structure of the Anglo-Norman Romanesque style is bloody gorgeous. We would definitely put it in our top-church-in-England list – as do many others, including Unesco, which declared it a World Heritage Site in 1986.

The cathedral is enormous and has a pretty fortified look; this is due to the fact that although it may have been built to pay tribute to God and to house the holy bones of St Cuthbert, it also needed to withstand any attack by the Scots and Northumberland tribes who weren't too thrilled by the arrival of the Normans a few years before.

The superb nave is dominated by massive, powerful piers – every second one round, with an equal height and circumference of 6.6m, and carved with geometric designs. The central tower dates from 1262, but was damaged in a fire caused by lightning in 1429, and was unsatisfactorily patched up until it was entirely rebuilt in 1470. The western towers were added in 1217–26. Built in 1175 and renovated 300 years later, the **Galilee Chapel** is one of the most beautiful parts.

The cathedral has worthwhile **guided tours** (adult/child/student £4/free/3; 🕙 10.30am, 11.30am & 2.30pm Mon & Sat).

There's a splendid view from the top of the **tower** (adult/child £3/1.50; 🕙 10am-4pm Mon-Sat mid-Apr–Sep, to 3pm Oct-Mar), but you have got to climb 325 steps to enjoy it.

Things you need to know: ☎ 0191-386 4266; www.durhamcathedral.co.uk; donation requested; 🕙 9.30am-8pm mid-Jun–Aug, 9.30am-6.15pm Mon-Sat & 12.30-5pm Sun Sep–mid-Jun, private prayer & services only 7.30-9.30am Mon-Sat & 7.45am-12.30pm Sun year-round

5pm Feb, Mar, Oct & Nov) offers a fascinating glimpse into the daily life of a Roman garrison town. The time-capsule museum displays leather sandals, signature Roman toothbrush-flourish helmet decorations, and countless writing tablets such as a student's marked work ('sloppy'), and a parent's note with a present of socks and underpants (things haven't changed – in this climate you can never have too many).

It's 1.5 miles north of Bardon Mill between the A69 and B6318 and a mile from Once Brewed.

HOUSESTEADS ROMAN FORT & MUSEUM

The wall's most dramatic site – and the best-preserved Roman fort in the whole country – is at **Housesteads** (EH; ☎ 01434-344363; admission £4.50; ☿ 10am-6pm Apr-Sep, to 4pm Oct-Mar). From here, high on a ridge and covering 2 hectares, you can survey the moors of Northumberland National Park, and the snaking wall, with a sense of awe at the landscape and the aura of the Roman lookouts.

Housesteads is 2.5 miles north of Bardon Mill on the B6318, and about 3 miles from Once Brewed.

NORTHUMBERLAND

Take a deep breath and prepare yourself for the last great 'undiscovered' wilderness in England, the utterly wild and stunningly beautiful landscapes of Northumberland.

NORTHUMBERLAND NATIONAL PARK

England's last great wilderness is the 398 sq miles of natural wonderland that make up Northumberland National Park; spread about the soft swells of the Cheviot Hills are spiky moors of autumn-coloured

---

THE PENNINE WAY

The North Pennines are billed as 'England's last wilderness', and if you like to walk in quiet and fairly remote areas, these hills are the best in England. Long routes through this area include the famous Pennine Way, which crosses the region between the Yorkshire Dales and the Scottish border. The whole route is over 250 miles, but the 70-mile section between Bowes and Hadrian's Wall would be a fine four-day taster.

---

heather and gorse, and endless acres of forest guarding the deep, colossal Kielder Water (Europe's largest artificial lake, which holds 200,000 million litres and has a shoreline of 27 miles).

The park runs from Hadrian's Wall in the south, takes in the Simonside Hills in the east and runs into the Cheviot Hills along the Scottish border.

For information, contact the **Northumberland National Park** (☎ 01434-605555; www.northumberland-national -park.org.uk; Eastburn, South Park, Hexham). Besides the tourist offices mentioned in this section, there are relevant offices in **Once Brewed** (☎ 01434-344396; ☿ 10am-5pm mid-Mar–May, Sep & Oct, 9.30am-6pm Jun-Aug) as well as **Ingram** (☎ 01665 578890; ingram@ nnpa.org.uk; ☿ 10am-5pm Easter-Oct). All the tourist offices handle accommodation bookings.

ALNWICK

The outwardly imposing **Alnwick Castle** (☎ 01665-510777; www.alnwickcastle.com; adult/child/concession £10.50/4.50/9; ☿ 10am-6pm Apr-Oct), ancestral home of the Duke of Northumberland and a favourite set

Bamburgh Castle

CHRIS MELLOR

Alnwick Garden (☎ 01665-510777; www
.alnwickgarden.com; adult/child/concession £10/
free/7.50; ☹ 10am-7pm Jun-Sep, to 6pm Apr, May
& Oct, to 4pm Nov-Jan, to 5pm Feb & Mar) is one of
the northeast's great success stories. Since
the project began in 2000, the 4.8-hectare
walled garden has been transformed from
a derelict site into a spectacle that easily
exceeds the grandeur of the castle's 19th-
century gardens, a series of magnificent
green spaces surrounding the breathtaking Grand Cascade – 120 separate jets
spurting over 30,000L of water down 21
weirs for everyone to marvel at and kids
to splash around in.

BAMBURGH

Bamburgh Castle (☎ 01668-214515; www
.bamburghcastle.com; adult/child £7/2.40;
☹ 10am-5pm Mar-Oct) is built around a powerful 11th-century Norman keep probably
built by Henry II, although its name is a
derivative of Bebbanburgh, after the wife
of Anglo-Saxon ruler Aedelfrip, whose fortified home occupied this basalt outcrop
500 years earlier. The castle played a key
role in the border wars of the 13th and
14th centuries, and in 1464 was the first
English castle to fall as the result of a sus-
tained artillery attack, by Richard Neville,
Earl of Warwick, during the Wars of the
Roses. It was restored in the 19th century
by the great industrialist Lord Armstrong,
who also turned his passion to Cragside,
1 mile north of Rothbury, and was the
owner of Jesmond Dene House (p238)
in Newcastle. The great halls within are
still home to the Armstrong family.

for film-makers (it was Hogwarts for
the first couple of *Harry Potter* films) has
changed little since the 14th century. The
interior is sumptuous and extravagant;
the six rooms open to the public – staterooms, dining room, guard chamber and
library – have an incredible display of
Italian paintings, including Titian's *Ecce
Homo* and many Canalettos. The castle
is set in parklands designed by Lancelot
'Capability' Brown.

As spectacular a bit of green-thumb art-
istry as you'll see anywhere in England,

↘WALES

Castle Arcade, Cardiff (p256)

NEIL SETCHFIELD

WALES

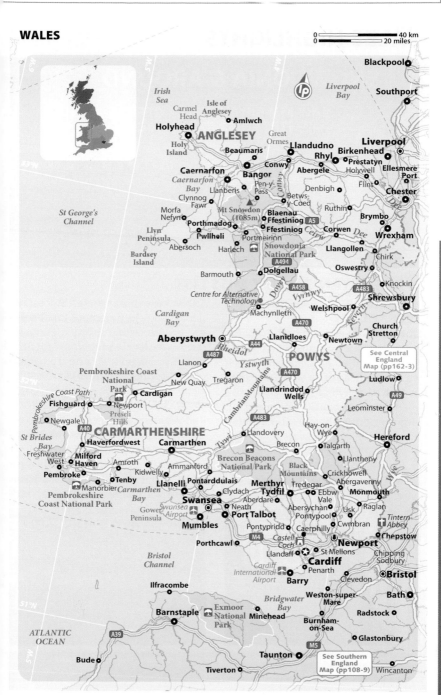

WALES HIGHLIGHTS

2

⬀ CARDIFF

After decades in the doldrums, the Welsh **capital** (p256) is very much a city on the up. Boasting a brand spanking new stadium, a shiny new opera house and a burgeoning cultural scene (not to mention a striking new architectural showpiece for the devolved Welsh parliament), Cardiff is Wales' coolest city by a long stretch – you'll need at least a couple of days to take in all the sights.

3

⬀ CAERNARFON CASTLE

Wales certainly isn't short on fortresses, but the top of the heap has to be **Caernarfon** (p274), lodged between the Menai Strait and the snowy peaks of Snowdonia. Part of a special World Heritage Site designated by Unesco, it's a real showstopper – ringed by dramatic battlements and moody watchtowers supposedly modelled on the ancient city of Constantinople.

4

⬈ MOUNT SNOWDON

The highest peak in Wales (and the second highest in Britain, topped only by Ben Nevis in Scotland), **Mt Snowdon** (p274) is a must-climb even if you're not a hardcore hiker. There are six main trails to the top, or you can cheat by taking a cable-car!

5

⬈ GOWER PENINSULA

For coastal scenery, there's nowhere better than gorgeous **Gower** (p262), which stretches out into the Bristol Channel just to the east of Swansea. It was the first spot in the UK to be earmarked as an Area of Outstanding Natural Beauty in 1956, and it's littered with secluded beaches and lovely cliff-top walks.

6

⬈ PORTMEIRION

Wales' wackiest attraction is the seaside fantasy-land of **Portmeirion** (p273), created by the eccentric Welsh architect Sir Clough Williams-Ellis. Brimming with follies, colonnades, pastel-coloured palaces and other architectural oddities, it provided the perfect setting for the classic cult TV series *The Prisoner* in the 1960s.

2 DAVID ELSE; 3 GREG GAWLOWSKI; 4 GRANT DIXON; 5 CHERYL FORBES; 6 NEIL SETCHFIELD

2 Wales Millennium Centre (p259), Cardiff; 3 Caernarfon Castle (p274); 4 Mt Snowdon ranges (p271); 5 Rhossili Bay (p262), Gower Peninsula; 6 Portmeirion (p273)

WALES' BEST...

⬧ MONUMENTS

- **Cardiff Castle** (p258) The capital's stronghold has a chequered past.
- **Caerphilly** (p261) Classic 13th-century fortress.
- **Castell Coch** (p261) The Bute family's summer retreat.
- **Conwy** (p269) Romantic ruins built to defend the Welsh border.
- **St David's Cathedral** (p264) One of Wales' finest cathedrals.

⬧ PLACES WITH A VIEW

- **Brecon Beacons** (p266) Explore grassy moors and sunlit uplands.
- **Pembrokeshire Coast** (p263) Savour coastal splendour.
- **Skomer Island** (p264) Spot puffins, guillemots and cormorants.
- **Conwy Castle** (p269) See all the way to Snowdon on a clear day.
- **Mount Snowdon** (p271) Where else?

⬧ TRAIN TRIPS

- **Heart of Wales Line** (p262) Catch Wales' most scenic train ride.
- **Llangollen Steam Railway** (p270) Vintage steam trains ply the Llangollen-Carrog line.
- **Great Orme Tramway** (p268) Catch the cable-car up Llandudno's landmark.
- **Snowdon Mountain Railway** (p272) The easy way to the top!

⬧ CULTURAL EXPERIENCES

- **Hay on Wye** (p266) Britain's biggest book festival.
- **Eisteddfod** (p272) Wales' major Celtic celebration, held annually in Llangollen.
- **National Museum Cardiff** (p256) World-class art meets Welsh history galore.
- **Laugharne** (p263) Dylan Thomas' old stomping ground.

LEFT: GREG GAWLOWSKI; RIGHT: EOIN CLARKE

Left: National Museum Cardiff (p256); Right: Crib Goch (p274), Snowdonia National Park

THINGS YOU NEED TO KNOW

⬖ VITAL STATISTICS

- **Area** 8043 sq miles
- **Population** 2.7 million
- **Best time to go** Spring or Autumn

⬖ AREAS IN A NUTSHELL

- **North Wales** (p267) Moodily marvellous.
- **Mid Wales** (p265) The Welsh heartland.
- **Snowdonia National Park** (p271) Britain's third biggest national park.
- **South Wales** (p262) Where coal and coast collide.
- **Cardiff** (p256) Wales' first city.
- **Powys** (p267) Rolling countryside chock-full of wildlife.

⬖ ADVANCE PLANNING

- **Two months before** Make accommodation plans – especially if you're interested in the Eisteddfod (p272) and other major celebrations.
- **One month before** Book train and bus tickets for the best deals.
- **Two weeks before** Confirm opening times and prices for the major sights.

⬖ RESOURCES

- **Visit Wales** (www.visitwales.co.uk) The major tourist site.
- **Visit Cardiff** (www.visitcardiff.com) The capital low-down.
- **Snowdonia National Park** (www.eryri-npa.co.uk) In Welsh and English.
- **Pembrokeshire Coast** (www.visitpembrokeshirecoast.org.uk)
- **Visit South Wales** (www.visitsouthwales.com)

⬖ GETTING AROUND

- **Bus** Can be erratic outside the big cities.
- **Train** Wales has good rail links.
- **Car** Gives you maximum freedom, but be prepared for some challenging driving.

⬖ BE FOREWARNED

- **Festivals** Accommodation is practically impossible to find during major festivals such as the Eisteddfod and the Hay Book Festival.
- **Weather** Wales is one of the wettest areas in Britain, so remember to leave space in your suitcase for wellies and wet-weather gear.
- **Welsh** Speaking a few words in Welsh can help break the ice, but remember not everyone's a Welsh speaker! Try hello – *sut mae* (pronounced sit mai), thanks – *diolch* (pronounced dee-olkh) and goodbye – *hwyl fawr* (hueyl vowrr).

WALES ITINERARIES

CARDIFF Three Days

Three days isn't long to take in all Wales has to offer, so it's probably a good idea to dedicate yourself to exploring **(1) Cardiff** (p256) in depth. The Welsh capital has received a new lease of life since devolution in the late 1990s, and it's bursting with things to see and do: the city's stately **castle** (p258) makes a great place to start on day one, and you should also have time for the **National Museum** (p256). On day two explore the revitalised area around Cardiff Bay, home to the Welsh Parliament, **Y Senedd** (p259) and the landmark **Millennium Centre** (p259) and **Llandaff Cathedral** (p259). Day three's reserved for a day trip to two of Wales' most charismatic castles: **(2) Castell Coch** (p261) and **(3) Caerphilly** (p261).

NORTHERN EXPOSURE Five Days

This five-day stint sticks mainly to Wales' scenic northern corners, beginning at the stately home of **(1) Erddig** (p271) in the east before visiting **(2) Llangollen** (p269), which famously hosts the annual Celtic knees-up known as the International Eisteddfodd held every July. Then it's on to lovely **(3) Llandudno** (p268), one of North Wales' prettiest seaside towns, and a useful base for exploring the nearby castle at **(4) Conwy** (p269). Swing round via **(5) Caernarfon Castle** (p274), where you'll be treated to views over the Menai Strait all the way to the island of Anglesey. Venture onwards to the Welsh version of Wonderland at **(6) Portmeirion** (p273). From here it's a short hop to **(7) Harlech Castle** (p273) and Wales' greenest tourist attraction, **(8) Centre for Alternative Technology** (p270). Alternatively you could head inland to explore the superb scenery of **(9) Snowdonia National Park** (p271).

WILD WALES One Week

The regal, rugged Welsh landscape has long been a favourite playground for lovers of the great outdoors. Britain's rock-climbers, mountaineers and hardy hikers have been testing their mettle around the hills and valleys of Wales for decades, and if you like your hills high and your views grand, you won't find a finer spot. (1) Snowdonia National Park (p271) is the obvious place to begin your outdoors adventure: the three activity centres can help you try out a whole host of adventure sports, ranging from white-water rafting to rock-climbing. Once you've settled your nerves, a hike up to the top of (2) Snowdon (p274) is a rite of passage for every Welsh visitor: most people cheat and take the Snowdon Mountain Railway (p272), but you'll feel a whole lot better about yourself if you reach the summit under your own steam.

Once you've explored Snowdonia, you'll find plenty of other wild spots scattered around Wales. The (3) Offa's Dyke Path (p267) is one of the most popular long-distance walks in Wales; if you haven't got time to attempt the whole thing, you could always take it in small day-long chunks instead. Further south, there's more world-class walking in the (4) Brecon Beacons (p266) and around the spectacular coastal paths of the (5) Gower Peninsula (p262), (6) Carmarthen Bay and the picturesque (7) Pembrokeshire Coast (p263).

WALES

DISCOVER WALES

For centuries, Wales – or *Cymru*, to give it its Welsh name – was an independent nation, governed by its own laws, language and Celtic customs. Although Welsh culture was dealt a blow following the English conquest in the 13th century, the flame of independence never quite died and, following the long-awaited acts of devolution in 1998, Wales finally regained control over its own political destiny. You can feel the crackle of change all over Wales these days; after decades in the doldrums, this is a country that is really rediscovering its sense of self. Crumbling castles and cultural landmarks have been restored; Cardiff's dilapidated waterfront has been polished up; and even Wales' most celebrated landmark, Mt Snowdon, has received a brand-spanking-new 21st-century visitor centre. Whether it's stalking the cliffs of the Gower Peninsula or tackling the trails of Snowdonia, you certainly won't regret a week or two devoted to Wales' wonderlands.

CARDIFF (CAERDYDD)

CARDIFF (CAERDYDD)

☎ 029 / pop 320,000

The capital of Wales since only 1955, the city has embraced its new role with vigour, emerging as one of Britain's leading urban centres in the 21st century. Post devolution, Cardiff has gone from strength to strength with a redefined cityscape, a creative buzz, a cultural renaissance and a vibrant nocturnal life that punches well above its weight for a city of its size.

HISTORY

You can thank the Romans for Cardiff. They built a fort here in AD 75, and the city's name is most likely derived from Caer Tâf (Taff Fort) or Caer Didi (Didius' Fort), referring to a Roman general, Aulus Didius.

Following the Norman Conquest of 1066 Robert Fitzhamon, conqueror of Glamorgan, built a castle (the remains of which stand in the grounds of Cardiff Castle) and a small town soon developed. When the southern Welsh valleys kickstarted the iron-making and coal-mining boom in the 19th century, Cardiff started to flourish under the aristocratic Bute family of Scotland.

Cardiff was proclaimed the first ever capital of Wales in 1955. Renovations began in the mid-1980s to convert the forlorn dockside, giving rise to Cardiff Bay, the new Senedd (Wales' independent parliament) and the stunning Wales Millennium Centre.

INFORMATION

Cardiff Bay Visitor Centre (☎ 2046 3833; Harbour Dr, Britannia Quay; ☽ 9.30am-5pm Mon-Sat, 10.30am-5pm Sun, to 6pm May-Oct)
Police station (☎ 2022 2111; King Edward VII Ave)
Tourist office (☎ 0870 121 1258; www.visit cardiff.com; Old Library, The Hayes; ☽ 9.30am-6pm Mon-Sat, 10am-4pm Sun; ▣)

SIGHTS & ACTIVITIES

NATIONAL MUSEUM CARDIFF

Sitting proudly at the northern edge of the city centre is the fantastic **National Museum Cardiff** (☎ 2039 7951; www.mu seumwales.ac.uk; Cathays Park; admission free; ☽ 10am-5pm Tue-Sun). With international-quality galleries and enthralling natural history exhibits, this museum, which recently completed a major refurbishment program, is a treat for adults and kids alike.

The **national art gallery** houses the largest Impressionist collection outside Paris, featuring works by Claude Monet, Camille Pissarro, Paul Cézanne, Henri Matisse and Pierre-Auguste Renoir. Welsh artists hold their own: Richard Wilson, Thomas Jones and Gwen and Augustus John feature prominently, the latter's portrait of Dylan Thomas being a beguiling treasure.

WALES

CARDIFF (CAERDYDD)

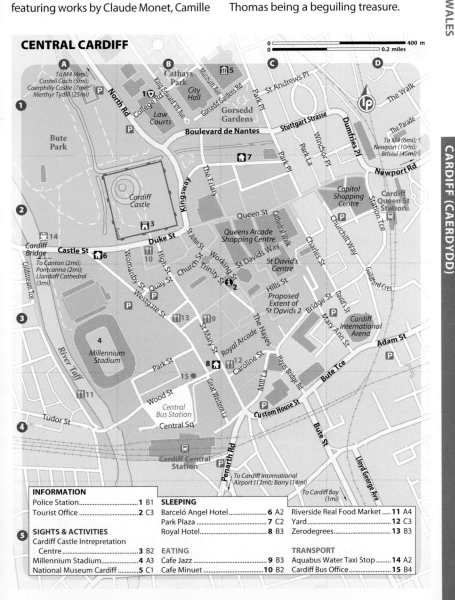

CENTRAL CARDIFF

INFORMATION			
Police Station.................................**1** B1	**SLEEPING**		
Tourist Office...............................**2** C3	Barceló Angel Hotel.....................**6** A2	Riverside Real Food Market.....**11** A4	
	Park Plaza..**7** C2	Yard...**12** C3	
SIGHTS & ACTIVITIES	Royal Hotel.......................................**8** B3	Zerodegrees......................................**13** B3	
Cardiff Castle Intrepretation			
Centre...**3** B2	**EATING**	**TRANSPORT**	
Millennium Stadium...................**4** A3	Cafe Jazz..**9** B3	Aquabus Water Taxi Stop.........**14** A2	
National Museum Cardiff.........**5** C1	Cafe Minuet.....................................**10** B2	Cardiff Bus Office........................**15** B4	

MANFRED GOTTSCHALK

Cardiff Castle

⟩ CARDIFF CASTLE

Dazzling Victorian style and mock-Gothic folly make Cardiff Castle an entertaining visit. Although far from a traditional Welsh castle (it's more a collection of disparate castles around a central green), the site encompasses practically the whole history of Cardiff and is, rightly, the city's leading attraction.

To the right of the entrance the remains of a 3rd-century-AD Roman fort (that guarded the River Taff) contrast with the motte-and-bailey of the 12th-century Norman castle. Opposite the fort, the neo-Gothic Victorian main buildings house the reconstructed home of the coal-rich Butes.

The romantic decor that adorns their residence is a particular highlight, medieval in style following the whims of the eccentric third marquis. It includes a gloriously over-the-top fireplace, a 199-mirrored bedroom ceiling, a minstrels' gallery and a clutch of decorative knights.

Things you need to know: ☎ 2087 8100; www.cardiffcastle.com; Castle St; adult/child grounds only £3.50/2.20, incl castle tour £8.95/6.35; ☼ 9am-6pm Mar-Oct, 9.30am-5pm Nov-Feb

Animal treats include a 9m-long humpback whale skeleton and the world's largest turtle (2.9m by 2.7m). In the mineral world, booming films of volcanic eruptions and footage of the soaring Welsh landscape trace evolution through 4600 million years.

MILLENNIUM STADIUM

The scepticism that greeted the decision to build a £110m new stadium on

the grounds of the old Cardiff Arms Park disappeared with the first drop-kick at the spectacular **Millennium Stadium** (☎ tours 2082 2228, box office 0870 558 2582; www.millenniumstadium.co.uk; tours adult/child £6.50/4; ☼ 10am-5pm Mon-Sat, 10am-4pm Sun & bank holidays).

CARDIFF BAY

Thirty years ago Cardiff Bay was derelict and forlorn, its industrial backbone broken and its soul ravaged. Today Cardiff Bay has gone from industrial wasteland to yuppie fantasy. To reach the Bay, walk 1 mile south from Central station down Bute St, or take the Cardiff Bus 6, the Baycar, which loops between the Bay and the city (£1.20, 15 minutes, every 10 to 15 minutes daily).

Another great way to approach the Bay is by the **Aquabus water taxi** (☎ 07500 556556; adult/chlld return £5/3), which shuttles around Mermaid Quay and heads up the Taff via South Barrage to the city (30 minutes, hourly from 10.30am to 5.30pm).

THE WATERFRONT
Cardiff Bay is home to the new building for the National Assembly for Wales, **Y Senedd** (☎ 0845 010 5500; www.assemblywales .org; Cardiff Bay), a distinctive glass, steel and slate construction with a canopy roof on the waterfront.

WALES MILLENNIUM CENTRE
In November 2004, the belated opening of the **Wales Millennium Centre** (☎ box office 0870 040 2000; www.wmc.org.uk; Bute Pl) sealed the renaissance of the Bay. The venue was designed by Welsh architect Jonathan Adams. Today it is Wales' premier arts complex and home to, among others, the Welsh National Opera.

LLANDAFF CATHEDRAL
In a peaceful suburb, 2 miles north of the city following Cathedral Rd to the A4119, Llandaff is home to the fine-looking **Llandaff Cathedral** (☎ 2056 4554; www.lland affcathedral.org.uk; Cathedral Rd; admission free).

Built on the site of a 6th-century monastery, the cathedral itself dates from 1130 and has fulfilled various roles over the centuries. Today its mishmash of styles is testimony to its disturbed history – one tower dates from the 15th century, the other from the 19th.

FESTIVALS & EVENTS
Cardiff Festival (☎ 2087 2087; www.cardiff -festival.com) The highlight of the summer is a multievent festival, from late June to early August around Cardiff Bay, with attractions from open-air theatre, via an international food and drink festival to the Cardiff Big Weekend (early August) with the Lord Mayor's Parade.

SLEEPING
Barceló Angel Hotel (☎ 2064 9200; www .barceloangelcardiff.com; Castle St; s/d from £65/115; ▣) Now under new management and recently refurbished, the Victorian Angel Hotel retains its stately rooms, many with castle views.

Royal Hotel (☎ 2055 0750; www.theroy alhotelcardiff.com; 10 St Mary St; standard/deluxe d £154/174; P ▣) Central Cardiff's latest boutique hotel, located just across from the train station, has all the modernist looks and urban style but at the time of our visit was let down by poor service and erratic internet access.

Park Plaza (☎ 2011 1111; www.parkplaza cardiff.com; Greyfriars Rd; d from £125; P ▣ wi-fi) The most luxurious property in town has all the five-star facilities you would expect from a business-oriented hotel. It's the only hotel in central Cardiff to offer free wi-fi internet, and boats a deservedly popular spa, health and leisure centre.

our pick Jolyons Hotel (☎ 2048 8775; www .jolyons.co.uk; Bute Cres, Cardiff Bay; d £90-150; ▣) Budget boutique accommodation at the heart of the Bay, this stylish town house currently boasts six rooms with period furniture and stylish fittings.

St David's Hotel & Spa (☎ 2045 4045; www.thestdavidshotel.com; Havannah St, Cardiff Bay; r from £260; P ▣) Epitomising Cardiff Bay's transformation from wasteland to stylish place-to-be, this landmark development is now under new management

WALES

CARDIFF (CAERDYDD)

Waterfront (p259), Cardiff

DAVID ELSE

and emerging from renovation works. It's five-star all the way, with a particularly popular spa and treatment centre.

EATING

our pick **Cafe Minuet** (☎ 2034 1794; 42 Castle Arcade; mains £5-7; ⏰ 10am-5pm Mon-Sat) A classical music-themed cafe with an Italian-influenced menu of dishes named after the great composers.

Yard (☎ 2022 7577; 42-43 St Mary St; mains £7-12; 🖥) The stand-out option in the chain-heavy Brewery Quarter, located on the site of the old Brains Brewery dating from 1713, this bar attracts a chilled-out daytime crowd, cranking up the music and the vibe by night.

Cafe Jazz (☎ 2023 2161; www.cafejazzcardiff.com; St Mary St; 2-/3-course set menus from £7.95/10.95; ⏰ lunch & dinner, Sun noon-5pm) Cool jazz joint by night, relaxed cafe by day. You can kick back here with decent food and a regular program of jazz events, high-profile gigs and informal jam sessions.

Zerodegrees (☎ 2022 9494; www.zerodegrees.co.uk; 27 Watergate St; pizzas & pastas £7-9)

This huge microbrewery-cum-restaurant combines all-day food with six, lip-smacking, artisan-crafted beers.

For an alfresco Sunday brunch, the **Riverside Real Food Market** (☎ 2019 0036; Fitzhamon Embankment; ⏰ 10am-2pm Sun) is a weekly haven of local goodies, located opposite the Millennium Stadium.

Woods Bar & Brasserie (☎ 2049 2400; www.woods-brasserie.com; Pilotage Bldg, Stuart St, Cardiff Bay; mains £16-21.50; ⏰ lunch & dinner Mon-Sat year-round, dinner Sun Jun-Sep) Featuring floor-to-ceiling windows and light-wood touches, Woods is a very classy eatery located in a converted dockside building.

Bayside Brasserie (☎ 2035 8444; www.baysidebrasserie.com; Unit Upper 14, Mermaid Quay, Cardiff Bay; mains around £17, 2-course set menus £14.95) Classy and defiantly chic, the Bayside is built around a light-filled atrium with panoramic views across the bay.

GETTING THERE & AWAY
AIR
Cardiff International Airport (☎ 01446-711111; www.cwlfly.com), 12 miles southwest

of the centre in Rhoose, near Barry, now has direct connections to over 50 destinations. Main flight operators:

Aer Arann (☎ 0800 587 2324; www.aerarran.com)

bmibaby (☎ 0871 224 0224; www.bmibaby.com)

Eastern Airways (☎ 0870 366 9100; www.easternairways.com)

Highland Airways (☎ 0870 777 0915; www.highland airways.co.uk)

KLM (☎ 0870 507 4074; www.klm.com)

Skybus (☎ 01736-334224; www.skybus.co.uk)

Thomsonfly (☎ 0870 190 0737; www.thomsonfly.com)

Zoom (☎ 0870 240 0055; www.flyzoom.com)

BUS

Buses currently congregate at Central bus station, located on Wood St opposite Cardiff Central train station, but work is now under way to demolish the terminus buildings. Pick up bus maps and details of changes at the **Cardiff Bus office** (☎ 20 666 444; www.cardiffbus.com; Wood St; ☼ 8.30am-5.30pm Mon-Fri, 9am-4.30pm Sat).

The First bus Shuttle100 travels from Cardiff to Swansea (peak/off-peak £6/5 return, one hour, hourly Monday to Saturday, reduced services Sunday).

National Express (☎ 0871 81 81 81; www.nationalexpress.com) bus 202 serves Bristol (£7.20, one hour, seven daily), and coach 509 serves London (£21.30, 3½ hours, hourly).

TRAIN

Cardiff Central train station, in the south of town, handles mainline services; **Valley Lines** (☎ 20 44 99 44; www.arrivatrainswales.com) local services also use Queen St Station to the northeast.

Regular services include Birmingham (£13.50, two hours, at least half-hourly),

London Paddington (£24, two hours, at least half-hourly) and Shrewsbury (£29.50, two hours, half-hourly).

GETTING AROUND
TO/FROM THE AIRPORT
Bus X91 Airport Express shuttles between the airport and Central bus station (30 minutes, at least hourly). Regular trains run between Cardiff International Airport station (bus link to the airport) and Cardiff Central station (35 minutes, hourly). A taxi to the city centre costs about £25.

AROUND CARDIFF

To the north of Cardiff the hills and valleys bear testimony to Wales' industrial heritage, and are home to some of its impressive castles.

CASTELL COCH
Fairy tales could be made at **Castell Coch** (Cadw; ☎ 2081 0101; adult/child £3.70/3.30; ☼ 9.30am-5pm Apr, May & Oct, 9am-6pm Jun-Sep, 9.30am-4pm Mon-Sat & 11am-4pm Sun Nov-Mar), a Victorian fantasy built on the foundations of a real fortress. This was the summer retreat of Cardiff's coal kings, the Bute family and, as with Cardiff Castle (p258), the architect William Burges did a fine job of creating a fairy-tale hideaway. The castle is gloriously over-the-top, featuring a tremendous drawing room decorated with mouldings from *Aesop's Fables*. Located 5 miles northwest of Cardiff on the A470.

CAERPHILLY CASTLE
It would be difficult to find a more beautiful medieval fortress than 13th-century **Caerphilly Castle** (Cadw; ☎ 2088 3143; adult/child £3.50/3; ☼ 9.30am-5pm Apr, May & Oct, 9.30am-6pm Jun-Sep, 9.30am-4pm Mon-Sat, 11am-4pm Sun Nov-Mar), complete with three

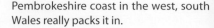

moats, six portcullises and five defensive doorways, not to mention a leaning tower that puts Pisa to shame (gashed open by subsidence). Located 7 miles northwest of Cardiff on the A469.

Stagecoach (www.stagecoachbus.com) bus 26 runs on to Caerphilly Castle from Castell Coch (45 minutes).

The new **Three Castles Pass (adult/child £12/8)** offers reduced-price entry to Castell Coch, Caerphilly Castle and Cardiff Castle.

SOUTH WALES

Stretching over 100 miles from historic border-town Chepstow in the east, via the industrial heritage of the valleys, to the big-sky and sea views of the jagged

Lady Bute's bedroom, Castell Coch (p261)

GREG GAWLOWSKI

Pembrokeshire coast in the west, south Wales really packs it in.

GETTING THERE & AROUND

Frequent train and bus services run from England, especially to Cardiff and Swansea. The famously scenic **Heart of Wales line** (☎ 01597-822053; www.heart-of -wales.co.uk) terminates in Swansea.

Arriva Trains (☎ 0845 6061 660; www.ar rivatrains wales.co.uk) offers the Freedom of Wales Flexi Pass (All Wales/South Wales £69/47) with four days of train and eight days of bus-based unlimited travel, plus discounts on attractions, available at most railway stations and online at www.wales flexipass.co.uk.

For more details contact **Traveline Cymru** (☎ 0871 200 2233; www.traveline-cymru .org.uk).

GOWER PENINSULA

With its precipitous cliff-top walks, golden-hued Blue Flag beaches and rugged, untamed uplands, the Gower's 15-mile sweep of peninsula west of Mumbles Head feels a million miles away from Swansea's urban bustle – yet it's just on the doorstep.

Today the National Trust (NT) owns 26 miles of Gower coast, operating a **Visitor Centre** (☎ 01792-390707; www.gower heritagecentre.co.uk; ☼ 10.30am-6pm Mon-Fri, 10.30am-5pm Sat & Sun Mar-Oct, 10.30am-5pm Wed-Sun Nov-Mar) at Rhossili, across the car park from the Bay Bistro & Coffee House.

Heading west along the south coast from the family-magnet beach of **Port Eynon**, the village of **Rhossili** looks north along the 3-mile sweep of **Rhossili Bay** at the western tip of the peninsula.

From Rhossili village follow the 1-mile tidal causeway to rocky, wave-blasted **Worm's Head** (from Old English *wurm*, meaning dragon) but *only* for a two-hour period either side of low tide. The **sea-bird colony** at the Outer Head includes razorbills, guillemots and oystercatchers, while seals often bob in the swell.

Above the village of **Reynoldston**, a colossal 25-ton quartz boulder is the fallen capstone of a neolithic burial chamber known as **Arthur's Stone**. **Cefn Bryn** (186m) in the central uplands affords sweeping 360-degree views of the Gower.

The **Gower Way**, a 35-mile marked path through the centre of the peninsula, is the most popular walking route.

GETTING THERE & AROUND

The various bus services to Gower destinations are coordinated from Swansea's Quadrant Bus Station – ask for the latest timetable.

The **Gower Day Explorer ticket** (adult/child £4/2.40) covers multiple journeys – buy it on the bus.

LAUGHARNE (LACHARN)

pop 2200

One of Wales' greatest writers, Dylan Thomas, spent his final years in this attractive coastal town and produced much of his best work here.

Built around The Grist, a makeshift town square with an ancient cross and views of Laugharne's 12th-century **castle** (Cadw; ☎ 01994-427906; adult/child £3.10/2.70; ☯ 10am-5pm Apr-Sep), the town is alleged to have inspired Llareggub, the small Welsh town in which Thomas' signature work, *Under Milk Wood* (1954) is set. The name is 'bugger all' spelt backwards – but appeared in print as 'Llaregyb' so as not to offend delicate postwar sensibilities.

Many are surprised to find that today Laugharne is no Dylan Thomas theme park. You can, however, follow a trail along the Taff Estuary from the castle to Thomas' erstwhile seafront home, check out his

gorgeously located gazebo in the castle grounds and visit St Martin's churchyard, the final resting place of Thomas and his wife Caitlin Macnamara.

The heritage centre **Dylan Thomas Boathouse** (☎ 01994-427420; www.dylanthomasboathouse.com; adult/child £3.50/1.75; ☯ 10am-5.30pm May-Oct, 10.30am-3.30pm Nov-Apr) is the ultimate pilgrimage for Thomas devotees. He lived in this simple house with his wife Caitlin and their three children from 1949 to 1953, but the exhibition about his life feels rather stale. More evocative is the garage, the first building you come to following the coast-hugging path, which Thomas used as his writing den, converted from an old garden shed.

ourpick **Boat House** (☎ 01994-427992; www.theboathousebnb.co.uk; 1 Gosport St; r £70-80; 🖳) Friendly, homely and tastefully decorated, this relative newcomer has become the smartest address in town for B&B, with four superior rooms. The building was converted from the former Corporation Arms pub and what is now the Gwendraeth room is allegedly where Thomas sat by the window telling stories in return for free drinks.

PEMBROKESHIRE COAST NATIONAL PARK

Rocky, sandy, sparkling and remote, the wonders of the Pembrokeshire Coast National Park are unmissable. Covering 240 sq miles in Wales' far-flung southwest, the park sits firmly in a region that the inhabitants proudly refer to as west Wales.

The **Pembrokeshire Coast National Park Authority** (☎ 0845 345 7275; www.pcnpa.org.uk) has its head office by the ferry terminal at Pembroke Dock.

On arrival, pick up a free copy of *Coast to Coast,* the excellent newspaper for visitors, or visit www.visitpembrokeshirecoast.com.

WALES

SOUTH WALES

GETTING THERE & AROUND

Once in Pembrokeshire, use buses to get around rather than trains but note that Sunday services are limited, especially from October to April.

Arriva Trains (☎ 0845 6061 660; www.arrivatrainswales.co.uk) has a Freedom of Wales Flexi Pass (All Wales/South & Mid Wales £69/47) with four days of train and eight days of bus-based unlimited travel, plus discounts on attractions, available at most railway stations and online at www.walesflexipass.co.uk.

Between May and September a group of local buses operate under the auspices of **Pembrokeshire Greenways** (☎ 01437-776313; www.pembrokeshiregreenways.co.uk), a collective to promote sustainable modes of transport through walking, cycling, bus and train travel.

SKOMER, SKOKHOLM & GRASSHOLM ISLANDS

Rocky and exposed, these three little islands off St Brides Bay's southern headland are a marine nature reserve and home to some of Wales' largest **sea-bird colonies**, most active from April to mid-August.

The largest and easiest island to reach, Skomer is home to over half a million breeding seabirds, including puffins, guillemots and cormorants, plus **grey seal pups, porpoises** and **dolphins**.

Regular trips run from Easter to October. **Dale Sailing Co** (☎ 01646-603123; www.dale-sailing.co.uk; cruises adult/child £30/15) runs a range of round-island cruises and landing trips to Skomer, departing from Martin's Haven near Marloes, for wildlife spotting.

ST DAVIDS (TY-DDEWI)

pop 2000

Charismatic St Davids (yes, it has dropped the apostrophe from its name) is Britain's smallest city, its status ensured by the magnificent 12th-century **St David's Cathedral** (☎ 01437-720199; www.stdavidscathedral.org.uk; The Close; donation invited; 8.30am-5.30pm Mon-Sat, 12.45-5.30pm Sun).

Across the river from the cathedral, the atmospheric ruined **Bishop's Palace** (Cadw;

Pembrokeshire Coast National Park (p263)

MARK DAFFEY

☎ 01437-720517; adult/child £3.10/2.70; ☼ 9am-5pm Apr-Oct, 9.30am-4pm Mon-Sat & 11am-4pm Sun Nov-Mar) is mostly due to Henry de Gower, bishop from 1327 to 1348.

Just off St Davids Head, **Ramsey Island** plays host to Atlantic grey seals and thousands of nesting seabirds, while porpoises and dolphins frolic near spectacular sea caves. **Aquaphobia** (☎ 01437-720471; www .aquaphobia-ramseyisland.co.uk; Grove Hotel, High St; adult/child £20/10) runs round-Ramsey tours and evening trips to see shearwaters, while **Thousand Islands Expeditions** (☎ 01437-721721; www.thousandislands.co.uk; Cross Sq; adult/child £15/7.50) offers evening puffin- and shearwater-spotting, whale-watching and guided walks.

Y Glennydd Hotel (☎ 01437-720576; www .yglennydd.co.uk; 11 Nun St; s/d £37/62) With its range of maritime memorabilia and traditional feel, this 10-room guesthouse mixes modern rooms with a period setting. The restaurant serves a decent three-course evening meal (£18.50) with lots of fresh fish options.

Alandale (☎ 01437-720404; www.stdavids .co.uk/guesthouse/alandale.htm; 43 Nun St; s/d £36/72) Homely and welcoming, Alandale is a smart town house with a cosy Victorian parlour-style lounge.

CARDIGAN (ABERTEIFI)

A contrasting vision of ragged stone, rampant ivy and plastic tarpaulin, the town's medieval **Cardigan Castle** is slowly emerging from decades of neglect. In more-glorious times, some 800 years ago, the castle hosted the first competitive eisteddfod, held by Lord Rhys ap Gruffydd in 1176 to select his court musicians (see Essential Eisteddfod, p272). Today restoration work is ongoing, with only limited public access.

Llety Teifi (☎ 01239-615566; www.llety .co.uk; Pendre; s/d/f from £45/70/95; P ▣) New

and stylish with a very contemporary interior, this is Cardigan's first boutique B&B. The 10 en suite rooms boast cable internet and DVD players for style seekers, but the B&B is also open to children, has wheelchair access on the ground floor and is the only place in town to welcome pets.

our pick **Ultracomida Deli** (Market Hall; ☼ cafe 10am-4pm, deli 10am-3pm) The sister cafe to Aberystwyth's Ultracomida, this new branch maintains the winning combination of Welsh, French and Spanish deli-style cuisine.

MID WALES

Ignore Mid Wales at your peril. While generations of visitors have traditionally viewed the region as a staging post en route to elsewhere, this region has more hidden gems than any other and is the crucible for the new Welsh movements championing green issues and local, organic food.

GETTING AROUND

Public transport is less frequent than in other regions, especially in the more remote areas – check details with **Traveline Cymru** (☎ 0871 200 2233; www.traveline-cymru .org.uk).

Train-wise, the Cambrian Main Line dissects Mid Wales, travelling from Shrewsbury to Aberystwyth via Machynlleth, while the scenic Heart of Wales line skirts the Brecon Beacons.

Arriva Trains (☎ 0845 6061 660; www.arrivat rains wales.co.uk) offers Freedom of Wales Flexi Pass tickets (All Wales/South & Mid Wales £69/47) with four days of train and eight days of bus travel, plus discounts on attractions, available at most railway stations and online at www.walesflexipass .co.uk.

BRECON BEACONS NATIONAL PARK (PARC CENEDLAETHOL BANNAU BRYCHEINIOG)

Soaring majestically in a wave of dappled pastel tones, the Brecon Beacons (www .breconbeacons.org) roll in a sea of greens, blues, reds and browns across a large slice of Mid Wales. Swaddled with grassy moors and uplands, the Beacons provide a striking contrast to rock-strewn Snowdonia in the north, but offer comparable thrills and excitement.

Walking is a major activity, with three key trails: Offa's Dyke Path, along the eastern border, the Taff Trail, which heads south from Brecon, and the Beacons Way, a 100-mile linear walk across the national park.

The **National Park Visitor Centre** (☎ 01874-623366; Mountain Centre, Libanus; ⏱ 9.30am-6pm May-Sep, to 5pm Oct-Mar) has a wealth of information and an excellent restaurant for coffee and a light lunch with lots of vegetarian and children's options. It's located in open countryside near the village of Libanus, 5 miles southwest of Brecon off the A470.

There are two other dedicated park information centres:

Abergavenny (☎ 01873-853254; ⏱ 9.30am-5.30pm Easter-Oct, 10am-4pm Nov-Easter) Sharing space with the town tourist office.

Llandovery (☎ 01550-720693; ⏱ 9.30am-1pm & 1.45-5pm daily Easter-Oct, 10am-1pm & 1.45-4pm Mon-Sat, 10am-noon Sun Oct-Easter)

HAY-ON-WYE (Y GELLI)

pop 1500

Hay-on-Wye, a pretty little town on the banks of the River Wye just inside the Welsh border, has become the stuff of legend. A festival of literature and culture was established in 1988, growing in stature each year to take in all aspects of the creative arts. Today the **Hay Festival**, as it is now known, is a major attraction in its own right, famously endorsed by the former American president Bill Clinton in 2001 when he described it as the 'Woodstock of the mind'. Accommodation during the festival is now fully booked several years ahead.

The 10-day event, in late May/early June, has grown to include a slew of readings, lectures, concerts and workshops across several stages, attracting a diverse, artistic crowd and some heavyweight star turns.

SLEEPING

Start (☎ 01497-821391; www.the-start.net; s/d £35/70; Ⓟ) Peacefully set on the fringes of town, this beautiful 18th-century stone cottage is a five-minute walk from the centre across Hay Bridge. Patchwork quilts adorn the pleasant country-style rooms, some with a view of the river.

Swan at Hay Hotel (☎ 01497-821188; www.swanathay.co.uk; Church St; d/tw/f £125/135/155; Ⓟ) The smartest place in Hay, and the most likely to be booked out during the festival, the Swan is still undergoing refurbishment, although the revamp downstairs is now finished.

EATING & DRINKING

Granary (☎ 01497-820790; Broad St; mains around £6; ⏱ 9am-5.30pm year-round, 8am-9pm school holidays & festival; 💻 wi-fi) Popular and welcoming, this bustling country-kitchen cafe is the staple choice for breakfasts, snack lunches and coffees.

Blue Boar (☎ 01497-820884; Castle St; mains around £11) The pick of the pubs in town, this cosy and traditional place is ideal for whiling away an afternoon with a decent pint of Timothy Taylor's ale, a home-cooked lunch of Glamorgan sausage with plum chutney and new potatoes, and a good book.

Three Tuns (☎ 01497-821855; www.threetuns .com; Broad St; mains around £12; ⏱ food noon-2pm

& 6.30-9pm Wed-Sat, 12.30-4pm Sun) This smart new gastropub was rebuilt and expanded after a fire partially destroyed the old building, which dates from the 16th century.

POWYS

This verdant, rural region offers good walking and cycling country, plus plenty of wildlife, notably Wales' burgeoning red-kite community.

Powys is crossed by two long-distance national trails: **Offa's Dyke Path** (www .nationaltrail.co.uk/OffasDyke) and **Glyndŵr's Way** (www.nationaltrail.co.uk/GlyndwrsWay). The former is a 177-mile trail skirting the Anglo-Welsh border from Prestatyn to Sedbury Cliff; the latter a 135-mile path from Knighton to Welshpool, based around sites related to Owain Glyndŵr, Wales' warrior-statesman famed for rebelling against English rule in the early 15th century.

For details of both, contact the **Offa's Dyke Centre** (☎ 01547-528753; www.offasdyke .demon.co.uk/odc.htm; West St, Knighton; ☼ 10am-5pm Easter-Oct, 10am-4pm Mon, Wed, Fri & Sat, 10am-5pm Tue & Thu Nov-Easter), part of the tourist office in the border town of Knighton.

MACHYNLLETH

pop 2200

Tiny Machynlleth (ma-*khun*-khleth) punches well above its weight. The town is rich in historical importance as it is here that nationalist hero Owain Glyndŵr defied the English to establish the country's first parliament in 1404. His legacy still lends Machynlleth a noble air but, more recently, the town has reinvented itself as the green capital of Wales and a centre for alternative communities.

Built on the site of the 1404 Parliament, **Owain Glyndŵr Parliament House** (☎ 01654-702214; www.canolfanowainglynd wrcentre.org.uk; Maengwyn St; adult/child £1.50/ free; ☼ 10am-4.30pm Mon, Tue & Thu-Sat, 10am-

4pm Wed Easter-Sep), is pretty low-key given Glyndŵr's pivotal royal in Welsh history.

A combined art gallery and converted chapel, the **Museum of Modern Art for Wales** (MOMA; ☎ 01654-703355; www.moma wales.org.uk; Penrallt St; admission free; ☼ 10am-4pm Mon-Sat) has two galleries: one for Welsh and one for international works.

Quarry Wholefood Cafe (☎ 01654-702624; Maengwyn St) A well-run vegetarian and organic-food joint, owned by the folks from the CAT. The delicious vegetarian lunch specials (around £6), plus child-friendly facilities and menu, make this place perennially busy.

Wynnstay (☎ 01654-702941; www.wynn stayhotel.com; Maengwyn St; pizzas £8, mains around £14; ☼ bar meals noon-2pm & 6.30-9.30pm; P 🖳) The town's best all-rounder combines comfortable rooms (single/double from £55/85) and a gastropub-style dining area, all set in a character-filled Georgian coaching inn.

GETTING THERE & AWAY

Machynlleth is on the Cambrian Main Line with services running to Shrewsbury (£10.90, 80 minutes, every two hours, six on Sunday) and Aberystwyth (40 minutes, every two hours).

Bus X32 runs north to Dolgellau (35 minutes, about every two hours Monday to Friday, two on Sunday) via CAT (six minutes), and south to Aberystwyth (45 minutes).

NORTH WALES

Feeling vast despite its relatively small area, North Wales really packs it in. The majestic, moody mountains of the Snowdonia National Park, the highest British peaks outside of Scotland, dominate the north of Wales, and provide a

WALES

NORTH WALES

GARETH MCCORMACK

White-water rafting, River Tryweryn (p271)

Flexi Pass tickets (All Wales/North Wales £69/47) with four days of train and eight days of bus unlimited travel (including the Ffestiniog Railway), plus discounts on attractions. It is available at most railway stations and online at www.walesflexi pass.co.uk.

NORTH COAST & BORDERS

The North Wales coast has both perennial charms and cultural blackspots in equal measure. Stick with the former and you'll not be disappointed – from a glorious castle at Conwy to the Victorian elegance of Llandudno.

LLANDUDNO

pop 15,000

Handsome Llandudno is Wales' largest Victorian seaside resort, with a fantastic location and spectacular period architecture along a sweeping bay. It's a busy place in summer, but still manages to retain a dignified air. The American-born travel writer Bill Bryson was moved to describe Llandudno as his 'favourite seaside resort'.

The premier attraction is the **Great Orme** (207m), a spectacular 2-mile-long limestone headland jutting in to the Irish Sea. The headland is a designated country park, boasting a cornucopia of flowers, butterflies and seabirds, and its own **visitor centre** (☎ 01492-874151; ☼ 9.30am-5pm mid-Mar-Oct) with picnic tables, a cafe and gift shop.

You can walk to the summit; take the **Great Orme Tramway** (☎ 01492-879306; www.greatormetramway.co.uk; adult/child return £5.20/3.60; ☼ 10am-6pm Easter-Sep, to 5pm Mar & Oct), which leaves every 20 minutes from Church Walks, or ride Britain's longest **cable car** (☎ 01492-877205; adult/child return £6.50/4.50) from Happy Valley above the pier – departures are weather dependent.

stark contrast with the candyfloss frippery of the northern coastline.

GETTING THERE & AROUND

An extensive network of bus routes is in operation, but Sunday services are usually limited (especially in more-remote areas). Check details with **Traveline Cymru** (☎ 0871 200 2233; www.traveline-cymru.org.uk).

Major rail routes include the North Wales Coast Line from Chester to the ferry terminal at Holyhead, the Cambrian Coast Line from Machynlleth to Pwllheli, and the Conwy Valley Line from Llandudno to Blaenau Ffestiniog. Check with **National Rail Enquiries** (☎ 0845 748 4950; www .nationalrail.co.uk) for times and fares.

Arriva Trains (☎ 0845 6061 660; www.arri vatrainswales.co.uk) offers Freedom of Wales

SLEEPING & EATING

ourpick Escape B&B (☎ 01492-877776; www
.escapebandb.co.uk; 48 Church Walks; r weekend from £115, midweek £85-110; ℗ ▯)
Llandudno's first boutique B&B has bags
of style and urban-cool swagger. The
individual rooms have a funky feel and
lots of high-tech gadgets to play with,
while breakfast is a hearty affair.

Osborne House (☎ 01492-860330; www
.osbornehouse.com; 17 North Pde; ste £145-175;
℗ ▯) This small luxury hotel is big on
grand gestures – from the lavish Italian
marble bathrooms to the huge beds clad
in Egyptian-cotton sheets. It's stylish, yet
modern – rooms have DVDs and internet
access – although some may find the frou-
frou design a bit over the top.

Number 1 Bistro (☎ 01492-875424; Old Rd;
set menu £12; ☙ 5.30-9.30pm Mon-Sat) This well-
established dark-wood bistro has a touch
of French style. The imaginative menu
takes in such dishes as baked guinea fowl
and venison medallions.

GETTING THERE & AWAY

Regional buses stop on the corner of
Upper Mostyn and Gloddaeth Streets.
Arriva bus 5/X5 runs every 15 minutes
(hourly on Sunday) to Caernarfon (one
hour 20 minutes) via the railway inter-
change at Llandudno Junction (15 minutes) and Conwy (20 minutes).

Conwy Valley Line trains serve Blaenau
Ffestiniog (£6, 75 minutes, five daily
Monday to Saturday) via Betws-y-Coed
(50 minutes). Arriva Trains services run
to Manchester Piccadilly (£22, 2¼ hours,
hourly Monday to Saturday, six Sunday)
via Chester (£13, one hour). Most Sunday
services require a change at Llandudno
Junction; the latter also has Virgin Trains
connections to London Euston (£30,
around four hours, three hourly, fewer on
Sunday) and Holyhead (£10, one hour).

CONWY

pop 4000

Conwy is all about the castle, one of Wales'
finest and a Unesco World Heritage Site.

Another great bastion in Edward I's
Welsh defences, **Conwy Castle** (Cadw;
☎ 01492-592358; adult/child £4.70/4.20; ☙ 9am-
5pm Apr-Oct, 9.30am-4pm Mon-Sat & 11am-4pm Sun
Nov-Mar) was built in just five years (1282-87)
following the conquest of Gwynedd. From
the battlements, views across the estuary
and to the peaks of Snowdonia – when not
veiled in cloud – are exhilarating.

The 1200m-long **town wall** was built
simultaneously with the castle, guarding
Conwy's residents at night. You can walk
part way round the wall; the best views
are at Upper Gate.

GETTING THERE & AWAY

The Castle St bus stop is the hub for Arriva
bus 5/5X to Llandudno (20 minutes, every
20 minutes Monday to Saturday, hourly
Sunday) and Arriva bus 19/X19 to Llangollen
(one hour 50 minutes, three daily Monday
to Saturday, two on Sunday).

LLANGOLLEN

pop 3500

Scenic Llangollen (lan-goch-len), huddled
in the fertile Vale of Llangollen around the
banks of the tumbling River Dee, is evolv-
ing from a day-trip destination for the
blue-rinse brigade to a centre for white-
water sports and cultural tourism.

Today the town is best known for the annual **International Eisteddfod** (see boxed
text, p272), held every July at the **Royal
International Pavilion** to promote world
peace through music, song and dance.

SIGHTS & ACTIVITIES

Ornate **Plas Newydd** (☎ 01978-861314; adult/
child £3.50/2.50; ☙ 10am-5pm Easter-Oct) was
home to the Ladies of Llangollen, Lady

Low-energy house, Centre for Alternative Technology

PATRICK HORTON

⬊ CENTRE FOR ALTERNATIVE TECHNOLOGY

A small but dedicated band of people has spent 30 years practising sustainability at the thought-provoking Centre for Alternative Technology (CAT), set in a beautiful wooded valley near Machynlleth (p267).

CAT is a virtually self-sufficient cooperative where more than 3 hectares of displays demonstrate how wind, water and solar power provide food, heating and telecommunications. Kids love the interactive displays and adventure playground, and there's a great organic-wholefood restaurant. To explore the whole site takes about two hours – take rainwear as it's primarily outdoors.

CAT is 3 miles north of Machynlleth on the A487. Hourly buses (four on Sunday) run from the clock tower in Machynlleth; bus 34 stops directly at the visitor centre, while bus X32 drops off in Pantperthog, five minutes' walk away. Arriving by train to Machynlleth gets 50% off admission, and by bus or bike £1 off.

Things you need to know: ☎ 01654-705950; www.cat.org.uk; adult/child £8.40/4.20; 🕑 10am-5.30pm Easter-mid-Jul, Sep & Oct, 10am-6pm mid-Jul–Aug, 10am-dusk Nov-Easter

Eleanor Butler and Miss Sarah Ponsonby. A romantic mix of Gothic and Tudor styles, the house has pleasant formal gardens, and audio guides are included in the admission price. The house lies a fifth of a mile uphill southeast of the town centre.

Llangollen Steam Railway (☎ 01978-860979; www.llangollen-railway.co.uk; return trip £9) chugs through another era on its 8-mile route to Carrog, passing the Horseshoe Falls en route. The timetable

of departures changes monthly (check the website). There are regular special services, including Santa and Thomas the Tank Engine excursions for kids (free up to 15 years).

SLEEPING

Glasgwm (☎ 01978-861975; Abbey Rd; s/d from £32.50/50; Ⓟ) A friendly, family-home guesthouse with a cosy lounge dominated by a traditional Welsh dresser, Glasgwm is a reliable midrange option. Four cosy rooms and a hearty breakfast, catering for all dietary needs, plus evening meals and packed lunches if required, make this an all-round winner.

Cornerstones Guesthouse (☎ 01978-861569; www.cornerstones-guesthouse.co.uk; 15 Bridge St; d/ste £70/85; P ▣) Still the smartest place in town, this converted 16th-century house has three individually styled rooms with sloping floorboards and oak beams, but also internet access and DVDs.

EATING & DRINKING

OURPICK Gales of Llangollen (☎ 01978-860089; www.galesofllangollen.co.uk; 18 Bridge St; mains around £10; ☺ lunch & dinner Mon-Sat) With rustic tables, chalk-board menus of daily changing specials, an exhaustive wine list, and Ryan Adams on the stereo to add a relaxed after-dark vibe, this place is hard to beat.

GETTING THERE & AWAY

Arriva bus 19/X19 runs to Betws-y-Coed (one hour, three daily, two on Sunday) and Llandudno (two hours). Arriva bus X94 runs to Dolgellau (1½ hours, every two hours Monday to Saturday, three on Sunday).

AROUND LLANGOLLEN

The Yorke family home for over two centuries (until 1973), **Erddig** (NT, ☎ 01978-355314; adult/child/family £9.40/4.70/23.50; ☺ grounds 10am-6pm Sat-Thu Jul & Aug, 11am-6pm Sat-Wed Apr-Jun & Sep, to 4pm Mar, Oct & Nov; house noon-5pm Sat-Thu Jul & Aug, noon-5pm Sat-Wed Apr-Jun & Oct, to 4pm Mar, to 4pm Sat & Sun Nov & Dec) offers an illuminating glimpse into 19th-century life for the British upper class. Much of the family's original furniture is on display in the fine staterooms, while a formal, walled garden has been restored in Victorian style, featuring rare fruit trees, a canal and the National Ivy Collection. Erddig lies 12 miles northeast of Llangollen on the A483 in the village of Rhostyllen.

SNOWDONIA NATIONAL PARK (PARC CENEDLAETHOL ERYRI)

In a country overflowing with uplands, Snowdonia National Park reigns supreme, with the highest mountains and steepest valleys of any Welsh region. Mt Snowdon (1085m) is the highest piece of rock in Wales and England. Scaling the summit, on foot or by mountain railway, is the goal of many visitors – the park was created in 1951 as much to prevent the peak from being over-loved as from being neglected or built upon.

ORIENTATION & INFORMATION

Snowdonia is the third-largest of Britain's 14 national parks. National Park information centres can be found at Betws-y-Coed and Dolgellau (both open year-round), and from Easter to October at Aberdyfi, Blaenau Ffestiniog, Harlech and Beddgelert. Excellent online information is available at www.eryri-npa.gov.uk and www.visitsnowdonia.info.

For the latest weather report, check the Met Office mountain forecast at www.metoffice.gov.uk/loutdoor/mountain safety/snowdonia.html.

ACTIVITIES

ACTIVITY CENTRES

Canolfan Tryweryn – the National Whitewater Centre (☎ 01678-521083; www.ukrafting.co.uk) A trusty 1½-mile stretch of the River Tryweryn, near Bala, provides top rafting, canoeing and kayaking. For aquaphobes, try activities such as clay-pigeon shooting or bushcraft skills.

Plas y Brenin – the National Mountain Centre (☎ 01690-720214; www.pyb.co.uk)

WALES

NORTH WALES

WALES

NORTH WALES

Based at Capel Curig, this is the place to learn climbing, mountain biking and summit leadership.

Plas Menai – the National Water Sports Centre (☎ 01248-670964; www.plasmenai.co.uk) A year-round range of water-based courses for all ability levels – from sailing to powerboating; based near Caernarfon.

WALKING

Mt Snowdon is the main destination for walkers, many basing themselves at Llanberis to tackle one of the numerous routes to the top (see boxed text, p274). But other hikes around the region are just as exhilarating – and less crowded. If in doubt about your abilities, consider a national park walk; ask at tourist offices, check the *Eryri/Snowdonia* newspaper, or download details of day walks from the national park website www.eryri- npa.gov.uk.

ESSENTIAL EISTEDDFOD

The **National Eisteddfod** (www.eisteddfod.org.uk), pronounced *ey-steth-vot*, a celebration of Welsh culture, is Europe's largest festival of competitive music-making and poetry. Descended from ancient bardic tournaments, it attracts more than 150,000 visitors and 6000 competitors annually. Conducted in Welsh, the festival welcomes all.

Most famous of all is the **International Eisteddfod** (www.international-eisteddfod.co.uk), established after WWII to promote international harmony. Held every July at Llangollen's Royal International Pavilion, the event pulls up to 5000 participants from more than 40 countries, transforming the town into a global village.

Prestatyn, on the north coast, is the end of **Offa's Dyke Path**, a long-distance national trail along the Wales–England border.

GETTING THERE & AROUND

Bus services between regional towns are adequate (but limited on Sunday). Colourful **Snowdon Sherpa** (☎ 01286-870880; day tickets adult/child £4/2) buses serve the mountain areas and Mt Snowdon trailheads. The Snowdon Sherpa day ticket is for hop-on, hop-off access to the network of buses throughout a 24-hour period.

LLANBERIS

pop 2000

Opened in 1896, the **Snowdon Mountain Railway** (☎ 0870-4580033; www.snowdonrailway.co.uk; ⌚ 9am-5pm Mar-Oct) is the UK's highest and only public rack-and-pinion railway. The 5-mile journey climbs 900m and takes an hour, but schedules are weather-dependent and summertime queues can be long. The railway was still undergoing major construction work at the time of writing, with trains running only to **Clogwyn station** (adult/child return £11/7). A new summit station, complete with a cafe and visitor centre, is due to open around May 2009 – depending on the weather.

ourpick **Pen-y-Gwryd** (☎ 01286-870211; www.pyg.co.uk; Nant Gwynant; s/d £35/45; ⌚ Jan-Oct) Eccentric but full of atmosphere, Pen-y-Gwryd has a great sense of living history. The 1953 Everest team used the inn as a training base, and memorabilia from their stay, including their signatures on the ceiling of the dining room, lends the place the atmosphere of a hidden-gem museum.

GETTING THERE & AWAY

Padarn bus 85 runs to Bangor (45 minutes, hourly Monday to Saturday, six on Sunday); bus 88 runs to Caernarfon (25 minutes, hourly, eight on Sunday). Snowdon Sherpa bus S1 runs to the Snowdon trailhead at Pen-y-Pass (15 minutes, half-hourly).

HARLECH
pop 1800

Finished in 1289 by Edward I, Harlech Castle is a Unesco World Heritage Site. Despite its strategic location and hefty construction, the **castle** (Cadw; ☎ 01766-780552; adult/child £3.70/3.30; 🕑 9am-5pm Apr-Oct, 9.30am 4pm Mon-Sat, 11am-4pm Sun Nov-Mar) has been called the 'Castle of Lost Causes' because it fell so often during battle. It was captured by Owain Glyndŵr in 1404, but the future Henry V usurped him just four years later. During the Wars of the Roses the castle fell to the Yorkists in 1468, and fell again in 1647 when Cromwell's men took control during the Civil War. The fortress's great natural defence is the seaward cliff face. When it was built, ships could sail supplies right to the base.

Fine dining and five-star accommodation by the castle characterise the excellent **Castle Cottage** (☎ 01766-780479; Y Llech; www.castlecottageharlech.co.uk; s/d £73/106; **P**). Ongoing refurbishment work keeps facilities top notch, while the restaurant menu features local seafood and heavenly desserts (three-course dinner £34).

GETTING THERE & AWAY

Arriva bus 38 runs to Barmouth (30 minutes, hourly, two on Sunday) and Blaenau Ffestiniog (30 minutes). Cambrian Coast trains serve Machynlleth (£8.20, 1½ hours, about every two to three hours, three on Sunday) and Porthmadog (20 minutes).

PORTMEIRION

The **Portmeirion** (☎ 01766-770000; www.portmeirion-village.com; adult/child £7/3.50; 🕑 9.30am-5.30pm) site was founded in 1926 by the Welsh architect Sir Clough

Caernarfon Castle (p274)
GARETH MCCORMACK

Williams-Ellis, who spent 50 years perfecting his Utopian masterpiece. The resulting group of disparate Italianate buildings is a seaside fairy tale that testifies to the power of imagination. There's glorious attention to detail and absurdity in each and every one of the nooks and crannies.

An **audiovisual show** (🕑 10am-5pm), located just off the central Piazza to the right of the Arc de Triomphe, has a commentary by Sir Williams-Ellis himself.

The village formed the ideally surreal stage set for the 1960s cult TV series, *The Prisoner*, which was filmed here from 1966 to 1967; it still draws fans of the show in droves and Prisoner conventions are held annually in March. The **Prisoner Information Centre** (🕑 9am-5.30pm Apr-Oct) has a raft of memorabilia for fans.

SUMMIT SPECIAL

No Snowdonia experience is complete without tackling one of the region's awe-inspiring mountains. At 1085m, Mt Snowdon is the biggest and also the busiest, thanks in no small part to the second-generation Snowdon Mountain Railway (p272).

Six paths of varying length and difficulty lead to the summit. Simplest (and dullest) is the **Llanberis Path** (10 miles, six hours), running beside the railway track. The **Snowdon Ranger Path** (7 miles, five hours) starts at the Snowdon Ranger YHA near Beddgelert; this is the shortest and also the safest in winter.

Two options start at Pen-y-Pass (and involve the least amount of ascent): the **Miners Track** (7 miles, six hours) starts gently and ends with a steep section; the **Pyg Track** (7 miles, six hours) is more interesting, and meets the Miners Track where it steepens. The classic **Snowdon Horseshoe** route (7.5 miles, six to seven hours) combines the Pyg Track to the summit (or via the precipitous ridge of Crib Goch if you're very experienced) with a descent route over the peak of Llewedd and a final section down on the Miners Track.

The straightforward **Rhyd Ddu Path** (8 miles, six hours) approaches from the west. Most challenging is the **Watkin Path** (8 miles, six hours), involving an ascent of more than 1000m on its southerly approach from Nantgwynant.

Snowdon Sherpa buses (see p272) drop off at the trailheads, and there are also options for accommodation near them all.

There are three accommodation options (☎ 01766 770000; www.portmeirion-village.com) – guests are excused the admission fee to Portmeirion:

Hotel Portmeirion (s/d/ste from £155/188/209) Has classic, elegant rooms and a contemporary dining room designed by Sir Terence Conran.

ourpick **Castell Deudraeth** (r £175-245) A fairy-tale castle with an informal grill and more modern rooms better suited to families.

Self-catering cottages (per week for 3-8 people £657-1760) Individually styled cottages dotted around in nooks and crannies of the village. Facilities and size vary between properties – check the website for deals.

Portmeirion lies 2 miles east of Porthmadog across the Cob, then a mile south off the main road. The Ffestiniog Railway and Cambrian Coast Line trains run to the village of Minffordd, from where it's a 1-mile walk.

CAERNARFON

Wedged between the gleaming swell of the Menai Strait and the deep-purple mountains of Snowdonia, **Caernarfon Castle** (Cadw; ☎ 01286-677617; adult/child £5.10/4.70; ☷ 9am-5pm Easter-Oct, 9.30am-4pm Mon-Sat, 11am-4pm Sun Nov-Mar) was built between 1283 and 1301, standing as Edward I's most impressive stronghold. Almost impregnable, the polygonal towers and colour-banded masonry were based on Constantinople's 5th-century walls, and set it apart from other castles of North Wales. The castle is a Unesco World Heritage Site.

EDINBURGH & GLASGOW

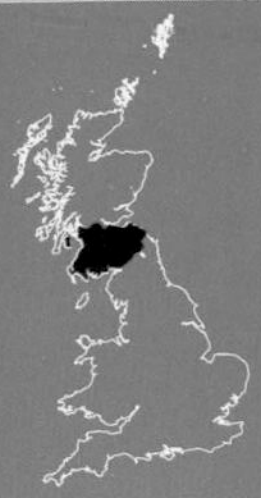

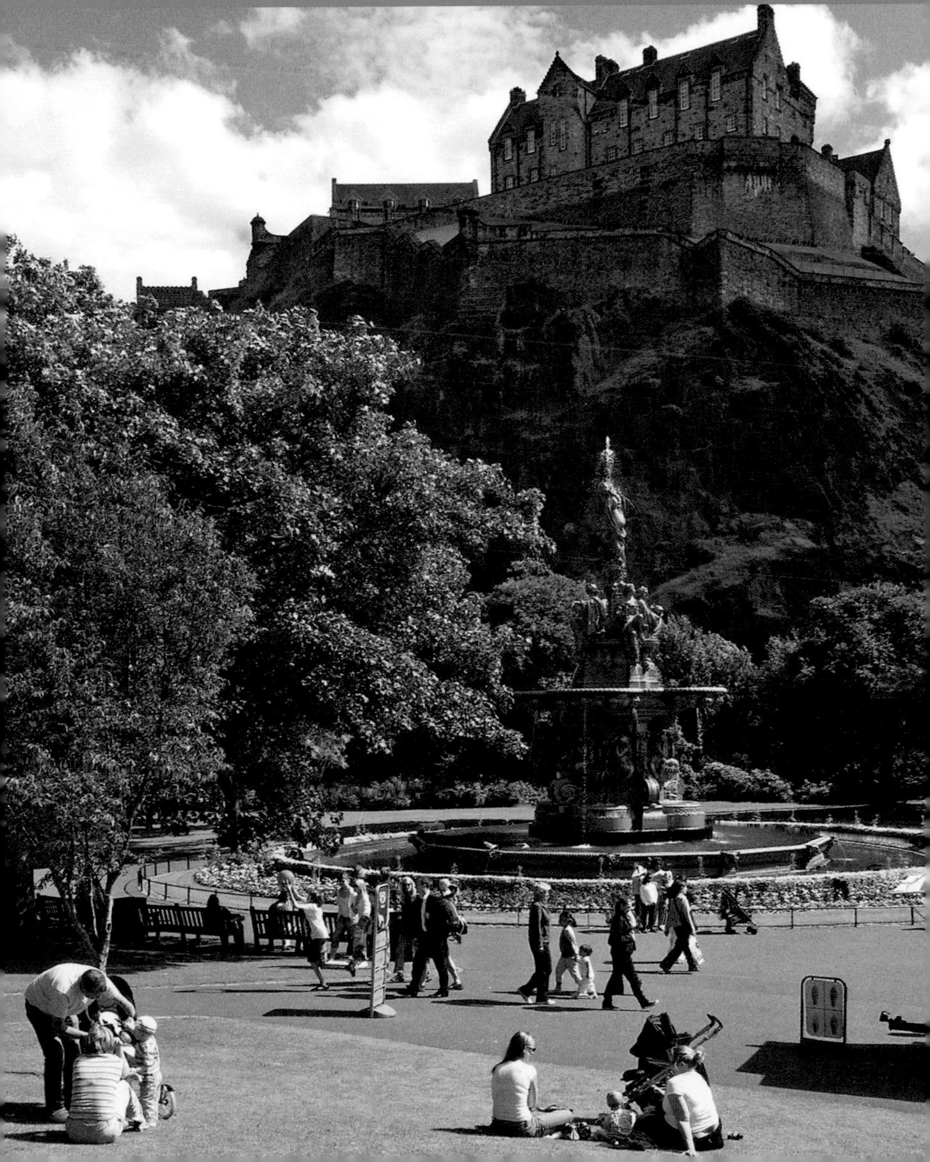

WILL SALTER

Palace of Holyroodhouse (p291)

EDINBURGH & GLASGOW

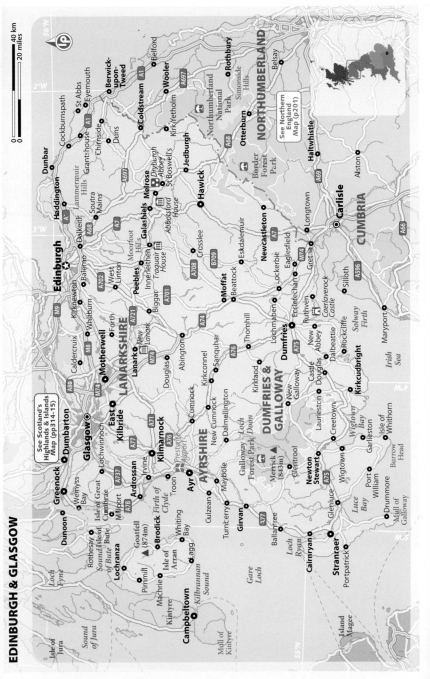

EDINBURGH & GLASGOW HIGHLIGHTS

1 EDINBURGH & AROUND

BY JAN HENDERSON, TOUR GUIDE FOR BLACK HART

I feel very lucky to live in Edinburgh. I've worked as a tour guide here for years and never get tired of it. It's a city filled with secret places and constant surprises, fascinating history and sites of unparalleled beauty.

⬊ JAN HENDERSON'S DON'T MISS LIST

❶ CAMERA OBSCURA

Many visitors miss this fascinating little **observatory** (p287) at the top of the Royal Mile. It's filled with optical illusions, and the obscura – using mirrors and lenses to project a bird's eye view of the city – is one of only two working in Britain.

❷ GREYFRIARS GRAVEYARD

By day, this **cemetery** (p290) is a lovely place, but after dark you won't find a spookier spot in Edinburgh. Many famous characters are buried in here,

including the city's most celebrated pooch, Greyfriars Bobby. I've had some pretty peculiar experiences up there on our ghost tours!

❸ UNDERGROUND EDINBURGH

Walking around Edinburgh, it's hard to believe there's another city right beneath your feet. During the 18th and 19th centuries the city's poor lived in a maze of alleyways and vaults beneath the Old Town. Recently rediscovered, the best way to see them is on a guided tour (see **Mercat Tours**, p293).

Clockwise from top: Funhouse mirror, Camera Obscura (p287); Rosslyn Chapel (p299); South Bridge underground vaults; Gravestone, Greyfriars Kirkyard (p290)

CLOCKWISE FROM TOP: MARGIE POLITZER; MICAH WRIGHT; JONATHAN SMITH; NEIL WILSON

❹ CRAIGMILLAR CASTLE

Edinburgh Castle is obviously a must-see sight, but it gets pretty crowded in summer, especially during the Festival in August. To dodge the crowds, Edinburgh's other **castle** (p293) is less well-known. On the outskirts of the city, it's over 600 years old and has fantastic views to boot.

❺ ROSSLYN CHAPEL

You might recognise this **chapel** (p299) from the movies – it recently took a starring role in the film version of *The Da Vinci Code*. The ancient building, covered in strange carvings and symbols, has played a pivotal role in some of Scotland's most important historical events. A magical, mysterious place.

❶ Camera Obscura
❷ Greyfriars Graveyard
❸ Mercat Tours
❹ Craigmillar Castle
❺ Rosslyn Chapel

0 — 800 m
0 — 0.5 miles

↘ THINGS YOU NEED TO KNOW

Survival tip Beat the queues and book ahead for guided city tours and the Camera Obscura **Top photo op** You're spoilt for choice in Edinburgh, but the castle, Arthur's Seat and Calton Hill are all picture-perfect **Times to avoid** July and August can be a nightmare for sightseeing

EDINBURGH & GLASGOW HIGHLIGHTS

↘ PALACE OF HOLYROODHOUSE

Scotland boasts a higher castle quota than practically any other corner of the British Isles, but few can match up to **Holyroodhouse** (p291) in terms of sheer regal splendour. The royal family's official Edinburgh residence is a must-see, and is brimming with fascinating artworks, antiques and architecture. Afterwards you can stroll over to Holyrood Abbey or wander around Holyrood Park.

↗ MACKINTOSH HOUSE

Glasgow's most famous son was the pioneering architect, artist, designer and decorative trendsetter Charles Rennie Mackintosh. The city is littered with examples of his influential work (look out for the Glasgow School of Art and Queen's Cross Church), but nowhere is the Mackintosh spirit more in evidence than his own Glasgow **home** (p301), a painstaking reconstruction of the original.

4

↘ CLIMBING ARTHUR'S SEAT

Clambering up to the summit of this long-dormant **volcano** (p290) is an Edinburgh rite of passage, and you really haven't seen the city till you've done it. There's a fantastic panorama all the way across the city, and it makes a fantastic spot for a picnic on those elusive sunny Scottish days.

5

↘ CULZEAN CASTLE

This stunning **stately home** (p311) – considered by many to be Scotland's finest – is the work of the Scottish architect Robert Adam, known for his show-stopping neoclassical designs. Its famous features include palatial suites, intricate plasterwork and an amazing staircase, not to mention a top-drawer cliff-top location.

6

↘ GALLOWAY FOREST PARK

If you're a sucker for green spaces, this **nature park** (p312) makes an ideal getaway. Rippled with hills, cloaked in pines and spotted with crystal-clear lochs, it's home to some of Scotland's most elusive wild inhabitants, such as wild goats, deer and red kites.

2 Palace of Holyroodhouse (p291); 3 Mackintosh House (p301); 4 Arthur's Seat (p290); 5 Culzean Castle (p311); 6 Galloway Forest Park (p312)

EDINBURGH & GLASGOW'S BEST...

↘ FREE THINGS

- Exploring Edinburgh's Royal Mile (p287).
- Getting lost in the National Museum of Scotland (p291).
- A picnic in Glasgow's Winter Gardens (p301).
- Taking to the hills in the Galloway Forest Park (p312).
- Wandering around Edinburgh's Royal Botanic Garden (p293).

↘ HISTORIC SPOTS

- New Lanark (p309) A pioneering social experiment.
- Grassmarket and Cowgate (p290) Explore Edinburgh's oldest areas.
- Melrose Abbey (p310) The most beautiful Border abbey.
- Caerlaverock Castle (p312) A classic Scottish stronghold.
- Calton Hill (p292) Enjoy Edinburgh views from the Nelson Monument.

↘ HOUSES

- Abbotsford House (p310) Sir Walter Scott's former house.
- Traquair House (p310) The Stuarts' stately home.
- Pollok House (p304) Upstairs-downstairs life in a Glasgow townhouse.
- The Georgian House (p292) See how Edinburgh's elite once lived.
- Mackintosh House (p301) Replica of Charles Rennie Mackintosh's Glasgow home.

↘ ARTISTIC EXPERIENCES

- Kelvingrove Art Gallery & Museum (p304) Glasgow's eclectic art gallery.
- The Burrell Collection (p304) See the catch-all-collection of Sir William Burrell.
- The Mackintosh Trail (p301) Admire Mackintosh's Glaswegian landmarks.

LEFT: IZZET KERIBAR; RIGHT: MARGIE POLITZER

Left: Cycling on the Royal Mile; Right: Glasgow School of Art (p301)

THINGS YOU NEED TO KNOW

⬎ VITAL STATISTICS

- **Area** 7509 sq miles
- **Population** 3.1 million
- **Best time to go** Summer for festivals, autumn for peace and quiet

⬎ AREAS IN A NUTSHELL

- **Edinburgh** (p286) The cutting-edge capital.
- **Glasgow** (p300) Scotland's second city.
- **Scottish Borders** (p309) Littered with castles and abbeys.
- **Dumfries & Galloway** (p312) Rolling hills and green, green valleys.

⬎ ADVANCE PLANNING

- **Three months before** Start planning for Edinburgh's big festivals.
- **One month before** Sort those transport tickets and restaurant bookings.
- **One week before** See what the weather's up to, but take it with a pinch of salt.

⬎ RESOURCES

- **Edinburgh** (www.edinburgh.org) The official tourist site.
- **See Glasgow** (www.seeglasgow.com) Online info for Glasgow.
- **Visit Southern Scotland** (www.visitsouthernscotland.com) Plan your southern Scottish adventure.
- **Scottish Borders** (www.scot-borders.co.uk) Great resource for the Borders area.

⬎ GETTING AROUND

- **Airports** Shuttle buses link Glasgow and Edinburgh with the airports.
- **Bus** Great for getting round Edinburgh and Glasgow; slow and infrequent in rural areas.
- **Train** Train links are good across most of Southern Scotland. The West Coast line links Glasgow and Edinburgh to major English cities, and continues north to the Highlands as the West Highland line.
- **Car** Expensive parking and mind-bending one-way systems mean driving in the two big cities is not a good idea.

⬎ BE FOREWARNED

- **Festivals** Edinburgh's festivals are enormously popular – start planning at least three months ahead and expect big crowds in August and around New Year.
- **Weather** No matter when you visit, chances are you won't escape a Scottish shower. Plan accordingly.
- **Prices** Everything takes a hefty price hike in busy periods, so avoid July, August and New Year if you're on a budget.

EDINBURGH & GLASGOW

THINGS YOU NEED TO KNOW

EDINBURGH & GLASGOW ITINERARIES

GLASGOW Three Days

If you've only got a limited time you'd be wise to concentrate on one area. **(1) Glasgow** (p300) is a good choice – three days should allow you to cover all the big-ticket sights.

Base yourself in the city for the first two days, ticking off the **Kelvingrove Art Gallery & Museum** (p304), the **Hunterian Museum** (p304), **Mackintosh House** (p301), the **Burrell Collection** (p304) and the **Gallery of Modern Art** (p301). Our top tips for dining out include **Cafe Gandolfi** (p306), **Two Fat Ladies at the Buttery** (p306) or, if you're feeling flush, the multi-award-winning **Ubiquitous Chip** (p306).

On the third day take a day trip to fascinating **(2) New Lanark** (p309), a model settlement established by the pioneering social reformer Robert Owen during the Industrial Revolution.

EDINBURGH & AROUND Five Days

If you've got a bit more time you'll be able to cover the **(1) Scottish capital** (p286) and some of the surrounding area. Start off with Edinburgh's **Royal Mile** (p287) on day one, allowing time for the **Camera Obscura** (p287), **St Giles Cathedral** (p290) and, of course, **Edinburgh Castle** (p287). After dark take a **ghost tour** (p293) and dine at **Apartment** or **Tower** (p296).

On day two tackle the **New Town** (p292). Indulge in some shopping on **Princes St** (p292), visit the **National Gallery** (p292) and the **Scottish National Portrait Gallery** (p292) and climb to the top of the **Scott Monument** (p292). Try out **Fishers** or **Howie's** (p296) for supper.

On day three you could visit **Holyroodhouse** (p291), climb **Arthur's Seat** (p290), wander around the **Botanical Gardens** (p293) or visit **Craigmillar Castle** (p293). Round things off in style at **Kitchin** (p296).

On the last two days hop in the car and head for either the **(2) Scottish Borders** (p309) or, if you're up for a road trip, **(3) Dumfries & Galloway** (p312) and the **(4) Galloway Forest Park** (p312).

HISTORIC HIGHLIGHTS One Week

This week-long trip covers the main historic sights Southern Scotland has to offer. (1) Edinburgh (p286) is the obvious starting point – the twin landmarks of the castle (p287) and Holyroodhouse (p291) are both essential, but just wandering around the city itself is a historical treat. On the outskirts, don't miss Craigmillar Castle (p293) and the mysterious Rosslyn Chapel (p299).

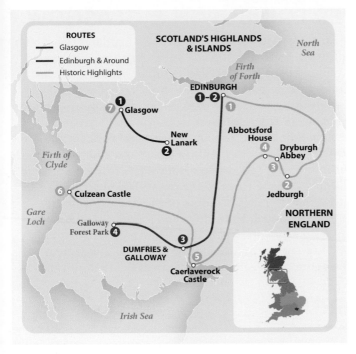

After a couple of days in Edinburgh it's time to head south for the Scottish Borders (p309), where you'll find some of the region's oldest abbeys and castles. (2) Jedburgh Abbey (p311) was dealt a heavy blow during the Dissolution – it's little more than a romantic ruin these days – but the abbey at (3) Dryburgh (p310) is much better preserved. The great Scottish writer Sir Walter Scott is buried in the grounds of the abbey, and if you've got time a visit to his mansion at (4) Abbotsford House (p310) is extremely worthwhile; look out for Rob Roy's gun and a lock of hair belonging to Bonnie Prince Billy as you wander round the rooms.

Then it's time to explore some of the region's castles – our favourites are rosy-hued (5) Caerlaverock (p312), just south of Dumfries, and (6) Culzean (p311), 12 miles south of Ayr.

Finish up the trip with a couple of days exploring Charles Rennie Mackintosh's home city, (7) Glasgow (p300) – we've picked out a few of our favourite Mackintosh landmarks on p301.

DISCOVER EDINBURGH & GLASGOW

Few corners of Britain boast a stormier past than Scotland's southern border. Some of the bloodiest battles of British history were played out along this tempestuous frontier, and countless towers, castles and fortified houses sit as reminders of the area's martial past – including the imposing fortresses of Craigmillar and Culzean, the crumbling abbeys of Dryburgh and Jedburgh and Scotland's fascinating first city, Edinburgh. The Scottish capital is obviously an essential stop on any itinerary, but before you make a headlong dash for the Highlands, you won't regret spending a few days in Scotland's second city, Glasgow – home town of the great designer Charles Rennie Mackintosh, not to mention some of the country's finest galleries and museums. Beyond the cities you'll find peace and quiet in the delightful Galloway Forest Park and a brace of fascinating country estates: Traquair House, with its pint-sized brewery, and Abbotsford House, the former home of the great Scottish novelist Sir Walter Scott.

EDINBURGH

☎ 0131 / pop 430,000

Not only is Edinburgh one of the most beautiful cities in Europe, it also enjoys one of Europe's most beautiful settings. It's a town entangled in its landscape, where the rocky battlements of Salisbury Crags overlook one end of the Old Town, and the Water of Leith snakes along only yards from the elegant Georgian terraces of the New Town.

HISTORY

The first effective town wall was constructed around 1450 and circled the Old Town and the Grassmarket. The city played an important role in the Reformation, led by the firebrand John Knox (p290), but later, when James VI of Scotland succeeded to the English crown in 1603, he moved the court to London. Edinburgh's importance waned, to be further reduced by the Act of Union in 1707.

In the second half of the 18th century the New Town was created and the popu-lation soon exploded. A new ring of crescents and circuses was built south of the New Town, and grey Victorian terraces spread to the south.

Following WWII, the city's cultural life blossomed, stimulated by the Edinburgh International Festival and its fellow traveller the Fringe, both held for the first time in 1947 and now recognised as world-class arts festivals.

Edinburgh entered a new era following the 1997 referendum vote in favour of a devolved Scottish parliament, which first convened in July 1999.

ORIENTATION

The city's most prominent landmarks are Arthur's Seat, southeast of the centre, and Edinburgh Castle at the western end of the Old Town. The Old and New Towns are separated by Princes Street Gardens, with Waverley train station at their eastern end.

Edinburgh's main shopping street, Princes St, runs along the northern side of the gardens. The Royal Mile (Lawnmarket, High St and Canongate), the parallel equivalent in the Old Town, is roughly bookended by the Palace of Holyroodhouse to the east and the castle to the west.

INFORMATION

City of Edinburgh Council (www.edinburgh.gov.uk)

Edinburgh & Scotland Information Centre (ESIC; ☎ 0845 225 5121; info@visitscotland.com; Princes Mall, 3 Princes St; 🕐 9am-9pm Mon-Sat, 10am-8pm Sun Jul & Aug, 9am-7pm Mon-Sat, 10am-7pm Sun May, Jun & Sep, 9am-5pm Mon-Wed, 9am-6pm Thu-Sun Oct-Apr)

Your Edinburgh (www.youredinburgh.info)

SIGHTS

OLD TOWN

EDINBURGH CASTLE

Edinburgh Castle (HS; ☎ 225 9846; www.edinburghcastle.gov.uk; Castlehill; adult/child £12/6; 🕐 9.30am-6pm Apr-Oct, 9.30am-5pm Nov-Mar) has played a pivotal role in Scottish history, both as a royal residence – King Malcolm Canmore (r 1057–93) and Queen Margaret first made their home here in the 11th century – and as a military stronghold. The castle last saw military action in 1745; from then until the 1920s it served as the British army's main base in Scotland.

Highlights of the castle include: **St Margaret's Chapel** (the oldest building in Edinburgh), a simple stone building that was probably built by David I or Alexander I around 1130 in memory of their mother; the **Royal Palace** (including the Stone of Destiny and the Scottish Crown Jewels); and the **National War Museum of Scotland** (☎ 225 7534; admission incl in Edinburgh Castle ticket; 🕐 9.45am-5.30pm Apr-Sep, to 4.45pm Oct-Mar).

ROYAL MILE

Edinburgh's Old Town stretches along a ridge to the east of the castle, and tumbles down Victoria St to the broad expanse of the Grassmarket. It's a jumbled maze of masonry riddled with closes (alleys) and wynds (narrow lanes), cleft along its spine by the cobbled ravine of the Royal Mile.

At the top of the Royal Mile the **Camera Obscura** (☎ 226 3709; Outlook Tower, Castlehill; adult/child £7.95/5.50; 🕐 9.30am-7.30pm Jul & Aug, 9.30am-6pm Apr-Jun, Sep & Oct, 10am-5pm Nov-Mar) is a curious 19th-century device – in constant use since 1853 – that uses lenses and mirrors to throw a live image of the city onto a large horizontal screen. Stairs lead up through various displays on optics to the Outlook Tower, which offers great views over the city.

GARETH MCCORMACK

Performer, Edinburgh International Festival (p294)

EDINBURGH

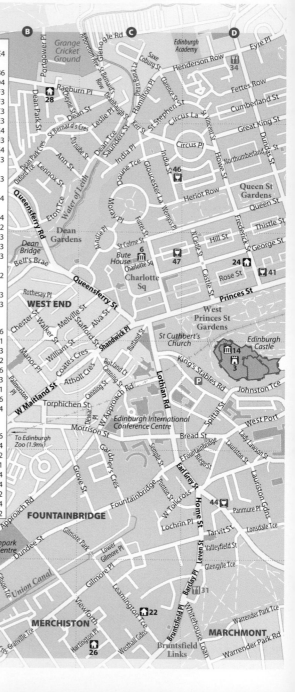

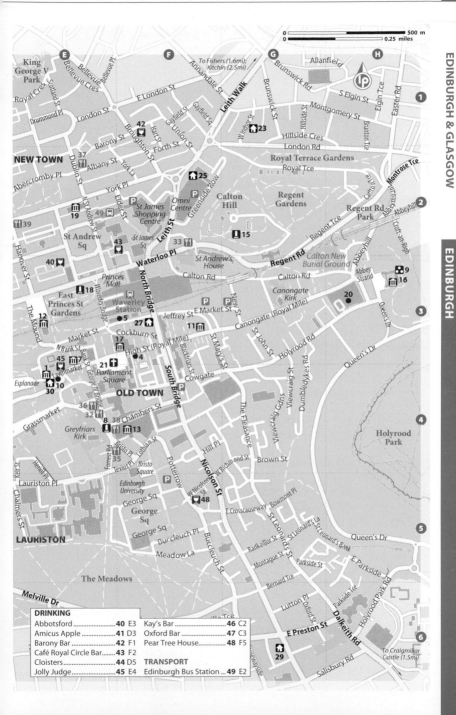

A typical Old Town tenement building, **Gladstone's Land** (NTS; ☎ 226 5856; 477 Lawnmarket; adult/child £5/4; ☺ 10am-7pm Jul & Aug, 10am-5pm Easter-Jun, Sep & Oct) offers a fascinating glimpse into the past. The narrow, six-storey house was built in the mid-16th century and extended around 1617 by wealthy merchant Thomas Gledstanes.

Parliament Square, largely filled by St Giles Cathedral, is in the middle part of the Royal Mile. **St Giles Cathedral** (High St; admission free, £3 donation suggested; ☺ 9am-7pm Mon-Fri, 9am-5pm Sat, 1-5pm Sun May-Sep, 9am-5pm Mon-Sat, 1-5pm Sun Oct-Apr) dates largely from the 15th century – the beautiful crown spire was completed in 1495 – but much of it was restored in the 19th century. St Giles was at the heart of the Scottish Reformation, and John Knox served as minister here from 1559 to 1572.

Sealed off for 250 years beneath the City Chambers, **Real Mary King's Close** (☎ 0870 243 0160; 2 Warriston's Close; adult/child £10/6; ☺ 9am-9pm Aug, 10am-9pm Apr-Jul, Sep & Oct, 10am-4pm Sun-Fri & 10am-9pm Sat Nov-Mar) is a spooky, subterranean labyrinth that gives a fascinating insight into the daily life of 16th- and 17th-century Edinburgh. Costumed characters give tours through a 16th-century town house and the plague-stricken home of a 17th-century gravedigger.

One of the oldest surviving buildings on the Royal Mile is **John Knox House** (☎ 556 9579; 43-45 High St; adult/child £3.50/1; ☺ 10am-6pm Mon-Sat year-round, noon-6pm Sun Jul & Aug), built in 1490 and once home to John Knox.

SCOTTISH PARLIAMENT

Built on the site of a former brewery, the controversial **Scottish Parliament Building** (☎ 348 5200; www.scottish.parliament.uk; Holyrood Rd; admission free, tours adult/concession £6/3.60; ☺ 9am-6pm Tue-Thu, 10am-5pm Mon & Fri in session, 10am-5pm Mon-Fri in recess Apr-Oct, 10am-4pm Mon-Fri in recess Nov-Mar) opened for business in 2005. The strange forms of the exterior are all symbolic in some way, from the oddly shaped windows on the west wall (inspired by the silhouette of the Reverend Robert Walker Skating on Duddingston Loch, one of Scotland's most famous paintings), to the ground plan of the whole complex, which represents a 'flower of democracy rooted in Scottish soil' (best seen looking down from Salisbury Crags).

HOLYROOD PARK & ARTHUR'S SEAT

In **Holyrood Park**, Edinburghers can enjoy a little wilderness in the heart of the city. The former hunting ground of Scottish monarchs, the park covers 263 hectares of varied landscape, including crags, moorland and loch. The highest point is the 251m summit of **Arthur's Seat**, the deeply eroded remnant of a long-extinct volcano; you can hike from Holyrood to the summit in 30 to 45 minutes.

SOUTH OF THE ROYAL MILE
GRASSMARKET & AROUND

The site of a former cattle market, the **Grassmarket** has always been a focal point of the Old Town. It was also the city's main place of execution, and over 100 martyred Covenanters are commemorated by a monument at the eastern end, where the gallows used to stand.

Cowgate – the long, dark ravine leading eastwards from the Grassmarket – was once the road along which cattle were driven from the pastures around Arthur's Seat to the safety of the city walls. Today it is the heart of Edinburgh's nightlife, with around two dozen clubs and bars within five minutes' walk of each other.

GREYFRIARS KIRK & KIRKYARD

Hemmed in by high walls, **Greyfriars Kirkyard** is one of Edinburgh's most

Holyrood Abbey

WILL SALTER

↘ PALACE OF HOLYROODHOUSE & HOLYROOD ABBEY

The Palace of Holyroodhouse is the royal family's official residence in Scotland, but is most famous as the 16th-century home of the ill-fated Mary Queen of Scots. The oldest surviving part of the building, the northwest tower, was built in 1529 as a royal apartment for James V and his wife, Mary of Guise. The palace is closed to the public when the royal family is visiting and during state functions (usually in mid-May, and mid-June to early July; check website for exact dates).

The exit from the palace leads into the ruins of Holyrood Abbey. King David I founded the abbey here in the shadow of Salisbury Crags in 1128. It was probably named after a fragment of the True Cross (rood is an old Scots word for cross), said to have been brought to Scotland by his mother, St Margaret.

Things you need to know: ☎ 556 5100; www.royal.gov.uk; Canongate; adult/child £9.80/5.80; ☾ 9.30am-6pm Apr-Oct, 9.30am-4.30pm Nov-Mar

evocative cemeteries, a peaceful green oasis dotted with elaborate monuments. Many famous Edinburgh names are buried here, including the poet Allan Ramsay (1686–1758), architect William Adam (1689–1748) and William Smellie (1740–95), the editor of the 1st edition of the *Encyclopaedia Britannica*.

The memorial that draws the biggest crowds is the tiny **Greyfriars Bobby statue**, a Skye terrier who, from 1858 to 1872, maintained a vigil over the grave of his master, an Edinburgh police officer.

NATIONAL MUSEUM OF SCOTLAND

Broad, elegant Chambers St stretches eastwards from Greyfriars Bobby, and is dominated by the **National Museum of Scotland** (☎ 247 4422; www.nms.ac.uk; Chambers St; admission free, special exhibitions extra; ☾ 10am-5pm).

The golden stone and striking modern architecture of the **Museum of Scotland** houses five floors of exhibits tracing the history of Scotland from geological beginnings to the 1990s. The neighbouring Victorian **Royal Museum of Scotland**, dating from 1861, houses an eclectic collection covering natural history, archaeology, scientific and industrial technology, and the decorative arts of ancient Egypt, Islam, China, Japan, Korea and the West.

NEW TOWN

Edinburgh's New Town lies north of the Old Town, separated from it by the valley of Princes Street Gardens. Its regular grid of elegant, Georgian terraces is a contrast to the chaotic tangle of the Old Town.

PRINCES STREET

Princes St is one of the world's most spectacular shopping streets. The eastern half of the street is dominated by the massive Gothic spire of the **Scott Monument** (☎ 529 4068; East Princes Street Gardens; admission

JONATHAN SMITH
Scott Monument

£3; ☺ 9am-6pm Mon-Sat, 10am-6pm Sun Apr-Sep, 9am-3pm Mon-Sat, 10am-3pm Sun Oct-Mar), built by public subscription in memory of the novelist Sir Walter Scott after his death in 1832. Inside you can see an exhibition on Scott's life, and climb the 287 steps to the top for a superb view of the city.

The **National Gallery of Scotland** (☎ 624 6200; www.nationalgalleries.org; The Mound; admission free; ☺ 10am-5pm Fri-Wed, 10am-7pm Thu) is another imposing neoclassical building, housing a significant collection of European art.

GEORGE STREET & CHARLOTTE SQUARE

Charlotte Square, the architectural jewel of the New Town, was designed by Robert Adam shortly before his death in 1791. The northern side of the square is Adam's masterpiece and one of the finest examples of Georgian architecture anywhere. **Bute House**, in the centre at No 6, is the official residence of Scotland's first minister.

Next door is the **Georgian House** (☎ 226 2160; 7 Charlotte Sq; adult/child £5/4; ☺ 10am-6pm Jul & Aug, 10am-5pm Apr-Jun, Sep & Oct, 11am-3pm Mar & Nov), which has been beautifully restored and furnished to show how Edinburgh's wealthy elite lived at the end of the 18th century.

Near St Andrew Sq, at the opposite end of George St, is the Venetian Gothic palace of the **Scottish National Portrait Gallery** (☎ 624 6200; www.nationalgalleries.org; 1 Queen St; admission free; ☺ 10am-5pm daily, to 7pm Thu). Its galleries illustrate Scottish history through portraits and sculptures of famous Scottish personalities, from Robert Burns and Bonnie Prince Charlie to Sean Connery and Billy Connolly.

CALTON HILL

Rising dramatically above the eastern end of Princes St, Calton Hill (100m) is

Edinburgh's acropolis; its summit scattered with grandiose memorials mostly dating from the first half of the 19th century.

Looking a bit like an upturned telescope – the similarity is intentional – and offering even better views, the **Nelson Monument** (☎ 556 2716; Calton Hill; admission £3; ☺ 1-6pm Mon, 10am-6pm Tue-Sat Apr-Sep, 10am-3pm Mon-Sat Oct-Mar) was built to commemorate Admiral Lord Nelson's victory at Trafalgar in 1805.

GREATER EDINBURGH
ROYAL BOTANIC GARDEN
North of the New Town lies the lovely **Royal Botanic Garden** (☎ 552 7171; www.rbge.org.uk; 20a Inverleith Row; admission to gardens free, to glasshouses £3.50; ☺ 10am-7pm Apr-Sep, 10am-6pm Mar & Oct, 10am-4pm Nov-Feb). Twenty-eight beautifully landscaped hectares include splendid Victorian palm houses, colourful swaths of rhododendron and azalea, and a world-famous rock garden. Take Lothian bus 8, 17, 23 or 27 to the East Gate.

EDINBURGH ZOO
Opened in 1913, **Edinburgh Zoo** (☎ 334 9171; www.edinburghzoo.org.uk; 134 Corstorphine Rd; adult/child £11.50/8; ☺ 9am-6pm Apr-Sep, 9am-5pm Oct & Mar, 9am-4.30pm Nov-Feb) is one of the world's leading conservation zoos. Edinburgh's captive breeding program has saved many endangered species, including Siberian tigers, pygmy hippos and red pandas.

The zoo is 2.5 miles west of the city centre; take Lothian bus 12, 26 or 31, First bus 16, 18, 80 or 86, or the Airlink bus 100 westbound from Princes St.

CRAIGMILLAR CASTLE
If you want to explore a Scottish fortress away from the crowds that throng Edinburgh Castle, try **Craigmillar Castle** (HS; ☎ 661 4445; Craigmillar Castle Rd; adult/child £4.20/2.10; ☺ 9.30am-5.30pm Apr-Sep, 9.30am-4.30pm Oct, 9.30am-4.30pm Sat-Wed Nov-Mar). Dating from the 15th century, the tower house rises above two sets of machicolated curtain walls. Mary Queen of Scots took refuge here after the murder of Rizzio; it was here too that plans to murder her husband Darnley were laid.

The castle is 2.5 miles southeast of the city centre. Take bus 33 eastbound from Princes St to Old Dalkeith Rd and walk 500m up Craigmillar Castle Rd.

TOURS
Black Hart Storytellers (☎ 225 9044; www.blackhart.uk.com; adult/concession £8.50/6.50) Not suitable for young children. The 'City of the Dead' tour of Greyfriars Kirkyard is probably the best of Edinburgh's 'ghost' tours.

Cadies & Witchery Tours (☎ 225 6745; www.witcherytours.com; adult/child £7.50/5) These entertaining tours are famous for their 'jumper-ooters' – costumed actors who 'jump oot' when you least expect it.

Edinburgh Literary Pub Tour (☎ 226 6665; www.edinburghliterarypubtour.co.uk; adult/student £9/7) An enlightening two-hour trawl through Edinburgh's literary history – and its associated *howffs* (pubs) – in the entertaining company of Messrs Clart and McBrain.

Edinburgh Tour (☎ 555 6363; adult/child £10/4) Lothian Buses' bright red buses depart every 20 minutes from Waverley Bridge.

Mercat Tours (☎ 557 6464; www.mercattours.com; adult/child £7.50/4) Mercat offers a wide range of fascinating tours including history walks in the Old Town and Leith, 'Ghosts & Ghouls' tours and visits to haunted underground vaults.

LEFT: MARGIE POLITZER; RIGHT: WILL SALTER

Left: Funhouse mirror, Camera Obscura (p287); Right: Outdoor cafe, Royal Mile

FESTIVALS & EVENTS

First held in 1947 to mark a return to peace after the ordeal of WWII, the **Edinburgh International Festival** (☎ 473 2099; www .eif.co.uk) is festooned with superlatives – the oldest, the most famous, the best in the world – as hundreds of the world's top musicians and performers congregate in Edinburgh for three weeks of diverse and inspirational music, opera, theatre and dance. You can buy tickets at the **Hub** (☎ 473 2000; Highland Tolbooth Kirk, Castlehill; ☻ 10am-5pm Mon-Sat), or by phone, fax or internet.

When the first Edinburgh Festival was held in 1947, there were eight theatre companies who didn't make it onto the main program. Undeterred, they grouped together and held their own minifestival, on the fringe, and an Edinburgh institution was born. Today the **Edinburgh Festival Fringe** (☎ 226 0026; www.edfringe .com; Edinburgh Festival Fringe Office, 180 High St) is *the* biggest festival of the performing arts anywhere in the world.

Also in August, the hugely popular **Edinburgh Military Tattoo** is a spectacular display of marching bands, massed pipes and drums, acrobats, cheerleaders and motorcycle display teams, all played out in front of the magnificent backdrop of the floodlit castle. Contact the **Edinburgh Tattoo Office** (☎ 225 1188; www.edintattoo .co.uk; 33 Market St) for tickets.

Hogmanay (New Year) is also a peak party time. You can find info on all of Edinburgh's main festivals on the umbrella website www.edinburgh-festivals.com.

SLEEPING

There's plenty of accommodation in Edinburgh, but during festival times the city still fills up, so pre-booking is a must.

OLD TOWN & SOUTH OF THE ROYAL MILE

Cluaran House (☎ 221 0047; www.cluaran -house-edinburgh.co.uk; 47 Leamington Tce; s from £50, d & tw from £80) Bright and arty, this re-stored town house is a stylish guesthouse known for its welcoming owners. Period features and wooden floorboards are kept, but the bold decoration makes this place an explosion of colour.

Greenhouse (☎ 622 7634; www.greenhouse -edinburgh.com; 14 Hartington Gardens; s/d from £65/70) The award-winning Greenhouse is a wholly vegetarian and vegan guesthouse, which uses organic and genetically modi-fied-free foods as much as possible.

Southside Guest House (☎ 668 4422; www.southsideguesthouse.co.uk; 8 Newington Rd; s/d from £60/88; 🖳 wi-fi) Though set in a typical Victorian terrace, the Southside transcends the traditional guesthouse category and feels more like a modern boutique hotel.

Witchery by the Castle (☎ 225 5613; www.thewitchery.com; Castlehill, Royal Mile; ste £295) Set in a 16th-century Old Town house in the shadow of Edinburgh Castle, the Witchery's seven lavish suites are extrava-gantly furnished with antiques, oak pan-elling, tapestries, open fires and roll-top baths, and supplied with flowers, choco-lates and complimentary champagne. It's overwhelmingly popular – you'll have to book several months in advance to be sure of getting a room.

Scotsman Hotel (☎ 556 5565; www.the scotsmanhotel.com; North Bridge; r £300-375, ste from £500; Ⓟ 🖳) The former offices of the *Scotsman* newspaper – opened in 1904 and hailed as 'the most magnificent news-paper building in the world' – are now home to this luxury hotel.

NEW TOWN & NORTHERN EDINBURGH

Frederick House Hotel (☎ 226 1999; www .townhousehotels.co.uk; 42 Frederick St; s/d from £50/70; 🖳 wi-fi) This well-positioned hotel is decked out in lovely interior wallpaper with roomy double beds and large baths to soak away the day's walking aches.

Dukes of Windsor Street (☎ 556 6046; www.dukesofwindsor.com; 17 Windsor St; d £90-170;

🖳 wi-fi) A relaxing eight-bedroom Georgian town house set on a quiet side street, only a few paces from Princes St, Dukes offers an appealing blend of modern sophistica-tion and period atmosphere.

ourpick Six Mary's Place (☎ 332 8965; www.sixmarysplace.co.uk; 6 Mary's Pl, Raeburn Pl; s/d/f from £45/94/150; 🖳 wi-fi) Six Mary's Place is an attractive Georgian town house with a designer mix of period features, contem-porary furniture and modern colours. Breakfasts are vegetarian-only, served in an attractive conservatory with a view of the garden, while the lounge, with its big, comfy sofas, offers free coffee and newspapers.

Glasshouse (☎ 525 8200; www.theetoncol lection.com; 2 Greenside Pl; d/ste £295/450; Ⓟ) A palace of cutting-edge design perched atop the Omni Centre at the foot of Calton Hill, and entered through the preserved facade of a 19th-century church, the Glasshouse sports luxury rooms with floor-to-ceiling windows, leather sofas, marble bathrooms and a rooftop garden.

EATING
OLD TOWN & SOUTH OF THE ROYAL MILE

Elephant House (☎ 220 5355; www.elephant house.biz; 21 George IV Bridge; snacks £3-6; 🕑 8am-11pm; 🖳) Brilliant cafe that does baguettes, pastries and coffees powerful enough to inspire JK Rowling to pen *Harry Potter* (she used to sit and write in the back room, with a view of Edinburgh Castle).

ourpick Monster Mash (☎ 225 7069; www .monstermashcafe.co.uk; 4a Forrest Rd; mains £5-7; 🕑 8am-10pm Mon-Fri, 9am-10pm Sat, 10am-10pm Sun) Classic British grub of the 1950s – bangers and mash, shepherd's pie, fish and chips – is the mainstay of the menu at this nostalgia-fuelled cafe.

Outsider (☎ 226 3131; 15 George IV Bridge; mains £8-12; 🕑 noon-11pm) This Edinburgh stalwart is known for its rainforest interior (potted ferns in atmospheric dimness) and has a brilliant menu that jumps straight in with mains such as chorizo and chickpea casserole.

Apartment (☎ 228 6456; 7-13 Barclay Pl; mains £8-12; ☺ dinner, lunch Sat & Sun) Whether it's in the decor or the menu, simple yet modish is the order of the day at this eatery. Dishes are divided into 'things': succulent fish things such as the baked sea bass papillote with king prawns and pepped up with chilli and lime is our favourite.

Tower (☎ 225 3003; Chambers St; mains £16-25; ☺ noon-11pm) Grand views of the castle are accompanied by a menu of top-quality Scottish produce, simply prepared – try half a dozen Scottish oysters followed by a chargrilled Aberdeen Angus fillet steak.

NEW TOWN & NORTHERN EDINBURGH

our pick Urban Angel (☎ 225 6215; www.urban-angel.co.uk; 121 Hanover St; snacks £3-7, mains £8-11; ☺ 10am-10pm Mon-Thu, 10am-11pm Fri & Sat, 10am-5pm Sun) A wholesome deli that puts the emphasis on fair-trade, organic and locally sourced produce, Urban Angel also has a delightfully informal cafe-bistro that serves a wide range of light, snacky meals including an unusual Scottish combination of smoked salmon and tattie scone.

L'Alba D'Oro (☎ 557 2580; www.lalba doro.com; 5-7 Henderson Row; fish supper £6-7; ☺ 5-11pm) Pronouncing any place as Edinburgh's best chippie is always contentious, but with a busy knot of cars waiting for a parking space outside, this place gets the nod from many locals.

Fishers (☎ 554 5666; 1 The Shore, Leith; mains £9-22; ☺ noon-10.30pm) This cosy little bar-turned-restaurant, tucked beneath a 17th-century signal tower, is one of the city's best seafood places. Fishers' fish cakes are an Edinburgh institution.

Howie's (☎ 556 5766; 29 Waterloo Pl; mains £10-15; ☺ lunch & dinner) A bright and airy Georgian corner-house provides the elegant setting for this, the most central of Howie's four hugely popular Edinburgh restaurants. Its recipe for success includes fresh Scottish produce, good-value, fixed-price menus, and eminently quaffable house wines for around £12 a bottle.

Stac Polly (☎ 556 2231; www.stacpolly.co.uk; 29-33 Dublin St; mains £18-20; ☺ lunch Mon-Fri, dinner) Named after a mountain in northwestern Scotland, Stac Polly's kitchen adds sophisticated twists to fresh Highland produce. Dishes such as loin of venison with redcurrant and rosemary jus keep the punters coming back for more.

our pick Kitchin (☎ 555 1755; www.the kitchin.com; 78 Commercial Quay; ☺ noon-2.30pm Tue-Sat, 7.30-10pm Tue-Thu, 6.45-10.30pm Fri & Sat) Fresh, seasonal Scottish produce, locally sourced, is the philosophy that has won a Michelin star for this elegant but unpretentious restaurant.

DRINKING
OLD TOWN & SOUTH OF THE ROYAL MILE

Jolly Judge (☎ 225 2669; 7a James Court) Tucked away down an Old Town close, the Judge exudes a cosy 17th-century ambience with its low, timber-beamed, painted ceilings and numerous nooks and crannies.

Cloisters (☎ 221 9997; 26 Brougham St; ☺ noon-midnight) Housed in a converted manse (minister's house) that once belonged to the next-door church, and furnished with well-worn, mismatched wooden tables and chairs, Cloisters now ministers to a mixed congregation of students, locals and real-ale connoisseurs.

Pear Tree House (☎ 667 7533; 38 West Nicolson St) The Pear Tree is another student favourite, with comfy sofas and board games inside, plus the city centre's biggest beer garden outside.

NEW TOWN & NORTHERN EDINBURGH

Kay's Bar (☎ 225 1858; 39 Jamaica St West) Tired of pubs where the TV's always blaring in the background? This former wine merchant's office (walls are decorated with old wine barrels) is a cosy little place whose rustic ambience is designed not to get in the way of sampling real ales and malt whiskies.

Amicus Apple (☎ 226 6055; 15 Frederick St) Cream leather sofas and dark-brown armchairs, bold design and funky lighting make this laid-back cocktail lounge the hippest hang-out in the New Town.

Barony Bar (☎ 557 0546; 81 Broughton St) Worn tables, a jovial crowd and warming fires mean that this pub remains a firm favourite, especially for reading the Sunday papers.

Oxford Bar (☎ 539 7119; 8 Young St) 'The Ox' has been immortalised by Ian Rankin, author of the Inspector Rebus novels, who is a regular here, as is his fictional detective.

ENTERTAINMENT

The comprehensive source for what's-on info is the *List* (£2.20; www.list.co.uk), an excellent listings magazine covering both Edinburgh and Glasgow. It's available from most newsagents, and is published fortnightly on a Thursday.

GETTING THERE & AWAY

AIR

Edinburgh airport (☎ 333 1000; www.edinburghairport.com), 8 miles west of Edinburgh, has flights to many parts of the UK, Ireland and continental Europe. The main airlines serving the city are **British Airways** (☎ 084 493 0787; www.ba.com), **bmi baby** (☎ 0870 60 70 555; www.bmibaby.com) and **easyJet** (☎ 0870 600 0000; www.easyjet.com), with direct flights from London, Bristol, Birmingham, Manchester, Belfast and Cardiff.

BUS

Edinburgh Bus Station is at the northeast corner of St Andrew Sq, with pedestrian entrances from the square and from Elder St.

IZZET KERIBAR

Edinburgh pub scene

For timetable information, call **Traveline** (☎ 0871 200 22 33; www.traveline.org.uk).

National Express (☎ 08717 818181; www.nationalexpress.com) runs to London (from £34, nine hours, three daily). There are also services to Newcastle (£17, 2¾ hours, three to five daily) and York (£34, 5¾ hours, one daily).

Scottish Citylink (☎ 08705 505050; www .citylink.co.uk) buses connect Edinburgh with all of Scotland's major cities and towns, including Aberdeen (£24, 3¼ hours, hourly); Dundee (£13, 1¾ hours, every 30 minutes); Fort William (£24, four hours, three daily); Glasgow (£6, 1¼ hours, four an hour); Inverness (£10, four hours, hourly); Portree (£32, eight hours, two daily); and Stirling (£6, one hour, hourly).

Stagecoach (☎ 01698 870 768; www.stage coachbus.com) runs the Motorvator bus to Glasgow (£6, 1¼ hours, every 20 minutes Monday to Saturday, hourly Sunday).

CAR & MOTORCYCLE

Arriving in or leaving Edinburgh by car during the morning and evening rush hours (7.30am to 9.30am and 4.30pm to 6.30pm Monday to Friday) is an experience you can live without.

TRAIN

The main train station in Edinburgh is Waverley station, in the heart of the city. Trains arriving from, and departing for, the west also stop at Haymarket station, which is more convenient for the West End. You can buy tickets, make reservations and get travel information at the **Edinburgh Rail Travel Centre** (☽ 4.45am-12.30am Mon-Sat, 7am-12.30am Sun) in Waverley station.

First ScotRail (☎ 08457 55 00 33; www .firstscotrail.com) operates a regular shuttle service between Edinburgh and Glasgow (£11, 50 minutes, every 15 to 30 minutes),

and frequent daily services to all Scottish cities including Aberdeen (£38, 2½ hours), Dundee (£19, 1½ hours) and Inverness (£38, 3¼ hours).

National Express East Coast (☎ 08457 225 333; www.nationalexpresseastcoast.com) operates the Edinburgh to London Kings Cross route (£126, 4½ hours, at least hourly), calling at Newcastle (£42, 1½ hours) and York (£72, 2½ hours).

GETTING AROUND
TO/FROM THE AIRPORT

The Lothian Buses **Airlink** (www.flybybus .com) service 100 runs from Waverley Bridge, just outside the train station, to the airport (one way/return £3/5, 30 minutes, every 10 to 15 minutes) via the West End and Haymarket.

Edinburgh Shuttle Minibus (☎ 0845 500 5000; www.edinburghshuttle.com; one way £9 per person) will drop you at your hotel (or any other address in central Edinburgh).

An airport taxi to the city centre costs around £15 and takes about 20 minutes.

PUBLIC TRANSPORT

The two main bus operators are **Lothian Buses** (☎ 554 4494; www.lothianbuses.co.uk) and **First Edinburgh** (☎ 08708 72 72 71; www.firstedinburgh.co.uk). Buy your ticket as you board buses – on Lothian services you need the exact change.

AROUND EDINBURGH
QUEENSFERRY & INCHCOLM

Queensferry is located at the narrowest part of the Firth of Forth, where ferries have crossed to Fife from the earliest times. The village takes its name from Queen Margaret (1046–93), who gave pilgrims free passage across the firth on

GARETH MCCORMACK

Edinburgh Military Tattoo (p294), Edinburgh Castle

their way to St Andrews. Ferries continued to operate until 1964 when the graceful **Forth Road Bridge** – now Europe's fifth longest – was opened.

Pre-dating the road bridge by 74 years, the magnificent **Forth Bridge** – only outsiders ever call it the Forth Rail Bridge – is one of the finest engineering achievements of the 19th century. Completed in 1890 after seven years' work, its three huge cantilevers span 1447m and took 59,000 tonnes of steel, eight million rivets and the lives of 58 men to build.

Two miles west of Queensferry, **Hopetoun House** (☎ 0131-331 2451; www .hopetounhouse.com; adult/child £8/4.25, grounds only £3.70/2.20; ⌚ 10.30am-5pm Apr-Sep) is one of Scotland's finest stately homes, with 150 acres of stunning landscaped grounds beside the Firth of Forth. There are two parts: the older built between 1699 and 1702 to Sir William Bruce's plans and dominated by a grand stairwell; and the newer designed between 1720 and 1750 by William Adam and his sons, Robert and John.

ROSSLYN CHAPEL

The success of Dan Brown's novel *The Da Vinci Code* and the subsequent Hollywood film has seen a flood of visitors descend on Scotland's most beautiful and enigmatic church – **Rosslyn Chapel** (Collegiate Church of St Matthew; ☎ 0131-440 2159; www .rosslynchapel.com; Roslin; adult/child £7.50/free; ⌚ 9.30am-6pm Mon-Sat, noon-4.45pm Sun Apr-Sep, 9.30am-5pm Mon-Sat, noon-4.45pm Sun Oct-Mar). The chapel was built in the mid-15th century for William St Clair, third earl of Orkney, and the ornately carved interior is a monument to the mason's art, rich in symbolic imagery. As well as flowers, vines, angels and biblical figures, the carved stones include many examples of the pagan 'Green Man'; other figures are associated with Freemasonry and the Knights Templar.

The chapel is on the eastern edge of the village of Roslin, 7 miles south of Edinburgh's centre. Lothian bus 15 (not 15A) runs from St Andrew Sq in Edinburgh to Roslin (30 minutes, every 30 minutes).

GLASGOW

pop 581,000

Scotland's biggest city has shrugged off its shroud of industrial soot and shimmied into a sparkling new designer gown. Ten years on from being named UK City of Architecture and Design 1999, Glasgow is flaunting its reputation as a capital of cool and has branded itself as 'Scotland with Style'.

HISTORY

Glasgow grew up around the church (later a cathedral) founded by St Mungo in the 6th century, and the University of Glasgow, established in 1451 (Britain's fourth university, after Cambridge, Oxford and St Andrews).

George Square

JONATHAN SMITH

Mosaic ceiling, City Chambers

MARTIN MOOS

Glasgow prospered in the 18th century on the wealth created by the tobacco trade between Europe and North America, much of which passed through its sprawling docks along the River Clyde. In the postwar years, however, the docks and heavy industries dwindled, and by the early 1970s the city seemed to be in terminal decline. But since the 1990s there has been increasing confidence in the city as it determinedly set about the process of regeneration.

ORIENTATION

The city centre is built on a grid system on the northern side of the River Clyde. The two train stations (Central and Queen St), the Buchanan bus station and the tourist office are all on, or within, a few blocks of George Sq, the main city square. Merchant City is the main commercial and entertainment district, east of George Sq.

INFORMATION

St Enoch Square Travel Centre (St Enoch Sq; ⏱ 8.30am-5.30pm Mon-Sat) Travel information only.

Tourist Office City Centre (☎ 0141-204 4400; www.seeglasgow.com; 11 George Sq; ⏱ 9am-6pm Mon-Sat Oct-Jan & Easter-May, 9am-7pm Mon-Sat Jun & Sep, 9am-8pm Mon-Sat Jul & Aug, 10am-6pm Sun Easter-Sep); Glasgow Airport (☎ 0141-848 4440; ⏱ 7.30am-5pm)

SIGHTS

CITY CENTRE

GEORGE SQUARE

Glasgow's main square is a grand public space, built in the Victorian era to show off the city's wealth and dignified by statues of notable Glaswegians and famous Scots, including Robert Burns, James Watt, General Sir John Moore and, atop a column, Sir Walter Scott. Overlooking the east side is the **City Chambers** (☎ 0141-287 4018; George Sq; admission & tours free) – the seat

CHARLES RENNIE MACKINTOSH, GLASGOW'S GENIUS

Wherever you go in Glasgow, you'll see the quirky, geometric designs of this famous Scottish architect, artist and designer. His best-known building is the **Glasgow School of Art** (☎ 0141-353 4526; www.gsa.ac.uk/tour; 167 Renfrew St; tours adult/ concession £7.75/5.75; ☽ tours hourly 10am-noon & 2-5pm Apr-Sep, 11am & 3pm only Oct-Mar), which was named one of the world's 100 greatest artistic achievements of the 20th century by the BBC.

North of the city centre, **Queen's Cross Church** (☎ 0141-946 6600; 870 Garscube Rd; adult/child £2/free; ☽ 10am-5pm Mon-Fri year round, 2-5pm Sun Mar-Oct), lit by dazzling stained glass and drawing on both Gothic and Japanese motifs, is Mackintosh's only church design to be built (1896). On a more intimate scale, **Mackintosh House** (☎ 0141-330 5431; www.hunterian.gla.ac.uk; 82 Hillhead St; admission £3, after 2pm Wed free; ☽ 9.30am-5pm Mon-Sat) is a reconstruction of the architect's (now demolished) Glasgow home, housed in the Hunterian Museum and Art Gallery.

The **Scotland Street School** (☎ 0141-287 0500; 225 Scotland St; admission free; ☽ 10am-5pm Mon-Thu & Sat, 11am-5pm Fri & Sun), dating from 1906, was Mackintosh's last major architectural commission in Glasgow, and is filled with his telltale design touches.

of local government – built in the 1880s at the high point of the city's prosperity.

GALLERY OF MODERN ART

The grandiose neoclassical exterior of the Royal Exchange, which now houses this **gallery** (GoMA; ☎ 0141-229 1996; www.glasgow museums.com; Queen St; admission free; ☽ 10am-5pm Mon-Wed & Sat, 10am-8pm Thu, 11am-5pm Fri & Sun), contrasts with the contemporary paintings and sculpture within. Outside, local smart-artists do a daily 'installation' of a traffic cone on the statue of the Duke of Wellington, despite the local council's regular removal of their handiwork.

GLASGOW CATHEDRAL

A shining example of pre-Reformation Gothic architecture, **Glasgow Cathedral** (HS; ☎ 0141-552 6891; www.glasgowcathedral .org.uk; admission free; ☽ 9.30am-6pm Mon-Sat, 1-5pm Sun Apr-Sep, 9.30am-4pm Mon-Sat, 1-4pm Sun Oct-Mar) is the only mainland cathedral in Scotland to survive the Reformation.

It's a 20-minute walk to the cathedral from George Sq, but numerous buses pass by, including buses 11, 12, 36, 37, 38 and 42.

PEOPLE'S PALACE & WINTER GARDENS

Not just a local museum for local people, the **People's Palace & Winter Gardens** (☎ 0141-271 2951; Glasgow Green; admission free; ☽ 10am-5pm Mon-Thu & Sat, 11am-5pm Fri & Sun) showcases what it means to be Glaswegian. From the goofy 1970s portrait of Billy Connolly to dance cards from the former Barrowland dance hall, this place is a monument to social history, with displays on language, comedy and the now-demolished Glasgow slums, charting the city's development from the 1750s to the present day. The neighbouring Winter Gardens is an elegant Victorian glasshouse where you can enjoy a cup of coffee among the tropical palms.

EDINBURGH & GLASGOW

GLASGOW

GLASGOW CITY CENTRE

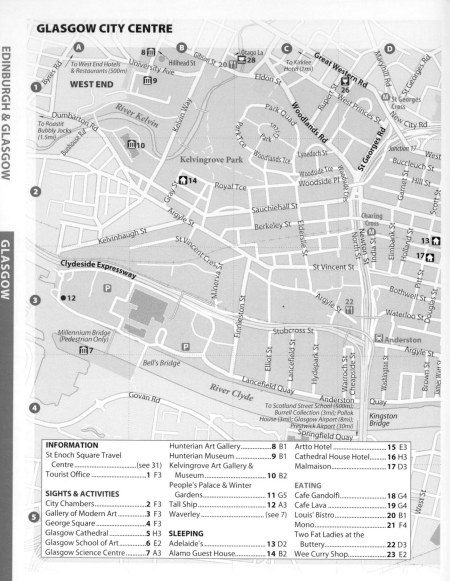

GLASGOW SCIENCE CENTRE

Glasgow's flagship millennium project, the **Glasgow Science Centre** (☎ 0141-420 5000; www.glasgowsciencecentre.org; 50 Pacific Quay; adult/child £7.95/5.95; ☼ 10am-6pm) brings science and technology alive through hundreds of interactive exhibits and kid-friendly activities. As well as the main science mall, there's an IMAX cinema (admission £2 extra), a planetarium (£2 extra) and 127m-tall, rotating observation tower (also £2 extra). Take Arriva bus 24

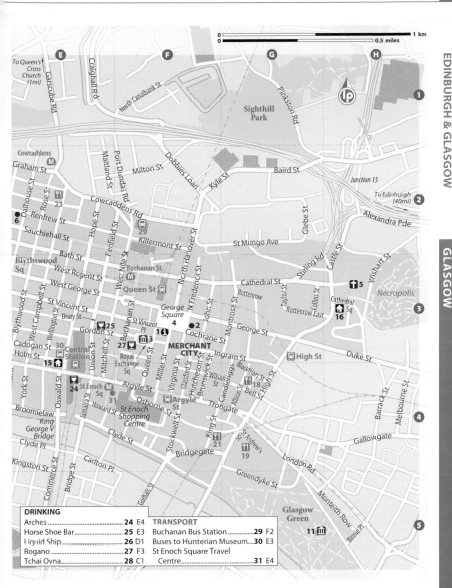

from Renfield St or First Glasgow bus 89 or 90 from Union St.

TALL SHIP

Across the Clyde from the Science Centre is the **Tall Ship** (☎ 0141-222 2513; www.thetall ship.com; Stobcross Rd; adult/child £4.95/3.75, 1 child per adult free; ☺ 10am-5pm Mar-Oct, 10am-4pm Nov-Feb), one of five Clyde-built sailing ships still afloat. Launched in 1896, the *Glenlee* is an impressively restored three-masted vessel that contains displays on

EDINBURGH & GLASGOW

GLASGOW

Kelvingrove Art Gallery & Museum

PAUL BIGLAND

↘ KELVINGROVE ART GALLERY & MUSEUM

Recently reopened after an enormous refurbishment program, Glasgow's much-loved cultural icon the Kelvingrove Art Gallery & Museum is the most visited museum in the UK outside of London. Its magnificent Edwardian building houses a superb collection of Scottish and European art – must-see masterpieces include Dali's sublime *Christ of St John of the Cross* and Rembrandt's *Man in Armour,* as well as works by the Scottish Colourists and the Glasgow Boys.

Things you need to know: ☎ 0141-276 9599; Argyle St; admission free; ⊙ 10am-5pm Mon-Thu & Sat, 11am-5pm Fri & Sun

her history, restoration and life on board in the early 20th century.

WEST END

Housed in two buildings on either side of University Ave, the **Hunterian Museum** (☎ 0141-330 4221; www.hunterian.gla.ac.uk; University Ave; admission free; ⊙ 9.30am-5pm Mon-Sat) was opened in 1807 as Scotland's first public museum, based on the collection of William Hunter (1718–83), physician, medical teacher and former student of the university.

Across the road, the Scottish Colourists (Samuel Peploe, Francis Cadell, JD Fergusson) are well represented in the **Hunterian Art Gallery** (☎ 0141-330 5431; 82 Hillhead St; admission free; ⊙ 9.30am-5pm Mon-Sat), which also displays Sir William MacTaggart's impressionistic Scottish landscapes, and a gem by Thomas Millie Dow. Also located here is the unmissable **Mackintosh House** (see p301).

Buses 11, 44 and 44A pass this way from the city centre (Hope St); or it's a short walk from Hillhead underground station.

GREATER GLASGOW

One of Glasgow's most famous attractions, the **Burrell Collection** (☎ 0141-287 2550; Pollok Country Park, Pollokshaws Rd; admission free, parking £1.50; ⊙ 10am-5pm Mon-Thu & Sat, 11am-5pm Fri & Sun) is an idiosyncratic treasure house of art and artefacts amassed by wealthy industrialist Sir William Burrell (1861–1958) and donated to the city in 1944. The collection ranges from Chinese porcelain and medieval furniture to paintings by Renoir and Cézanne and sculpture by Rodin.

There are occasional guided tours. Many buses pass the park gates (including buses 45, 47, 48 and 57 from the city centre), and there's a twice-hourly bus service between the gallery and the gates (a pleasant 10-minute walk).

The Burrell Collection stands in the grounds of **Pollok House** (NTS; ☎ 0141-616 6410; www.nts.org.uk; Pollok Country Park, 2060 Pollokshaws Rd; admission Apr-Oct £8, Nov-Mar free; ⊙ 10am-5pm), a sumptuous Edwardian mansion brimful of period furniture, its walls graced with paintings by El Greco and Murillo. The extensive servants' quarters give an idea of how the British aristocracy once lived, and there's an atmospheric cafe in the old Edwardian kitchen. The house is less than half a mile's walk from the Burrell Collection.

TOURS

City Sightseeing (☎ 0141-204 0444; www .citysightseeingglasgow.co.uk; adult/child £9/3) has a bus tour starting at George Sq – get on and off as you wish.

Offering cruises on the world's last ocean-going paddle steamer, the **Waverley** (☎ 0845 130 4647; www.waver leyexcursions.co.uk; Anderston Quay; cruises from £17; ⏲ Apr-Sep) goes from Glasgow to the Firth of Clyde and the Islands of Bute, Great Cumbrae and Arran. It departs from Glasgow Science Centre.

SLEEPING

CITY CENTRE

Adelaide's (☎ 0141-248 4970; www.adelaides .co.uk; 209 Bath St; s £32-45, d £54; 🖳) Adelaide's is an unusual place – a simple, family-friendly (and relatively cheap) guesthouse on prestigious Bath St set in an historic church conversion.

Artto Hotel (☎ 0141-248 2480; www.artto hotel.com; 37 Hope St; s/d £70/90; 🖳 wi-fi) Everything is squeaky clean and gleaming in this fashionable hotel. The high-ceilinged rooms have light subtle tones combined with earthy, darkish maroons, giving them a modish appeal, and slick, sparkling en suites with power showers complete the happy picture.

ourpick **Cathedral House Hotel** (☎ 0141-552 3519; www.cathedralhousehotel.org; 28-32 Cathedral Sq; s/d from £60/90; 🖳 wi-fi) In the heart of the leafy, dignified East End stands this 19th-century Scottish baronial-style hotel, complete with turrets and eight individual and beautifully furnished rooms.

Malmaison (☎ 0141-572 1000; www.mal maison-glasgow.com; 278 West George St; d/ste from £109/£210; 🖳 wi-fi) Part of a boutique chain that's conquering the UK, the Glasgow branch is as swanky as you'd expect. Housed in a converted Episcopalian church built in the style of a Greek temple, the rooms have been individually styled with private CD collections and sunken baths.

WEST END

Alamo Guest House (☎ 0141-339 2395; www.alamoguesthouse.com; 46 Gray St; s/d from £32/52; 🖳 wi-fi) This elegant Victorian town house is a great place to stay, dripping with period detail and offering rooms larger than you'd get in a city-centre hotel, plus a beautiful breakfast room overlooking leafy Kelvingrove Park.

Kirklee Hotel (☎ 0141-334 5555; www .kirkleehotel.co.uk; 11 Kensington Gate; s/d £59/75) This grand Edwardian town house is a quiet little gem of a place that combines the luxury of a classy hotel with the warmth of staying in someone's home.

Hotel du Vin (☎ 0141-339 2001; www .hotelduvin.com; 1 Devonshire Gardens; r/ste from £145/395; 🖳 wi-fi) Glasgow's first boutique hotel was made famous as One Devonshire Gardens. A study in elegance, it spreads through three classical terraced town houses offering individually furnished designer bedrooms with monsoon showers, and two fine restaurants.

EATING

CITY CENTRE

Cafe Lava (☎ 0141-553 1123; 24 St Andrew's St; mains £2-6; ⏲ 8am-6pm Mon-Fri, 10am-5pm Sat & Sun; 🖳 wi-fi) Everyone wants to live next door to a cafe like this. The understated menu delivers delicious home cooking, including a breakfast of Stornoway black pudding and eggs Benedict.

Mono (☎ 0141-553 2400; 12 Kings Ct; mains £3-7; ⏲ noon-10pm) Not content to be one of Glasgow's best vegetarian cafes, this place also crams in an indie record store and an organic grocery shop, and serves as an occasional live-music venue.

Wee Curry Shop City (☎ 0141-353 0777; 7 Buccleuch St; 2-course lunches £6, dinner mains £11;

Restaurants on Ashton Lane, Glasgow

MARGIE POLITZER

⏱ lunch Mon-Sat, dinner daily); West End (☎ 0141-357 5280; 29 Ashton Lane; dinner mains £11; ⏱ lunch, dinner) Could there be a better illustration of Scotland's infatuation with Indian cuisine than a curry shop decked out in tartan?

Cafe Gandolfi (☎ 0141-552 6813; 64 Albion St; mains £8-16; ⏱ 9am-11.30pm Mon-Sat, noon-11.30pm Sun) This Merchant City pioneer (opened in 1979) maintains its place in the pecking order of this busy eating precinct by working innovative magic with Modern Scottish and Mediterranean cuisine – very busy at weekends, so book ahead.

Two Fat Ladies at the Buttery (☎ 0141-221 8188; 652-4 Argyle St; mains £18-22; ⏱ lunch & dinner) Now under new management, Glasgow's oldest restaurant (opened 1856) has toned down the tartanry and shrugged off its air of formality – you can now enjoy its ancient oak-panelled rooms, magnificent carved bar and antique stained glass without having to don jacket and tie.

WEST END

Louis' Bistro (☎ 0141-339 7915; 18 Gibson St; mains £8-13; ⏱ lunch & dinner Tue-Sat) Well placed to take the award for best burger in town, this unpretentious neighbourhood bistro also serves perfectly prepared steaks. But vegetarians have not been forgotten, with a selection of tasty and inventive meat-free dishes.

Gambrino (☎ 0141-339 4111; 333 Great Western Rd; mains £8-13; ⏱ noon-2.30pm & 5.30-11pm Mon-Fri, noon-11pm Sat, noon-11pm Sun) A rustic Italian trattoria with weathered timber beams, bare brickwork and candlelit tables. Gambrino's deliciously authentic pizza and pasta mean that it is often busy – there's a queue for tables at weekends, but it always seems to fit everyone in.

Roastit Bubbly Jocks (☎ 0141-339 3355; 450 Dumbarton Rd; mains £9-14; ⏱ lunch Fri-Sun, dinner) Lively and informal, this bustling bistro takes traditional Scottish dishes such as Scotch broth, braised lamb and roast venison and gives them a gourmet twist. It's a bit out of town, but close to the Partick underground station.

Ubiquitous Chip (☎ 0141-334 5007; 12 Ashton Lane; 3-course lunch/dinner £30/40; ⏱ lunch & dinner) The original champion of quality

Scottish produce, this restaurant has won lots of awards for its unparalleled Scottish cuisine, and for its lengthy wine list.

DRINKING

Some of Scotland's best nightlife is to be found in the din and roar of Glasgow's crowded pubs and bars.

Rogano (☎ 0141-248 4055; 11 Exchange Pl) Opened in 1935, the Rogano is a gem of art-deco design, based on the decor in the *Queen Mary* ocean liner, which was built on the Clyde in the 1930s.

Horse Shoe Bar (☎ 0141-221 3051; 17 Drury St) This legendary city pub and popular meeting place dates from the late 19th century and has hardly changed its appearance since then.

Arches (☎ 0141-565 1035; 253 Argyle St) A one-stop culture, entertainment and refreshment venue, this bar and club doubles as a theatre showing contemporary and experimental productions.

Tchai Ovna (☎ 0141-357 4524; 42 Otago Lane) More rustic than your grannie's woodshed, this Bohemian-style tea house is frequented by local students and Indie kids sipping on speciality teas, nibbling on vegetarian snacks, or puffing on apple-scented tobacco in hubble-bubble pipes.

Liquid Ship (☎ 0141-332 2840; 171-175 Great Western Rd) The best of Glasgow's style bars distilled into a single venue, the Ship is built from reclaimed architectural salvage – everything from school desks to an old bank counter to a brick with the 120-year-old imprint of a dog's paw.

GETTING THERE & AWAY
AIR
Ten miles west of the city on the M8, **Glasgow International airport** (☎ 0141-887 1111; www.baa.co.uk/glasgow) handles domestic traffic and international flights, including some direct transatlantic routes.

It's the main airport for most of the Scottish islands. **Glasgow Prestwick airport** (☎ 0871 223 0700; www.gpia.co.uk), 30 miles southwest of Glasgow near Ayr, is used by the budget carrier **Ryanair** (☎ 0871 246 0000; www.ryanair.com), which offers flights from London Stansted airport (1¼ hours, frequent) for around £25 plus taxes.

BUS
All long-distance buses arrive and depart from **Buchanan bus station** (☎ 0141-333 3708; Killermont St), just 300m north of Queen St train station. Bus fares from London are very competitive – **Megabus** (☎ 0900 160 0900; www.megabus.com) should be your first port of call if you're looking for the cheapest fare, with one-way fares from around £10.

National Express (☎ 0870 580 8080; www.nationalexpress.com) coaches to London leave from the same bus station (single £34, nine hours, at least four daily). There's a daily direct overnight bus from Heathrow airport, usually departing at 11.05pm. National Express also has direct services to Birmingham (£48, six to seven hours, four daily), Manchester (£28, five hours, four daily), Newcastle (£30, four hours, one daily); and one from York (£34, seven hours, one daily).

Scottish Citylink (☎ 0870 550 5050; www.city link.co.uk) has buses to most major towns in Scotland, including a frequent service to Edinburgh (£8.40 return, 1¼ hours, every 20 minutes). Direct buses also run to Stirling (£6, 45 minutes, hourly), Inverness (£23, 3¾ hours, one daily) and Aberdeen (£24, three hours, hourly).

TRAIN
Glasgow has two train stations. Generally, Central Station serves southern Scotland, England and Wales, and Queen St serves the north and east of Scotland. There are buses

between the two every 10 minutes (free with a through train ticket), or it's a 10-minute walk.

There are direct trains from London's King's Cross and Euston stations; they're not cheap, but they're much quicker (£101, 5½ hours, 12 daily) and more comfortable than the bus.

First ScotRail (☎ 08457 55 00 33; www .firstscotrail.com) runs the West Highland line heading north to Oban and Fort William, and has other direct links to Dundee (£22, one hour 20 minutes, hourly), Aberdeen (£38, 1¾ hours, hourly) and Inverness (£38, three hours, one direct service daily). There are trains every 15 to 30 minutes to/from Edinburgh (£11, 50 minutes).

GETTING AROUND
TO/FROM THE AIRPORT
First Glasgow's 757 AirLink bus runs between Glasgow International airport and Buchanan bus station (£2.90, 30 minutes, every 20 minutes 6am to 11pm) via the SECC and Central and Queen St train stations. The 24-hour Glasgow Flyer (www. glasgowflyer.com) is slightly faster (£4.20,

25 minutes) and more frequent (every 10 to 15 minutes, and every 30 minutes through the night). A taxi to the city centre costs around £20.

You can get to Prestwick airport by bus on the X77 route (£9, 45 minutes, every 30 minutes, hourly on Sunday), which operates from 7.30am to midnight; for earlier or later arrivals get the X99 airport express. You can also get to Prestwick by train from Central Station (£6.25, 50 minutes, every 30 minutes).

CAR
A convoluted one-way system that will leave you feeling like you're trying to navigate a pretzel, plus expensive and limited parking, makes driving an unattractive proposition, though parking is easier in the West End. The motorway (M8) makes getting into/out of the city easy, as long as you avoid rush hour.

PUBLIC TRANSPORT
The **St Enoch Square Travel Centre** (☎ 0141-226 4826; ☺ 8.30am-5.30pm Mon-Sat), just off

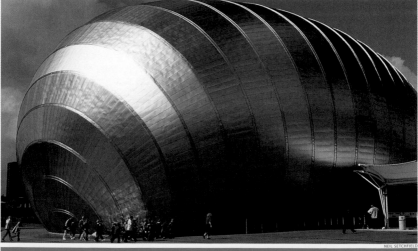

Glasgow Science Centre (p302)

NEIL SETCHFIELD

Argyle St, provides information on all public transport in the Glasgow region. You can buy tickets when you board local buses, but on most you must have exact change.

The tiny trains on the circular **Underground** (www.spt.co.uk/subway) line serve 15 stations in the city's centre, west and south (£1.10 single). The Discovery ticket (£2.50) gives a day's unlimited travel after 9.30am.

LANARKSHIRE

Historically, Lanarkshire is the county that contained Glasgow. Today, its northern parts have been swallowed up by Glasgow's urban sprawl, but the southern part of the county encompasses the valley of the River Clyde, a mainly rural district of market gardens and dairy farms surrounded by low, rolling hills.

LANARK & NEW LANARK

pop 8250

Set in a beautiful wooded gorge on the banks of the River Clyde, the former cotton-spinning village of New Lanark is a monument to one of the most forward-thinking industrialists of the 19th century. Welshman Robert Owen (1771–1858), who married the mill-owner's daughter and co-owned and managed New Lanark from 1800 to 1828, was a philanthropist and social reformer who kicked against the rampant capitalism and exploitation of the early 19th century by providing his workers with good-quality housing, a cooperative store (the inspiration for the modern cooperative movement), a school with adult-education classes, the world's first infant school, a sick-pay fund for workers and a social and cultural centre.

Once the largest cotton-spinning complex in Britain, built in 1785 to take advantage of water power provided by the fast-flowing Clyde, New Lanark finally closed down in 1968. The site was restored and opened to the public, and was awarded Unesco World Heritage Site status in 2001.

At the **visitor centre** (☎ 01555-661345; www.newlanark.org; adult/child £6.95/5.95; ⏱ 11am-5pm) you can buy a ticket for all the main attractions. These include the **New Millennium Experience** – aimed mainly at kids – a slightly naff but thought-provoking multimedia ride that reminds us of Robert Owen's utopian vision.

Nearby, Robert Owen's **Historic School** contains an innovative, high-tech journey to New Lanark's past via a 3-D hologram of the spirit of Annie McLeod, a 10-year-old mill girl who describes life here in 1820. Also included in your admission is entry to a **millworker's house**, Robert Owen's **home** and exhibitions on 'saving New Lanark'. There's also a 1920s-style **village store**.

After you've seen New Lanark you can walk up to the **Falls of Clyde** (1 mile) through the beautiful nature reserve managed by the Scottish Wildlife Trust; the 28m high Corra Linn is the highest waterfall on the Clyde, and an impressive sight in full flood.

GETTING THERE & AROUND

Lanark is 25 miles southeast of Glasgow. There are frequent trains from Glasgow's Central Station (£5.25, one hour, two an hour) – you may have to change at Holytown – or take bus 240X from Glasgow's Buchanan bus station (one hour, hourly Monday to Saturday).

SCOTTISH BORDERS

Much of Scotland's history has been played out along the Borders, from centuries of territorial battles and border raids to the building of imposing castles and grand abbeys, all lovingly dramatised by local poet and novelist Sir Walter Scott.

TRAQUAIR HOUSE

One of Britain's great country houses, **Traquair House** (☎ 01896-830323; www .traquair.co.uk; adult/child £6.50/3.50; ⊙ noon-5pm Apr-May & Sep, 10.30am-5.30pm Jun-Aug, 11am-4pm Oct) – pronounced tra-*kweer* – is the oldest inhabited house in Scotland; parts are believed to have been constructed long before the first official record of its existence in 1107.

Since the 15th century the house has belonged to various branches of the Stuart family, whose unwavering Catholicism and loyalty to the Jacobite cause is largely why development ceased when it did. One of the most fascinating features is the hidden room where priests secretly lived and conducted Mass – right up to the passing of the 1829 Catholic Emancipation Act. Other beautiful time-worn rooms hold precious relics, including the cradle that Mary Queen of Scots used for her son, James VI of Scotland (later James I of England).

More-recent attractions will appeal to kids, including a maze and adventure playground, while adults will appreciate the produce of the 18th-century brewery.

The house is set in beautiful parkland with woodland walks and secluded picnic spots about 6 miles southeast of Peebles.

MELROSE

Founded by King David I in 1136 for Cistercian monks from Rievaulx in Yorkshire, **Melrose Abbey** (HS; ☎ 01896-822562; admission £5.20; ⊙ 9.30am-5.30pm Apr-Sep, 9.30am-4.30pm Oct-Mar) is perhaps the most beautiful of the Borders abbeys. It was sacked repeatedly by the English in the 13th and 14th centuries, and was rebuilt on the orders of Robert the Bruce. After his death, Bruce's heart was sealed in a lead casket and, according to his wishes, borne by the Black Douglas into battle against the Moors during the Spanish Reconquista. Despite Douglas' death, the well-travelled heart was returned to Scotland and buried in the chapter house of the abbey.

DRYBURGH ABBEY

The most complete of all the Borders abbeys is **Dryburgh Abbey** (HS; ☎ 01835-822381; admission £4.70; ⊙ 9.30am-5.30pm Apr-Sep, 9.30am-4.30pm Oct-Mar). Partly due to its out-of-the-way location by the Tweed, Dryburgh was only ransacked three times by the English. Dating from about 1150, it belonged to the Premonstratensians, a religious order founded in France, and conjures up images of 12th-century monastic life more successfully than its counterparts in nearby towns. The pink-hued stone ruins were chosen as the burial place of Sir Walter Scott. A mile and a half north of the abbey on the B6356 is the famous **Scott's View**, looking across the Tweed Valley to the Eildon Hills; it was Sir Walter Scott's favourite spot, and it is said that his horse, which pulled his hearse on the way to his burial at Dryburgh Abbey, paused here for several minutes out of habit.

The abbey is 5 miles southeast of Melrose.

ABBOTSFORD HOUSE

For a window into Sir Walter Scott's life drop by his former residence, **Abbotsford House** (☎ 01896-752043; www.scottsabbotsford .co.uk; adult/child £6.20/3.10; ⊙ 9.30am-5pm late Mar-Oct). The writer lived here for 20 years until his death in 1832, amassing an intriguing collection of literature, with a library that numbers 9000 volumes, and historic relics such as Rob Roy's gun, dirk (dagger) and sword, and a lock of Bonnie Prince Charlie's hair.

The house is about 2 miles west of Melrose between the River Tweed and the B6360.

JEDBURGH

Dominating the town skyline, **Jedburgh Abbey** (HS; ☎ 01835-863925; adult/child £5.20/2.60; ⏱ 9.30am-5.30pm Apr-Sep, 9.30am-4.30pm Oct-Mar) was the first great Borders abbey to be passed into state care, and it shows – audio and visual presentations

GR. RICHARDSON/ PHOTOLIBRARY

Culzean Castle

⬂ CULZEAN CASTLE

Magnificent Culzean Castle – pronounced cull-*ane* – is one of the most impressive of Scotland's stately homes. Perched dramatically on a coastal cliff-top, it is a monument to its designer Robert Adam, the king of neoclassical architecture.

The superb **oval staircase** is regarded as one of his finest achievements, leading to an opulent circular **drawing room** with views of Arran and Ailsa Craig. Everywhere you look there are classical friezes and roundels in delicate 18th-century plasterwork, and even the bathrooms are palatial – the dressing room beside the **state bedroom** is equipped with a state-of-the-art Victorian multidirectional shower.

The top-floor apartment is known as the **Eisenhower Suite** – it was gifted to the American general for his lifetime at the end of WWII to salute his role in that conflict. Today it's the NTS's flagship holiday property, and you can stay the night in the general's suite for £250/375, single/double occupancy.

Culzean is 12 miles south of Ayr, accessible by bus 60 from Ayr (30 minutes, 11 daily Monday to Saturday), which passes the park gates, from where it's a 1-mile walk through the grounds to the castle.

Things you need to know: NTS; ☎ 01655-884455; www.culzeanexperience.org; adult/child £12/8, park only £8/5; ⏱ castle 10.30am-5pm Apr-Oct, park 9.30am-sunset year-round

telling the abbey's story are scattered throughout the carefully preserved ruins (good for the kids or if it's raining). The abbey was founded in 1138 by David I as a priory for Augustinian canons. The red-sandstone walls are roofless but relatively intact, and the ingenuity of the master mason can be seen in some of the rich (if somewhat faded) stone carvings in the nave (be careful of the staircase in the nave – it's slippery when wet).

DUMFRIES & GALLOWAY

Some of southern Scotland's finest attractions lie in the gentle hills and lush valleys of Dumfries & Galloway. Galloway Forest with its sublime views, mountain-biking and walking trails, red deer, kites and other wildlife is a highlight, as are the dreamlike ruins of Caerlaverock Castle.

CAERLAVEROCK CASTLE

The ruins of **Caerlaverock Castle** (HS; ☎ 01387-770244; adult/child £5.20/2.60; 9.30am-5.30pm Apr-Sep, 9.30am-4.30pm Oct-Mar) are among the loveliest in Britain. Surrounded by a moat, neatly groomed lawns and stands of trees, the unusual pink-hued, triangular, stone castle looks impregnable – but it fell several times. The curtain walls date from the late 13th century, but inside there are chambers with an extraordinary Scottish Renaissance facade built in 1634. The castle is 8 miles southeast of Dumfries by Glencaple on the B725.

A mile further on is **Caerlaverock Wildfowl & Wetlands Centre** (☎ 01387-770200; www.wwt.org.uk; Eastpark Farm; adult/child £5.95/2.95; 10am-5pm), a 1400-acre nature reserve with observation towers and CCTV spy cameras to spot badgers, wild swans and hen harriers. The highlight of the year

is in October, when vast flocks of migrating barnacle geese stop to feed.

NEW ABBEY

The small, picturesque village of New Abbey lies 7 miles south of Dumfries on the A710, clustered around the gaunt, red sandstone remains of 13th-century **Sweetheart Abbey** (HS; ☎ 01387-850397; adult/child £3/1.50; 9.30am-5.30pm Apr-Sep, 9.30am-4.30pm Sat-Wed Oct-Mar). The abbey was founded by Devorgilla de Balliol in honour of her dead husband (with whom she had founded Balliol College, Oxford). On his death, she had his heart embalmed and carried it with her until she died 22 years later. She and the heart are buried in the presbytery of the abbey church – hence the name.

GALLOWAY FOREST PARK

The Galloway Hills are one of Scotland's best-kept secrets – a range of whale-backed, heather-clad granite mountains fringed with pine forests and dotted with trout-filled lochs. Rising to their highest point at **The Merrick** (843m), they bring a little taste of Highland scenery to the southern Uplands, and provide a playground for hikers, mountain bikers, anglers and wildlife-watchers. The hills form the centrepiece of the 300-sq-mile **Galloway Forest Park** (www.forestry .gov.uk/gallowayforestpark), which stretches from Newton Stewart in the south to Dalmellington in the north.

Wildlife-wise, the park is famous for its red kites (www.gallowaykitetrail.com) and herds of wild goats and red deer. Halfway between Newton Stewart and New Galloway on the A712 is the **Galloway Red Deer Range** (☎ 07771-748401; adult/child £3.50/2.50; 1-2.30pm Sun-Thu mid-Jun–mid-Sep). Guided walks with a ranger (included in the admission fee) begin at 1pm.

↘ SCOTLAND'S
HIGHLANDS &
ISLANDS

SCOTLAND'S HIGHLANDS & ISLANDS

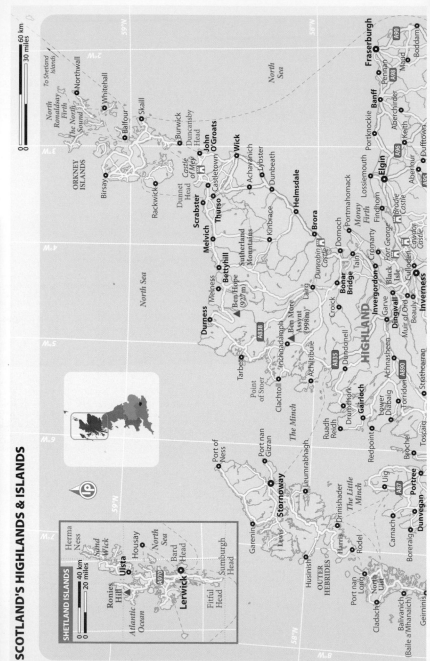

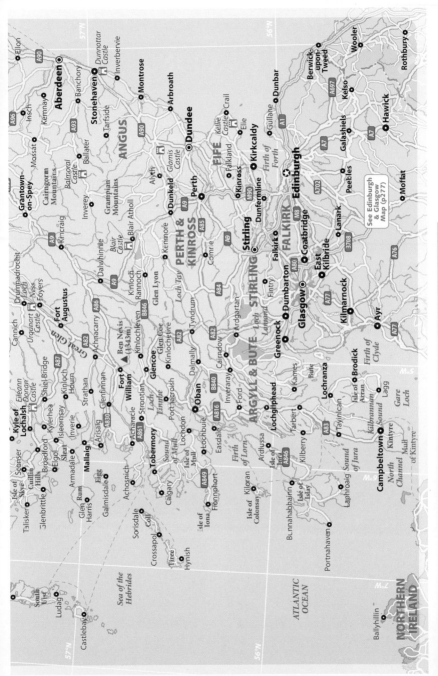

HIGHLANDS & ISLANDS HIGHLIGHTS

1 SPEYSIDE & AROUND

BY IAN LOGAN FROM CHIVAS BROTHERS

I suppose you could say whisky's in my blood. I'm absolutely passionate about the stuff! For me it's a great honour to be living and working in Speyside, the spiritual home of whisky making, which is where you'll find some of the country's most historic distilleries.

⤵ IAN LOGAN'S DON'T MISS LIST

❶ A WHISKY TOUR

You really mustn't miss visiting one of our famous distilleries. One of my favourites is run by the **Aberlour Distillery** (p337). Its intimate and personal two-hour tour covers the whisky making process and includes a chance to sample six different products, including three which aren't for sale beyond the distillery. Best of all, you get the chance to hand-fill and sign your own bottle of cask strength single malt – priceless!

❷ LOCH NESS

Everyone who comes to the Highlands makes the pilgrimage to Scotland's most celebrated **loch** (p334). It's been inspiring people's imaginations since Nessie was supposedly first spotted in the 1930s. While I'm afraid I can't promise you'll see the monster, there are boat trips across the loch if you fancy trying your luck!

❸ BALMORAL

Scotland is famous for its castles, but for me there's nowhere as impressive

Clockwise from top: Urquhart Castle (p335) and Loch Ness; Reindeer, Cairngorms National Park (p338); Balmoral Castle (p332); Cairngorms National Park (p338); Laphroaig distillery (p326)

CLOCKWISE FROM TOP IZZET KERIBAR; DAVID TIPLING; JONATHAN SMITH; ANDREW PARKINSON; IMAGEBROKER / ALAMY

as **Balmoral** (p332), the royal family's Scottish retreat. It's full of royal memorabilia and the setting is absolutely wonderful. If you get bitten by the castle bug, you could follow it with a drive along the Castle Trail in Aberdeenshire (see www.aberdeen-grampian.com).

❹ DOLPHIN WATCHING ON THE MORAY FIRTH

Many people aren't aware that the **Moray Firth** (p339) is home to a year-round population of dolphins. You can see them at close quarters at the **Whale and Dolphin Conservation Society Centre** (☎ 01463 731 866; www.wdcs.org.uk; ⏰ 9.30am-4.30pm Jun-Sep) at North Kessock, near Inverness, or you can catch a boat from Cromarty on the Black Isle.

❺ THE CAIRNGORMS

This beautiful **national park** (p338) is one of the last pockets of wilderness left in Britain. It's full of spectacular scenery and wonderful walks – I've travelled all over the world, but for me nowhere stirs the blood quite like the Cairngorms!

⤵ THINGS YOU NEED TO KNOW

Driving Remember to arrange a designated driver if you're planning on whisky tasting! **Whisky tours** Distillery tours are very popular, so prebooking is essential **What to say** Scots never call whisky Scotch, and they spell it without an 'e' **For more on whisky tours, see p337**

HIGHLANDS & ISLANDS HIGHLIGHTS

↘ STIRLING CASTLE

Edinburgh Castle tops the visitor stakes, but in terms of history and heritage its sister fortress at **Stirling** (p330) is arguably more rewarding. This sturdy bastion has played a pivotal role in many key events of Scottish history, and was once a residence for the Stuart monarchs; today you can wander its stately halls, drink in the scenery from the battlements and check out the castle's magnificent kitchens.

↘ GLEN COE

If you're searching for Scotland's most scenic corner, you'll be hard pushed to find anywhere that measures up to **Glen Coe** (p334). Massive glaciers carved out the area's deep valleys and peaks during the last ice age, and today the heather-clad hills provide some of Britain's most spectacular hiking country – and a wealth of photo ops. Don't forget warm clothing, sturdy boots and wet-weather gear!

4

⬎ BEN NEVIS

In England it's Scafell Pike, in Wales it's Snowdon, and in Scotland it's **Ben Nevis** (p333); collectively they're the three highest peaks in Britain. For many walkers, the Scottish summit is the most scenic of all, with panoramic views from the top (assuming the weather decides to play ball, that is…).

5

⬎ ISLE OF SKYE

Travellers have been 'going over the sea to **Skye**' (p340) for centuries, although these days the journey's rather more straightforward thanks to a controversial road bridge. While it's not quite the island escape it once was, it's still an irresistibly romantic spot.

6

⬎ SCONE PALACE

This fabulous **stately home** (p329) near Perth exudes history from every corniced cranny. Kenneth MacAilpin, the first king of a united Scotland, was crowned on the site in AD 838, and the famous Stone of Destiny subsequently became a powerful symbol of Scottish nationhood. The house is now owned by the aristocratic Murray family.

2 Stirling Castle (p330); 3 Glen Coe (p334); 4 Climbers, Ben Nevis (p333); 5 Cuillin Hills (p341), Isle of Skye; 6 Scone Palace (p329)

HIGHLANDS & ISLANDS' BEST...

↘ VIEWPOINTS

- **Urquhart Castle** (p335) Keep a lookout for Nessie.
- **Dunnet Head** (p340) Mainland Britain's most northerly point.
- **Cuillin Hills** (p341) Beautiful mountains above Skye.
- **Fort George** (p339) Spy dolphins in the Moray Firth.
- **Duncansby Head** (p339) Forget John O'Groats – this blustery headland has far finer views.

↘ ISLANDS

- **Shetland Islands** (p329) Oozing old-fashioned charm.
- **Islay** (p326) For whisky lovers.
- **Orkney** (p329) Fantastically remote and full of history.
- **Mull, Iona, Coll & Tiree** (p327 & p328) Romantic specks just a ferry ride from the mainland.
- **Jura** (p329) Untamed wilderness attracts walkers aplenty.

↘ LANDMARKS

- **Wallace Monument** (p330) Pay your dues to Braveheart.
- **John O'Groats** (p339) Touristy, but still an essential photo op.
- **Glamis Castle** (p331) One of Scotland's most photographed (and haunted) castles.
- **Ben Nevis** (p333) Needs no introduction.
- **Culloden** (p337) Where Bonnie Prince Billy and the Scottish Clans made their last stand.

↘ TRIPS

- Driving up the **Great Glen** (p333).
- Cruising on **Loch Lomond** (p325) or **Loch Ness** (p335).
- Crossing the sea to **Skye** (p340).
- Exploring the north coast route from **John O'Groats** (p339) round to Ullapool.
- Catching the Kyle of Lochalsh Railway from **Inverness** (p336).

Left: View from Ben Nevis (p333); Right: Whisky barrels

LEFT: GARETH MCCORMACK; RIGHT: MARTIN MOOS

THINGS YOU NEED TO KNOW

⭘ VITAL STATISTICS

- **Area** 22521 sq miles
- **Population** 1.8 million
- **Best time to go** Spring or summer

⭘ AREAS IN A NUTSHELL

- **Central Scotland** (p324) Gateway to the Highlands.
- **The Great Glen** (p333) Mountains and lochs loom on every side.
- **East & North Coast** (p339) Where the views get really wild.
- **Isle of Skye** (p340) Scotland's most famous island.
- **Speyside** (p337) The heartland of Scottish whisky making.

⭘ ADVANCE PLANNING

- **Two months before** Plan accommodation and car hire.
- **One month before** Book up for your whisky and wildlife tours.
- **Two weeks before** Check opening times and scan the net for the latest Nessie sightings.

⭘ RESOURCES

- **Visit Highlands (www.visithighlands .com)** Comprehensive tourist info.
- **Malt Whisky Trail (www.maltwhisky trail.com)** Online guide to the strong stuff.
- **Historic Scotland (www.historic-scot land.gov.uk)** The main organisation for Scotland's historic monuments.

⭘ GETTING AROUND

- **Bus** Cheap, but erratic timetables can make it slow-going.
- **Train** Northern Scotland is crossed by several scenic railways, including the main West Highland Coast line from Glasgow and several scenic routes from Inverness.
- **Car** You'll need wheels if you want to explore the more remote areas.

⭘ BE FOREWARNED

- **Midges** The Highlands are plagued by these biting insects, especially in summer. Cover up at dawn and dusk, and bring repellent.
- **Weather** Heavy rain, high winds and even snow can strike the Highlands at practically any time of year. Plan accordingly.
- **Roads** Many of the region's roads are narrow and twisty, and petrol stations are few and far between.

SCOTLAND'S HIGHLANDS & ISLANDS ITINERARIES

INVERNESS & AROUND Three Days

This quick Highland fling is a good option if time's short. Kick off in the lively town of **(1) Inverness** (p336) with a visit to the **castle**, a **dolphin-spotting trip** and a night in the sexy **Rocpool Reserve**.

Hop in the car and head southwest for a boat trip across **(2) Loch Ness** (p334), a wander around **Urquhart Castle** (p335) and a night in Fort William at the **Grange** (p334) or **Lime Tree An Ealdhain** (p334). The last day's left for exploring the southern half of the **Great Glen** (p333), with sightseeing stops at **(3) Glen Coe** (p334), and **(4) Loch Lomond** (p325) and a final night's stay in **(5) Glasgow** (p300).

CASTLE TRAIL Five Days

This itinerary connects Scotland's most fabulous fortresses, beginning with a visit to the capital castle in **(1) Edinburgh** (p286). From the big city it's only a short drive along the coast to strategic **(2) Stirling Castle** (p330), the ancestral seat of the Stuart family. **(3) Kellie Castle** (p328) was originally medieval, but received a thorough makeover during Victorian days, while nearby **(4) Scone Palace** (p329) stands on the site where Scottish monarchs were crowned until the 13th century.

North of Scone is **(5) Blair Castle** (p331), which provides a fascinating glimpse into the well-to-do lives of the Highlands aristocracy, and **(6) Glamis Castle** (p331), an imposing turret-topped pile notorious for its resident spooks and spectres. Trundle on along the A93 to **(7) Balmoral** (p332), where HRH Elizabeth II and family have been taking their annual Highlands holiday for over five decades; Prince Charles set his whimsical children's fable on the nearby peak of Lochnagar.

Aberdeen is surrounded by several castles (including Dunnottar, Kildrummy and Craigievar), but for our trip we continue north via the book-lined library of **(8) Brodie Castle** (p339) and nearby **(9) Cawdor** (p338), where Shakespeare set his 'Scots Play', *Macbeth*. If you have time it's worth making the pilgrimage north to the **(10) Castle of Mey** (p339), crammed with mementoes, photos and knick-knacks left behind by the castle's former resident, the Queen Mum.

SCENIC SCOTLAND One Week

This fabulous road-trip packs in some of the most glorious landscapes Scotland has to offer, but there's a lot of driving involved so you'll need to get your skates on; alternatively you could just concentrate on a single section and spend a few extra days in each area. Pick up

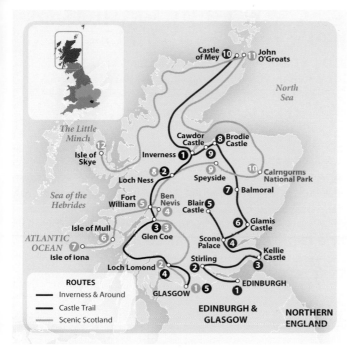

a car in **(1) Glasgow** (p300) and spin north via the first of Scotland's great lochs, **(2) Loch Lomond** (p325), gateway to the **Trossachs National Park**. Take a boat trip around the loch, then head onwards into the **Great Glen** (p333). Watch in wonder as the peaks stack up around **(3) Glen Coe** (p334) en route to Scotland's mountainous monarch, **(4) Ben Nevis** (p333). Nearby **(5) Fort William** (p333) makes a handy base.

Next up you've got a choice of veering south to Oban to catch the ferry over to the **(6) Isle of Mull** (p327) and **(7) Iona** (p328), or heading north via **(8) Loch Ness** (p334) into whisky-centric **(9) Speyside** (p337) and the stunning **(10) Cairngorms** (p338).

Still haven't satisfied your scenic craving? Scotland's east coast still awaits, with eye-popping views around **(11) John O'Groats** (p339) and **Dunnet Head** (p340), followed by the region's most beautiful stretch of coast road en route to **(12) Skye** (p340).

DISCOVER SCOTLAND'S HIGHLANDS & ISLANDS

If anywhere can lay a claim on Scotland's heart and soul, it's the Highlands. It's here where you'll find many of the quintessential Scottish images, from the lonely peaks and heather-clad hills of the Cairngorms and Glen Coe to the shimmering waters of Loch Ness and Loch Lomond. Hikers have been heading to this splendid scenic playground in search of solitude and escape for decades, but long before their boots tramped across the landscape, generations of hill-farmers were raising their flocks on the Highland slopes while Scotch moonshiners were perfecting the fine art of illicit whisky-making.

These days you'll find some of the most hallowed names of Scotch whisky scattered around Speyside, including Aberlour, Glenlivet and Glenfiddich. If time allows, it's worth making the pilgrimage west to the Isle of Skye and north to Britain's last stop at Dunnet Head; on a clear day you'll be rewarded with views all the way to the Orkney Islands.

CENTRAL SCOTLAND

Anything you ever dreamed about Scotland you can find here: lochs aplenty, from romantic Lomond to the steely fjords of the western coastline; castles ranging from royal Balmoral to noble Stirling or desolately picturesque Dunnottar; whiskies from the honeyed lotharios of Speyside to the peaty clan chiefs of Islay; and islands from brooding, deer-studded Jura to emerald Iona, birthplace of Scottish Christianity.

GETTING AROUND
BOAT

Ferries to the west-coast islands are run by **Caledonian MacBrayne** (CalMac; ☎ 0870 565 0000; www.calmac.co.uk). Island Rover Passes cover the whole system. Available for eight/15 consecutive days, costing £53/76 for passengers and £253/379 for vehicles, these represent value if you want to see a lot of islands fast.

BUS

Citylink (☎ 08705 50 50 50; www.citylink .co.uk) is the major intercity bus operator. Most local bus transport is operated by **Stagecoach** (☎ 0871 200 2233; www.stage coachbus.com). **Postbuses** (☎ 08457 740 740; www.postbus.royalmail.com) serve remote communities.

TRAIN

First Scotrail (☎ 08457 484950; www.first group.com/scotrail) runs three north–south lines, including the spectacular West Highland line, running from Glasgow to Fort William with a branch to Oban.

The Central Scotland Rover pass allows unlimited travel for three days out of seven between Edinburgh and Glasgow and the Fife and Stirling areas. It costs £31 and is available from all train stations. Similarly, the Highland Rover (£68) gives four days out of eight and includes Oban, Aberdeen, and buses on Mull.

LOCH LOMOND

Legendary Loch Lomond, not 20 miles from central Glasgow, gives you the first taste of the epic scenery awaiting you in Britain's northern reaches. **Sweeney's Cruises** (☎ 01389-752376; www.sweeneycruises .com) offers a wide range of trips from £6.50 an hour. From Tarbet, on the western shore, **Cruise Loch Lomond** (☎ 01301-702356; www.cruiselochlomond.co.uk) runs various trips around the northern half of the loch, including one that drops you on the West Highland Way and picks you up 9 miles further up the track (£14.50).

Drover's Inn (☎ 01301-704234; www.the droversinn.co.uk; Inverarnan; most mains £7-10; ⏰ 11.30am-10pm Mon-Sat, noon-9.30pm Sun; **P**) This authentically historic inn at the northern end of the loch shouldn't be missed. Fully three centuries old, it oozes character and oddness, with kilt-wearing staff, a menagerie of stuffed animals, and a palpable sense that it hasn't changed a jot since Rob Roy dropped in for a pint.

Oak Tree Inn (☎ 01360-870357; www .oak-tree-inn.co.uk; Balmaha; dm/d £25/75; **P**)

Balmaha is an inviting Loch Lomond base, both for its appealing lochside location and for this pub, a haven for walkers, travellers and locals alike.

GETTING THERE & AWAY

Citylink buses link Glasgow with Balloch (40 minutes, 12 daily) and on up the western shore to Tarbet; many continue to Ardlui (£11.30, one hour 20 minutes). Buses run around eight times daily from Balloch to Balmaha (25 minutes) via Drymen.

Trains from Glasgow run to Balloch (45 minutes, half-hourly) and three to five times daily to Tarbet and Ardlui (£11.70, one hour 20 minutes).

INVERARAY

pop 510

A lovely place to spend a night, though a little clogged with coach parties by day, wee whitewashed Inveraray preserves an 18th-century feel and sits pretty as a postcard on the shores of Loch Fyne, its buildings almost blinding the casual visitor on a sunny day.

CHRIS MELLOR

Loch Lomond

Tobermory, Isle of Mull

MARTIN MOOS

Half a mile north of town, **Inveraray Castle** (☎ 01499-302203; www.inveraray-castle .com; admission £6.80; ☉ 10am-5.45pm Mon-Sat, noon-5.45pm Sun Apr-Oct) has housed the chiefs of Clan Campbell, the dukes of Argyll, since the 15th century. The current 18th-century building includes whimsical turrets and fake battlements; inside is the armoury hall, whose walls are patterned with numerous lances, dirks and halberds, many of which were stuck into Jacobites back in the day.

George Hotel (☎ 01499-302111; www .thegeorgehotel.co.uk; Main St; s/d £35/70, superior d £90-140; Ⓟ) This wonderfully restored historic hotel boasts fabulous superior rooms, tastefully evoking a period charm with exposed stone, antique furniture, quirky Scottish features, and comfortable beds, some in the four-poster class.

our pick **Loch Fyne Oyster Bar** (☎ 01499-600264; www.lochfyne.com; mains £9-15; ☉ 9am-7.30pm Nov-Easter, 9am-8.30pm Easter-Oct) The success of this oyster cooperative, 8 miles north of Inveraray on the A83, is such that it now lends its name to some 40 restaurants throughout the UK. But the original's still the best, with salty oysters straight out of the lake, and fabulous salmon dishes: order an 'ashet' to try a few different types.

GETTING THERE & AWAY
Citylink buses connect Glasgow to Inveraray (£8.20, 1¾ hours, three to five daily), some continuing to Tarbert and Campbeltown. Buses also run to Oban (£6.90, 70 minutes, two to three daily).

ISLE OF ISLAY
pop 3460

The home of the world's greatest and peatiest whiskies, whose names reverberate on the tongue like a pantheon of Celtic deities, Islay is a wonderfully friendly place whose warmly welcoming inhabitants offset its lack of majestic scenery.

The eight **whisky distilleries** welcome visitors for guided tours. Most cost £4 to £5 (redeemable on a bottle) and some you have to book. The most charming to visit is **Bruichladdich** (☎ 01496-850190; www .bruichladdich.com; tours £5; ☉ tours 11.30am & 2.30pm Mon-Fri, 11.30am Sat Nov-Easter, 10.30am, 11.30am, 2.30pm Mon-Fri, 10.30am & 2.30pm Sat Easter-Oct), pronounced brook-*laddie,* located near Port Charlotte. Independently owned, it runs on palpable enthusiasm, and refuses to compromise on quality. To get there, take a Port Charlotte–bound bus and jump off when you see the distinctive turquoise gates.

The three famous southerners are, in order of distance from Port Ellen, **Laphroaig** (☎ 01496-302418; www.laphroaig .com; tours 10.15am & 2.15pm Mon-Fri, plus 11.45am

& 3.30pm Mon-Fri & 10am Sat Jun-Sep), **Lagavulin** (☎ 01496-302730; www.discovering-distiller ies.com; tours by appointment 9.30am, 11.15am & 2.30pm Mon-Fri) and **Ardbeg** (☎ 01496-302244; www.ardbeg.com; tours 10.30am & 3pm Mon-Fri Sep-May, 10.30am, noon, 1.30pm & 3pm daily Jun-Aug). Peat content is high in these cult whiskies, all of which pack a punch and get aficiona-dos debating over their medal positions.

ourpick Lambeth Guest House (☎ 01496-810597; lambethguesthouse@tiscali.co.uk; Jamieson St, Bowmore; r per person £28; ☐) If the whisky hasn't given you that glow of warm con-tentment yet, this great little guesthouse surely will.

ourpick Harbour Inn (☎ 01496 810330; www.harbour-inn.com; Bowmore; d £115-145; ☐ wi-fi) Right by the water in the heart of Bowmore, this special place fills fast: book it or miss it. Spacious, ultra-commo-dious rooms furnished with a light touch provide proper relaxation, and the classy restaurant (mains £14 to £24) offers ex-cellent local game, lamb and seafood; try matching local malts to your meal.

GETTING THERE & AWAY
Flybe/Loganair (☎ 0871 700 2000; www.flybe .com) operates one to three flights per day from Glasgow to Islay (£38 to £76 one way, 45 minutes).

CalMac runs daily ferries (per per-son/car return £15/77, 2¼ hours) from Kennacraig to either Port Ellen or Port Askaig. Citylink buses running between Glasgow and Campbeltown connect with the ferry. In summer there's a Wednesday ferry from Port Askaig to Colonsay (per person/car one way £4.50/23.30, 1¼ hours) and Oban.

ISLE OF MULL
pop 2667
Just a short ferry hop from the west coast, Mull has long enchanted visitors with its majestic hillscapes and the almost mysti-cal appeal of little Iona, the holy island off its western end.

Most Mull residents live in Tobermory in the north. The Oban ferry arrives at Craignure, on the east coast. The island is large, and has mostly single-track roads, so don't try to 'do' it in a day – you'll end up exhausted.

Craignure is basically just a ferry stop, but from here you can catch the **Mull Rail** (☎ 01680-812494; www.mullrail.co.uk; adult/child return £4.75/3.25) miniature steam train 1.5 miles south to **Torosay Castle** (☎ 01680-812421; www.torosay.com; admission £6; ☻ 10.30am-5pm mid-Mar–Oct). A typical Victorian Scottish baronial mansion with its turrets and step gables, its grand but comfortably homelike interior gives an in-sight into British aristocratic families, and David Guthrie James, father of the current laird, whose interesting life included two daring escapes from a Stalag, polar explo-ration and film-making.

Two miles further, **Duart Castle** (☎ 01680-812309; www.duartcastle.com; admis-sion £5; ☻ 11am-4pm Sun-Thu Apr, 10.30am-5.30pm May–mid-Oct) is the ancestral seat of the Maclean clan and enjoys a spectacular position on a rocky outcrop overlooking the Sound of Mull. Originally built in the 13th century, it was abandoned for 160 years before a 1912 restoration.

Mull's capital is **Tobermory**, a sparkling little fishing port in the island's north. The brightly painted houses strung out along a sheltered bay surrounded by wooded hills make this one of the prettiest villages in Scotland.

SLEEPING & EATING
Highland Cottage (☎ 01688-302030; www .highland cottage.co.uk; Breadalbane St; d £150-185; ☻ mid-Mar–Oct; P) Intimate and persona-ble, this small luxurious hotel sits on the hill

above the harbour and offers friendly elegance, a warm welcome and great food.

ourpick Achnadrish House (☎ 01688-400388; www.achnadrish.co.uk; Dervaig Rd; r per person from £37.50; P ☐ wi-fi) It's tough to think of a more inviting place to stay on the west side of Scotland than this offbeat and upmarket fusion of historic shooting lodge and Indochinese guesthouse, located between Tobermory and Dervaig.

ourpick Mishnish Hotel (☎ 01688-302009; Main St; bar meals £5-9; ☺ lunch & dinner, bar open till 1am/2am weeknights/weekends) Spend your life savings on ferry tickets, but you might not find a better island pub than the legendary Mishnish, a nook-and-cranny set up behind a black facade. Large pub meals offer plenty of value; posher fare is served upstairs.

Cafe Fish (☎ 01688-301253; The Pier; dinner mains £8-14; ☺ lunch & dinner) Upstairs at the far end of the harbour, this fabulous newcomer offers simply prepared, delicious seafood. At lunchtime you can chow down on lobster wraps or crab sandwiches; the dinner options include a delicious fish pie and aromatic bowls of steamed mussels.

GETTING THERE & AWAY

CalMac ferries go from Oban to Craignure (per person/car £4.50/38, 45 minutes, five to seven daily). Another crossing links Fishnish with Lochaline (per person/car £2.60/11.50, 15 minutes, at least hourly) on the Morvern Peninsula.

ISLE OF IONA

pop 125

Like an emerald teardrop off Mull's western shore, enchanting Iona, holy island and burial place of kings, is a magical place that lives up to its lofty reputation.

Iona's status dates back to 563, when St Columba came here from Ireland and established a monastic community, with the aim to christianise Scotland. Around 1200, a Benedictine monastery was founded on or near the site of Columba's church. **Iona Abbey** (HS; ☎ 01681-700512; admission £4.70; ☺ 9.30am-6.30pm Apr-Sep, 9.30am-4.30pm Oct-Mar) was remodelled in the 15th century and rebuilt in the 20th, but is still a dramatic place and the island's focal point. In the ancient **graveyard** next door a mound marks the burial place of 48 of Scotland's early kings, including Macbeth; the ruined **nunnery** nearby was established at the same time as the abbey.

From Fionnphort, at the southwestern extremity of Mull, a CalMac ferry takes you to Iona (return £4, 10 minutes, frequent).

KELLIE CASTLE

A magnificent example of Lowland domestic architecture, **Kellie Castle** (NTS; ☎ 01333-720271; adult/child £8/5; ☺ 1-5pm Easter-Oct, garden & grounds 9.30am-5.30pm year-round) dates partly from the 14th century but had an extensive makeover in Victorian times; the combination of creaky floors and crooked little doorways, with elegant plasterwork and marvellous works of art, is a winning one.

It's 3 miles northwest of Pittenweem on the B9171.

FALKLAND

Below the soft ridges of the Lomond Hills in the centre of Fife is the charming village of Falkland. It developed around its magnificent centrepiece, the 16th-century **Falkland Palace** (NTS; ☎ 01337-857397; adult/child £10/7; ☺ 10am-5pm Mon-Sat, 1-5pm Sun Mar-Oct), a country residence of the Stuart monarchs. Mary Queen of Scots spent the happiest days of her life 'playing the country girl in the woods and parks' at Falkland. The palace is visually stunning, a masterpiece of Scottish Gothic, and with much French influence evident in the decoration and furnishings.

DUNFERMLINE

Historic, monastic Dunfermline is Fife's largest population centre, sprawling eastwards through once-distinct villages. Its noble history is centred on evocative **Dunfermline Abbey** (HS; ☎ 01383-739026; admission £3.70; ⏰ 9.30am-5.30pm Apr-Sep, call for winter hours), founded by David I in the 12th century as a Benedictine monastery. Dunfermline was already favoured by religious royals; Malcolm III married the exiled Saxon princess Margaret here in the 11th century, and both chose to be interred here. There were many more royal burials, none more notable than Robert the Bruce, whose remains were discovered here in 1818.

What's left of the abbey is the ruins of the impressive three-tiered refectory building, and the atmosphere-laden nave of the church, endowed with geometrically patterned columns and fine Romanesque and Gothic windows.

PERTH

Fabulous **Scone Palace** (☎ 01738-552300; www.scone-palace.net; adult/child £8/5; ⏰ 9.30am-5.30pm Apr-Oct), pronounced skoon, is 2 miles north of Perth. It was built in 1580 on a site intrinsic to Scottish history. Here in 838, Kenneth MacAilpin became the first king of a united Scotland and brought the Stone of Destiny, on which Scottish kings were ceremonially invested, to Moot Hill. In 1296 Edward I of England carted the talisman off to Westminster Abbey, where it remained for 700 years before being returned to Scotland. Scone has belonged for centuries to the Murray family, earls of Mansfield, and many of the objects have fascinating history attached to them (friendly guides are on hand).

GARETH MCCORMACK
Skara Brae, Orkney Islands

⬎ IF YOU LIKE...

Fallen for the island life while exploring **Mull** and **Iona**? Then you might like to investigate some of Scotland's more isolated outposts...

- **Jura** George Orwell penned *1984* while living on this moody and mountainous island; these days it's mainly favoured by hardy hikers and hillwalkers.
- **Orkney Islands** This idyllic island archipelago off Scotland's northern tip is famous for its ancient settlements, including Skara Brae, the oldest Stone Age settlement ever discovered.
- **Shetland Islands** These isolated specks of land are just about as far as you can get from the British mainland – in fact, they're actually closer to Norway.
- **Outer Hebrides** Scotland's westerly frontier is the place to give the outside world the slip; wild, windswept and wonderfully romantic.

our pick **Parklands** (☎ 01738-622451; www.theparklandshotel.com; 2 St Leonard's Bank; s/d £99/119; P ⬚ wi-fi) Tucked away near the train station, this relaxing hotel sits amid a lush hillside garden overlooking the parklands of South Inch.

Cannon, Stirling Castle

GRAEME CORNWALLIS

↘ STIRLING

Hold Stirling and you control the country. This maxim has ensured that **Stirling Castle** has existed here in one form or another since prehistoric times. Commanding superb views, Stirling invites parallels with Edinburgh Castle – but many find the former's fortress more atmospheric; the location, architecture and historical significance combine to make it a grand and memorable visit.

The current building dates from the late 14th to the 16th century, when it was a residence of the Stuart monarchs. The spectacular palace was constructed by French masons in the reign of James V. The **Great Kitchens** are especially good, bringing to life the bustle and scale of the enterprise of cooking for the king.

Towering over Scotland's narrow waist, the **National Wallace Monument** commemorates the bid for Scottish independence depicted in the film *Braveheart*. From the visitors centre, walk or shuttle-bus it up the hill to the building itself. Once there, break the climb up the narrow staircase inside to admire Wallace's 66 inches of broadsword and see the man himself recreated in a 3-D audiovisual display. Buses 62 and 63 run from Murray Place in Stirling to the visitors centre; otherwise it's a half-hour walk from the centre.

Citylink bus services to/from Stirling include Dundee (£10.20, hourly, 1½ hours), Edinburgh (£5.40, one hour, hourly, also operated by First), Glasgow (£5.40, 45 minutes, hourly) and Perth (£6.30, 50 minutes, at least hourly).

Half-hourly train services run to Edinburgh (£6.50, 55 minutes) and Glasgow (£6.70, 40 minutes); hourly trains to Perth (£9.80, 30 minutes), Dundee (£15, 55 minutes) and Aberdeen (£37, 2¼ hours).

Things you need to know: Stirling Castle (HS; ☎ 01786-450000; adult/child £8.50/4.25, audio tour £2; ◷ 9.30am-6pm Apr-Sep, 9.30am-5pm Oct-Mar); National Wallace Monument (☎ 01786-472140; www.nationalwallacemonument.com; adult/child £6.50/4; ◷ 10am-5pm Mar-May & Oct, 10am-6pm Jun, 9am-6pm Jul & Aug, 9.30am-5.30pm Sep, 10.30am-4pm Nov-Feb)

our pick Breizh (☎ 01738-444427; www.cafe
breizh.co.uk; 28 High St; galettes £6-8, mains £9-15;
⏰ 9am-9pm Mon-Sat, 11am-9pm Sun) This warmly
decorated bistro is a treat. Dishes such as
bouillabaisse (soupy seafood stew) are
served with real panache, and the house
salad, featuring poached salmon, seared
scallops and fresh asparagus, is a feast of
colour, texture and subtle flavours.

63 Tay Street (☎ 01738-441451; www.63tay
street.com; 63 Tay St; lunch/dinner mains
£9.95/16.95; ⏰ lunch & dinner Tue-Sat) In a culinary Auld Alliance, French influence is
applied to the best of Scottish produce
to produce memorable game, seafood,
beef and vegetarian plates.

GETTING THERE & AWAY
From the bus station, Citylink operates
hourly buses to/from Edinburgh (£8.50,
1½ hours) and Glasgow (£8.70, 1½ hours).
There are also buses to/from Inverness
(£15.40, 2½ hours, at least five daily).

Trains hit Edinburgh (£12.20, 1½ hours,
two hourly) and Glasgow (Queen St;
£12.20, one hour, at least hourly Monday
to Saturday, two-hourly Sunday), as well
as Inverness (£20.40, 2¼ hours, nine daily
Monday to Saturday, five Sunday) via
Pitlochry and Aviemore.

BLAIR CASTLE
Noble **Blair Castle** (☎ 01796-481207;
www.blair-castle.co.uk; adult/child £7.90/4.90;
⏰ 9.30am-6pm Apr-Oct, last admission 4.30pm,
check website for winter hours), and the 108
square miles it sits on, is the seat of the
Duke of Atholl, head of the Murray clan.
The original tower was built in 1269, but
the castle has undergone significant re-
modelling since. Thirty rooms are open to
the public and they present a wonderful
picture of upper-class Highland life from
the 16th century on. The dining room is
sumptuous – check out the nine-pint wine

glasses – and the ballroom is a vaulted
chamber that's a virtual stag cemetery.

Blair Castle is 7 miles north of Pitlochry,
and a mile from the village of **Blair Atholl**.

LOCH TAY & KENMORE
elev 476m
Serpentine and picturesque, long Loch Tay
reflects the powerful forests and mountains around it. The bulk of mighty **Ben
Lawers** (1214m) looms above and is part of
a National Nature Reserve that includes the
nearby Tarmachan range. The **Ben Lawers
visitors centre** (NTS; ☎ 0844 493 2136; admission £2; ⏰ 10am-5pm Easter-Sep), which sells the
Ben Lawers Nature Trail booklet describing
the area's flora and fauna, is 5 miles east of
Killin, a mile off the A827.

Pretty **Kenmore** lies at Loch Tay's eastern end, and is dominated by a church,
clock tower and the striking archway of
the privately owned **Taymouth Castle**.
Just outside town, on the loch, is the
fascinating **Scottish Crannog Centre**
(☎ 01887-830583; www.crannog.co.uk; adult/child
tour £5.75/4; ⏰ 10am-5.30pm mid-Mar–Oct, 10am-
4pm Sat & Sun Nov). A crannog, perched on
stilts in the water, was a favoured form
of defence-minded dwelling in Scotland
from the 3rd millennium BC onwards. This
one has been superbly reconstructed, and
the guided tour (last tour one hour before
closing) includes an impressive demon-
stration of firemaking.

GLAMIS CASTLE
Looking every bit the Scottish castle, with
turrets and battlements, **Glamis Castle**
(glamis; ☎ 01307-840393; www.glamis-castle.co.uk;
adult/child £8/5, grounds only £4/3; ⏰ 10am-6pm
mid-Mar–Oct, 11am-5pm Nov-Dec) was the legendary setting for Shakespeare's *Macbeth*
but its medieval origins have been ob-
scured and most of what you now see
dates from the 17th and 18th centuries.

Home of the earls of Strathmore, this was where the Queen Mother grew up.

Entry is by child-friendly guided tour; the most impressive room is the drawing room, with its arched plasterwork ceiling, while the frescoes on the roof of the chapel (haunted, naturally) are magnificent. There's a display of armour and weaponry in the crypt (also haunted).

The castle is 12 miles north of Dundee in the village of Glamis. There are Strathtay Scottish buses from Dundee (35 minutes, one to three daily) to the castle itself, and a couple more that stop in the adjacent village. The Dundee tourist office has a leaflet on reaching the castle by bus.

BALMORAL CASTLE

This **castle** (☎ 01339-742534; www.balmoralcastle.com; adult/child £7/3, parking 70p; ☯ 10am-5pm Easter-Jul) was built for Queen Victoria in 1855 as a private royal residence. It sits in a privileged and beautiful position by the entrancing Dee. In truth, the somewhat hefty entrance fee is mainly for the grounds, as visitors are only allowed into one room of the castle – a ballroom stocked with rather uninteresting memorabilia. Walking around the gardens, however, is delightful on a nice day, although the flowers don't bloom until the Queen's stay in August.

Balmoral is just off the A93 (where there's a tourist office) and can be reached on buses running between Aberdeen and Braemar. The website details self-catering cottages in the grounds, let out by the week.

THE HIGHLANDS

Scotland's vast and melancholy soul is in its northernmost reaches, a land whose stark beauty leaves an indelible imprint on the hearts of those who journey here. Mist and peat, heather and whisky, and long sun-blessed summer evenings that are the deserved reward for so many days of horizontal drizzle: it's a magical land.

For outdoor-lovers, especially walkers, the Highlands are heaven. As well as incorporating part of the West Highland Way and Speyside Way, the region offers numerous possibilities for anything from a stroll to a serious trek. The Great Glen Way is a 73-mile trip from Fort William to Inverness via the Caledonian Canal and Loch Ness, and places like Glen Coe, Skye and the Cairngorms offer opportunities for walkers of all abilities.

Walk Scotland (www.walkscotland.com) has good leaflets and a comprehensive website to get you planning.

GETTING THERE & AROUND
BUS
Inverness is the main transport hub, and has onward bus services connecting with ferries to the islands at Scrabster and Ullapool. **Citylink** (☎ 08705 50 50 50; www.citylink.co.uk) and **Stagecoach** (☎ 01463-239292; www.stagecoachbus.com) are the main operators; **postbuses** (☎ 08457-740 740; www.postbus.royalmail .com) serve remote communities.

CAR & MOTORCYCLE
To explore some of the more remote areas consider hiring a car; it will significantly increase your flexibility. Roads are single-track in many areas, so duck into passing places when you spot oncoming traffic.

TRAIN
The Highland railway lines from Inverness – north along the east coast to Wick and Thurso, and west to Kyle of Lochalsh – are justly famous. The West Highland railway also follows a spectacular route from Glasgow to Fort William and Mallaig. Services are run by **First Scotrail** (☎ 08457-484950; www.firstgroup.com/scotrail); its Highland Rover pass allows unlimited

travel for four days out of eight (£68), including some bus and ferry services.

THE GREAT GLEN

The spectacular chain of long, thin lochs stretching from Inverness to Fort William could be axe wounds, bleeding crystal-blue water. An ancient geological fault line was gouged by glaciers until the end of the last ice age, creating the majestic, humbling backdrops of Lochs Linnhe, Lochy, Oich and Ness, which are connected by the Caledonian Canal, creating a link between the east and west coasts.

FORT WILLIAM & AROUND

pop 9908

Fort William styles itself 'Outdoor Capital of the UK', and there's much to do. Trot up Ben Nevis and you can look down on everyone in Britain; if downhill's more your thing, try mountain-biking or skiing at the nearby Nevis Range.

INFORMATION

Tourist office (☎ 0845 2255121; fortwilliam@visitscotland.com; 15 High St; ☺ 9am-6pm Mon-Sat, 10am-5pm Sun Jun-Sep, 9am-5pm Mon-Sat Oct-May) Helpful. Internet access (£1 per 20 minutes).

SIGHTS & ACTIVITIES

The most obvious hike is up Britain's highest mountain, **Ben Nevis** (1344m), 5 miles east of town. Even though it's but a pimple on a global scale you should prepare thoroughly. At the top, the weather's often bad (snow-covered at least six months of the year, and foggy 70% of the time), even if it's sunny down below. Take warm clothes, a detailed map, food and water. Guides can be found via the visitor centre.

The three principal trailheads in Glen Nevis start from the car park by Achintee Farm (reached by the road through Claggan), from the Glen Nevis Visitor Centre, and from the youth hostel. The trails join, then head up to the summit and ruins of the old observatory. It takes at least 5½ hours return, but allow eight to be sure.

Other, less strenuous walks exist in the beautiful glen. From the end of the Glen Nevis road, 7 miles from town, you can follow the River Nevis gorge along a slippery

GLENN BEANLAND

Nevis Range

path until it opens out into a spectacular mountain meadow, with the **An Steall** falls visible ahead. Or else walk part of the **West Highland Way** from Fort William to Kinlochleven via Glen Nevis (14 miles).

The **Great Glen Way** concludes in Fort William and many walkers hike the Fort William–Gairlochy section (21 miles return) in a day.

SLEEPING

our pick **Lime Tree An Ealdhain** (☎ 01397-701806; www.limetreefortwilliam.co.uk; Achintore Rd; s/d £60/100; P ⛝ 💻 wi-fi) This staggeringly imaginative gallery/hotel in a former manse is a tour de force of the artistic spirit. Foodies rave about the restaurant, while the gallery space, a triumph of sensitive design, does everything from serious touring exhibitions (they were packing away Goyas on last visit) to folk concerts.

Grange (☎ 01397-705516; www.thegrange-scotland.co.uk; Grange Rd; d £98-110; 🕒 Mar–mid-Oct; P) The gorgeous antique furniture in the opulent rooms, the elegant tiered lawn surrounded by carefully tended flowering shrubs, the loch views and the country-house feel place this firmly in the boutique hotel class.

Inverlochy Castle Hotel (☎ 01397-702177; www.inverlochycastlehotel.com; Torlundy; s £350, d £410-510; P 💻 wi-fi) This magnificently opulent hotel sits in expansive grounds below Ben Nevis, some 3 miles north of town. Fulfilling everyone's dreams of Highland luxury, it's a classic Victorian castle, with hunting trophies, log fires, a trout loch and noble old furniture.

GETTING THERE & AWAY

BUS

Citylink operates services to Edinburgh (£25.20, four hours, one direct daily) and Glasgow (£17.80, three hours, eight daily) via Glencoe (30 minutes); Inverness (£11.30, two hours, five to seven daily); Oban (£10.40, 1½ hours, two to four daily Monday to Saturday); and Portree (£22.90, three hours, four daily).

Stagecoach runs to Kinlochleven (50 minutes, three to 10 daily) via Glencoe.

TRAIN

Trains run between Fort William and Glasgow (£22.20, 3¾ hours, three to four daily) and to Mallaig (£9.20, 1½ hours, three or four daily). An overnight service heads here from London Euston (seat/sleeper £86/141, 13 hours).

From May to October consider the **Jacobite Steam Train** (☎ 01524-737751; www.steamtrain.info; adult/child day-return £29/16.50) from Fort William to Mallaig.

GLEN COE

Even by the Highlands' lofty standards, Glen Coe is magnificent, with soaring mountains flanking heathered valleys cut by bright rivers and waterfalls. Three brooding spurs, the Three Sisters, dominate the south, while the rim of the Aonach Eagach ridge, at 900m, looms in the north. This is serious walking country; take maps, warm clothes, food and water.

Glen Coe's bloody place in history came in 1692, when the MacDonalds were murdered by the Campbells in the Glen Coe Massacre. About 1.5 miles from the village, on the main road, **Glencoe Visitor Centre** (NTS; ☎ 01855-811307; admission £5; 🕒 10am-4pm Mar, 9.30am-5.30pm Apr-Aug, 10am-5pm Sep & Oct, 10am-4pm Thu-Sun Nov-Feb) has a focus on the geology, ecology and environmental issues of the valley rather than past bloodshed, although an audiovisual presentation does give the history of the massacre.

LOCH NESS

The legend of the beastie in this steely loch's brooding depths has brought

Loch Ness worldwide fame, and Nessie still draws a crowd. But there are other attractions to Scotland's second-largest loch (and second deepest, at 230m); pretty Fort Augustus at its southern end is bisected by the impressive 19th-century Caledonian Canal, and the quieter eastern shore of the loch is worth exploring away from the west's heavy traffic.

FORT AUGUSTUS
pop 508

The Fort Augustus Flight raises and lowers boats on the **Caledonian Canal** a total of 12m through five picturesque locks down the middle of town. You can watch boats being led on ropes, like obedient Labradors, through the locks; it's even more spectacular when skyscraper-like cruise liners pass through. The canal, built in the early 19th century to an original Thomas Telford design, linked Scotland's east and west coasts, ending the need for the stormy passage around the top.

To get on the water yourself, **Cruise Loch Ness** (☎ 01320-366277; www.cruiseloch ness.com; adult/child £9.50/5.50) does a one-hour jaunt, leaving hourly from 10am to 4pm from March to October; there's also an evening cruise in summer.

Citylink buses running between Inverness (£10.20, one hour) and Fort William (£10.40, one hour) stop at Fort Augustus five to seven times daily each way. Stagecoach services on the same route are half the price but less frequent.

DRUMNADROCHIT
pop 813

Nessie's heartland is here, with two competing visitor centres a fixture on the tour-bus circuit although, ironically, the town itself isn't actually on the loch. Much the better of the two neighbouring rival monster exhibits, **Loch Ness Centre** (☎ 01456-450573;

www.lochness.com; adult/child £5.95/3.50; ☺ 9am-8pm) seeks to explain the Nessie phenomenon rather than hype it. The multilingual presentation walks you through a series of audiovisuals, including an interesting overview of the loch's ecology.

With its sublime location overlooking Loch Ness, **Urquhart Castle** (HS; ☎ 01456-450551; admission £6.50; ☺ 9.30am-6pm Apr-Sep, 9.30am-5pm Oct-Mar) sees its fair share of tour buses. The entrance fee includes a short film and exhibition but is a little steep considering the fortress is in ruins. The castle was repeatedly sacked, damaged and rebuilt over the centuries. It was finally blown up in 1692 to prevent Jacobites using it; what remains perches dramatically over the loch.

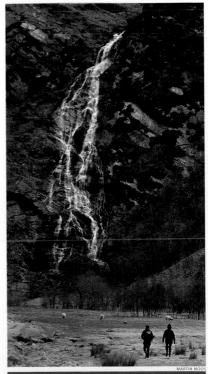

MARTIN MOOS

An Steall falls, Glen Nevis

INVERNESS

pop 44,500

By far the region's largest settlement, friendly Inverness is an important service centre for Highlanders and visitors alike, as well being as a transport hub: you're bound to pass through at some point in your wanderings. It's taking on quite a sophisticated air these days, with posh hotels and restaurants popping up, especially along its glorious riverbank.

On a riverside hillock, **Inverness Castle** is a johnny-come-lately lightweight compared with more ancient and muscly Highland fortifications. Finished in 1847, it's rather grand nonetheless, and its rosy walls are beautiful at sunset.

The delight of Inverness is strolling along the river, with its regularly spaced bouncy bridges, stately houses and peaceful parkland. Just over half a mile south of the centre, you come to the **Ness Islands**, a top picnic spot.

CRUISES

Inverness Dolphin Cruises (☎ 01463-717900; www.inverness-dolphin-cruises.co.uk; Shore St; 1½hr cruise adult/child £12.50/9; ☺ 10.30am-6pm Mar-Oct) Spot dolphins, seals and bird life; great commentary. Free pick-up from tourist office.

Jacobite (☎ 01463-233999; www.jacobite .co.uk) Various Loch Ness cruises, including Urquhart Castle and pick-up from the tourist office. Options from £16.

SLEEPING

Trafford Bank Guest House (☎ 01463-241414; www.traffordbankguesthouse.co.uk; 96 Fairfield Rd; s/d £75/100; P ☐ wi-fi) Victorian elegance, garden tables and tasteful tartan give way to individually decorated colour-themed rooms bursting with little luxuries like iPod speaker docks, DVD players and Arran Aromatics toiletries.

our pick **Rocpool Reserve** (☎ 01463-240089; www.rocpool.com; Culduthel Rd; d £195-365; P ☐ wi-fi) A far cry from the antlers and creaky wooden staircases of most upmarket Highland hotels, this luxury boutique option is slick, modern and sexy, the perfect place to take someone you want to seduce, or re-seduce.

EATING, DRINKING & ENTERTAINMENT

Kitchen (☎ 01463-259119; www.kitchenrestau rant.co.uk; 15 Huntly St; lunch £5.95, mains £10-15; ☺ lunch & dinner) A contented buzz and positive attitude emanate from this striking glass-fronted riverside restaurant.

Mustard Seed (☎ 01463-220220; www .themustardseedrestaurant.co.uk; 16 Fraser St; 2-course lunch £5.95, mains £11-19; ☺ lunch & dinner) This visionary conversion of a riverside church has kept locals bright-eyed and well fed for years now. It combines with aplomb a lofty open-plan dining area, flowered balcony, cordial service and smart Med-Scottish cuisine.

our pick **Hootananny** (☎ 01463-233651; www.hootananny.co.uk; 67 Church St; ☺ 11am-late) A real mix of people patronise this huge former bank, where three floors offer something for everyone. Young Celts in love, sturdy octogenarian couples and curious backpackers dance to Scottish folk and ceilidh bands downstairs, cooler cats prowl the upstairs rock bar and top-floor armchair chill-out area.

GETTING THERE & AROUND

AIR

Ten miles east of town, **Flybe/Loganair** (☎ 0871-700 2000; www.flybe.com) has flights to London, Edinburgh, Orkney, Shetland and Stornoway; an **Aer Arann** (www.aera rann.com) route to Dublin, and services to London and other English cities run by easyJet, Ryanair, Eastern Airways, Flybe and Flybmi.

BLAZE YOUR OWN WHISKY TRAIL

A distillery visit can be memorable, but only hard-core malthounds will want to go to more than a couple. Some are great to visit; others depressingly corporate.

Aberlour (☎ 01340-881249; www.aberlour.com; tours £10; 🕙 10.30am & 2pm daily Easter-Oct, Mon-Fri by appointment Nov-Mar) has an excellent, detailed tour with a proper tasting session. It's on the main street in Aberlour.

Small, friendly and independent, **Glenfarclas** (☎ 01807-500257; www.glenfarclas .co.uk; admission £3.50; 🕙 10am-4pm Mon-Fri Oct-Mar, 10am-5pm Mon-Fri Apr-Sep, plus 10am-4pm Sat Jul-Sep) is 5 miles south of Aberlour on the Grantown road. The last tour leaves 90 minutes before closing.

Glenfiddich (☎ 01340-820373; www.glenfiddich.com; admission free; 🕙 9.30am-4.30pm Mon-Fri year-round, 9.30am-4.30pm Sat & noon-4.30pm Sun Easter-mid-Oct) is big and busy, but handiest for Dufftown and foreign languages are available.

Excellent sherry-casked malt is found at **Macallan** (☎ 01340-872280; www.the macallan.com; standard tours £5; 🕙 9.30am-4.30pm Mon-Sat Apr-Oct, ring for winter hours). Several small-group tours are available (last tour at 3.30pm), including an expert one (£15); all should be prebooked. Lovely location 2 miles northwest of Craigellachie.

BUS

Citylink runs from Edinburgh/Glasgow (both £21.20, four hours, hourly) via Perth, Pitlochry and Aviemore; Fort William (£11.30, two hours, five to seven daily); Portree (£18.60, 3¼ hours, three daily); Thurso (£16.50, 3½ hours, four daily); and Ullapool (£9.80, 1¼ hours, two daily Monday to Saturday). **National Express** (☎ 08450 130130; www.nationalex press.com) operates buses to/from London (£40, 13 hours, one daily). **Megabus** (☎ 08705 50 50 50; www.megabus.com) offers discounted fares on Edinburgh/Glasgow/Perth/London routes.

TRAIN

Destinations include Edinburgh (£38.20, 3¼ hours, six direct daily), Glasgow (£38.20, 3½ hours, three direct daily, more changing in Perth), Aberdeen (£23.50, 2¼ hours, five to 10 daily), London (£149, eight hours, daily) and Thurso (£15.30, 3¾ hours, two to three daily).

The Kyle of Lochalsh line (£17.30, 2½ hours, four daily Monday to Saturday, two on Sunday) is one of Britain's great scenic journeys.

TO/FROM THE AIRPORT

Stagecoach bus 11 runs from Falcon Square in Inverness (£1.90, 20 minutes, twice hourly). A taxi costs around £15.

CULLODEN

A name resonant with despair for many Scots, Culloden field was the arena for a short, brutal battle in 1746 that saw the defeat of Bonnie Prince Charlie and sounded the death knell for the Scottish clan system. Five miles east of Inverness, the forlorn 49-hectare moor where the conflict took place has scarcely changed. The smart new **visitors centre** (NTS; ☎ 01463-790607; admission £10; 🕙 9am-6pm Apr-Oct, 10am-4pm Nov-Mar) presents detailed information on the lead-up to the Culloden field battle, with perspective from both sides.

DAVID TIPLING

Cairngorms National Park

↘ THE CAIRNGORMS

At 1465 sq miles, **Cairngorms National Park** is the UK's largest, and encompasses the whole range as far east as Ballater in the Dee Valley. As well as harbouring a significant population of fauna, including rare bird species such as the osprey, the capercaillie and the golden eagle, its regenerated Caledonian forest and high-altitude subarctic vegetation are of particular ecological value and make the region a paradise for hikers and cyclists.

Apart from the spectacular scenery and world-class hiking, the area is also home to wild attractions including the **Highland Wildlife Park**, a drive-through safari-style park 1.5 miles south of the village of Kincraig, featuring shaggy European bison, wolves, lynxes and stately red deer.

Nearby in the village of Boat of Garten is the **Loch Garten Osprey Centre** (☎ 01479-831476; www.rspb.org.uk; adult/child £3/50p; ☺ 10am-6pm Apr-Aug) where you can watch for ospreys from a state-of-the-art hide equipped with telescopes and video monitoring. The centre is signposted about 2 miles from the village.

Things you need to know: Cairngorms National Park (www.cairngorms.co.uk); Highland Wildlife Park (☎ 01540-651270; www.highlandwildlifepark.org; adult/child £10.50/8; ☺ 10am-5pm Apr-Oct, till 6pm Jul-Aug, 10am-4pm Nov-Mar)

CAWDOR CASTLE

This entertaining **castle** (☎ 01667-404401; www.cawdorcastle.com; adult/child £7.90/4.90, gardens only £4; ☺ 10am-5.30pm May–mid-Oct), whose title Macbeth inherits in Shakespeare's play, actually had nothing to do with the Scottish king, who lived in the 11th century, as it was built three cen-

turies later. Shakespeare took his tale from 15th-century chronicles that were a little liberal transcribing names and locations from earlier texts. The central tower is original, but the wings are 17th-century additions. The castle is still inhabited, opulently furnished and casually includes treasures, like Dalí cartoons (in the Tower Room).

Explanatory notes are written in humorous style by a former earl of Cawdor.

Bus 12 runs from Strothers Lane in Inverness to Cawdor village via Culloden. The Cawdor Tavern in the village is an excellent pub for a meal or a whisky.

BRODIE CASTLE

Set in 70 hectares of parkland, **Brodie Castle** (NTS; ☎ 01309-641371; adult/child £8/5; ☼ 10.30am-5pm Apr, Jul & Aug, 10.30am-5pm Sun-Thu May, Jun & Sep) has several highlights, including an early-19th-century library, which has more than 6000 dusty, peeling books. There are some wonderful clocks, and a 17th-century dining room with extravagant mythological ceiling carvings. There's also a selection of fine 19th- and 20th-century Scottish art. The present structure was built in 1567, with many extensions added over the years. Entrance is by guided tour.

The castle is 8 miles east of Nairn.

FORT GEORGE

Muscular 18th-century **Fort George** (HS; ☎ 01667-462777; admission £6.70; ☼ 9.30am-6.30pm Easter-Sep, to 4.30pm Oct-Mar) guards the entrance to the **Moray Firth** and, with its numerous bastions and gun ports, does so most effectively. The austere but elegant symmetry of the Georgian buildings within its solid walls is striking, but more fun are the views from the ramparts; there's a sporting chance of spotting bottlenose dolphins frolicking in the firth.

It's off the A96 about 11 miles northeast of Inverness.

EAST COAST

As you work your way north along the scimitar blade of the east coast, the desolation that the Clearances created becomes apparent and the staggering emptiness of the Highlands is in evidence.

DUNROBIN CASTLE

A mile north of Golspie is **Dunrobin Castle** (☎ 01408-633177; www.dunrobincastle .co.uk; adult/child £7.50/5; ☼ 10.30am-5.30pm Mon-Sun Jun-Aug, 10.30am-4.30pm Mon-Sat, noon-4.30pm Sun Apr, May & Sep–mid-Oct), the largest Highland dwelling (187 rooms), dating from the 13th century. Most of the elaborate fairy-tale architecture that greets you at the end of a memorable driveway is a result of a French chateau–style expansion in 1841, but the building is better known for the pitiless first Duke of Sutherland, who cleared 15,000 people from the north of Scotland while residing here.

JOHN O'GROATS & AROUND
pop 512

A car park surrounded by tourist shops, John O'Groats offers little to the visitor beyond a means to get across to Orkney; even the pub has been shut for a while now. Though it's not the northernmost point of the British mainland (that's Dunnet Head), it still serves as the endpoint of the 874-mile trek from Land's End in Cornwall, a popular if arduous route for cyclists and walkers, many of whom raise money for charitable causes.

Two miles east, **Duncansby Head** provides a more solemn end-of-Britain moment with a small lighthouse and 60m cliffs sheltering nesting fulmars. From here a 15-minute walk through a sheep paddock yields spectacular views of the sea-surrounded monoliths known as **Duncansby Stacks**.

Stagecoach runs to John O'Groats from Thurso and Wick.

CASTLE OF MEY

Once a residence of the Queen Mother, this is more home than **castle** (☎ 01847-851473; www.castleofmey.org.uk; adult/child £8/3; ☼ 10.30am-5pm May, Jul & mid-Aug–Sep, last entry

4pm), 6 miles west of John O'Groats on the A836. The exterior may seem grand, but inside it feels domestic and everything is imbued with the character of the late Queen Mum: from a surprisingly casual lounge area with TV showing her favourite show (*Dad's Army,* since you asked) to a photo of the king in 1943 that's lovingly inscribed 'Bertie'. It's 6 miles west of John O'Groats.

DUNNET HEAD

Turn off 8 miles east of Thurso to reach the most northerly point on the British mainland, dramatic Dunnet Head, which banishes tacky pretenders with its majestic cliffs dropping into Pentland Firth. There are majestic views of the Orkneys, seals and nesting seabirds below, and a lighthouse built by Robert Louis Stevenson's granddad.

ISLE OF SKYE

Skye's romantic and lofty reputation is well deserved, as the scenic splendour of Scotland's largest island rarely disappoints, with lances of light penetrating the regular cloud cover bathing the rugged hillscapes in ethereal light. What you won't feel is lonely; Skye attracts legions of visitors, as summering families, grey-haired coach parties, courting couples, and grizzled walkers and climbers bagging a few more Munros all home in on this easily accessible island. Book accommodation ahead.

GETTING THERE & AROUND

Most visitors arrive across the bridge from Kyle of Lochalsh. CalMac operates ferries from mainland Mallaig to Armadale (person/car single £3.50/18.75, 30 minutes, eight Monday to Saturday, six Sunday mid-May to mid-September).

There's also the unusual turntable **Skye Ferry** (☎ 01599-522273; www.skyeferry.com; adult/car with 4 passengers £1.50/10; ☽ 10am-6pm Easter-Oct) from Glenelg to Kylerhea.

Citylink runs buses to Portree and on to Uig from Glasgow (£31.40, 6½ hours, three daily) and Inverness (£18.60, 3¼ hours, three daily).

Stagecoach operates the main island bus routes, linking most villages and towns. Its good-value Skye Roverbus ticket gives unlimited travel for one/three days for £6/15. Sunday services are scant.

PORTREE (PORT RÌGH)
pop 1917

Skye's capital is built above a picturesque harbour, the ideal spot for a stroll or a cruise, and has the largest selection of accommodation, eating places and other services.

Marmalade (☎ 01478-611711; www.marmaladehotels.com; Home Farm Rd; s/d/f £100/120/125; P ⌨ wi-fi) The modern cafe chic, funky wire chandeliers in the bar, above-average breakfast and laid-back staff are the perfect complements to the seven large light rooms, super-spacious bathrooms, grassy grounds and long views.

Bosville Hotel (☎ 01478-612846; www.macleodhotels.co.uk; 9 Bosville Tce; standard d £128; ⌨ wi-fi) From the welcome drink to your last gourmet breakfast, everything is done with aplomb at this busy and upmarket hotel. Split-level suites feature neutral furnishings and thoughtful touches, such as cosy slippers, armchairs and deep tubs in which to soak walk-worn muscles.

GETTING THERE & AROUND
Citylink runs to/from Inverness (£18.60, 3¼ hours, three daily); Glasgow (£31.40, 6½ hours, three daily) via Fort William; and Edinburgh (£38, eight hours, two daily).

ARMADALE (ARMADAIL)
pop 120
The Mallaig ferry arrives in wee Armadale. Near the ruins of **Armadale Castle** is the excellent **Museum of the Isles** (☎ 01471-

844305; www.clandonald.com; adult/child £5.60/4; ⏱ 9.30am-5.30pm Apr-Oct). This engrossing exhibition covers island prehistory through to Norse raids, the disintegration of Gaelic culture and mass emigration.

Sea.fari (☎ 01471-833316; www.seafari.co.uk; The Pier, Armadale) does whale-spotting trips (£27 for two hours) with plenty of scenery to enjoy if the cetaceans don't show.

The home of celebrated Scottish chef Claire MacDonald, **Kinloch Lodge** (☎ 01471-833214; www.kinloch-lodge.co.uk; d £150-275; Ⓟ) is a stately foodie treat (dinner £42). Rooms have an elegant country-house feel with bird watercolours on the walls, and plump beds. It's 10 miles north of Armadale, 5 miles before the turn-off to the A87.

CUILLIN HILLS & MINGINISH PENINSULA
Rising to the west of Broadford, the Cuillins are Britain's most impressive mountain range. Their jagged peaks and ridges could be a serrated knife sawing at the grey sky; climbers and walkers see them as *the* challenge in Scotland. The highest summit, **Sgurr Alasdair** (993m), is one of the biggest trophies for experienced mountaineers, but is off limits for most walkers.

Sample the excellent sweety, peaty malt once favoured by Robert Louis Stevenson on the slightly corporate 45-minute tour of Carbost's Diageo-owned **Talisker Distillery** (☎ 01478-614308; www.malts.com; adult/child £5/ free; ⏱ 9.30am-5pm Mon-Sat Easter Oct, 12.30 5pm Sun Jul & Aug, winter by appointment), which has been operating since 1830.

DUNVEGAN & AROUND
On the island's western side is the MacLeod stronghold of **Dunvegan Castle** (☎ 01470-521206; www.dunvegancastle.com; adult/child £7.50/4, gardens only £5/3; ⏱ 10am-5.30pm Apr–mid-Oct, 11am-4pm mid-Oct–Mar). It's stood firm since the 13th century, perhaps because it

holds the **Fairy Flag**, a silken Crusader relic from the Middle East that supposedly guarantees victory for the clan that holds it.

our pick **Three Chimneys** (☎ 01470-511258; www.threechimneys.co.uk; 2-course lunches £22.50, 3-course dinners £50; ⏱ lunch Mon-Sat, dinner daily), 5 miles from Dunvegan towards Glendale, has both a wonderful rural location and some of the finest food in the country.

From Monday to Saturday there are three to four bus services from Portree to Dunvegan Castle.

NORTH SKYE
North of Portree, Skye's coastal scenery opens into the magical Trotternish Peninsula. Look out for the rocky spike of the **Old Man of Storr**, a terrace of splayed skirtlike basalt at **Kilt Rock** and the ruins of **Duntulm Castle**.

Flodigarry Country House Hotel (☎ 01470-552203; www.flodigarry.co.uk; r per person £50-90; Ⓟ) Furnished with a venerable elegance appropriate to this noble building, the rooms here are memorable, particularly those in the 'flagship' class, which have majestic views.

At the peninsula's northern end at **Kilmuir**, the **Skye Museum of Island Life** (☎ 01470-552206; adult/child £2.50/50p; ⏱ 9.30am-5pm Mon-Sat Apr-Oct) recreates crofting life in a series of thatched cottages. Up the hill in the Kilmuir cemetery is **Flora MacDonald's grave**. Flora helped Bonnie Prince Charlie escape following his defeat at the Battle of Culloden in 1746. She dressed him up in drag to play her maid as they sailed over the sea to Skye. She was imprisoned in the Tower of London for a year for her pains.

Three miles south of Staffin, **Glenview Hotel** (☎ 01470-562248; www.glenviewskye .co.uk; d £90; Ⓟ 🖳 wi-fi), on the west side of the road, is a whitewashed hotel with notable comfort and hospitality.

ARCHITECTURE

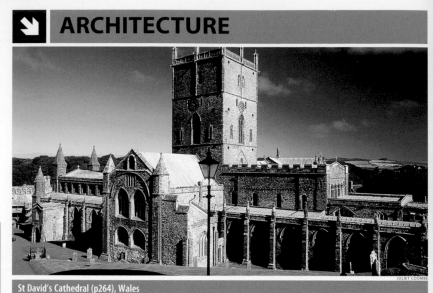

St David's Cathedral (p264), Wales

JULIET COOMBE

One of the highlights of visiting Britain is the chance to explore its architectural heritage – encompassing everything from 5000-year-old burial mounds and Stone Age circles to medieval cathedrals, thatched cottages and stunning stately homes. But don't make the mistake of thinking Britain's just one big museum piece. Landmark new buildings have sprung up in many of the nation's major cities in recent years, demonstrating that, despite her age, Britain is still capable of mustering up a spirit of architectural adventure when the mood takes her.

THE ANCIENTS TO THE ROMANS

Perhaps the best-known construction of prehistoric times is the mysterious stone circle of Stonehenge (p143) – top of the highlights list for many visitors – although the Callanish Standing Stones on Scotland's Isle of Lewis are even older. The Scottish islands also hold many of Europe's best surviving remains from the Bronze and Iron Ages, such as the stone villages of Skara Brae in Orkney and Jarlshof in Shetland.

Other highlights are the Roman ramparts of Hadrian's Wall (p240) and the well-preserved Roman swimming pools and steam rooms that gave the city of Bath its name. Bath is also top of the hit lists for most visitors thanks to architecture from a later time: the 18th- and early 19th-century Georgian period that produced grand houses, squares, parades and the famous Royal Crescent.

CASTLES, CHURCHES & STATELY HOMES

For much of the past millennium, Britain's architecture has been dominated by two aspects: worship and defence. This gives Britain its incredibly diverse and truly magnificent collection of cathedrals, minsters, abbeys and monasteries dotted across the country, not to mention an equally diverse collection of forts and castles.

Castles were good for keeping out the enemy, but there were few other benefits of living in a large damp pile of stones. As times grew more peaceful from around the 16th century, the landed gentry started to build fine residences – known simply as 'country houses'. There was a particular boom in the 18th century, and one of the most distinctive features of the British countryside today is the sheer number (not to mention size) of these grand and beautiful structures.

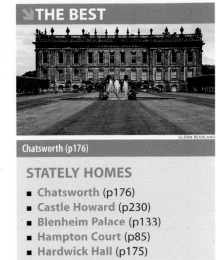

⬇ THE BEST

Chatsworth (p176)

STATELY HOMES

- **Chatsworth** (p176)
- **Castle Howard** (p230)
- **Blenheim Palace** (p133)
- **Hampton Court** (p85)
- **Hardwick Hall** (p175)
- **Erddig** (p271)
- **Balmoral** (p332)

GLENN BEANLAND

But it's not all about big houses. Alongside the stately homes, ordinary domestic architecture from the 16th century onwards can also still be seen in rural areas: black-and-white 'half-timbered' houses still characterise counties such as Worcestershire; brick-and-flint cottages pepper Suffolk and Sussex; and hardy, centuries-old structures built with slate or local gritstone are a feature of areas such as Derbyshire, north Wales and the Lake District.

MODERN BUILDINGS

The rebuilding that followed WWII showed scant regard for the aesthetics of cities, or for the lives of the people who lived in them, as 'back-to-back' terraces of slum houses were demolished and replaced by tower blocks (simply shifting horizontal rows of deprivation to the vertical, according to some critics). Public buildings of the 1960s were often little better; heavy concrete 'brutalism' – a style epitomised by London's South Bank Centre, although even this monstrosity has its fans today – was much beloved by architects of the time.

Perhaps the insensitivity of the 1960s and '70s is why, on the whole, the British are conservative in their architectural tastes and often resent ambitious or experimental designs. With this attitude in mind, over the last 15 years or so British architecture has started to redeem itself, and many big cities now have contemporary buildings their residents enjoy and admire.

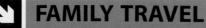

FAMILY TRAVEL

MARK DAFFEY

Playing in the water jets, Manchester

Britain's generally a great place for kids. There's no shortage of places and activities to keep the nippers occupied, ranging from fun-parks and theme rides through to nationally renowned museums. Many national parks and resort towns organise activities for children, especially during school-holiday periods, and tourist offices are a great source of information on kid-friendly attractions.

Accommodation can sometimes be a headache. Not all hotels are happy to accept kids (especially those at the boutique end), so it's worth checking their policy before you book. Many places also quote prices per person rather than per room, so you might find yourself having to pay extra (albeit at a reduced rate) even if the kids share your room. Likewise restaurants: some have child menus, crayons and highchairs, while others firmly say 'no children after 6pm'. Traditional pubs and bars generally aren't for under-18s, although there are an increasing number of specifically 'family-friendly' pubs (often if they serve food, they'll serve the kids too).

Breastfeeding in public remains mildly controversial, but if done modestly is usually considered OK. On the sticky topic of dealing with nappies (diapers) while travelling, most big museums and historical attractions have baby-changing facilities, but you probably won't be terribly impressed with the facilities in motorway service stations and city-centre toilets. For more advice see www.babygoes2.com or www.travelforkids .com.

There are usually hefty child discounts available on public transport, travel tickets and admission costs, so it's well worth doing a bit of pre-trip planning to make sure you make the most of your funds.

Great Britain has plenty of sights that will appeal to the younger set, from popular theme parks such as Alton Towers, in central England, to fascinating historic sites. London's mesmerising list of kid-friendly attractions includes the London Aquarium (p78), one of Europe's largest. The Science Museum (p79) has something for all ages, while the spooky London Dungeon (p77) might be a bit too much for the real littlies. See also p86 for more things do with the kids in London.

THE NITTY GRITTY

- **Changing facilities** In most large shopping centres, museums and attractions
- **Cots** Usually available at more expensive hotels, but rare in B&Bs
- **Health** Just do as you'd do back home
- **Highchairs** Common in chain restaurants, but ask elsewhere
- **Nappies (diapers)** Sold in every supermarket
- **Transport** Look out for kids' discounts on trains, buses and the tube

Sure hits in the south of England include Windsor Legoland (p138), a fun-filled theme park full of thrilling rides, and Longleat Safari Park (p144), a drive-through wildlife park. Eco-minded youngsters will enjoy a visit to Cornwall, which is home to the space-age Eden Project (p157), three biomes so large you can apparently even see them from space.

For those heading to the north of England, York is home to Jorvik (p226), a reconstruction of the Viking settlement which includes a smells-and-all ride through the 9th-century Jorvik (the Viking name for York).

It's also a good idea to have a stock of rainy-day activities just in case the great British weather rears its head…

FOOD & DRINK

Dining out, London

JONATHAN SMITH

Britain has taken pretty bad press for its grub, but there's been something of a culinary revolution going on over the last few years. In 2005 food bible *Gourmet* magazine famously singled out London as having the best collection of restaurants in the world. Michelin-starred restaurants, organic eateries and gourmet gastropubs seem to be springing up practically everywhere you look.

While the traditional staples of fish and chips and roast beef and Yorkshire pudding are still as popular as ever, Britain's gastronomic mix is an altogether more cosmopolitan affair. (A recent poll suggested that the nation's favourite takeaway food was in fact chicken tikka masala – a pungent curry that can trace its roots back to the heyday of the British Empire.) Mix in some spicy ingredients from the Commonwealth, a handful of culinary tips, tricks and techniques from its near-European neighbours, and the modern phenomenon of the 'celebrity chef' (epitomised by big names such as Jamie Oliver, James Martin, Gordon Ramsay, Hugh Fearnley-Whittingstall and Rick Stein) and you might start to understand why Britain has begun to transform itself from a culinary no-go to a taste trendsetter.

WHAT TO EAT
BREAKFAST
Most working people make do with toast or a bowl of cereal before dashing to the office or factory, but a weekend treat for many is the 'fry-up breakfast': bacon, sau-

sage, egg, mushrooms, baked beans and fried bread. Other additions may include tomatoes (also fried, of course) and black pudding – known in other countries as 'blood sausage'.

The same dish will inevitably be encountered at hotels and B&Bs, preceded by cereal and followed by toast and marmalade, where it's known as a Full English Breakfast (in England) and just a Full Breakfast in Wales and Scotland – although north of the border you might get oatcakes instead of fried bread. In Wales you may be offered laver bread – not a bread at all, but seaweed – a tasty speciality often served with oatmeal and bacon on toast.

If you don't feel like eating half a farmyard it's quite OK to ask for just the egg and tomatoes, for example. Some B&Bs offer other alternatives, such as kippers (smoked fish) – especially in Scotland – or a 'continental breakfast', which completely omits the cooked stuff and may even add something exotic like croissants.

LUNCH

One of the many great inventions that Britain gave the world is the sandwich, supposedly invented in the 18th century by the aristocratic Earl of Sandwich. Another speciality – especially in pubs – is the ploughman's lunch. Basically it's bread and cheese, usually accompanied by a spicy pickle, salad and some onions, although you'll also find other variations, such as farmer's lunch (bread and chicken), stockman's lunch (bread and ham), Frenchman's lunch (brie and baguette) and fisherman's lunch (er…fish).

For cheese and bread in a different combination, try Welsh rarebit – a sophisticated variation of cheese on toast, seasoned and flavoured with butter, milk and sometimes a little beer. *Cawl* (a thick broth) is another traditional Welsh dish; for a takeaway lunch in Scotland look out for *stovies* (tasty pies of meat, mashed onion and fried potato) and Scotch pies (hard-cased pies of minced meat, sometimes eaten cold). In restaurants and cafes, sample Scotch broth (a thick soup of barley, lentils and mutton stock), sometimes offered as a starter, but filling enough as a meal in itself.

DINNER

In the view of many outsiders, a typical British dinner is a plate of roast beef. Perhaps the most famous beef comes from Scotland's Aberdeen Angus cattle, while the best-known

---

⤵ THE BREAKFAST BLACK STUFF

Nothing divides the nation as much as Marmite, the dark, pungent yeast extract that the British have been happily spreading on their hot buttered toast since the 1930s. For some, it's the stuff of culinary nightmares; for others, it's practically a life-long passion, a fact that its makers have cunningly tapped into with an entire national advertising campaign geared around whether you 'Love It or Hate It'. Similar (but definitely not the same) to the Australian icon Vegemite, it's most often eaten at breakfast, but also makes a fine companion to a lunchtime cheese sandwich or all manner of late-night snacks.

food from Wales is lamb (although a lowly vegetable, the leek, is a national emblem). Venison – usually from red deer – is readily available in Scotland, as well as in parts of Wales and England, most notably in the New Forest.

The traditional accompaniment for British beef is Yorkshire pudding. It's simply roasted batter, but very tasty when properly cooked. Bring sausages and Yorkshire 'pud' together and you have another favourite dish: toad-in-the-hole.

But perhaps the best-known classic British staple is fish and chips, often bought from the 'chippie' as a takeaway wrapped in paper to enjoy at home, or 'open' to eat immediately as you walk back from a late night at the pub. Sometimes the fish can be greasy and tasteless (especially once you get far from the sea), but in towns with salt in the air this deep-fried delight is always worth trying.

Of course, the Scottish food that everyone knows is haggis, essentially a large sausage made from a sheep's stomach filled with minced meat and oatmeal. Some restaurants in Scotland serve haggis and it's also available deep-fried at takeaways.

Scottish salmon is also well known, and available everywhere in Britain smoked or poached, but there's a big difference between bland fatty salmon from fish farms and the lean, tasty, wild version. Other British seafood includes herring, trout and haddock; in Scotland the latter is best enjoyed with potato and cream in the old-style soup called Cullen skink.

REGIONAL SPECIALITIES

If fish is your thing, Yorkshire's coastal resorts are particularly famous for huge servings of cod – despite it becoming an endangered species, thanks to overfishing – while restaurants in Devon and Cornwall regularly conjure up prawns, lobster, oysters, mussels and scallops. Elsewhere, seafood specialities include Norfolk crab, Northumberland kippers, and jellied eels in London, while restaurants in Scotland, west Wales and south-

BETHUNE CARMICHAEL

Traditional Scottish meal of haggis and neeps (turnips)

west England regularly conjure up seafood such as oysters, scallops, prawns, lobster and mussels.

Meat-based treats in northern and central England include Cumberland sausage, a tasty mix of minced pork and herbs so large it has to be spiralled to fit on your plate. For a snack, try Melton Mowbray pork pies (motto: 'gracious goodness for over 100 years'): cooked ham compressed in a casing of pastry and always eaten cold, ideally with pickle. A legal victory in 2005 ensured that only pies made in the eponymous Midlands town could carry the Melton Mowbray moniker – in the same way that fizzy wine from regions outside Champagne can't claim that name.

> ## ⬐ MUST-TRY THINGS
> - Fish and chips
> - Roast beef and Yorkshire pudding
> - Welsh rarebit
> - A pint of ale
> - A dram of whisky
> - Tea and cake

Another British speciality that enjoys the same protection is Stilton – a strong white cheese, either plain or in a blue-vein variety. Only five dairies in the country – four in the Vale of Belvoir, and one in Derbyshire in central England – are allowed to produce cheese with this name. Bizarrely, the cheese *cannot* be made in the village of Stilton in Cambridgeshire, although this is where it was first sold – hence the name.

PUDDINGS

After the main course comes dessert or 'pudding'. Perhaps the best-known is Bakewell pudding, an English speciality that blundered into the recipe books around 1860 when a cook at the Rutland Arms Hotel in the Derbyshire town of Bakewell was making a strawberry tart, but mistakenly (some stories say drunkenly) spread the egg mixture on top of the jam instead of stirring it into the pastry. Especially in northern England, the Bakewell pudding (pudding, mark you, not 'Bakewell tart' as it's sometimes erroneously called) features regularly on local dessert menus and is certainly worth sampling.

More of a cake than a pudding, Welsh speciality *bara brith* (spicy fruit loaf) is a delight, while Scottish bakeries usually offer milk scones and griddle scones as well as plain varieties. Other sweet temptations include *bannocks* (half scone, half pancake), shortbread (a sweet biscuit) and Dundee cake (a rich fruit mix topped with almonds).

Then there's the dome-shaped plum pudding, full of fruit, nuts and brandy or rum, traditionally eaten at Christmas, when it's called – surprise, surprise – Christmas pudding. Rhubarb crumble is made from the stewed stem of a large-leafed garden plant, topped with a baked mix of flour, butter and sugar, and best served with custard or ice cream. You'll often find versions made with other fruits, especially apples and summer berries.

DRINKS
BEER

Among alcoholic drinks, Britain is best known for its beer. Typically ranging from dark brown to bright orange in colour, and generally served at room temperature, technically it's called 'ale' and is more commonly called 'bitter' in England and Wales. If you're used to the 'amber nectar' or 'king of beers', a local British

⬎ THE GREAT ENGLISH CUPPA

Nothing sums up the English more than their favourite tipple. Nationwide, the English get through an astonishing 165 million cuppas a day. It's been a staple since the 18th century, when trading links with tea plantations on the Indian subcontinent were established. Initially tea was considered a luxury commodity and heavily taxed, making it the preserve of the upper-class coffee houses. But within the space of a few decades, English from all echelons of society had taken it firmly to their heart.

One of the great innovations in tea drinking was an American invention: the first tea bags were accidentally invented in 1908 by a New York tea merchant who sent out samples to his customers in small silken bags.

brew may come as a shock. A warm, flat and expensive shock. Most important of all, though, is the integral flavour: traditional British beer doesn't *need* to be chilled or fizzed to make it palatable. In Scotland, ales are designated by strength – light, heavy, export and strong – or by a notional 'shilling' scale; so you'd order a 'pint of heavy' or a 'pint of 80-shilling'.

CIDER

If beer doesn't tickle your palate, try cider – available in sweet and dry varieties. In western parts of England, notably Herefordshire and the southwest counties, you could try 'scrumpy', a very strong dry cider made from local apples.

WINE

While not traditionally a wine-growing nation, Britain's vineyards are steadily gaining accolades. There are now 450 vineyards and wineries producing around two million bottles a year. English white sparkling wines have been a particular success story recently; many are produced in the southeast of the country where the chalky soil and climatic conditions are similar to those of the Champagne region in France.

WHISKY

The spirit most visitors associate with Britain – and especially Scotland – is whisky. (Note the spelling – it's *Irish* whiskey that has an 'e'.) More than 2000 brands are produced, but the two main kinds are single malt, made from malted barley, and blended whisky, made from unmalted grain blended with malts. Single malts are rarer (there are only about 100 brands) and more expensive. When ordering a 'dram' in Scotland remember to ask for whisky – only the English and other foreigners say 'Scotch'.

HISTORY

Roman baths (p145), Bath

SIMON GREENWOOD

It may be a small island on the edge of Europe, but Britain has never been on the sidelines of history. For thousands of years, invaders and incomers have arrived, settled and made their mark here. The result is a fascinating mix of landscape, culture and language – a dynamic pattern that shaped the state and continues to evolve today.

FIRST ARRIVALS

Stone tools discovered near the town of Lowestoft in Suffolk show that human habitation in Britain stretches back at least 700,000 years. As the centuries rolled on, ice ages came and went, sea levels rose and fell, and the island now called Britain was frequently joined to the European mainland.

Around 4000 BC a new group of migrants arrived and settled, most notably in open chalky hill areas such as the South Downs and Salisbury Plain in southern England. These early settlers used rocks and turf to build massive burial mounds, many of which can still be seen today, including the West Kennet Long Barrow in Wiltshire and the great

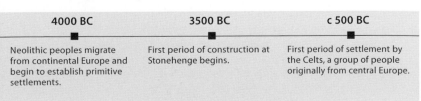

4000 BC	3500 BC	c 500 BC
Neolithic peoples migrate from continental Europe and begin to establish primitive settlements.	First period of construction at Stonehenge begins.	First period of settlement by the Celts, a group of people originally from central Europe.

passage grave at Maes Howe, Orkney. Stone circles (cromlechs) were another major landmark left behind by ancient settlers, including the great circles of Avebury (p148) and Stonehenge (p143).

CELTS & ROMANS

Move on a millennium or two to the Iron Age. The population expanded and began to divide into specific groups or tribes. By around 500 BC, the Celts had settled across much of the island of Britain, absorbing the indigenous people. A Celtic-British population – sometimes known as the 'ancient Britons' – developed, divided into about 20 different tribes.

Although there had been some earlier expeditionary campaigns, the main Roman invasion of the region they called Britannia was in AD 43. Within a decade most of the land was under Roman control, and most of the occupation was straightforward: several Celtic-British tribal kings realised collaboration was more profitable than battle.

By around AD 80 Britannia comprised much of today's England and Wales. Along with stability and wealth, the Romans introduced another cultural facet – a new religion called Christianity, after it was recognised by Emperor Constantine in the 4th century. But by this time, although Romano-British culture was thriving in Britannia, back in its heartland the Empire was already in decline.

THE EMERGENCE OF ENGLAND

When Roman power faded, the province of Britannia went into decline, and entered a period known by some historians as the Dark Ages. Romano-British towns were abandoned and rural areas became no-go zones as local warlords fought over fiefdoms. Historians disagree on what happened next; either the Anglo-Saxons largely overcame or absorbed the Romano-British and Celts, or the indigenous tribes simply adopted Anglo-Saxon language and culture. Either way, by the late 6th century much of England was predominantly Anglo-Saxon, divided into separate kingdoms dominated by Wessex (in today's southern England), Mercia (today's Midlands) and Northumbria (today's northern England and southern Scotland).

THE VIKING ERA

Just as the new territories of England, Wales and Scotland were becoming established, Britain was yet again invaded by a bunch of pesky Continentals. This time, Vikings appeared on the scene. The main wave of Vikings came from today's Denmark, and conquered east and northeast England. By the middle of the 9th century, they started to expand southwards into central England, but blocking their route were the Anglo-Saxon armies led by the king of Wessex, Alfred the Great. By 886, Alfred had garnered his forces

AD 43	122	c 410
Emperor Claudius orders the first major Roman invasion of England and conquers much of the country by AD 50.	Construction of Hadrian's Wall begins to protect Britannia from northern raids.	The end of Roman imperial control in the province of Britannia.

and pushed the Vikings back to the north. He was hailed as king of the English – the first time the Anglo-Saxons regarded themselves as a truly united people.

Meanwhile, Wales was also dealing with the Nordic intruders. Building on the initial cooperation forced upon them by Anglo-Saxon oppression, in the 9th and 10th centuries the small kingdoms of Wales began cooperating, through necessity, to repel the Vikings.

Around the same time, the warring factions of the Scots and Picts were unified by the coronation of Kenneth MacAilpin, born to a Scots father and a Pictish mother. In a surprisingly short time, the Scots gained cultural and political ascendancy. The Picts were absorbed, and Pictish culture simply – and quite suddenly – came to an end. As part of this process, Alba became known as Scotia.

⬊THE BEST

ANDREW MARSHALL & LEANNE WALKER

Hadrian's Wall (p240)

ROMAN REMAINS

- **Bath's Roman baths** (p145)
- **Hadrian's Wall** (p240)
- **Housesteads Roman Fort** (p243)
- **Chesters Roman Fort** (p241)
- **Fishbourne Roman Palace** (p126)
- **Dig** (p226)

In the 11th century, Scottish nation-building was further consolidated by King Malcolm III (whose most famous act was the 1057 murder of Macbeth – as immortalised by William Shakespeare). With his English queen, Margaret, he founded the Canmore dynasty that would rule Scotland for the next two centuries.

1066 & ALL THAT

While Wales and Scotland laid the foundations of nationhood, back in England things were unsettled, as the royal pendulum was still swinging between Saxon and Danish-Viking monarchs. When King Edward the Confessor died, the crown passed to Harold, his brother-in-law. That should've settled things, but Edward had a cousin in Normandy (the northern part of today's France) called William, who thought *he* should have succeeded to the throne of England.

The end result was the 1066 Battle of Hastings. William and his army sailed from Normandy, landing near the town of Hastings, on England's southern coast. The Saxons were defeated, and King Harold was killed – by an arrow in the eye, according to the traditional telling.

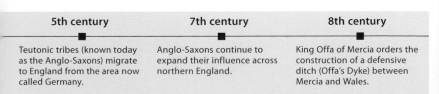

5th century	7th century	8th century
Teutonic tribes (known today as the Anglo-Saxons) migrate to England from the area now called Germany.	Anglo-Saxons continue to expand their influence across northern England.	King Offa of Mercia orders the construction of a defensive ditch (Offa's Dyke) between Mercia and Wales.

GRANT DIXON

Viking runic graffiti, Maes Howe burial mound (p354), Orkney Islands

William became king of England, earning himself the prestigious epithet Conqueror. In the years after the invasion, a strict class hierarchy developed, known as the feudal system. At the top was the monarch, below that the nobles (barons, bishops, dukes and earls), then knights and lords, and at the bottom were peasants or 'serfs', effectively slaves. The feudal system helped established the basis of a class system which to a certain extent still exists in England today.

ROYAL & HOLY SQUABBLING

When the rule of Henry I ended in 1135, the fight to take his place continued the enduring English habit of competition for the throne, and introduced an equally enduring tendency of bickering between royalty and the church. Things came to a head in 1170 when Henry II had 'turbulent priest' Thomas Becket murdered in Canterbury Cathedral (p119) – still an important shrine today.

Perhaps the next king, Richard I, wanted to make amends for his forebear's unholy actions by leading a crusade – a Christian 'Holy War' – to liberate Jerusalem and the Holy Land (Levant) from occupation by Muslim 'heathens' under their leader Saladin. Unfortunately, Richard's overseas activities meant he was too busy to bother about governing England – although his bravery, and ruthlessness, earned him the sobriquet Richard the Lionheart – and in his absence the country fell into disarray.

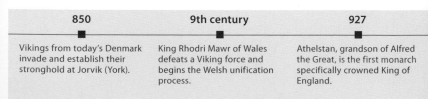

850	9th century	927
Vikings from today's Denmark invade and establish their stronghold at Jorvik (York).	King Rhodri Mawr of Wales defeats a Viking force and begins the Welsh unification process.	Athelstan, grandson of Alfred the Great, is the first monarch specifically crowned King of England.

Richard was succeeded as king by his brother John, but under his harsh rule things got even worse for the general population. According to legend, it was during this time that a nobleman called Robert of Loxley, better known as Robin Hood, hid in Sherwood Forest (p174) and engaged in a spot of wealth redistribution.

EXPANSIONIST EDWARD

Henry III was followed in 1272 by Edward I, a skilled ruler and ambitious general. During a busy 35-year reign he expounded English nationalism and was unashamedly expansionist in his outlook, leading campaigns into Wales and Scotland. In the end, Wales became a dependent principality, owing allegiance to England. There were no more Welsh kings, and just to make it clear who was boss, Edward made his own son the Prince of Wales. Ever since, the British sovereign's eldest son has been automatically given the title.

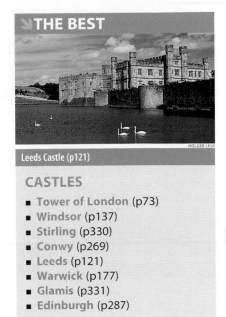

◥THE BEST

HOLGER LEUE

Leeds Castle (p121)

CASTLES

- **Tower of London** (p73)
- **Windsor** (p137)
- **Stirling** (p330)
- **Conwy** (p269)
- **Leeds** (p121)
- **Warwick** (p177)
- **Glamis** (p331)
- **Edinburgh** (p287)

Edward I then looked north. For the past 200 years, Scotland had been ruled by the Canmores, but the dynasty effectively ended in 1286 with the death of Alexander III. There followed a dispute for the Scottish throne for which there were 13 *tanists* (contestants), but in the end it came down to two: John Balliol and Robert Bruce of Annandale. Arbitration was needed and Edward I was called in; he chose Balliol.

Edward then sought to formalise his feudal overlordship and travelled through Scotland forcing clan leaders to swear allegiance. In a final blow to Scottish pride, Edward removed the Stone of Scone (also known as the Stone of Destiny or Fatal Stone), on which the kings of Scotland had been crowned for centuries, from Scone Abbey.

In response, Balliol got in touch with Edward's old enemy, France, and arranged a treaty of cooperation, the start of an anti-English partnership – the 'Auld Alliance' – that was to last for many centuries (and to the present day when it comes to rugby and football).

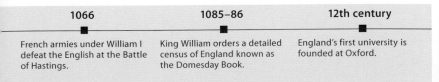

1066	1085–86	12th century
French armies under William I defeat the English at the Battle of Hastings.	King William orders a detailed census of England known as the Domesday Book.	England's first university is founded at Oxford.

Caerlaverock Castle (p312), Scotland

GRAEME CORNWALLIS

Edward wasn't the sort of bloke to brook opposition, though. In 1296 the English army defeated Balliol, forcing the Scottish barons to accept Edward's rule, and his ruthless retaliation earned him the title 'Hammer of the Scots'. But still the Scottish people refused to lie down: in 1297, at the Battle of Stirling Bridge, the English were defeated by a Scots army under the leadership of William Wallace. More than 700 years later, Wallace is still remembered as the epitome of Scottish patriots (see National Wallace Monument, p330) as well as the mullet-sporting central character of Mel Gibson's 1995 film, *Braveheart*.

HARD TIMES

Back in England, Edward I was succeeded by Edward II, but the new model lacked the military success of his forebear, and his favouring of personal friends over barons didn't help. Edward failed in the marriage department, too, and his rule came to a grisly end when his wife, Isabella, and her lover, Roger Mortimer, had him murdered in Berkeley Castle.

By this time, Robert the Bruce (grandson of Robert Bruce of Annandale) had crowned himself King of Scotland (1306), been beaten in battle, gone on the run, and, while hiding in a cave, been inspired to renew his efforts by a spider persistently spinning its web. Bruce's army went on to defeat Edward II and the English at the

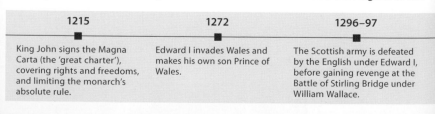

1215	1272	1296–97
King John signs the Magna Carta (the 'great charter'), covering rights and freedoms, and limiting the monarch's absolute rule.	Edward I invades Wales and makes his own son Prince of Wales.	The Scottish army is defeated by the English under Edward I, before gaining revenge at the Battle of Stirling Bridge under William Wallace.

Battle of Bannockburn in 1314, another milestone in Scotland's long fight to remain independent.

Next in line was Edward III. Highlights of his reign – actually lowlights – include the start of the Hundred Years' War with France in 1337 and the arrival of a plague called the Black Death about a decade later, which eventually wiped out 1.5 million people, more than a third of the country's population.

STEWARTS ENTER THE SCENE

While the Hundred Years' War raged (or rather, rumbled) between England and France, things weren't much better in Scotland. After the death of Robert the Bruce in 1329, the country was ravaged by endless internal conflicts and plague epidemics.

Bruce's son became David II of Scotland, but he was soon caught up in battles against fellow Scots disaffected by his father and aided by Edward III. When David died in 1371, the Scots quickly crowned Robert Stewart (Robert the Bruce's grandson) as king, marking the start of the House of Stewart, which was to crop up again in England a bit later down the line.

HOUSES OF YORK & LANCASTER

In 1399, the ineffectual Richard II, the last of the House of Plantagenet, was ousted by a powerful baron called Henry Bolingbroke, who became Henry IV – the first monarch of the House of Lancaster.

Less than a year later, his rule was disrupted by a final cry of resistance from the downtrodden Welsh, led by royal-descendant Owain Glyndŵr. It wasn't a good result for Wales: the rebellion was crushed, vast areas of farmland were destroyed, Glyndŵr died an outlaw and the Welsh elite were barred from public life for many years.

Henry IV was followed, neatly, by Henry V, who decided it was time to stir up the dormant Hundred Years' War. His defeat of France at the Battle of Agincourt and the patriotic tear-jerker speech he was given by Shakespeare ('cry God for Harry, England and St George') ensured his position among the most famous English kings of all time.

Still keeping things neat, Henry V was followed by Henry VI, whose main claim to fame was overseeing the building of great places of worship (including King's College Chapel, p189, in Cambridge, and Eton Chapel, p138, near Windsor), interspersed with great bouts of insanity.

WARS OF THE ROSES

When the Hundred Years' War finally ground to a halt in 1453, the English forces returning from France threw their energies into another battle: a civil conflict dubbed the Wars of the Roses.

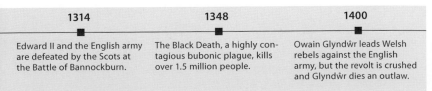

1314	1348	1400
Edward II and the English army are defeated by the Scots at the Battle of Bannockburn.	The Black Death, a highly contagious bubonic plague, kills over 1.5 million people.	Owain Glyndŵr leads Welsh rebels against the English army, but the revolt is crushed and Glyndŵr dies an outlaw.

JULIET COOMBE

Celebrations for Shakespeare's birthday, Stratford-upon-Avon (p177)

Briefly, it went like this: Henry VI of the House of Lancaster (whose emblem was a red rose) was challenged by Richard, Duke of York (symbolised by a white rose). Henry was weak and it was almost a walkover for Richard, but Henry's wife, Margaret of Anjou, was made of sterner mettle and her forces defeated the challenger. But it didn't rest there: Richard's son Edward entered with an army, turned the tables, drove out Henry, and became King Edward IV – the first monarch of the House of York.

DARK DEEDS IN THE TOWER

Life was never easy for the guy at the top. Edward IV hardly had time to catch his breath before facing a challenger to his own throne. Enter scheming Richard Neville, Earl of Warwick, who liked to be billed as 'the kingmaker'. In 1470 he teamed up with the energetic Margaret of Anjou to shuttle Edward into exile and bring Henry VI to the throne. But a year later Edward IV came bouncing back, and this time there was no messing about; he killed Richard Neville – Earl of Warwick, captured Margaret, and had Henry snuffed out in the Tower of London.

Although Edward IV's position seemed secure, he ruled for only a decade before being succeeded by his 12-year-old son, now Edward V. But the boy-king's reign was even shorter than his dad's: in 1483 he was mysteriously murdered, along with his brother, and once again the Tower of London was the scene of the crime.

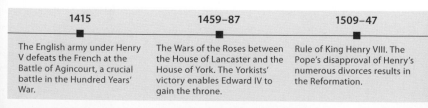

1415	1459–87	1509–47
The English army under Henry V defeats the French at the Battle of Agincourt, a crucial battle in the Hundred Years' War.	The Wars of the Roses between the House of Lancaster and the House of York. The Yorkists' victory enables Edward IV to gain the throne.	Rule of King Henry VIII. The Pope's disapproval of Henry's numerous divorces results in the Reformation.

With the 'little princes' dispatched, this left the throne open for their dear old Uncle Richard. Whether he was the princes' killer is still the subject of debate, but his rule as Richard III was also short-lived. Despite being rewarded with another famous Shakespearean sound bite ('A horse, a horse, my kingdom for a horse'), few tears were shed in 1485 when he was tumbled from the top job by a nobleman from Wales called Henry Tudor, who became Henry VII.

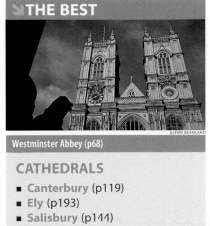

THE BEST

Westminster Abbey (p68)

GLENN BEANLAND

CATHEDRALS

- **Canterbury** (p119)
- **Ely** (p193)
- **Salisbury** (p141)
- **Westminster Abbey** (p68)
- **Durham** (p242)
- **Lincoln** (p194)

HENRY VIII VS THE CHURCH

There hadn't been a Henry on the throne for a while, and this new incumbent harked back to the days of his namesakes with a skilful reign. After the York-vs-Lancaster Wars of the Roses, Henry VII's Tudor neutrality was important. He also diligently mended fences with his northern neighbours by marrying off his daughter to James IV of Scotland, thereby linking the Tudor and Stewart lines.

Matrimony may have been more useful than warfare for Henry VII, but the multiple marriages of his successor, Henry VIII, were a very different story. Fathering a male heir was his problem – hence the famous six wives – but the Pope's disapproval of divorce and remarriage led in part to Henry's split with the Roman Catholic Church. Parliament made Henry the head of the Protestant Church of England – marking the start of a period known as the English Reformation – and the beginning of a pivotal division between Catholics and Protestants that still exists in some areas of Britain.

In 1536 Henry 'dissolved' many monasteries in Britain and Ireland, more a takeover of land and wealth than a symptom of the struggle between church and state.

EARLY UNIONS

At the same time, Henry signed the Acts of Union (1536 and 1543), formally uniting England and Wales for the first time. This was welcomed by the aspiring Welsh gentry, as it meant English law and parliamentary representation for Wales, plus plenty of

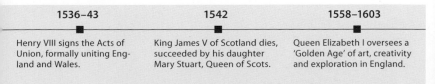

1536–43	1542	1558–1603
Henry VIII signs the Acts of Union, formally uniting England and Wales.	King James V of Scotland dies, succeeded by his daughter Mary Stuart, Queen of Scots.	Queen Elizabeth I oversees a 'Golden Age' of art, creativity and exploration in England.

GREAT BRITAIN IN FOCUS

HISTORY

Hampton Court Palace (p85), England

DOUG MCKINLAY

trade opportunities. The Welsh language, however, ceased to be recognised in the law courts.

ROUGH WOOING

In Scotland, James IV had been succeeded by James V, who died in 1542, broken-hearted, it is said, after yet another defeat at the hands of the English. His baby daughter Mary became queen and Scotland was ruled by regents.

From his throne in England Henry VIII sent a proposal that Mary should marry his son. But the regents rejected his offer and – not forgetting the Auld Alliance – Mary was sent to France instead. Henry was furious and sent his armies to ravage southern Scotland and sack Edinburgh in an (unsuccessful) attempt to force agreement to the wedding – the Rough Wooing, as it was called with typical Scottish irony and understatement.

THE ELIZABETHAN AGE

When Henry VIII died, he was succeeded by his son Edward VI, then by daughter Mary I, but their reigns were short. So, unexpectedly, Henry's third child, Elizabeth, came to the throne.

As Elizabeth I, she inherited a nasty mess of religious strife and divided loyalties, but after an uncertain start she gained confidence and turned the country around. Refusing

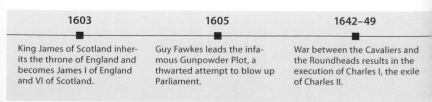

1603	1605	1642–49
King James of Scotland inherits the throne of England and becomes James I of England and VI of Scotland.	Guy Fawkes leads the infamous Gunpowder Plot, a thwarted attempt to blow up Parliament.	War between the Cavaliers and the Roundheads results in the execution of Charles I, the exile of Charles II.

marriage, she borrowed biblical imagery and became known as the Virgin Queen – perhaps the first English monarch to create a cult image.

Highlights of her 45-year reign included the naval defeat of the Spanish Armada, the far-flung explorations of English seafarers Walter Raleigh and Francis Drake and the expansion of England's increasingly global trading network – not to mention a cultural flourishing thanks to writers such as William Shakespeare and Christopher Marlowe.

MARY, QUEEN OF SCOTS

Meanwhile, Elizabeth's cousin Mary had stayed in France, and married the French dauphin (crown prince), thereby becoming queen of France as well as Scotland. After her husband's death, Mary returned to Scotland, and from there ambitiously claimed the English throne as well – on the grounds that Elizabeth was illegitimate.

Mary's plans failed; she was imprisoned and forced to abdicate, but then escaped to England and appealed to Elizabeth for help. In an uncharacteristic display of indecision, Elizabeth held Mary under arrest for 19 years, moving her frequently from house to house, so that today England has many stately homes (and even a few pubs) claiming 'Mary Queen of Scots slept here'. Eventually, Elizabeth ordered her cousin's execution.

UNITED & DISUNITED BRITAIN

When Elizabeth died in 1603, the Virgin Queen had failed to provide an heir. She was succeeded by her closest relative, the Scottish King James, the safely Protestant son of the murdered Mary. He became James I of England and VI of Scotland, the first English monarch of the House of Stuart (Mary's time in France had Gallicised the Stewart name). Most importantly, James united England, Wales and Scotland into one kingdom for the first time in history – another step towards British unity, at least on paper – although the terms 'Britain' and 'British' were still not yet widely used in this context.

But the divide between king and Parliament continued to smoulder, and the power struggle worsened during the reign of Charles I, eventually degenerating into the

◤**THE BEST**

Edinburgh (p286) from Arthur's Seat

JONATHAN SMITH

HISTORIC CITIES

- **London** (p51)
- **York** (p225)
- **Edinburgh** (p286)
- **Oxford** (p127)
- **Bath** (p145)

1665–66	1707	1721–42
The Great Plague kills 100,000 people; the Great Fire of London burns much of the city to the ground.	The Act of Union links the countries of England, Wales and Scotland under one parliament for the first time.	Leading member of Parliament Robert Walpole becomes Britain's first prime minister.

English Civil War. The antiroyalist forces were led by Oliver Cromwell, a Puritan who preached against the excesses of the monarch and established church, and his parliamentarian (or Roundhead) army was pitched against the king's forces (the Cavaliers) in a war that tore England apart. Fortunately, this would be the last such occurrence. It ended with victory for the Roundheads, the king executed, and England declared a republic – with Cromwell hailed as 'Protector'.

THE RETURN OF THE KING

By 1653 Cromwell was finding Parliament too restricting and assumed dictatorial powers, much to his supporters' dismay. On his death in 1658, he was followed half-heartedly by his son, but in 1660 Parliament decided to re-establish the monarchy – as republican alternatives were proving far worse.

Charles II (the exiled son of Charles I) came to the throne, and his rule – known as the Restoration – saw scientific and cultural activity bursting forth after the strait-laced ethics of Cromwell's time.

RICHARD I'ANSON

Oliver Cromwell statue, Houses of Parliament (p69)

The next king, James II, had a harder time. Attempts to ease restrictive laws on Catholics ended with his defeat at the Battle of the Boyne by William III, the Protestant ruler of Holland, better known as William of Orange. Ironically, William was married to James' own daughter Mary, but it didn't stop him doing the dirty on his father-in-law.

William and Mary both had equal rights to the throne and their joint accession in 1688 was known as the Glorious Revolution.

KILLIECRANKIE, GLEN COE & UNION

In Scotland, things weren't quite so glorious. Anti-English (essentially anti-William and anti-Protestant) feelings ran high, as did pro-James ('Jacobite') support. In 1689 Jacobite

1776–83	1799–1815	1837–1901
The American War of Independence damages British power and prestige.	Napoleon threatens invasion but is eventually defeated at the Battles of Trafalgar and Waterloo.	Under the reign of Queen Victoria, the British Empire expands its influence across the globe.

leader Graham of Claverhouse, better known as Bonnie Dundee, raised a Highlander army and routed English troops at Killiecrankie.

Then in 1692 came the infamous Glen Coe Massacre. On English-government orders, members of the Campbell clan killed most of the MacDonald clan for failing to swear allegiance to William. The atrocity further fuelled Catholic–Protestant divisions, and further tightened English domination of the island of Britain.

ANOTHER ACT OF UNION

In 1694 Mary died, leaving William as sole monarch. He died a few years later and was followed by his sister-in-law Anne (the second daughter of James II). In 1707, during Anne's reign, the Act of Union was passed, bringing an end to the independent Scottish Parliament, and finally linking the countries of England, Wales and Scotland under one parliament (based in London) for the first time in history.

In 1714 Anne died without leaving an heir, marking the end of the Stuart line. The throne was then passed to distant (but still safely Protestant) German relatives, the House of Hanover.

AGE OF EMPIRE

Stronger control over the British Isles was mirrored by even greater expansion abroad. The British Empire – which, despite its official title, was predominantly an *English* entity – continued to grow in America, Canada and India. The first claims were made to Australia after Captain James Cook's epic voyage in 1768.

The Empire's first major reverse came when the American colonies won the War of Independence (1776–83). This setback forced Britain to withdraw from the world stage for a while, a gap not missed by French ruler Napoleon. He threatened to invade Britain and hinder the power of the British overseas, before his ambitions were curtailed by navy hero Viscount Horatio Nelson and military hero the Duke of Wellington at the famous Battles of Trafalgar (1805) and Waterloo (1815).

THE INDUSTRIAL AGE

While the Empire expanded abroad, at home Britain had become the crucible of the Industrial Revolution. Steam power (patented by James Watt in 1781) and steam trains (launched by George Stephenson in 1825) transformed methods of production and transport, and the towns of the English Midlands became the first industrial cities.

This population shift in England was mirrored in Scotland. From about 1750 onwards, much of the Highlands region had been emptied of people, as landowners casually expelled entire farms and villages to make way for more-profitable sheep farming, a seminal event in Scotland's history known as the Clearances.

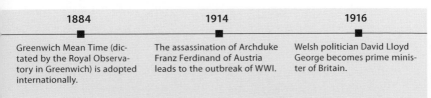

1884	1914	1916
Greenwich Mean Time (dictated by the Royal Observatory in Greenwich) is adopted internationally.	The assassination of Archduke Franz Ferdinand of Austria leads to the outbreak of WWI.	Welsh politician David Lloyd George becomes prime minister of Britain.

The same happened in Wales. By the early 19th century copper, iron and slate were being extracted in the Merthyr Tydfil and Monmouth areas. The 1860s saw the Rhondda valleys opened up for coal mining, and Wales soon became a major exporter of coal, as well as the world's leading producer of tin plate.

Across Britain, industrialisation meant people were on the move as never before. The rapid change from rural to urban society caused great dislocation, and although knowledge of science and medicine improved alongside industrial advances, it also meant a rapid rise in population. For many people the side effects of Britain's economic blossoming were poverty and deprivation.

Nevertheless, by the time Queen Victoria took the throne in 1837, Britain's factories dominated world trade and Britain's fleets dominated the oceans. The times were optimistic, but it wasn't all tub-thumping jingoism. The British Prime Minister Benjamin Disraeli and his successor William Gladstone introduced many social reforms to address the worst excesses of the Industrial Revolution. Education became universal, trade unions were legalised and the right to vote was extended to commoners. Well, to male commoners – women didn't get the vote for another few decades, and only then thanks to a pioneering group of female protestors known as the Suffragettes.

WWI

When Queen Victoria died in 1901, it seemed that Britain's energy fizzled out, and the country entered a period of decline. In continental Europe, other states were more active: the military powers of Russia, Austro-Hungary, Turkey and Germany were sabre-rattling in the Balkan states, a dispute that eventually culminated in WWI. When German forces entered Belgium on their way to invade France, Britain and the Allied countries were drawn in and the Great War became a vicious conflict of stalemate and slaughter – most infamously on the fields of Flanders and the beaches of Gallipoli. By the war's weary end in 1918 over a million Britons had died, not to mention millions more from the Commonwealth.

DISILLUSION & DEPRESSION

For soldiers who did return from WWI, disillusion led to questioning of the social order. Many supported the ideals of a new political force – the Labour Party, to represent the working class – upsetting the balance long enjoyed by the Liberal and Conservative parties since the days of Walpole.

The Labour Party was elected to government for the first time in 1923, in coalition with the Liberals, with James Ramsay MacDonald as prime minister. A year later, the Conservatives were back in power, but by this time the world economy was in decline. Industrial unrest was a common feature of the 1920s.

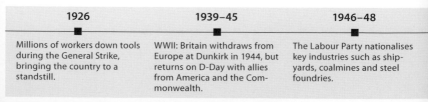

1926	1939–45	1946–48
Millions of workers down tools during the General Strike, bringing the country to a standstill.	WWII: Britain withdraws from Europe at Dunkirk in 1944, but returns on D-Day with allies from America and the Commonwealth.	The Labour Party nationalises key industries such as shipyards, coalmines and steel foundries.

LEFT: NEIL SETCHFIELD; RIGHT: RICHARD I'ANSON

Left: Queen Victoria Memorial, Buckingham Palace (p70); Right: Nelson's Column, Trafalgar Square (p65)

This worsened in the 1930s as the world economy slumped and the Great Depression took hold. Even the royal family took a knock when Edward VIII abdicated in 1936 so he could marry a woman who was twice divorced and – horror of horrors – American. The ensuing scandal was good for newspaper sales and hinted at the prolonged 'trials by media' suffered by royals in more recent times.

The throne was taken by Edward's less-than-charismatic brother George VI and Britain dithered through the rest of the decade, with mediocre government failing to confront the country's deep-set social and economic problems.

WWII

Meanwhile, on mainland Europe, Germany saw the rise of Adolf Hitler, leader of the Nazi party. Many feared another Great War, but Prime Minister Neville Chamberlain met the German leader in 1938 and promised Britain 'peace for our time' (a phrase still remembered, although usually misquoted as 'peace in our time'). He was wrong. The following year Hitler invaded Poland. Two days later Britain was once again at war with Germany.

The German army moved with astonishing speed, swept west through France, and pushed back British forces to the beaches of Dunkirk in northern France in June 1940,

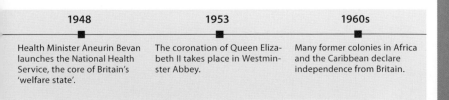

1948	1953	1960s
Health Minister Aneurin Bevan launches the National Health Service, the core of Britain's 'welfare state'.	The coronation of Queen Elizabeth II takes place in Westminster Abbey.	Many former colonies in Africa and the Caribbean declare independence from Britain.

NEIL SETCHFIELD

Queen Elizabeth II leaving the gates of Buckingham Palace (p70)

where they were miraculously rescued by a flotilla of makeshift vessels sent from back home in Blighty.

Chamberlain, reviled for his earlier 'appeasement', stood aside to let a new prime minister, Winston Churchill, lead a coalition government. In June 1940 the famous Battle of Britain, in which the Luftwaffe and the RAF fought it out in the skies over southern England, helped delay the planned German invasion of the British mainland, and in 1941 the tide finally began to turn. Following the Japanese attack on Pearl Harbour, the USA entered the war to support Britain, and Germany became bogged down on the eastern front fighting Russia. The D-Day landings in 1944 marked the start of the liberation of Europe from the west, and according to Churchill the beginning of the end of the war. By 1945 Hitler was dead, and his country ruined. Two atomic bombs forced the surrender of Germany's ally Japan, and finally brought WWII to a close.

SWINGING & SLIDING

In Britain, despite the victory, there was an unexpected swing on the political front. An electorate tired of war and hungry for change tumbled Churchill's Conservatives and voted in the Labour Party, led by Clement Attlee. This was the dawn of the 'welfare state'; key industries (such as steel, coal and railways) were nationalised, and the

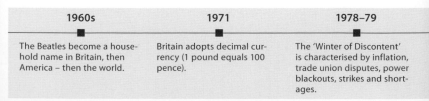

1960s	1971	1978–79
The Beatles become a household name in Britain, then America – then the world.	Britain adopts decimal currency (1 pound equals 100 pence).	The 'Winter of Discontent' is characterised by inflation, trade union disputes, power blackouts, strikes and shortages.

National Health Service was founded. But rebuilding Britain was a slow process, and the postwar 'baby boomers' experienced food rationing well into the 1950s.

The impact of depleted reserves were felt overseas, too, as parts of the British Empire became independent, including India and Pakistan in 1947 and Malaya in 1957, followed by much of Africa and the Caribbean.

But while the Empire's sun may have been setting, Britain's royal family was still going strong. In 1952 George VI was succeeded by his daughter Elizabeth II, who has remained on the throne for more than five decades, overseeing a period of massive social and economic change.

During the Swinging Sixties Britain became the centre of a new explosion in youth culture, but by the 1970s economic decline had set in once again. A deadly combination of inflation, an oil crisis and international competition revealed the weakness of Britain's economy, and a lot that was rotten in British society, too. The ongoing struggle between disgruntled working and ruling classes was brought to the boil once again; the rest of the decade was marked by strikes, disputes and general all round gloom – especially when the electricity was cut, as power stations went short of fuel or workers walked out.

Neither the Conservatives under Edward Heath, nor Labour under Harold Wilson and Jim Callaghan, proved capable of controlling the strife. The British public had had enough, and the elections of May 1979 returned the Conservatives, led by a little-known politician named Margaret Thatcher.

⬊ THREE IN ONE

The countries of England, Wales and Scotland make up the state of Great Britain. Three countries in one might seem a strange set-up, and visitors are sometimes confused about the difference between England and Britain.

Just for the record, the United Kingdom (UK) consists of Great Britain and Northern Ireland. The island of Ireland consists of Northern Ireland and the Republic of Ireland (also called Eire). 'British Isles' is a geographical term for the whole group of islands that make up the UK, the Republic of Ireland and some autonomous or semiautonomous islands, such as the Channel Islands and the Isle of Man.

THE THATCHER YEARS

Love her or hate her, no one could argue that her methods weren't direct and dramatic. The industries nationalised in the late 1940s were now seen as inefficient and a drain on

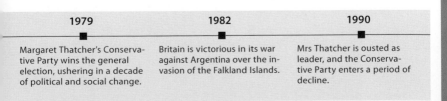

1979	1982	1990
Margaret Thatcher's Conservative Party wins the general election, ushering in a decade of political and social change.	Britain is victorious in its war against Argentina over the invasion of the Falkland Islands.	Mrs Thatcher is ousted as leader, and the Conservative Party enters a period of decline.

resources, and were sold off with a sense of purpose that made Henry VIII's dissolution of the monasteries seem like a Sunday-school picnic.

These moves were opposed by those working in the nationalised industries (and by many other sections of society) via strikes, marches and organised industrial disputes. But Mrs Thatcher's government waged a relentless assault on the power of trade unions, fronted by the closure of coalmines throughout Britain – most notably in the English Midlands, Yorkshire, south Wales and parts of Scotland. In response, the nationwide strike by miners in the early 1980s was one of the most bitter labour disputes in British history, but the pit closures went ahead.

By 1988, the 'Iron lady' had become the longest-serving British prime minister of the 20th century, but she was finally ousted when her introduction of the hugely unpopular 'poll tax' (a fixed, per-adult tax) in the early 1990s sparked nationwide riots and huge public discontent.

NEW LABOUR, NEW MILLENNIUM

Following an indecisive interim period under the leadership of Mrs Thatcher's successor, John Major, 'New' Labour swept to power in 1997 under fresh-faced leader Tony Blair. Amongst a host of other reforms, Blair's government established devolved parliaments in Scotland and Wales, granting both countries limited control over their own taxation, spending and public policy – something they hadn't enjoyed since the Act of Union in 1707.

Tony Blair and New Labour continued to dominate the political landscape over the next few years, enjoying another landslide victory at the 2001 election. But as the decade wore on a series of controversial issues – most notably the threat of international terrorism in the wake of 9/11 and the invasions of Iraq and Afghanistan – fed into a growing sense of public dissatisfaction and dissent. Despite the shocking events of 7 July 2005, when British-born bombers attacked underground trains and a bus, killing 52 people, Labour won a historic third term in 2005. A year later Mr Blair became the longest-serving Labour Party prime minister in British history, but was finally forced to resign in 2007 following continued questions about his leadership.

THE FUTURE'S BROWN?

After a decade of waiting for the top job, Gordon Brown, the chancellor of the exchequer (the British term for minister of finance) finally succeeded Tony Blair as prime minister in 2007. Mr Brown's first three months in office were promising, but before long the wheels came off the wagon: weakening opinion polls, mishandled plans for a 'snap' election, a series of disastrous by-elections and growing criticism of his leadership style were compounded by a massive global financial crash in late 2008. The subsequent

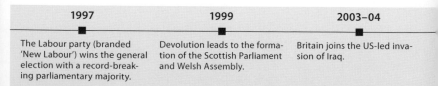

1997	**1999**	**2003–04**
The Labour party (branded 'New Labour') wins the general election with a record-breaking parliamentary majority.	Devolution leads to the formation of the Scottish Parliament and Welsh Assembly.	Britain joins the US-led invasion of Iraq.

Exterior of the Scottish Parliament Building (p290)

BETHUNE CARMICHAEL

economic downturn, rising costs of fuel and food, plummeting interest rates and falling house values all led to growing disillusionment with Brown's government, alongside a groundswell of support for the Conservatives under the leadership of David Cameron. With a general election pencilled for 2010 at the time of writing, it remains to be seen if the voters will award Labour another term in office or if the political pendulum will swing back the other way.

2005	2007	2008
Labour is re-elected for a third term with Tony Blair still at the helm. Tube bombs kill 52 people.	After more than a decade in the top job, Tony Blair resigns and Gordon Brown takes over as Labour leader and Britain's prime minister.	Gordon Brown's first year in office is dogged by problems, including a global financial meltdown and Britain's worst recession since the 1980s.

MUSIC

Music-goers, London

NEIL SETCHFIELD

Britain's been putting the world through its musical paces ever since a mop-haired four-piece from Liverpool tuned up their Rickenbackers and became 'bigger than Jesus', to quote John Lennon. Quite what it is that makes this little island such a musical powerhouse is still something of a mystery, but even in the days of falling CD sales, digital downloads and MySpace demos, British bands still seem hell bent on remaining top of the pops.

POP TO PUNK

Elvis may have brought rock-and-roll to the world, but it was the Fab Four who transformed it into a global phenomenon, backed by the Rolling Stones, the Who, Cream, the Kinks and the other bands of the 'British Invasion'.

Glam rock swaggered in to replace peace and love in the early 1970s, with Marc Bolan and David Bowie donning spandex and glittery guitars in a variety of chameleonic guises, succeeded by art-rockers Roxy Music and anthemic popsters Queen and Elton John. Meanwhile Led Zeppelin laid down the blueprint for heavy metal and hard rock, and 1960s psychedelia morphed into the spacey noodlings of prog rock, epitomised by Pink Floyd, Genesis and Yes.

By the late '70s the prog bands were looking out of touch in a Britain wracked by rampant unemployment, industrial unrest and the three-day-week. Flicking a giant two fingers to the establishment, punk exploded onto the scene, summing up the general air of doom and gloom with nihilistic lyrics and short, sharp, three-chord

GREAT BRITAIN IN FOCUS

MUSIC

tunes. The Sex Pistols produced one landmark album (*Never Mind the Bollocks: Here's the Sex Pistols*), a clutch of (mostly banned) singles and a storm of controversy, ably assisted by other punk pioneers such as the Clash, the Damned, the Buzzcocks and the Stranglers.

While punk burned itself out in a blaze of squealing guitars and earsplitting feedback, New Wave bands including the Jam and Elvis Costello took up the torch, blending spiky tunes and sharp lyrics into a poppier, more radio-friendly sound. Meanwhile the Specials, Selecter and baggy-trousered rude boys Madness mixed punk, reggae and ska into two-tone (a nod to the movement's cross-racial ethos).

NEW WAVE TO RAVE

The big money and conspicuous consumption of Thatcherite Britain in the early 1980s bled over into the decade's pop scene. Big hair, shiny suits and shoulder pads became the uniform of New Romantics such as Spandau Ballet, Duran Duran and Culture Club, while the advent of synthesisers and processed beats led to the development of a new electronic sound in the music of Depeche Mode and Human League. But the glitz and glitter of '80s pop concealed a murky underbelly: bands like the Cure, Bauhaus and Siouxsie and the Banshees were employing doom-laden lyrics and apocalyptically heavy riffs, while the rock heritage of Led Zeppelin inspired heavy metal acts such as Iron Maiden, Judas Priest and Black Sabbath. Meanwhile the arch-priests of miserabilism, the Smiths, fronted by extravagantly quiffed wordsmith Morrissey, summed up the disaffection of mid-'80s England in classic albums such as *The Queen Is Dead* and *Meat Is Murder*.

The beats and bleeps of eighties electronica fuelled the burgeoning dance music scene of the early 1990s. Pioneering artists such as New Order (risen from the ashes of Joy Division) and the Orb used synthesised sounds to create the soundtrack for the new ecstasy-fuelled rave culture, centred around famous clubs like Manchester's Haçienda and London's Ministry of Sound. Subgenres such as trip-hop, drum and bass, jungle, house and big-beat cropped up in other UK cities, with key acts including Massive Attack, Portishead, the Prodigy and the Chemical Brothers.

NINETIES & NOUGHTIES

Manchester was also a focus for the burgeoning British indie scene, driven by guitar-based bands such as the

⬊ LIVE & KICKING

You're never short of live music in Britain. Most major British cities have at least one stadium or concert hall that regularly hosts big-name acts and classical concerts, and right across the country there's a huge choice of smaller venues where the latest bands strut their musical stuff. Bands large and small are pretty much guaranteed to play in London, but often tour extensively, so a night out in Cardiff, Cambridge, Newcastle or Glasgow is just as likely to land you a decent gig. For tickets and listings, try countrywide agencies such as See (www.seetickets.com) and Ticketmaster (www.ticketmaster.co.uk), while Gigs in Scotland (www.gigsinscotland.com) is the absolute authority north of the border.

Charlatans, the Stone Roses, James, Happy Mondays and Manchester's most famous musical export, Oasis. In the late 1990s indie segued into Britpop, a catch-all term covering bands such as Oasis, Pulp, Supergrass and Blur, whose distinctively British music chimed with the country's new sense of optimism following the landslide election of New Labour in 1997 (Noel and Liam Gallagher were even invited for afternoon tea at Number 10). But the phenomenon of 'Cool Britannia' was short-lived; by the millennium, most of Britpop's big acts had self-destructed. Some bands survived, though, and others have risen from the ashes: Britpop pioneers Blur returned in triumphant style with a headline performance at the 2009 Glastonbury Festival.

So where does that leave us in the 2000s? The era of MySpace, iTunes and file sharing has seen Britain's music scene become more diverse and divided than ever. Jazz, soul, R&B and hip-hop beats have fused into a new urban sound (featuring artists such as Jay-Z, Jamelia, the Streets and Dizzee Rascal), while dance music continues to morph through new forms. On the pop side, singer-songwriters have made a comeback: Lily Allen, Duffy and self-destructive songstress Amy Winehouse are flying the flag for the female artists, while Damien Rice, Ed Harcourt and soppy ex-soldier boy James Blunt croon for the boys.

The spirit of shoegazing British indie is alive and well thanks to bands like Keane, Foals, Editors, We are Scientists and world-conquering Coldplay; traces of punk survive

thanks to Franz Ferdinand, Razorlight, Babyshambles, Muse, Dirty Pretty Things and download phenomenons Arctic Monkeys; and the swagger of the Manchester sound still echoes through the music of Primal Scream, Kaiser Chiefs, Kasabian, Doves and the (reformed) Verve.

And as ever, alternative music continues to push the nation's musical boundaries: names to look out for include Elbow, British Sea Power, Archie Bronson Outfit, the Horrors and Britain's most wilfully eclectic band, Radiohead.

FOLK MUSIC

Scotland, England and Wales all have long histories of folk music, each with its own distinctive traditions, melodies and native instruments. Scotland has its bagpipes and bodhrán (a hand-held drum), England the Northumbrian pipes and brass bands, Wales the harp and male voice choirs. These days, though, folk music generally refers to a single musician or small group singing traditional songs live in a pub (or

NEIL SETCHFIELD

Guitarist, Glasgow

on stage), usually accompanied by instruments such as guitar, fiddle and penny whistle.

British folk music mines a rich seam of regional culture, from the rhythmic 'waulking songs' of the tweed weavers of the Outer Hebrides to the jaunty melodies of England's morris dancers. Local history plays its part too – many Welsh folk songs recall Owain Glyndŵr's battles against English domination, while English folk lyrics range from memories of the Tolpuddle Martyrs to sea shanties sung by Liverpool sailors. In Scotland, the Jacobite rebellion of 1745 was a rich source of traditional songs, while *Flower of Scotland* – written in 1967 by popular folk duo the Corries, and today the unofficial Scottish national anthem – harks back to the Battle of Bannockburn in 1314.

Scottish Gaelic and Welsh traditional music are celebrated annually in the **Mod** (www.the-mod.co.uk) and the **Eisteddfod** (www.eisteddfod.org.uk).

NEIL SETCHFIELD

Pipers, Scotland

GREAT BRITAIN IN FOCUS

MUSIC

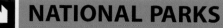

NATIONAL PARKS

Snowdonia National Park (p271)

EOIN CLARKE

In 1810, poet and outdoors-lover William Wordsworth suggested that the Lake District should be 'a sort of national property, in which every man has a right'.

More than a century later, the Lake District became a national park, along with the Brecon Beacons, Cairngorms, Dartmoor, Exmoor, Loch Lomond and the Trossachs, the New Forest, the Broads (in Norfolk and Suffolk – often known as the Norfolk Broads), Northumberland, the North York Moors, the Peak District, the Pembrokeshire Coast, Snowdonia and the Yorkshire Dales. A new park, the South Downs in southern England, is in the process of being created.

Combined, Britain's national parks now cover over 10% of the country. It's an impressive total, but the term 'national park' can cause confusion. First, these areas are not state owned: nearly all land is private, belonging to farmers, companies, estates and conservation organisations. Second, they are not total wilderness areas, as in many other countries. In Britain's national parks you will often find roads, railways, villages and even towns.

However, national parks still contain vast tracts of wild mountains and moorland, rolling downs and river valleys, and other areas of quiet countryside, all ideal for long walks, cycle rides, easy rambles, sightseeing or just lounging around. To help you get the best from the parks, they all have information centres and facilities (trails, car parks, camp sites etc) for visitors. For more details see www.nationalparks.gov.uk.

Some of the best national parks are the Lake District (p228), the Cairngorms (p338), Snowdonia (p271), the Yorkshire Dales (p224) and the Peak District (p174). There are also many beautiful spots that are *not* national parks (such as Mid Wales, the North Pennines in England, and many parts of Scotland).

NATIONAL PSYCHE

JULIET COOMBE

Flower seller, London

Calmness in the face of adversity, a laconic sense of humour, a sense of decency and fair play, and mastery of understatement are all fundamental facets of the British character – at least, as seen by the British themselves.

But the idea of 'British Identity' is a relatively recent creation, largely stemming from the empire-building of the 19th century and the two world wars of the 20th. This idealised British character – the plucky, stiff-upper-lipped, source-of-the-Nile-discovering, Everest-conquering, all-round hero and decent chap (or chapess) – is celebrated in countless films released in the decade or two following WWII.

You might think that much of this mythical Britishness is a thing of the past, but a lot lives on. *The British Character* by 'Pont' (one of *Punch* magazine's finest cartoonists) was first published in the late 1930s, but pretty much all the idiosyncrasies that are gently mocked in this collection of cartoons are still recognisable today, including the importance of forming an orderly queue, an unflinching belief in the miraculous cure-all properties of a nice cup of tea, and a love of animals that borders on the clinically insane.

But today, as the prime minister is promoting the idea of 'citizenship ceremonies' and 'celebrations of Britishness', British identity seems to be disintegrating. Scotland and Wales have always had a strong sense of themselves, nurturing their differences in the face of centuries of English cultural dominance. Since the creation of separate parliaments in Edinburgh and Cardiff in the late 1990s, this process has accelerated, forcing the English to rediscover their own national identity. Today, there is more celebration of individual Scots, English and Welsh identity than there is of a British one – even the Team GB brand used in the 2008 Olympics caused a controversy because it left out Northern Ireland.

⬊ SPORT

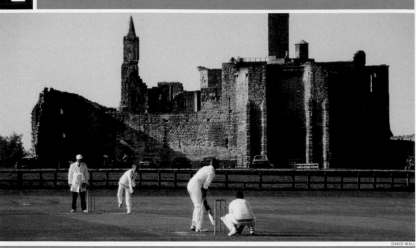

DAVID WALL

Playing cricket, England

If you want a short cut into the heart of British culture, watch the British at play. They're fierce and passionate about their sport, whether participating or watching. The mood of the nation is more closely aligned to the success of its international teams in major competition than to budget announcements from the chancellor of the exchequer, or even the weather.

The British invented – or at least laid down the modern rules for – many of the world's most popular spectator sports, including cricket, tennis, golf, rugby and football. Trouble is, the national teams aren't always so good at playing them (as the newspapers continually remind us), although recent years have seen some notable success stories. But a mixed result doesn't dull the fans' enthusiasm. Every weekend, thousands of people turn out to cheer their favourite team, and sporting highlights such as Wimbledon or the Derby keep the entire nation enthralled, while the biggest sporting event of all – the Olympic Games – is coming to London in 2012.

FOOTBALL (SOCCER)

Despite what the fans may say in Madrid or São Paulo, the English football league has some of the finest teams and players in the world. It's the richest too, with multimillion-pound sponsorship deals regularly clinched by powerful agents.

At the top of the tree is the **Premier League** (www.premierleague.com) for the country's top 20 clubs, although the hegemony enjoyed by superclubs Arsenal, Liverpool and globally renowned (and part US-owned) Manchester United has been challenged in recent years by former underdogs Chelsea, thanks to the seemingly bottomless budget of Russian owner Roman Abramovich.

Down from the premiership, 72 other teams play in the three divisions called the Championship, League One and League Two. The Scottish Premier League is dominated by Glasgow Rangers and Glasgow Celtic.

The football season lasts from August to May, so seeing a match can easily be included in most visitors' itineraries – but tickets for the big games in the upper division are like gold dust, and cost £20 to £50 even if you're lucky enough to find one.

RUGBY

A popular witticism holds that football is a gentlemen's game played by hooligans, while rugby is the other way around. True or not, rugby is very popular, especially since England became world champions in 2004; it's worth catching a game for the display of skill (OK, and brawn), and the fun atmosphere on the terraces. Tickets cost around £15 to £40 depending on the club's status and fortunes.

There are two variants of the game: **rugby union** (www.rfu.com) is played in southern England, Wales and Scotland, while **rugby league** (www.therfl.co.uk) is the main sport in northern England, although there is a lot of crossover. Many rules and tactics of both codes are similar. In league there are 13 players in each team (ostensibly making the game faster), while rugby union sides have 15 players each.

The main season for club matches is roughly September to Easter, while the international rugby union calendar is dominated by the annual Six Nations Championship (England, Scotland, Wales, Ireland, France and Italy) between January and April. It's usual for the Scots to support Wales, or vice versa, when either team is playing the 'old enemy' England.

CRICKET

Cricket has its origins in southeast England, with the earliest written record dating to 1598. It became an international game during Britain's colonial era, when it was exported to the countries of the Commonwealth, particularly the Indian subcontinent, the West Indies and Australasia.

To outsiders (and many locals) the rules and terminology may appear ridiculously arcane and confusing, but if you're patient and learn the intricacies, you could find cricket as enriching and enticing as the many thousands of Brits (especially the English) who remain glued to their radio or TV all summer.

⬟THE BEST

ADINA TOVY AMSEL

Old Trafford (p213)

SPORTING INSTITUTIONS

- **Lord's Cricket Ground** (p83)
- **Old Trafford** (p213)
- **Wimbledon** (p87)
- **Millennium Stadium** (p258)

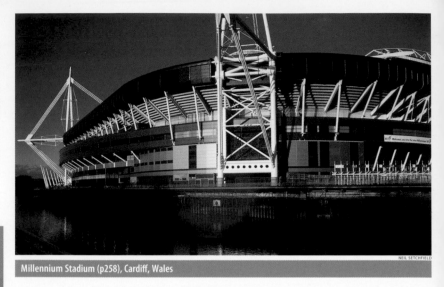

NEIL SETCHFIELD

Millennium Stadium (p258), Cardiff, Wales

County cricket (www.ecb.co.uk) is the mainstay of the domestic game, while international one-day games and five-day test matches are played against sides such as Australia and the West Indies at landmark grounds like Lords in London, Edgbaston in Birmingham and Headingley in Leeds. Test match tickets cost £25 to £100 and tend to sell fast. County championships usually charge £10 to £15, and rarely sell out. Watching a local game on the village green is free of charge.

Twenty20 cricket is a short form of the game, introduced in Britain in 2003. Matches last only 2½ hours, encouraging batsmen to go all out for big scores. Purists look down on it as an inferior sport, but it makes a good introduction for anyone who lacks the inclination to sit through five days of test-match stalemate.

TENNIS

Tennis is widely played at club and regional levels, but the best-known tournament is the All England Lawn Tennis Championships at **Wimbledon** (www.wimbledon.org), when tennis fever sweeps through the country for the last week of June and the first week of July. In between matches, the crowds traditionally feast on strawberries and cream; that's 28 tonnes of strawberries and 7000L of cream annually, to be precise.

Current British tennis darlings are Andy Murray (ranked number three in the world at time of research) and 14-year-old Laura Robson (who won the girls' junior championship in 2008). Demand for seats at Wimbledon always outstrips supply, but to give everyone an equal chance the tickets are sold through a public ballot. You can also take your chance on the spot: about 6000 tickets are sold each day (but not the last four days) and queuing at dawn should get you into the ground.

➘ DIRECTORY & TRANSPORT

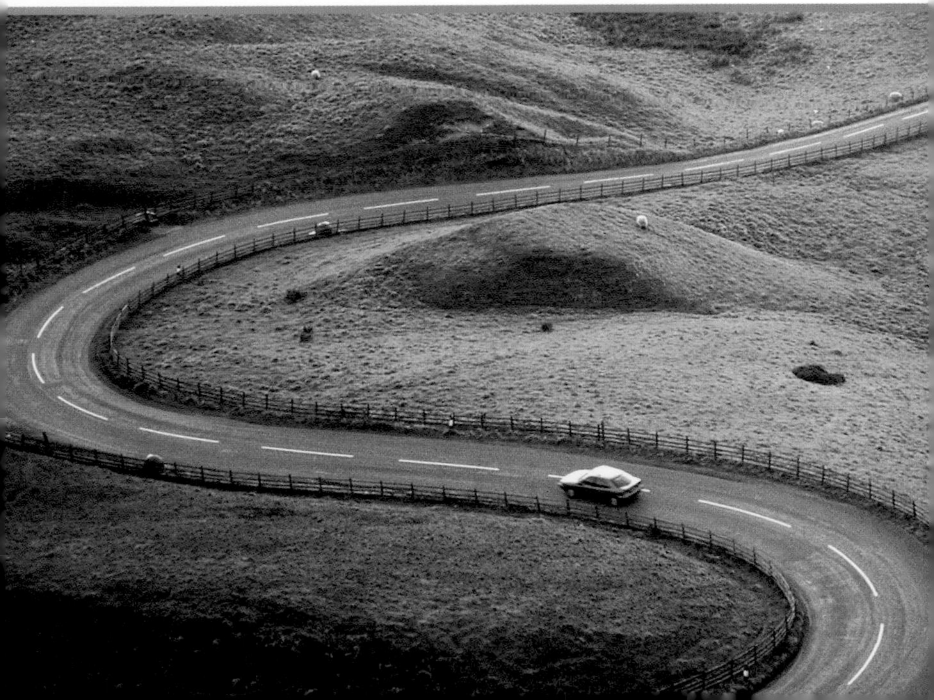

DIRECTORY

Country-wide practical information is given in this Directory. For details on specific areas, flip to the relevant regional chapter.

ACCOMMODATION

Accommodation in Britain is as varied as the sights you visit. From hip hotels to basic barns, the wide choice is all part of the attraction.

As in other countries, hotels and B&Bs (and even hostels) in Britain are awarded stars by the national tourist board and main motoring organisations, according to their levels of quality and service.

For a country-wide view, an excellent first stop is **Stilwell's** (www.stilwell.co.uk), a huge user-friendly database, listing holiday cottages, B&Bs, hotels, camp sites and hostels. Good agencies include **Bed & Breakfast Nationwide** (☎ 01255-831235; www.bedandbreakfastnationwide.com) and **Hoseasons** (☎ 01502-502588; www.hoseasons.co.uk), the latter covering cottages and holiday parks.

B&BS & GUESTHOUSES

The B&B (bed and breakfast) is a great British institution. Basically, you get a

room in somebody's house, and at smaller places you'll really feel part of the family. Larger B&Bs may have around 10 rooms and more facilities.

B&B prices are usually quoted per person, based on two people sharing a room. Solo travellers have to search for single rooms and pay a 20% to 50% premium.

Here are some more B&B tips:

- Advance reservations are always preferred at B&Bs, and essential during popular periods. Many require a minimum two nights at weekends.
- In country areas, most B&Bs cater for walkers and cyclists, but some don't, so let them know if you'll be turning up with dirty boots or wheels.
- Some places reduce rates for longer stays (three nights plus).
- Most B&Bs serve enormous breakfasts; some also offer packed lunches (around £5) and evening meals (from around £10 to £15).
- When booking, check your B&B's actual position. In country areas, addresses include the nearest town, which may be 20 miles away – important if you're walking!

CAMPING

The opportunities for camping in Britain are numerous – ideal if you're on a tight budget or simply enjoy the great outdoors. In rural areas, camp sites range from farmers' fields with a tap and a basic toilet, costing as little as £3 per person per night, to smarter affairs with hot showers and many other facilities charging up to £10.

If you're planning more than a few nights in a tent, or touring Britain with a campervan (motor home), it's worth joining the well-organised **Camping & Caravanning Club** (☎ 0845 130 7632;

↘ BOOK YOUR STAY ONLINE

For more accommodation reviews and recommendations by Lonely Planet authors, check out the online booking service at www.lonelyplanet.com. You'll find the true, insider lowdown on the best places to stay. Reviews are thorough and independent. Best of all, you can book online.

PRACTICALITIES

- Be ready for a bizarre mix of metric and imperial measures in Britain; for example, petrol is sold by the litre, but road-sign distances are given in miles.
- Use plugs with three flat pins to connect appliances to the 220V (50Hz AC) power supply.
- Follow current events in the *Sun, Mirror* or *Record* tabloids, or get more incisive views in the (right to left, politically) *Telegraph, Times, Independent* or *Guardian* quality papers.
- Turn on the TV and watch some of the finest programs in the world from multichannel BBC, closely followed by boundary-pushing Channel 4.
- Tune into BBC radio for a wide range of shows, and no adverts. Half the households in Britain have digital radio and TV, but for those still on analogue, main stations and wavelengths are Radio 1 (98-99.6MHz FM); Radio 2 (88-92MHz FM); Radio 3 (90-92.2MHz FM); Radio 4 (92-94.4MHz FM); and Radio 5Live (909 or 693 AM).
- National commercial stations include Virgin Radio (1215kHz MW) and non-highbrow classical-specialist Classic FM (100-102MHz FM). Both are also on digital, with at least 40 other stations.

www.campingandcaravanningclub.co.uk), which owns almost 100 camp sites and lists thousands more in the invaluable *Big Sites Book* (free to members). Annual membership costs £35 and includes discounted rates on club sites and various other services – including insurance and ferries.

HOSTELS

Britain has two types of hostel: those run by the **Youth Hostels Association** (**YHA;** ☎ 01629-592 700; www.yha.org.uk) or **Scottish Youth Hostels Association** (**SYHA;** ☎ 0870 155 3255; www.syha.org.uk); and independent hostels.

You'll find hostels in rural areas, towns and cities. They're aimed at all types of traveller – whether you're a long-distance walker or touring by car – and you don't have to be young or single to use them. The YHA also handles bookings for many bunkhouses and camping barns around the country.

HOTELS

A hotel in Britain might be a small and simple place, perhaps a former farmhouse now stylishly converted, where peace and quiet – along with luxury – are guaranteed. Or it might be a huge country house with fancy facilities, grand staircases, acres of grounds and the requisite row of stag-heads on the wall. With such a great choice your only problem will be deciding where to stay.

How much is a hotel in Britain? It depends. At the bargain end, you can find singles/doubles costing £30/40. Move up the scale and you can easily pay up to £100/150 or beyond.

PUBS & INNS

As well as selling drinks, many pubs and inns offer lodging, particularly in country areas. Staying in a pub can be good fun – you're automatically at the centre of the community – although accommodation varies enormously, from stylish suites to

↘ CLIMATE CHANGE & TRAVEL

Travel – especially air travel – is a significant contributor to global climate change. At Lonely Planet, we believe that all who travel have a responsibility to limit their personal impact. As a result, we have teamed with Rough Guides and other concerned industry partners to support Climate Care, which allows people to offset the greenhouse gases they are responsible for with contributions to energy-saving projects and other climate-friendly initiatives in the developing world. Lonely Planet offsets all staff and author travel.

For more information, turn to the responsible travel pages on www.lonely planet.com. For details on offsetting your carbon emissions and a carbon calculator, go to www.climatecare.org.

threadbare rooms. You'll pay around £20 per person at the cheap end, and £30 to £35 for something better.

RENTAL ACCOMMODATION

If you want to slow down and get to know a place better, renting for a week or two can be ideal. Cottages for four people cost from around £200 to £300 per week in high season. Rates fall at quieter times, and you may be able to rent for a long weekend.

BUSINESS HOURS

BANKS, SHOPS & POST OFFICES

Monday to Friday, most shops and post offices operate 9am to 5pm (or 6pm in cities). Most banks open 9.30am to 4pm or 5pm. On Saturdays, shops open 9am to 5pm, banks (main branches only) 9.30am to 1pm, and post offices may open all or half-day. Sunday shopping hours are around 10am to 4pm or 11am to 5pm, but banks and post offices are closed.

MUSEUMS & SIGHTS

Large museums and places of interest are usually open every day. Some smaller places open just five or six days per week, usually including Saturday and Sunday, but may be closed on Monday and/or

Tuesday. Much depends on the time of year too; they'll open daily in high season, but just at weekends (or shorter hours) in quieter periods.

PUBS, BARS & CLUBS

Pubs in towns and country areas in England and Wales usually open daily from 11am to 11pm Sunday to Thursday, sometimes to midnight or 1am Friday and Saturday. Most open all day, although some may shut from 3pm to 6pm. In Scotland, pubs tend to close later; 1am is normal, and 3am is not unusual. Throughout this book, we don't list pub opening and closing times unless they vary significantly from these hours.

In cities, some pubs open until midnight or later, but it's mostly bars and clubs that have taken advantage of relatively recent licensing laws ('the provision of late-night refreshment', as it's officially called) in England and Wales to stay open to 2am or beyond.

RESTAURANTS & CAFES

Restaurants in Britain open for lunch (about noon to 3pm) *and* dinner (about 6pm to 11pm – earlier in smaller towns; midnight or later in cities), or for lunch *or* dinner – usually every day of the week, although some close Sunday evenings or all day Monday.

In towns and cities, cafes may open from 7am, providing breakfast for people on their way to work. In country areas, teashops will open in time for lunch, and may stay open until 7pm or later in the summer, catering to tourists leaving stately homes or hikers down from the hills. In winter months, country cafe and restaurant hours are cut back, while some places close completely from October to Easter.

CLIMATE CHARTS

These charts give details for specific regions.

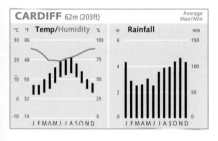

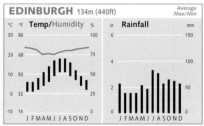

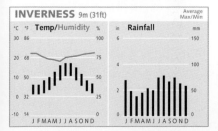

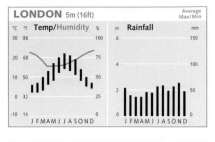

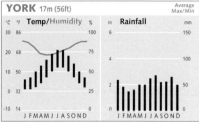

DIRECTORY

CLIMATE CHARTS

CUSTOMS

Britain has a two-tier customs system – one for goods bought in another European Union (EU) country where taxes and duties have already been paid, and the other for goods bought duty-free outside the EU. For more details go to www.hmce.gov .uk and search on Customs Allowances.

DUTY FREE

If you bring duty-free goods from *outside* the EU, the limits include 200 cigarettes, 2L of still wine, plus 1L of spirits or another 2L of wine, 60cc of perfume, and other duty-free goods (including beer) to the value of £145.

TAX & DUTY PAID

There is no limit to the goods you can bring from *within* the EU (if taxes have been paid), but customs officials use the following guidelines to distinguish personal use from commercial imports: 3200 cigarettes, 200 cigars, 10L of spirits, 20L of fortified wine, 90L of wine and 110L of beer – still enough to have one hell of a party.

DANGERS & ANNOYANCES

Britain is a remarkably safe country, but crime is certainly not unknown in London and other cities, so you should take care – especially at night. When travelling by tube, tram or urban train service, choose a carriage containing other people. It's also best to avoid some deserted suburban tube stations at night; a bus or taxi can be a safer choice.

As well as licensed taxis and minicabs (see p399), unlicensed minicabs – essentially a bloke with a car earning money on the side – operate in large cities, but these are worth avoiding unless you know what you're doing.

On the main streets of big cities, mugging or bag-snatching is rare, but money and important documents are best kept out of sight and out of reach. Pickpockets operate in crowded public places such as stations or bars (bags and jackets hanging on chair-backs are popular targets), so make sure your stuff is secure here as well.

In large hotels, don't leave valuables lying around; put them in your bag or use the safe if there is one. In hostel dorms, especially independent/backpacker hostels in cities, keep your stuff packed away and carry valuables with you.

If driving, remove luggage from the car when parking overnight in cities and towns. The same applies even in some apparently safe rural locations. While you're out walking in the countryside, someone may well be walking off with your belongings.

DISCOUNT CARDS

There's no specific discount card for visitors to Britain, although travel cards are discounted for younger and older people. Membership of the YHA/SHYA (see p383)

can get you discounts in bookshops and outdoor-gear shops, and on some public transport.

EMBASSIES & CONSULATES

For a complete list of foreign embassies in the UK, see the website of the **Foreign & Commonwealth Office** (www.fco.gov.uk), which also lists Britain's diplomatic missions overseas. Your embassy, consulate and high commission will be useful if, for example, you've lost your passport, but they won't be much help if you're in trouble for committing a crime; remember, even as a foreigner, you're bound by British laws.

Australia (Map pp66-7; ☎ 020-7379 4334; www.australia.org.uk; Strand, WC2B 4LA)

Canada (Map p80; ☎ 020-7258 6600; www.canada.org.uk; 1 Grosvenor Sq, W1X 0AB)

China (Map p84; ☎ 020-7299 4049; www.chinese-embassy.org.uk; 49-51 Portland Pl, London W1B 4JL)

France (Map p80; ☎ 020-7073 1000; www.ambafrance-uk.org; 58 Knightsbridge, SW1 7JT)

Germany (Map p80; ☎ 020-7824 1300; www.london.diplo.de; 23 Belgrave Sq, SW1X 8PX)

Ireland (Map p80; ☎ 020-7235 2171; www.embassyofireland.co.uk; 17 Grosvenor Pl, SW1X 7HR)

Japan (Map pp66-7; ☎ 020-7465 6500; www.uk.emb-japan.go.jp; 101 Piccadilly, W1J 7JT)

Netherlands (Map p80; ☎ 020-7590 3200; www.netherlands-embassy.org.uk; 38 Hyde Park Gate, SW7 5DP)

New Zealand (Map pp66-7; ☎ 020-7930 8422; www.nzembassy.com/uk; 80 Haymarket, SW1Y 4TQ)

USA (Map p80; ☎ 020-7499 9000; www.usembassy.org.uk; 24 Grosvenor Sq, W1A 1AE)

FOOD

Throughout this book, Eating reviews are divided into three price bands: budget (up to £8), midrange (£8 to £16) and top end (over £16).

GAY & LESBIAN TRAVELLERS

Britain is a generally tolerant place for gays and lesbians. London, Manchester and Brighton have flourishing gay scenes, and in other sizable cities (even some small towns) you'll find communities not entirely in the closet. That said, you'll still find pockets of homophobic hostility in some areas too.

For info, listings and contacts, see monthly magazines (and websites) **Gay Times** (www.gaytimes.co.uk) and **Diva** (www.divamag.co.uk), or the twice-monthly **Pink Paper** (www.pinkpaper.com). In the capital, a useful source of information is the **London Lesbian & Gay Switchboard** (☎ 020-7837 7324; www.llgs.org.uk); there are similar services in cities and regions across the country.

HEALTH

Britain is a healthy place to travel, and the excellent National Health Service (NHS) is free on the point of delivery, which – although Brits may complain – is better than most other countries offer. Across the country, hygiene standards are high (despite what your nose tells you on a crowded tube train) and there are no unusual diseases to worry about. Your biggest risks will be from overdoing activities – physical, chemical or other.

BEFORE YOU GO

No immunisations are mandatory for visiting Britain. Travel insurance, however, is highly recommended for the reasons outlined under Insurance (p389).

You should also check reciprocal medical arrangements between the UK and your own country. Everyone gets emergency treatment (see In Britain, p388) and European Economic Area (EEA) nationals get free non-emergency treatment (ie the same service British citizens receive) with a European Health Insurance Card (EHIC) validated in their home country. Reciprocal arrangements between the UK and some other countries (including Australia) allow free medical treatment at hospitals and surgeries, and subsidised dental care. For details see the **Department of Health** (www.doh.gov.uk) website – follow links to Health Care, Entitlements and Overseas Visitors.

INTERNET RESOURCES

Useful sites include the following:
Age Concern (www.ageconcern.org.uk) Advice on travel (and much more) for the elderly.
Center for Disease Control and Prevention (www.cdc.gov)
Foreign & Commonwealth Office (www.fco.gov.uk) The Travelling & Living Overseas section is for Brits going abroad, but useful for incomers.
Marie Stopes International (www.mariestopes.org.uk) Sexual health and contraception.
MD Travel Health (www.mdtravelhealth.com) Worldwide recommendations, updated daily.
World Health Organization (www.who.int) Go to the International Travel and Health section.

IN TRANSIT

DEEP VEIN THROMBOSIS (DVT)

Deep Vein Thrombosis (DVT) refers to blood clots that form in the legs during plane flights, chiefly because of prolonged immobility. The longer the flight, the greater the risk. The chief symptom is swelling or pain in the foot, ankle or calf. When a blood clot travels to the lungs, it may cause chest pain and breathing difficulties. To prevent DVT on long flights you should walk about the cabin, contract and release leg muscles while sitting, drink plenty of fluids and avoid alcohol.

JET LAG
To avoid jet lag (common when crossing more than five time zones), try drinking plenty of nonalcoholic fluids and eating light meals. Upon arrival, get exposure to natural sunlight and readjust to a local schedule (for meals, sleep etc) as soon as possible.

IN BRITAIN
AVAILABILITY & COST OF HEALTH CARE
Regardless of nationality, everyone receives free emergency treatment at accident and emergency (A&E) departments of state-run NHS hospitals.

If you don't need full-on hospital treatment, chemists (pharmacies) can advise on minor ailments such as sore throats and earaches. In large cities, there's always at least one 24/7 chemist.

ENVIRONMENTAL HAZARDS
SUNBURN
In summer in Britain, you can get sunburnt quickly – even under cloud cover and especially on water. Use sunscreen, wear a hat and cover up with a shirt and trousers.

WATER
The tap (faucet) water in Britain is safe to drink unless there is a sign that states to the contrary (eg on trains). Don't drink from streams in the countryside – you never know if there's a dead sheep upstream.

WOMEN'S HEALTH
Emotional stress, exhaustion and travel through time zones can upset the menstrual pattern. If using oral contraceptives, remember that some antibiotics, diarrhoea and vomiting can stop them from working.

If you're already pregnant, travel is usually possible, but you should consult your doctor. The most risky times are the first 12 weeks of pregnancy and after 30 weeks.

HERITAGE ORGANISATIONS
For many visitors, a highlight of a journey through Britain is visiting the numerous castles and other historic sites that pepper the country. Membership of Britain's heritage organisations gives you free entry to properties as well as reciprocal arrangements with similar bodies, maps, information handbooks and so on.

The main organisations are: National Trust (NT), and its partner organisation National Trust for Scotland (NTS); English Heritage (EH) and its equivalent organisations Historic Scotland (HS) and Cadw. You can join at the first site you visit, or online in advance. If you are a member of a similar organisation in your own country, this may get you free or discounted entry at sites in Britain.

Cadw (☎ 01443-336000, 0800 0743121; www.cadw.wales.gov.uk) The Welsh historic monuments agency. (The name means 'to keep'.) Membership costs £35.

English Heritage (☎ 0870 333 1181; www.english-heritage.org.uk) A state-funded organisation responsible for numerous historic sites. Membership costs £42 and an Overseas Visitors Pass allows free entry to most sites for seven/14 days for £19/23.

Historic Scotland (☎ 0131-668 8600; www.historic-scotland.gov.uk) Manages more than 330 historic sites. Membership costs £38, and 'Explorer' passes cost £20 for three days in five, £28 for seven days in 14, or £34 for 10 days in 30.

National Trust (☎ 0844 800 1895; www.nationaltrust.org.uk) Protects hundreds of historic buildings plus vast tracts of land with scenic importance in England and Wales. Membership costs £46 and a Touring Pass for one/two weeks is £19/24.

National Trust for Scotland (☎ 0844 493 2100; www.nts.org.uk) The NT's sister organisation north of the border, caring for over 100 properties and almost 80,000 hectares of countryside. Membership costs £44.

HOLIDAYS
PUBLIC HOLIDAYS
New Year's Day 1 January
Easter (Good Friday to Easter Monday inclusive) March/April
May Day First Monday in May
Spring Bank Holiday Last Monday in May
Summer Bank Holiday Last Monday In August
Christmas Day 25 December
Boxing Day 26 December

If a public holiday falls on a weekend, the nearest Monday is usually taken instead. In England and Wales, most businesses and banks close on official public holidays (hence the quaint term 'bank holiday'). In Scotland, bank holidays are just for the banks, and many businesses stay open. Instead, Scottish towns normally have a spring and autumn holiday, but the dates vary from town to town.

On public holidays, some small museums and places of interest close, but larger attractions specifically gear up and have their busiest times, although nearly everything closes on Christmas Day. Generally speaking, if a place closes on Sunday, it'll probably be shut on bank holidays as well.

As well as attractions, virtually everything – shops, banks, offices – closes on Christmas Day, although pubs are open at lunchtime. There's usually no public transport on Christmas Day, and a very restricted service on Boxing Day.

SCHOOL HOLIDAYS
Most schools have three main terms, interspersed with three main holidays (when roads get busy and hotel prices go up), although the exact dates vary from year to year and region to region:
Easter Holiday Week before and week after Easter.
Summer Holiday Third week of July to first week of September.
Christmas Holiday Mid-December to first week of January.

There are also three weeklong 'half-term' school holidays – usually late February (or early March), late May and late October. Some regions are moving towards six terms (and six holidays) of more equal length.

INSURANCE
Regardless of nationality, everyone receives free *emergency* medical treatment at state-run National Health Service (NHS) hospitals – if they've got an accident and emergency (A&E) department. For other medical treatment, many countries have reciprocal health agreements with the UK, meaning visitors from overseas get the same standard of care from hospitals and doctors as any British citizen. But travel insurance is still highly recommended because it offers greater flexibility over where and how you're treated.

INTERNET ACCESS

Internet cafes are surprisingly rare in Britain, especially once you get away from tourist spots. Most charge from £1 per hour, and out in the sticks you can pay up to £5 per hour. Public libraries often have computers with free internet access, but only for 30-minute slots, and demand is high.

Sockets are thankfully becoming a thing of the past though as an increasing number of hotels, hostels, stations and coffee shops (even some trains) have wi-fi access, charging anything from nothing to £5 per hour. Throughout this book, we use an 'internet' icon to show if a place has PCs for public use, and the word 'wi-fi' if it has…you guessed it…wi-fi.

LEGAL MATTERS
AGE RESTRICTIONS

The age of consent in Britain is 16 (gay and straight). You can also get married at 16 (with permission from parents), but you'll have to wait two years for the toast – you must be over 18 to buy alcohol. Over-16s may buy cigarettes, so you can have a celebratory smoke instead.

You usually have to be 18 to enter a pub or bar, although the rules are different if you have a meal. Some bars and clubs are over-21 only, so you won't see many highchairs.

DRIVING CRIMES & TRANSPORT FINES

Drink-driving is a serious offence. For more information about speed limits and parking rules, see p398.

On buses and trains (including the London Underground), people without a valid ticket for their journey may be fined – usually around £20 – on the spot.

DRUGS

Illegal drugs are widely available, especially in clubs. All the usual dangers apply and there have been much-publicised deaths associated with ecstasy. Cannabis possession is a criminal offence, but the punishment for carrying a small amount is usually a warning. Dealers face far stiffer penalties, as do people caught with any other 'recreational' drugs.

MAPS

For a map of the whole country, a road atlas is handy – especially if you're travelling by car. The main publishers are Ordnance Survey (OS) and Automobile Association (AA), with atlases in all sizes and scales. If you plan to use minor roads, you'll need a scale of about 1:200,000 (3 miles to 1in).

If you're spending any length of time in London, the iconic **A-Z maps** (www.a-zmaps .co.uk) are incredibly detailed – online and in book form. The books are sold at newsagents and souvenir shops, but remember to pronounce it 'A to Zed'. Similar street maps are available for other cities and big towns across the country.

MONEY

The currency of Britain is the pound, officially called the 'pound sterling'. Paper money comes in £5, £10, £20 and £50 denominations (and £1 in Scotland), although £50s can be difficult to change because fakes circulate.

In England and Wales, notes are issued by the Bank of England, and in Scotland by Clydesdale Bank, Bank of Scotland and Royal Bank of Scotland. All notes are legal tender on both sides of the border, but you might have trouble using Scottish notes in England, especially southern and central England, so try to spend all your Scottish notes before you leave Scotland, or just head to a bank and swap them one-for-one at no charge.

ATMS

Debit or credit cards are perfect companions – the best invention for travellers since the backpack. You can use them in most shops, and withdraw cash from ATMs (often called 'cash machines'), which are easy to find in cities and even small towns. But ATMs aren't fail-safe, and it's a major headache if your only card gets swallowed, so take a back-up. And watch out for ATMs that might have been tampered with; a common ruse is to attach a card-reader to the slot; your card is scanned and the number used for fraud.

CREDIT & DEBIT CARDS

Visa and MasterCard credit and debit cards are widely accepted in Britain, and are good for larger hotels, restaurants, shopping, flights, long-distance travel, car hire etc.

Since 2006, nearly all credit and debit cards use the 'chip and pin' system; instead of signing, you enter a PIN (personal identification number). If you're from overseas and your card isn't chip-and-pin enabled, you should be able to sign in the usual way – but some places will not accept your card.

MONEYCHANGERS

Finding a place to change your money (cash or travellers cheques) into pounds is never a problem in cities, where banks and bureaus compete for business. Be careful using bureaus, however; some offer poor rates or levy outrageous commissions. You can also change money at some post offices – very handy in country areas, and exchange rates are fair (and usually commission free).

TIPPING & BARGAINING

In restaurants you're expected to leave around a 10% tip, but at smarter restaurants in larger cities waiters can get a bit sniffy if the tip isn't nearer 12% or even 15%. At smarter cafes and teashops with table service around 10% is fine. In pubs, when you order drinks at the bar, or order and pay for food at the bar, tips are not expected.

Taxi drivers also expect tips (about 10%, or rounded up to the nearest pound), especially in London.

Bargaining is rare, although it's occasionally encountered at markets.

TRAVELLERS CHEQUES

Travellers cheques (TCs) offer protection from theft, so are safer than wads of cash, but are rarely used in Britain, as credit/debit cards and ATMs have become the method of choice. If you prefer TCs, note that they are rarely accepted for purchases (except at large hotels), so for cash you'll still need to go to a bank or bureau.

POST

There are two classes of post within Britain: a standard letter costs 36p 1st-class (normally delivered next day) and 27p 2nd-class (up to three days). The cost goes up if the letter is heaver than 100g or larger than 240x165mm or thicker than 5mm, and up again if heavier than 750g and bigger than 353x250x25mm. Letters by airmail cost 50p to EU countries and 56p to the rest of the world (up to 10g). For details on all prices, see www.post office.co.uk.

TELEPHONE

Britain's iconic red phone boxes can still be seen in city streets and especially in conservation areas, although many have been replaced by soulless glass cubicles.

Either way, public phones accept coins, and usually credit/debit cards. The minimum charge is 20p or 40p.

Area codes in Britain don't have a standard format and vary in length, which can be confusing for foreigners (and locals). For example ☎ 020 for London, ☎ 029 for Cardiff, ☎ 0131 for Edinburgh, ☎ 0161 for Manchester, ☎ 0113 for Leeds, ☎ 01225 for Bath, ☎ 015394 for Ambleside, followed as usual by the individual number. For clarity, area codes and individual numbers are separated by a hyphen.

As well as the geographical area codes, other 'codes' include ☎ 0500 or ☎ 0800 for free calls and ☎ 0845 for calls at local rates, wherever you're dialling from within the UK. Numbers starting with ☎ 087 are charged at national-call rates, while numbers starting with ☎ 089 or ☎ 09 are premium rate, and should be specified by the company using the number (ie in their advertising literature), so you know the cost before you call.

Note that many numbers starting with 08 or 09 do not work if you're calling from outside the UK, or if they do you'll be charged for a full international call – and then some.

Codes for mobile phones usually start with ☎ 07. Calling a mobile phone is more expensive than calling a landline.

INTERNATIONAL CALLS

To call outside the UK dial ☎ 00, then the country code (☎ 1 for USA, ☎ 61 for Australia, etc), the area code (you usually drop the initial zero) and the number. For country codes, see the inside front cover of this book.

Direct-dialled calls to most overseas countries can be made from most public telephones, and it's usually cheaper between 8pm and 8am Monday to Friday and at weekends. You can usually save money by buying a phonecard (usually denominated £5, £10 or £20) with a PIN that you use from any phone by dialling an access number (you don't insert it into the machine). There are dozens of cards, usually available from city newsagents, with rates of the various companies often vividly displayed.

To make reverse-charge (collect) calls, dial ☎ 155 for the international operator. It's expensive, but what the hell – the person at the other end is paying.

To call Britain from abroad, dial your country's international access code, then ☎ 44 (the UK's country code), then the area code (dropping the first 0) and the phone number.

Most internet cafes now have Skype or some other sort of VOIP system, so you can make international calls for the price of your time online.

LOCAL & NATIONAL CALLS

From public phones the weekday rate is about 5p per minute; evenings and weekends are cheaper – though still with a minimum charge of 20p. Local calls (within 35 miles) are cheaper than national calls. All calls are cheaper between 6pm and 8am Monday to Thursday, and from 6pm Friday to 8am Monday. From private phones, rates vary between telecom providers.

For the operator, call ☎ 100. For directory inquiries, a host of agencies compete for your business and charge from 10p to 40p; numbers include ☎ 118 192, ☎ 118 118, ☎ 118 500 and ☎ 118 811.

MOBILE PHONES

Phones in the UK use GSM 900/1800, which is compatible with Europe and Australia but not with North America or Japan (although phones that work globally are increasingly common).

Even if your phone works in the UK, because it's registered overseas a call to someone just up the road will be routed internationally and charged accordingly. An option is to buy a local SIM card (around £30), which includes a UK number, and use that in your own handset (as long as your phone isn't locked by your home network).

A second option is to buy a pay-as-you-go phone (from around £50, including SIM and number); to stay in credit, you buy 'top-up' cards at newsagents.

TIME

Wherever you are in the world, time is measured in relation to Greenwich Mean Time (GMT, or Universal Time Coordinated, UTC as it's more accurately called). If it is noon in London, it is 4am on the same day in San Francisco, 7am in New York and 10pm in Sydney. British summer time (BST) is Britain's daylight saving; one hour ahead of GMT from late March to late October.

TOURIST INFORMATION

Before leaving home, check the informative, comprehensive and wide-ranging website **VisitBritain** (www.visitbritain.com) or the more specific sites www.enjoy england.com, www.visitscotland.com and www.visitwales.com. Between them, they cover all angles of national tourism, with links to numerous other sites.

LOCAL TOURIST OFFICES

All British cities and towns (and some villages) have a tourist information centre (TIC). Some TICs are run by national parks and often have small exhibits about the area. These places have helpful staff, books and maps for sale, leaflets to give away and loads of advice on things to see

or do. They can also assist with booking accommodation.

TRAVELLERS WITH DISABILITIES

If you happen to be in a wheelchair, use crutches or just find moving about a bit tricky, Britain is a mixed bag. All new buildings have wheelchair access, and even hotels in grand old country houses often have lifts, ramps and other facilities added, although smaller B&Bs are often harder to adapt, so you'll have less choice here. In the same way, you might find a restaurant with ramps and excellent wheelchair-access toilet, but tables so close you can't get past.

When getting around in cities, new buses have low floors for easy access, but few have conductors who can lend a hand when you're getting on or off. Many taxis take wheelchairs, or just have more room in the back, so that might be a better way to go.

For long-distance travel, coaches present problems if you can't walk, but National Express (the main operator) has wheelchair-friendly coaches on many routes, with plans for more, and a dedicated **Disabled Passenger Travel Helpline** (☎ 0121-423 8479). Or see www .nationalexpress.com/coach/ourservice/ disabled.cfm.

All Go Here (www.allgohere.com) Comprehensive info on hotels and travel.

Disability UK (www.disabilityuk.com) Excellent information resource; shopping, benefits, diseases, drugs and more.

Good Access Guide (www.goodaccess guide.co.uk) The name says it all.

Holiday Care Service (☎ 0845 124 9971; www.holidaycare.org.uk) Travel and holiday information; publisher of numerous booklets on UK travel.

Royal Association for Disability & Rehabilitation (RADAR; ☎ 020-7250 3222; www.radar.org.uk) Published titles include *Holidays in Britain and Ireland*. Through RADAR you can get a key for 7000 public disabled toilets across the UK.

Shopmobility (www.shopmobilityuk.org) Directory of cities and towns across Britain where manual or powered wheelchairs can be hired – often for free.

VISAS

If you're a European Economic Area (EEA) national, you don't need a visa to visit (or work in) Britain. Citizens of Australia, Canada, New Zealand, South Africa and the USA are given leave to enter at their point of arrival for up to six months (three months for some nationalities), but are prohibited from working.

Visa and entry regulations are always subject to change, so it's vital to check before leaving home. Your first stop should be www.ukvisas.gov.uk or www.ukba.homeoffice.gov.uk and if you still have queries contact your local British embassy, high commission or consulate.

WEIGHTS & MEASURES

Britain is in transition when it comes to weights and measures, as it has been for the last 30 years – and probably will be for 30 more. For length and distance, most people still use the 'imperial' units of inches, feet, yards and miles, although mountain heights on maps are given in metres.

For weight, many people use pounds and ounces, even though since January 2000 goods in shops must be measured in kilograms. And nobody knows their weight in pounds (like Americans) or kilograms (like the rest of the world); Brits weigh themselves in stones, an archaic unit of 14 pounds.

When it comes to volume, things are even worse: most liquids are sold in litres or half-litres, except milk and beer – available in pints. Garages sell petrol priced in pence per litre, but measure car performance in miles per gallon.

In this book we have reflected this wacky system of mixed measurements. Heights are given in metres (m) and longer distances in miles. For conversion tables, see the inside front cover.

TRANSPORT
GETTING THERE & AWAY

London is a global transport hub, so you can easily fly to Britain from just about anywhere in the world. Your other main option for travel between Britain and mainland Europe is ferry, either port-to-port or combined with a long-distance bus trip. International trains are much more comfortable, and another 'green' option; the Channel Tunnel allows direct rail services between Britain, France and Belgium, with onward connections to many other European destinations.

For information on climate change and travel, see the boxed text, p384.

AIR
AIRPORTS

London's main airports for international flights are Heathrow and Gatwick, while Luton and Stansted deal largely with charter and budget European flights.

GATWICK

The UK's No 2 airport, **Gatwick** (LGW; ☎ 0870 000 2468; www.gatwickairport.com), is 30 miles south of central London.

HEATHROW

Some 15 miles west of central London, **Heathrow** (LHR; ☎ 0870 000 0123; www

.heathrowairport.com) is the world's busiest international airport, so not surprisingly is often chaotic and crowded.

LONDON CITY
A few miles east of central London, **London City** (LCY; ☎ 020-7646 0088; www .londoncityairport.com) specialises in business flights to/from European and other UK airports.

LUTON
Some 35 miles north of central London, **Luton** (LTN; ☎ 01582-405100; www.london-luton .co.uk) is especially well known as a holiday-flight airport.

STANSTED
London's third-busiest airport, **Stansted** (STN; ☎ 0870 000 0303; www.stanstedairport .com) is 35 miles northeast of the capital, and one of Europe's fastest-growing airports.

REGIONAL AIRPORTS
If you're arriving in Britain from overseas, and plan to avoid London or spend more time in Scotland or northern England, it's worth looking for direct flights to major regional airports like Manchester, Glasgow and Edinburgh. Likewise, smaller regional airports such as Cardiff, Liverpool, Southampton and Birmingham are usefully served by flights to/from continental Europe and Ireland.

AIRLINES
Most mainstream airlines have services to Britain from many parts of the world, while budget airlines fly between Britain and other European countries. The best deals are usually available online, and to save going to every airline's site individually, it's worth using an internet travel agency or price comparison site; these include www.expedia.com, www.travel ocity.com, www.skyscanner.com, www .lowcostairlines.org, www.flightline.co.uk and www.cheapflights.co.uk.

LAND
BUS
You can easily get between Britain and other European countries via long-distance bus or coach. The international network **Eurolines** (www.eurolines.com) connects a huge number of destinations; the website is full of information on routes and options, and you can buy tickets online via one of the national operators. Services to/from Britain are operated by **National Express** (www.nationalexpress.com) and these are some sample journey times to/from London: Amsterdam 12 hours; Paris eight or nine hours; Dublin 12 hours; Barcelona 24 hours.

TRAIN
CHANNEL TUNNEL SERVICES
The Channel Tunnel makes direct train travel between Britain and continental Europe a fast and enjoyable option. High-speed **Eurostar** (☎ 08705 186 186; www.eurostar.com) passenger services hurtle at least 10 times daily between London and Paris (the journey takes 2½ hours) or Brussels (two hours). You can buy tickets from travel agencies, major train stations or direct from the Eurostar website. The normal single fare between London and Paris or Brussels is around £150, but if you buy in advance and travel at a less busy period, deals drop to around £90 return or less. You can also buy 'through fare' tickets from many cities in Britain – for example York to Paris, or Manchester to Brussels.

If you've got a car, use **Eurotunnel** (☎ 08705 353535; www.eurotunnel.com). At Folkestone in England or Calais in France, you drive onto a train, go through the tunnel, and drive off at the other end. The trains run about four times hourly from 6am to 10pm, then hourly. Loading and unloading is one hour; the journey takes 35 minutes.

SEA

Between Britain and mainland Europe, ferry routes include Dover to Calais or Boulogne (France), Harwich to Hook of Holland (Netherlands), Hull to Zeebrugge (Belgium) and Rotterdam (Netherlands), Portsmouth to Santander or Bilbao (Spain), and Newcastle to Bergen (Norway) or Gothenberg (Sweden).

Competition from Eurotunnel and budget airlines has forced ferry operators to discount heavily and offer flexible fares, meaning great bargains at quiet times of day or year. For example, the short cross-Channel routes such as Dover to Calais or Boulogne-sur-Mer can be as low as £20 for a car plus up to five passengers, although around £50 is more likely. If you're a foot passenger, or cycling, there's often less need to book ahead, and cheap fares on the short crossings start from about £10 each way. Some operators take only online bookings; others charge a supplement (up to £20) for booking by phone.

Brittany Ferries (www.brittany-ferries.com)
DFDS Seaways (☎ 0871 522 9955; www.dfds.co.uk)
Irish Ferries (☎ 08705 171717; www.irishferries.com)
Norfolkline (☎ 08701 450603; www.norfolkline.com)
P&O Ferries (☎ 08716 645 645; www.poferries.com)
Speedferries (☎ 0871 222 7456; www.speedferries.com)
Stena Line (☎ 08705 70 70 70; www.stenaline.com)
Transmanche (☎ 0800 917 1201; www.transmancheferries.com)

Another very handy option is www.ferrybooker.com, a single site covering all sea-ferry routes and operators, plus Eurotunnel.

GETTING AROUND

While having your own car helps make the best use of your time to reach remote places, rental and fuel costs can be expensive for budget travellers – and the trials of traffic jams and parking hit everyone – so public transport is often the better way to go.

Your main public transport options are train and long-distance bus (called coach in Britain). Services between major towns and cities are generally good, although at 'peak' (busy) times you must book in advance to be sure of getting a ticket. Conversely, if you book ahead early and/or travel at 'off-peak' periods, tickets can be very cheap.

Traveline (☎ 0871 200 2233; www.traveline.org.uk) is a very useful information service covering bus, coach, taxi and train services nationwide, with numerous links to help plan your journey. By phone, you get transferred automatically to an advisor in the region you're phoning from; for details on another part of the country, you need to key in a code number (☎ 81 for London, ☎ 874 for Cumbria, etc) – for a full list, go to the Traveline home page and click on 'call centre codes'.

AIR

Britain's domestic air companies include British Airways, BMI, bmibaby, easyJet and Ryanair. On some shorter routes (eg London to Newcastle, or Manchester to Newquay) trains can compare favourably with planes, once airport downtime is factored in.

TRANSPORT

GETTING AROUND

BUS & COACH

If you're on a tight budget, long-distance buses are nearly always the cheapest way to get around, although they're also the slowest. In Britain, long-distance express buses are called coaches, and in many towns there are separate bus and coach stations. Make sure you go to the right place!

National Express (☎ 08717 818181; www .nationalexpress.com) is the main operator, with a wide network and frequent services between main centres. North of the border, services tie in with those of **Scottish Citylink** (☎ 08705 505050; www.citylink.co.uk), Scotland's leading coach company.

Also offering fares from £1 is **Megabus** (www.megabus.com), operating a budget coach service between about 30 destinations around the country. Go at a quiet time, book early, and your ticket will be very cheap. Book last minute, for a busy time and…you get the picture.

BUS PASSES & DISCOUNTS

National Express offers discount passes to full-time students and under-26s, called Young Persons Coachcards. They cost £10, and get you 30% off standard adult fares. Also available are coachcards for people over 60, families and disabled travellers.

For touring Britain, National Express also offers Brit Xplorer passes, which allow unlimited travel for seven days (£79), 14 days (£139) and 28 days (£219). You don't need to book journeys in advance with this pass; if the coach has a spare seat – you can take it.

CAR & MOTORCYCLE

Travelling by private car or motorbike you can be independent and flexible, and reach remote places. Motorways and main A-roads are dual carriageways and deliver

HOW MUCH TO…?

When travelling long-distance by train or coach in Britain, it's important to note that there's no such thing as a standard fare. Just like with airlines, prices vary according to demand and when you buy your ticket. Book long in advance and travel on Tuesday mid-morning, and it's cheap. Buy on the spot on Friday late afternoon, and it'll be a lot more expensive. Ferries (eg to the Isle of Wight or Channel Islands) use similar systems. Throughout this book, to give you an idea, we have quoted *sample* fares somewhere in between the very cheapest and most expensive options. The price you pay will almost certainly be different.

you quickly from one end of the country to another. Lesser A-roads, B-roads and minor roads are much more scenic and fun, as you wind through the countryside from village to village – ideal for car or motorcycle touring.

HIRE

Compared to many countries (especially the USA), hire rates are expensive in Britain; you should expect to pay around £250 per week for a small car (unlimited mileage) but rates rise at busy times and drop at quiet times.

1car1 (☎ 0113-263 6675; www.1car1.com)

Avis (☎ 0844 581 0147; www.avis.co.uk)

Budget (☎ 0844 581 9998; www.budget .co.uk)

Europcar (☎ 0870 607 5000; www.europcar. co.uk)

Sixt (☎ 08701 567567; www.sixt.co.uk)

Thrifty (☎ 01494-751540; www.thrifty.co.uk)

Your other option is to use an internet search engine to find small local car-hire companies in Britain who can undercut the big boys. See under Getting Around in the main city sections for more details, or see a rental-broker site such as **UK Car Hire** (www.ukcarhire.net).

Another option is to hire a motor home or campervan. Sites to check include www.coolcampervans.com, www.wildhorizon.co.uk and www.justgo.uk.com.

MOTORING ORGANISATIONS

Large motoring organisations include the **Automobile Association** (www.theaa.com) and the **Royal Automobile Club** (www.rac.co.uk); annual membership starts at around £35, including 24-hour roadside breakdown assistance. A greener alternative is the **Environmental Transport Association** (www.eta.co.uk); it provides all the usual services (breakdown assistance, roadside rescue, vehicle inspections etc) but *doesn't* campaign for more roads.

PARKING

Britain is small, and people love their cars, so there's often not enough space to go round. 'Park & Ride' systems allow you to park on the edge of the city then ride to the centre on regular buses provided for an all-in-one price.

Yellow lines (single or double) along the edge of the road indicate restrictions. Find the nearby sign that spells out when you can and can't park. In London and other big cities, traffic wardens operate with efficiency; if you park on the yellow lines at the wrong time, your car will be clamped or towed away, and it'll cost you £100 or more to get driving again. In some cities there are also red lines, which mean no stopping at all. Ever.

ROAD RULES

A foreign driving licence is valid in Britain for up to 12 months. If you plan to bring a car from Europe, it's illegal to drive without (at least) third-party insurance. Some other important rules:

- drive on the left (!)
- wear fitted seat belts in cars
- wear crash helmets on motorcycles
- give way to your right at junctions and roundabouts
- always use the left-side lane on motorways and dual carriageways, unless overtaking (although so many people ignore this rule, you'd think it didn't exist)
- don't use a mobile phone while driving unless it's fully hands-free (another rule frequently flouted).

Speed limits are 30mph (48km/h) in built-up areas, 60mph (96km/h) on main roads and 70mph (112km/h) on motorways and most (but not all) dual carriageways. Drinking and driving is taken very seriously; you're allowed a blood-alcohol level of 80mg/100mL and campaigners want it reduced to 50mg/100mL.

All drivers should read the *Highway Code*. It's available at main newsagents and some tourist offices, and at www.direct.gov.uk/en/TravelAndTransport/Highwaycode.

LOCAL TRANSPORT
BUS

There are good local bus networks year-round in cities and towns. Buses also run in rural areas year-round, with more frequent services in tourist spots (especially national parks) from Easter to September. Elsewhere in the countryside, bus timetables are designed to serve schools and industry, so there can be few midday and

TRANSPORT

GETTING AROUND

weekend services (and they may stop running in school holidays).

In this book, along with local bus route number, frequency and duration, we have provided indicative prices if the fare is over a few pounds. If it's less than this, we have generally omitted the fare details.

BUS PASSES

If you're taking a few local bus rides in a day of energetic sightseeing, ask about day-passes (with names like Day Rover, Wayfarer or Explorer), which will be cheaper than buying several single tickets. Passes are mentioned in the regional chapters, and it's always worth asking ticket clerks or bus drivers about your options.

TAXI

There are two sorts of taxi in Britain: the famous black cabs (some with advertising livery in other colours these days) that have meters and can be hailed in the street; and minicabs that are cheaper but can only be called by phone. In London and other big cities, taxis cost £2 to £3 per mile. In rural areas, it's about half this. The best place to find the local taxi's phone number is the local pub. Alternatively, if you call **National Cabline** (☎ 0800 123444) from a landline phone, the service pinpoints your location and transfers you to an approved local taxi company. Also useful is www.traintaxi.co.uk.

TRAIN

For long-distance travel around Britain, trains are generally faster and more comfortable than coaches but can be more expensive, although with discount tickets they're competitive – and often take you through beautiful countryside.

About 20 different companies operate train services in Britain (for example: First Great Western runs from London

to Bristol, Cornwall and South Wales; National Express East Coast runs from London to Leeds, York and Edinburgh; Virgin Trains runs the 'west coast' route from London to Birmingham, Carlisle and Glasgow), while Network Rail operates track and stations.

Your first stop should be **National Rail Enquiries** (☎ 08457 48 49 50; www.nationalrail. co.uk), the nationwide timetable and fare information service. Once you've found the journey you need, links take you to the relevant train operator or to centralised ticketing services (www.thetrainline .com, www.qjump.co.uk, www.raileasy .co.uk) to buy the ticket.

You can also buy train tickets on the spot at stations, which is fine for short journeys (under about 50 miles), but for longer trips discount tickets are usually not available at the station and must be bought in advance by phone or online.

For planning your trip, some very handy maps of the UK's rail network can be downloaded from www.nationalrail. co.uk/tocs_maps/maps/network_rail _maps.html. The nationalrail.co.uk site also advertises special offers, and has real-time links to station departure boards, so you can see if your train is on time (or not).

CLASSES

There are two classes of rail travel: 1st and standard. First class costs around 50% more than standard and, except on very crowded trains, is not really worth it. However, at weekends some train operators offer 'upgrades' for an extra £10 to £15 on top of your standard-class fare, so you can enjoy more comfort and legroom.

COSTS & RESERVATIONS

For short journeys, it's usually best to buy tickets on the spot at train stations. For longer journeys, on-the-spot fares are always available, but tickets are much cheaper if bought in advance. Essentially, the earlier you book, the cheaper it gets. You can also save if you travel at 'off-peak' – ie avoiding commuter times, Fridays and Sundays. The cheapest fares are nonrefundable, though, so if you miss your train you'll have to buy a new ticket.

If you buy by phone or website, you can have the ticket posted to you (UK addresses only), or collect it at the originating station on the day of travel, either at the ticket desk (leave time to spare, as queues can be long) or via automatic machines.

Whichever operator you travel with and wherever you buy tickets, there are three main fare types:

Advance Buy ticket in advance, travel only on specific trains.

Anytime Buy at any time, travel at any time.

Off-peak Buy ticket at any time, travel off-peak.

For an idea of the price difference, an Anytime single ticket from London to York will cost around £100, and an Off-peak around £80, while an Advance single can be less than £20, and even less than £10 if you book early enough or don't mind arriving at midnight.

Off-peak and Anytime tickets are available as returns and the price can vary from just under double the single fare to just a pound more than the single fare.

Children under five years old travel free on trains; those aged between five and 15 pay half price, except on tickets already heavily discounted – but a Family & Friends Railcard is usually better value.

If the train doesn't get you all the way to your destination, a **PlusBus** (www.plus bus.info) supplement (usually around £2)

validates your train ticket for onward travel by bus.

And finally, it's worth a look at **Megatrain** (www.megatrain.com) – from the people who brought you Megabus – ultra-low train fares on ultra off-peak services between London and a few destinations in southwest England and the East Midlands.

TRAIN PASSES

Local train passes usually cover rail networks around a city (many include bus travel too), and are mentioned in the individual city sections throughout this book. If you're staying in Britain for a while, passes known as 'railcards' are available:

16-25 Railcard For those aged 16 to 25, or full-time UK students.

Family & Friends Railcard Covers up to four adults and four children travelling together.

Senior Railcard For anyone over 60.

These railcards cost around £25 (valid for one year, available from major stations or online) and get you a 33% discount on most train fares, except those already heavily discounted. With the Family card, adults get 33% and children get a 60% discount, so the fee is easily repaid in a couple of journeys. Proof of age and a passport photo may be required. For full details see www.railcard.co.uk.

A Disabled Person's Railcard costs £18. You can get an application form from stations or from the railcard website. Call ☎ 0191-281 8103 for more details.

If you're concentrating your travels on southeast England (eg London to Dover, Weymouth, Cambridge or Oxford), a Network Railcard covers up to four adults and up to four children travelling together outside peak times.

TRANSPORT

GETTING AROUND

For country-wide travel, BritRail Passes are good value, but they're only for visitors from overseas and not available in Britain. They must be bought in your country of origin from a specialist travel agency. There are many BritRail variants, each available in three different versions: for England only; for the whole of Britain (England, Wales and Scotland); and for the UK and Ireland. Following is an outline of the main options, quoting high-season adult prices.

BritRail Consecutive offers unlimited travel on all trains in England for four, eight, 15, 22 or 30 days, for US$259/375/559/709/839. Anyone getting their money's worth out of the last pass should earn some sort of endurance award.

With the **BritRail Flexipass**, you don't have to get on a train every day to get full value. Your options are four days of unlimited travel in England within a 60-day period for US$329, eight in 60 days for US$479, or 15 in 60 days for US$725.

Children's BritRail passes are usually half price (or you can get a family pass), and seniors get discounts too. Other deals include a rail pass combined with the use of a hire car, or travel in Britain combined with one Eurostar journey. For more details see www.britrail.com.

If you don't (or can't) buy a BritRail pass, an All Line Rover gives virtually unlimited travel for 14 days anywhere on the national rail network. You can travel at any time, but aren't guaranteed a seat (reservations cost extra), so it's best to travel at off-peak times if you can. The pass costs £565 and can be purchased in Britain, by anyone. For an idea of what's possible, do a search on All Line Rover in rail-enthusiast sites such as www.railforums.co.uk or www.railwayscene.co.uk.

Of the other international passes, an InterRail card is valid in Britain, as long as you bought it in another European country, but Eurail cards are not accepted in Britain.

⬎ GLOSSARY

bailey – outermost wall of a castle

bill – total you need to pay after eating in a restaurant ('check' to Americans)

bloke – man (colloquial)

bridleway – path that can be used by walkers, horse riders and cyclists

Cadw – the Welsh historic-monuments agency

CalMac – Caledonian MacBrayne, the main Scottish island ferry operator

circus – junction of several streets, usually circular

coach – long-distance bus

court – courtyard

croft – plot of land with adjoining house worked by the occupiers (Scotland)

downs – rolling upland, characterised by lack of trees

EH – English Heritage

Evensong – daily evening service (Church of England)

fen – drained or marshy low-lying area

flat – apartment

footpath – path through countryside and between houses, not beside a road (that's called a 'pavement')

gate – street (York, and some other northern cities)

graft – work (not corruption, as in American English; colloquial)

hire – rent

HS – Historic Scotland; organisation that manages historic sites in Scotland

kirk – church (N England and Scotland)

kyle – strait or channel (Scotland)

lift – machine for carrying people up and down in large buildings ('elevator' to Americans)

lock – part of a canal or river that can be closed off and the water levels changed to raise or lower boats

loch – lake (Scotland)

mad – insane (not angry, as in American English)

midge – mosquito-like insect

motorway – major road linking cities (equivalent to 'interstate' or 'freeway')

motte – mound on which a castle was built

Munro – hill or mountain over 912m (3000ft) especially in Scotland

naff – inferior, in poor taste (colloquial)

NT – National Trust; protects historic buildings and land with scenic importance in England and Wales

NTS – National Trust for Scotland

pitch – playing field

postbus – minibus delivering the mail, also carrying passengers

punter – customer (colloquial)

ramble – short easy walk

return ticket – round-trip ticket

single ticket – one-way ticket

ton – 100 (colloquial)

tor – pointed hill (Celtic)

tube, the – London's underground railway system (colloquial)

Underground, the – London's underground railway system

↘ BEHIND THE SCENES

THE AUTHORS

OLIVER BERRY

Coordinating author, This Is Great Britain, Great Britain's Top 25 Experiences, Great Britain's Top Itineraries, Planning Your Trip, Northern England, Great Britain in Focus

A born and bred Brit, Oliver lives and works in Cornwall as a writer and photographer. His travels for Lonely Planet have carried him from the mountains of Corsica to the beaches of the Cook Islands, but he never manages to stay away from the old home country for long. He has worked on several editions of Lonely Planet's bestselling guides to England and Great Britain, and has also written first editions for Lonely Planet's regional guides to Devon, Cornwall and Southwest England, and the Lake District. You'll find some of his latest work at www.oliverberry.com.

Author thanks First up, a heartfelt thanks to all the people who gave up their time to recommend their local tips: John Keohane, Paul Collins, Mark O'Kane, Sally Robinson, Pat Shelley, Peter Storey, Kim Bryan, Jan Henderson and Ian Logan. Over at the Planet, thanks to Cliff Wilkinson, Sam Trafford, Herman So and Dan Corbett for keeping me on the straight and narrow. But most of all, thanks to my brilliant coauthors for providing me with the backbone of this book: here's to you Fionn, Neil, Belinda, Peter, Nana, David E, David A, James, Andy and Etain. Look forward to doing it all again soon.

DAVID ELSE   Directory & Transport, Great Britain in Focus, Glossary

As a full-time professional travel writer, David has authored more than 20 books, including Lonely Planet's *England* and *Walking in Britain*. His knowledge of Britain comes from a lifetime of travel around the country, often on foot or by bike, a passion dating from university years when heading for the hills was always more attractive than visiting the library. Originally from London, David has lived in

LONELY PLANET AUTHORS

Why is our travel information the best in the world? It's simple: our authors are passionate, dedicated travellers. They don't take freebies in exchange for positive coverage so you can be sure the advice you're given is impartial. They travel widely to all the popular spots, and off the beaten track. They don't research using just the internet or phone. They discover new places not included in any other guidebook. They personally visit thousands of hotels, restaurants, palaces, trails, galleries, temples and more. They speak with dozens of locals every day to make sure you get the kind of insider knowledge only a local could tell you. They take pride in getting all the details right, and in telling it how it is. Think you can do it? Find out how at **lonelyplanet.com**.

Yorkshire, Wales and Derbyshire, and is currently based on the southern edge of the Cotswolds. For those interested in domestic matters: David is married with two young children – often found on the back of their dad's tandem whenever the sun shines.

DAVID ATKINSON   Wales
David Atkinson is a full-time freelance travel writer based in Chester, northwest England. He previously coauthored Lonely Planet's *Wales* and was subsequently asked to judge the 2007 National Tourism Awards for Wales. He writes about all aspects of travel from green issues to family journeys, and his stories appear in the *Observer*, the *Weekend Financial Times* and the *Daily Express*. David spent his early childhood holidays in Wales and returned after several years working overseas to find the new Wales is greener, chic-er and more compelling than ever before. He is now busy inspiring his two-year-old daughter with a sense of *hiraeth* (the longing to come home to Wales). More details at www.atkinsondavid.co.uk.

FIONN DAVENPORT   Northern England
Dublin-based Fionn has been visiting and writing about northern England for about a decade, which is a good thing considering that this is his favourite bit of the country – mostly because the people remind him of the folks across the puddle in Ireland. When he's not traipsing around Newcastle or Manchester – or watching his beloved Liverpool FC at Anfield – he's juggling his commitments to Irish radio and TV, where he doles out travel advice and gives out about globalisation fatigue. And when he's not doing that, he spends most of his time wondering where he'd like to go next.

BELINDA DIXON   Southern England
Belinda was drawn to England's southwest in the 1990s to do a post-grad (having been impressed there were palm trees on the campus) and, like the best Westcountry limpets, has proved hard to shift since. She spends as much time as possible in the sea, but can also be seen and heard writing and broadcasting in the region.

PETER DRAGICEVICH   London
After a dozen years working for newspapers and magazines in New Zealand and Australia, Peter could no longer resist London's bright lights and loud guitars. Like all good Kiwis, Peter got to know the city while surfing his way between friends' flats all over London. Now, living an even more nomadic life as a Lonely Planet writer, London is one of three cities that he likes to think of as home. He has contributed to many Lonely Planet titles, including writing the Thames Path section of *Walking in Britain*.

NANA LUCKHAM   Southern England, Central England
Nana spent most of her childhood in Brighton, aside from a few years in Tanzania, Ghana and Australia. After university, she worked as an editorial assistant in London and a UN press officer in New York and Geneva before becoming a fulltime travel writer. Now based in London, she spends most of her time on research trips in exotic faraway climes. Hence, she jumped at the chance to rediscover her home region of the southeast and

relive her university days in the Midlands, during which she developed a new-found enthusiasm for the old country.

ETAIN O'CARROLL

Southern England, Central England

Travel writer and photographer Etain grew up in small-town Ireland. Regular childhood trips to England were tinged with the excitement of eating gammon and pineapple in motorway service stations; examining the countless sparkly pens in swanky Woolies; and meeting all those cousins with funny accents. In between were the trips to the chocolate-box villages, stately homes, massive castles and ruined abbeys. Now living in Oxford, Etain's childish awe has become a long-term appreciation for the fine architecture, bucolic countryside and rich heritage of her adopted home. Work often takes her far away but she cherished the excuse to traipse around her own back yard searching for hidden treats.

ANDY SYMINGTON

Scotland's Highlands & Islands

Andy's Scottish forebears make their presence felt in his love of malt, a debatable ginger colour to his facial hair and occasional appearances in a kilt. From childhood slogs up the M1, he graduated to making dubious road-trips around the firths in a disintegrating Mini Metro and thence to peddling whisky in darkest Leith. Whilst living there, he travelled widely around the country in search of the perfect dram; now resident in Spain, Andy continues to visit several times a year.

NEIL WILSON

Northern England, Edinburgh & Glasgow, Great Britain in Focus

From rock-climbing trips to Yorkshire gritstone in his university days, to weekend getaways in York and Whitby in more recent years, Neil has made many cross-border forays into 'God's own country' from his home in Scotland. Whether hiking across the high tops of the Yorkshire Dales, savouring Britain's best fish and chips on the Whitby waterfront, or worshipping at the fountainhead of Theakston Ales in Masham, he's never short of an excuse for yet another visit. Neil is a full-time travel writer based in Edinburgh, and has written more than 40 guidebooks for various publishers.

THIS BOOK

This 1st edition of *Discover Great Britain* was coordinated by Oliver Berry, and researched and written by him, David Else, David Atkinson, Fionn Davenport, Belinda Dixon, Peter Dragicevich, Nana Luckham, Etain O'Carroll, Andy Symington and Neil Wilson. It was commissioned in Lonely Planet's London office, and produced by the following:

Commissioning Editor Clifton Wilkinson
Coordinating Editors Daniel Corbett, Sasha Baskett
Coordinating Cartographer Valentina Kremenchutskaya
Coordinating Layout Designer Yvonne Bischofberger
Managing Editor Bruce Evans
Managing Cartographer Herman So
Managing Layout Designer Laura Jane
Assisting Editor Paul Harding

SEND US YOUR FEEDBACK

We love to hear from travellers – your comments keep us on our toes and help make our books better. Our well-travelled team reads every word on what you loved or loathed about this book. Although we cannot reply individually to postal submissions, we always guarantee that your feedback goes straight to the appropriate authors, in time for the next edition. Each person who sends us information is thanked in the next edition and the most useful submissions are rewarded with a free book.

To send us your updates – and find out about Lonely Planet events, newsletters and travel news – visit our award-winning website: lonelyplanet.com/contact.

Note: we may edit, reproduce and incorporate your comments in Lonely Planet products such as guidebooks, websites and digital products, so let us know if you don't want your comments reproduced or your name acknowledged. For a copy of our privacy policy visit lonelyplanet.com/privacy.

Assisting Cartographer Anthony Phelan
Cover research Naomi Parker, lonelyplanetimages.com
Internal image research Aude Vauconsant, lonelyplanetimages.com
Project Manager Chris Girdler

Thanks to Glenn Beanland, Nicholas Colicchia, Eoin Dunlevy, Ryan Evans, Jane Hart, Suki Gear, Joshua Geoghegan, Mark Germanchis, Michelle Glynn, Brice Gosnell, Imogen Hall, James Hardy, Steve Henderson, Lauren Hunt, Paul Iacono, Chris Lee Ack, Nic Lehman, Alison Lyall, John Mazzocchi, Jennifer Mullins, Wayne Murphy, Darren O'Connell, Trent Paton, Piers Pickard, Howard Ralley, Kirsten Rawlings, Lachlan Ross, Wibowo Rusli, Julie Sheridan, Jason Shugg, Caroline Sieg, Cara Smith, Carlos Solarte, Naomi Stephens, Geoff Stringer, Jane Thompson, Sam Trafford, Stefanie Di Trocchio, Tashi Wheeler, Juan Winata, Emily K Wolman, Nick Wood

Internal photographs p4 Millennium Bridge, London, Doug McKinlay; p10 Hiker, Cornwall, Holger Leue; p12 Edinburgh Festival performance, Edinburgh Castle, Gareth McCormack; p31 Conwy Castle, Wales, Chris Mellor; p39 Hiker, Scottish Highlands, Eoin Clarke; p3, p50 Double-decker bus passing Houses of Parliament and Big Ben, London, Barbara Van Zanten; p54 Chief Yeoman Warder John Keohane, Historic Royal Palaces; p3, p107 The Cotswolds, Gloucestershire, Gavin Gough; p3, p161 Punting, Cambridge, Max Paoli & Ruth Eastham; p164 Actor Peter Shorey, Simon Annand; p3, p199 Lake District National Park, Hugh Watts; p3, p245 Snowdonia National Park, Gareth McCormack; p3, p275 Princes Street Gardens, Edinburgh, Will Salter; p3, p313 Scottish Highlands, Graeme Cornwallis; p342 St Ives, Cornwall, Glenn Beanland; p381 Peak District, Anders Blomqvist.

All images are copyright of the photographer unless otherwise indicated. Many of the images in this guide are available for licensing from Lonely Planet Images: www .lonelyplanetimages.com.

↘ INDEX

INDEX

R–S

MAP LEGEND

ROUTES

Tollway		One-Way Street
Freeway		Mall/Steps
Primary		Tunnel
Secondary		Pedestrian Overpass
Tertiary		Walking Tour
Lane		Walking Tour Detour
Under Construction		Walking Path
Unsealed Road		Track

TRANSPORT

Ferry		Rail/Underground
Metro		Tram
Monorail		Cable Car, Funicular

HYDROGRAPHY

River, Creek		Canal
Intermittent River		Water
Swamp/Mangrove		Dry Lake/Salt Lake
Reef		Glacier

BOUNDARIES

International		Regional, Suburb
State, Provincial		Marine Park
Disputed		Cliff/Ancient Wall

AREA FEATURES

Area of Interest		Forest
Beach, Desert		Mall/Market
Building/Urban Area		Park
Cemetery, Christian		Restricted Area
Cemetery, Other		Sports

POPULATION

CAPITAL (NATIONAL)		**CAPITAL (STATE)**
LARGE CITY		**Medium City**
Small City		Town, Village

SYMBOLS

Sights/Activities

	Buddhist
	Canoeing, Kayaking
	Castle, Fortress
	Christian
	Confucian
	Diving
	Hindu
	Islamic
	Jain
	Jewish
	Monument
	Museum, Gallery
	Point of Interest
	Pool
	Ruin
	Sento (Public Hot Baths)
	Shinto
	Sikh
	Skiing
	Surfing, Surf Beach
	Taoist
	Trail Head
	Winery, Vineyard
	Zoo, Bird Sanctuary

Information

	Bank, ATM
	Embassy/Consulate
	Hospital, Medical
	Information
	Internet Facilities
	Police Station
	Post Office, GPO
	Telephone
	Toilets
	Wheelchair Access

Eating

	Eating

Drinking

	Cafe
	Drinking

Entertainment

	Entertainment

Shopping

	Shopping

Sleeping

	Camping
	Sleeping

Transport

	Airport, Airfield
	Border Crossing
	Bus Station
	Bicycle Path/Cycling
	FFCC (Barcelona)
	Metro (Barcelona)
	Parking Area
	Petrol Station
	S-Bahn
	Taxi Rank
	Tube Station
	U-Bahn

Geographic

	Beach
	Lighthouse
	Lookout
	Mountain, Volcano
	National Park
	Pass, Canyon
	Picnic Area
	River Flow
	Shelter, Hut
	Waterfall

LONELY PLANET OFFICES

Australia
Head Office
Locked Bag 1, Footscray, Victoria 3011
☎ 03 8379 8000, fax 03 8379 8111
talk2us@lonelyplanet.com.au

USA
150 Linden St, Oakland, CA 94607
☎ 510 250 6400, toll free 800 275 8555,
fax 510 893 8572
info@lonelyplanet.com

UK
2nd fl, 186 City Rd,
London EC1V 2NT
☎ 020 7106 2100, fax 020 7106 2101
go@lonelyplanet.co.uk

Published by Lonely Planet
ABN 36 005 607 983

Printed by Markono Print Media Pte Ltd
Printed in Singapore